Redistribution through Public Choice

Redistribution through Public Choice

HAROLD M. HOCHMAN

and

GEORGE E. PETERSON

Editors

1974
Columbia University Press
NEW YORK and LONDON

Published in cooperation with The
Urban Institute, Washington, D.C.

Library of Congress Cataloging in Publication Data
Main entry under title:

Redistribution through public choice.

Includes bibliographical references.
Revised versions of papers presented at a con-
ference sponsored by the National Science Foundation
and The Urban Institute, held Mar. 23-24, 1972.
1. Income—Congresses. 2. Income—United States
—Congresses. I. United States. National Science
Foundation. II. Urban Institute. III. Hochman,
Harold M., ed. IV. Peterson, George E., ed.
HB601.R4   339.2'0973   73-19748
ISBN 0-231-03775-9

Preface

It is a measure of the changing emphasis of the economic profession that more and more attention is being devoted to the distribution of income. Shunted to the background for several decades, while economists concentrated on the level and rate of change of income rather than its division among the political community, distribution has once again come to the fore in the last decade. The emergence of distribution and redistribution, as a focus of research and policy discussion, doubtless is related to the sense of distributive injustice that has fostered dissatisfaction with existing rules and institutions among important segments of the American political community. In discussion of major issues of domestic economic policy—such as income maintenance and welfare plans, tax reform, the fiscal strain on cities, and the quality of public service provision—distributional issues almost always are the ones most fiercely debated. In a sense, the current resurgence of academic interest in distributional issues is motivated by contemporary events, just as the interest in macroeconomic policy grew out of the experience of the Great Depression.

Recent research on distributional topics has focused largely on the quantitative implications of various measures that the American society might undertake to reduce the inequality of its income distribution and guarantee a minimum income to all. Many of our colleagues at the Urban Institute have been active in these fields. There is, however, another stream of thought, differing in emphasis, that bears on the theory of distributional questions. Modeled on the writings of such scholars as James Buchanan, Anthony Downs, and Gordon Tullock, a considerable literature has emerged which treats distributional questions as a form of public choice. Our objectives in planning the Urban Institute conference on "Redistribution through Public Choice," where the papers in this book were originally presented, were to take stock of this literature, to which many of the authors and discussants at the conference have contributed, and to see what further light modern studies in political economy could shed on distributional questions.

The conference itself was held on March 23 and 24, 1972, and was sponsored by the National Science Foundation under Grant GS-33244X and by The Urban Institute under its institutional grant from the Ford Foundation. This book contains revised versions of the papers presented at that time. Although remarks of the discussants and other participants are not reproduced, many of the authors have incorporated them into the final versions of their papers. Indeed many of the papers differ substantially in content from the original presentations.

The chairman of the opening session of the conference was Alvin Klevorick. The papers presented by William Breit and James Buchanan were discussed by Martin Bronfenbrenner and Stephan Michelson, respectively. In the afternoon sessions four papers were presented. Terry Kelly discussed Richard Zeckhauser's paper on risk spreading; Peter Mieskowski discussed Mitchell Polinsky's paper; and Guido Calabresi and Burton Weisbrod discussed the papers of Harold Hochman and James Rodgers. The chairmen of these sessions were Benjamin Chinitz and Worth Bateman.

On the second day of the conference six papers were presented in two sessions. The morning session, chaired by William Niskanen, heard papers by George Peterson, William Baumol, and Martin Feldstein, with discussions by Mark Pauly, Richard Musgrave, and A. Myrick Freeman, III, respectively. In the afternoon Louis De Alessi presided over the final session, in which David Bradford and Wallace Oates presented a joint paper, Otto Davis and John Jackson presented a joint paper, and Julius Margolis gave the final paper. The Bradford-Oates paper was discussed by Henry Aaron, the Davis-Jackson paper by James Coleman, and the Margolis paper by Gordon Tullock.

It is incumbent on us, as editors of a book on distribution, to make sure that the distribution of credit for the conference itself be fair. We wish to acknowledge not only the participants but also the many others without whose effort and encouragement our plans for the conference and the publication of this book could not have been realized. Foremost among these are Dr. James Blackman, Director of the Economics Program of the National Science Foundation, and Dr. Worth Bateman, Senior Vice President for Research at The Urban Institute, who not only encouraged, guided, and goaded us into planning the conference, but also did much to provide the necessary financial support. At The Urban Institute itself, many of our colleagues in the Urban Public Finance group took on the responsibility for the logistical management of the conference, a matter far more complex than either of us could have contemplated. In this connection special thanks are due Cathy Gilson and Elaine Liang. Finally we wish to thank B.J. Stiles, Director of Publications at The Urban Institute for his continuing guidance in the preparation of the manuscript for publication.

Harold M. Hochman
George E. Peterson

Washington, D.C.
December, 1973

Contents

Introduction

No topic in economics generates so much controversy as the distribution of income. And it is altogether fitting that this be so, for the knowledge that poverty persists in the midst of national wealth ought to be a source of discomfort and questioning to a conscientious citizenry. John Stuart Mill no doubt drew too sharp a distinction when he contrasted the Production of Wealth, which he thought obeyed laws that had the character of physical truth, with the Distribution of Wealth, which he described as entirely a matter of human institutions;[1] but the idea that Mill meant to convey, that society bears more responsibility for the disposition of wealth than it does for the rest of the economic system, because the income distribution is in the end more easily subject to human alteration, rings true. Rights, in person and property, that are conferred by the body politic provide the legal ground rules for the economic behavior that determines individual incomes. Any act of public policy that alters these rights, by intent or inadvertence, is likely to have large consequences for the distribution of income.

Although Mill insisted that the shape of the income distribution was a matter of social choice, he also believed that analysis could be carried forward quite apart from personal preferences as to what the distribution of income ought to be. The task of the political economist, Mill thought, was to make clear the implications of choosing one form of income distribution over another. Or in Mill's words: "Society can subject the distribution of wealth to whatever rules it thinks best; but what practical results will flow from the operation of those rules must be discovered, like any other physical or mental truths, by observation and reasoning." This book adheres to the distinction that Mill laid down. It is concerned with observation and reasoning, with what might be called "positive analysis" of the income distribution, rather than with advocacy. In this, it reflects the current state of economic thinking, which holds that economists are no better equipped than other citizens, and less well equipped than elected political leaders, to judge which distributions of income are "desirable." The only substantial agreement that exists among economists is that any redistribution of income that can make everyone better off (that is to say, that satisfies the criterion of Pareto optimality) ought to be carried out.

For an explicit consideration of the rules that should determine the distribution of income in the first place we must turn from economics either to the everyday world (where all men seem to have an opinion) or to the works of moral and political philosophers. In the first paper in this book William Breit discusses the attempts that have been made by utilitarian philosophers and economists to ground a recommendation of income equality on the principle of utility maximization for all citizens. As Breit notes, after more than a century of intellectual experimentation, this effort has been abandoned, victim of the realization that a man's "utility" level cannot be quantified or added to another citizen's utility to compute a national sum of happiness that decision makers can judge to have grown or diminished with alternative income-distribution policies.

More promising as a guideline for distribution policy—or at least more thought provoking to modern-day scholars—are attempts to revive social contract theory for the purpose of framing a set of fair rules to regulate the distribution of income. John Rawls is perhaps the most influential advocate of this viewpoint.[2] In his important treatise on justice Rawls has argued that the "right" or "just" distribution of income is that to which free men would willingly consent in the absence of any knowledge of the roles that they would occupy within society. In old-fashioned contract theory this hypothetical state of affairs was called the "state of nature." In Rawls's treatment, which is in some ways similar to arguments advanced in the writings of such economists as Buchanan and Tullock, Harsanyi, and Lerner, the veneer of historical anthropology has been replaced by frank acknowledgment that the situation prior to the formation of society can be imagined only as an abstraction, albeit an instructive one. If men labored behind a veil of ignorance, not knowing whether they would be endowed with wealthy parents or poor ones, given an abundance of marketable skills or saddled with physical disabilities that rendered them incapable of self-support, what rules would they agree upon for distributing the national income? Rawls advances two contentions: first that the set of rules to which men would voluntarily consent under these conditions should be accepted as determining the distribution of income that is "fair" and, that the rules rational men would settle upon can be deduced *a priori*. According to Rawls, men who set up rules under these conditions would stipulate that no inequalities of income are to be tolerated unless the existence of the inequality makes everyone, especially those at the bottom of the economic ladder, better off. Rawls tries to show that this rule-making behavior follows from the very definition of rationality, which implies risk-averse behavior on the part of rational individuals. That is to say, as long as men could equally well find themselves within the class of those who are discriminated against as within the class of those who benefit from discriminatory treatment, and since the unfortunate consequences of falling into the former class outweigh the benefits of falling into the latter in the eyes of the rational individual, the thoughtful citizen, Rawls maintains, will opt for strict equality of treatment, unless all men can be made better off by the introduction of inequality. Several of the esssays in this book attempt to extend Rawls's approach. Richard Zeckhauser analyzes the consequences of the fact that men do not labor behind a veil of ignorance when reaching agreement on the rules that will determine the income distribution, but do so in knowledge of the relative advantages that each possesses. Harold Hochman analyzes the consequences of the fact that in practice we cannot start *de novo* in setting up a fair society but must adjust the rules that have governed conduct in the past. Consequently, it is not enough to maintain an objective that is "fair" in Rawls's sense; some precautions have to be taken to ensure that men are treated fairly during the period of transition.

Rawls's analysis makes clear that in order to uncover the sources of inequality in the distribution of income we must examine carefully the rules or laws that a society adopts. In a society of laws and markets, like ours, there is a body of rights or entitlements that in effect assigns every income stream to an owner. It is this body of law that determines that the laborer has the "right" to keep the earnings that his skills command on the market, or that the capitalist has the "right" to the earnings that flow from the assets he controls. Often it is the right to put an asset to productive use that commands a price, rather than the physical asset itself. Urban land that is zoned for commercial use may sell at several times the price of similar land, sold without the right to commercial development, just as in tobacco states land sold with the right to grow tobacco (which requires governmental authorization) may sell for $20,000 per acre whereas neighboring land, similar in every respect, except that it is sold without a tobacco permit, is worth hardly $200 per acre. Every time that society alters the bundle of rights that accompany property ownership, whether it be by imposing new obligations on the owners of property or by removing old tax burdens, there are substantial wealth effects. At several points the essays in this book touch upon the legal delimitation of property rights and their distributional consequences. But many of the participants in The Urban Institute conference felt that a more careful scrutiny of the relationship between legal rules and the distribution of wealth should be the next priority item for economic research.

As William Breit points out in his review of economists' attitudes toward income redistribution, strictly positive analysis of the income distribution has dwelt historically on a presumed trade-off between more nearly equal distribution of wealth or incomes and the total magnitude of wealth that is available for distribution. From the nineteenth century to now the mainstream of economics has held that unequal rewards are a necessary part of the incentive structure that leads to the maximal production of wealth for society as a whole. If this is so, the choice of the optimal degree of income inequality may be interpreted in a way that closely resembles other economic choices. Citizens can be supposed to have preferences regarding both average income levels and the degree of income inequality. There will be some rate of utility trade-off at which the representative citizen is willing to exchange one desideratum, greater income equality, for the other, average income level. If, in addition, there is a production possibility schedule showing the rate at which average incomes must decline in order to obtain more distributional equality, society can adjust its rules until the optimal degree of inequality is reached, given the cost in terms of total output that a further leveling of incomes would require. Although this approach conforms to traditional economics, it must be confessed that for over a century the presumption that greater equality means lesser total output has survived on theoretical speculation rather than sound empirical evidence. One of the principal tasks of positive analysis of income distribution would seem to be to quantify the terms of the trade-off between work and investment incentives, on the one hand, and more equal distribution of economic rewards, on the other.

It is also the task of positive analysis to identify the constraints that markets place on the feasible scope for income distribution. In his paper James Buchanan shows that the existence of a market in residential location both severely constrains the amount of pure redistribution that can be carried out at the local level, whatever the desires of individual jurisdictions may be, and constrains the manner in which localities can share the gains from local public goods production among their residents. As long as those whom public policy would convert into unwilling benefactors have the option of moving to another locality, where tax policies are more lenient, towns that attempt to use the local tax structure to redistribute income will find themselves frustrated by the flight of the wealthy householders who were to finance the planned redistribution. Income redistribution at the national level does not encounter the same constraints because the migration alternative in this case is much more difficult to exercise.

Of course the scope for local redistribution would be enlarged if rich communities were prevented from insulating themselves, by means of municipal borders, from the poor. It is often claimed that the existence of upper-class suburbs, to which wealthy families can flee and remain safe from the taxing powers of poor families who would use the local public sector for redistributive purposes, contributes greatly to income inequality. In their paper, the third in the volume, David Bradford and Wallace Oates explore both the distributional and efficiency implications of the present fragmented arrangement of local jurisdictions, and contrast these with the outcome that might ensue under the opposite extreme of unified metropolitan fiscal structures. To give their analysis empirical content, they illustrate the effects of the change to a unified metropolitan structure by examining a sample of New Jersey cities and suburban communities.

As Bradford and Oates point out, the current system of fragmented governments offers households a wider choice as to the mix and level of local public services than would a metropolitan-wide government. For this reason, any shift to area-wide governance would involve an efficiency loss associated with diminished consumer choice. Over the long run, however, this might be offset by the productivity gains to be secured from less income homogeneity. Elimination of local financing would remove some of the incentive to income or wealth segregation, and the resulting income mixture might increase the total benefits from such basic services as public schooling. The transition to a unitary system also would have complex distributional effects. Bradford and Oates show that the redistribution of tax burdens would occur primarily among property owners rather than between these groups and poorer ones. Concerning expenditure, they show that an equalization of per pupil spending on public schools would aid the poor and equalization of spending on noneducational functions would produce some redistribution from rich to poor in the suburbs. However, equalizing expenditures on services other than education would work to the disadvantage of city dwellers, who count disproportionate numbers of poor among their population.

The papers by Buchanan and Bradford and Oates examine the effect that institutional and governmental structures have on income distribution. The second set of papers looks at income distribution in the context of specific policy decisions. The papers by William Baumol and George Peterson consider the distributional side effects of public programs that are undertaken for other reasons. Neither pollution control (the subject of Baumol's paper) nor efforts to improve the efficiency of schooling (the subject of Peterson's paper) have been undertaken primarily with an eye to redistribution. But like most important policy decisions, these measures prove to have sizable distributional consequences. In fact, the distributional effects may be so strong that the devotion of significant resources to these programs is acceptable only if explicit mechanisms are created to guard against undesirable distributional outcomes.

Baumol points out that the apparent lack of enthusiasm of the poor for environmental protection policies is well grounded in their self-interest. Because environmental quality is a normal good, the demand for which increases with family income, the poor suffer a deadweight loss when they are taxed to pay for environmental quality, which in Baumol's model must be provided in uniform quantity for all members of the community, if it is provided at all. This welfare loss is due to the public-goods nature of environmental protection that makes the poor "buy," through the tax system, more environmental quality than they would choose to pay for on their own. Other aspects of environmental-protection policies may be even less attractive to lower-income households. Baumol cites, in particular, the employment-restricting effects of environmental protection, which are likely to fall most heavily on the poor. He argues, moreover, that any effort to implement environmental policies through geographic differentiation that sets aside some areas as "forever wild" will not only afford the poor fewer benefits than the wealthy, because the poor reside disproportionately in central cities and industrial areas, but if implemented by restrictions on the location of industrial centers are likely to bring about a further concentration of pollution-producing activities in areas where the poor now reside. This skewing of the benefits from environmental protection in favor of the well-to-do is likely to more than offset the relative advantage that the poor may derive from the fact that such programs are financed by progressive revenue sources. On balance, then, the poor will be less likely to favor expenditures on environmental quality than the wealthy.

Peterson discusses performance contracting in education. Performance contracting is an experiment in which private firms are hired to operate public schools and are paid according to the results that their students achieve on standard tests. The rationale underlying performance contracting is that educational attainment can be improved if public-service provision is harnessed to the same profit incentives that have proved useful in the private market. Although the objective of the performance-contract system has been to improve the efficiency of school instruction for all pupils, Peterson shows that for at least some payment systems the structure of profit incentives also helps determine which pupils receive most attention in school. In the Banneker School System in Gary, Indiana, which Peterson examines in detail, the profit incentives were set up so as to concentrate resources disproportionately on students in the middle of the ability range to the relative neglect of the students farthest ahead and farthest behind in the classroom. Actual achievement data are analyzed to show that the results of the experiment conform to the structure of profit incentives that was built into the payment contract. In this case, the distributional consequences of the profit incentives seem to have outweighed the efficiency effects.

One conclusion to be drawn from the Baumol and Peterson papers is that decision makers have to take into account the distributional implications of public programs at the same time that they consider their efficiency advantages. The paper by Martin Feldstein is intended to provide policy makers with a means of combining distributional and efficiency considerations in a single analysis. Feldstein focuses on public-expenditure programs. What is needed, he argues, is a means of aggregating the benefits and costs that accrue to individuals in different income classes into a single measure, which can be used like a cost-benefit ratio when determining the desirability of a public-investment program. Feldstein does this by devising a *numéraire,* which he refers to as the "UDD" or "uniformly distributed dollar." This measures the equivalent benefits, in terms of pure efficiency gains, of a project which has both distributional and efficiency effects. It provides a one-number measure of total benefits, which can be analyzed in dollar terms. It should be emphasized that the Feldstein formula provides a convenient way for the economist to help the decision maker to incorporate his distributional preferences into the choice of public-investment projects, not a means for inserting the economist's value judgments into the decision-making process.

The third group of papers turns to the consideration of what motivates the observed pattern of income redistribution in countries like the United States. Economists, in recent years, have devoted considerable effort to reconciling both the existence and the form of income redistribution with the postulates of human behavior that are implicit in economic theory, and, where it has been necessary, modifying these postulates to accommodate income transfers as a fact of social life. James Rodgers, in his contribution to this book, examines in depth three main types of positive behavioral models that have been put forward to explain real-world redistribution. These models explain redistribution in terms of: (1) self-interested behavior on the part of the majority who benefit from redistribution away from the rich (this model has been developed by Anthony Downs and a sophisticated version of it is used by Otto Davis and John Jackson in paper 10 of this book); (2) voluntary agreements among individuals to insure themselves against unfavorable contingent events (dealt with, in detail, by Richard Zeckhauser in paper 8); and (3) utility interdependence, which postulates that benefactors make transfers because they are genuinely desirous of relieving the plight of the poor, or at least modifying the more conspicuous signs of their poverty (Rodgers himself, with one of the editors of this book, has considered this hypothesis in a number of earlier papers). Then, in a discussion that is both informal and heuristic, Rodgers examines the overall magnitude of poverty-alleviating transfers in the United States and the social mechanisms through which these are effected, and evaluates the empirical usefulness of the three alternative theories in explaining the observed facts.

The notion that the benefits of redistribution are really designed to be "intrapersonal," for the purpose of redistributing a man's income from good times to bad times, or from periods of high earnings to periods of low earnings, has an established place in the distributional choice literature. Redistribution of this sort, which is worked out over a person's lifetime, would have the appearance, of course, at any one time, of involving interpersonal redistribution, since at any one time men who are well off would be net contributors to such redistribution schemes whereas men who are poorly off would be net recipients. This idea is studied in more detail in the models that Richard Zeckhauser and Michell Polinsky develop in their papers.

The paper by Zeckhauser, very much in the spirit of Rawls, discusses the factors that determine why and how individuals might use redistribution as a means of spreading and reducing risk. One rationale for risk reduction emphazised by Zeckhauser but neglected in previous discussions of gambling, including the "gambles" that comprise the decision-making experience of human life, is the disutility of anxiety. The unresolved possibility that some catastrophic event will transpire, even though the probability is very low, creates anxiety that men want to eliminate. In order to alleviate this anxiety, they are likely to agree to finance some system that successfully identifies those who will suffer from the catastrophic event and those who will not. The desire to reduce anxiety in this way seems such a natural urge that it is surprising that none of the formal economic models of risk reduction acknowledges its existence. All these models treat prolonged uncertainty as identical with immediately resolved uncertainty, so long as the probability of a successful outcome in each case is the same.

As Zeckhauser points out, if men are equally likely to experience a disaster, they will be inclined to insure one another against its consequence. Once the event occurs, the insurance payments may make for substantial income redistribution, although before the event no redistribution of expected incomes is involved at all. However, the possibilities of arranging a mutually satisfactory insurance scheme diminish, the more information individuals have about their current and future status. Men who expect higher incomes are unlikely to contract with men who expect prolonged unemployment when insuring against the risk of low earnings, just as low-risk individuals are unlikely to join the same health-insurance pool as high-risk individuals, unless they get substantial "price" reductions. If men literally labored behind a "veil of ignorance" they would insure one another against almost all risks, at a uniform price. But starting from an initial position of considerable knowledge about life's prospects, the scope for income redistribution through voluntary insurance is much reduced.

Polinsky considers the possible role of the fiscal structure as an instrument of intertemporal redistribution. He demonstrates that the maximization of a person's lifetime utility may well require that he consume ahead of his income stream. If it is imposible to borrow current funds against one's expected future income, it may be desirable for the government to intervene and act as a lending agent for its citizens, by extending them more money in times of low income and taxing them at a higher rate when their income streams are greater. Some such rationalization underlies the social-security programs of this country. Where incomes are measured on a full lifetime basis such intertemporal redistribution need imply no interpersonal redistribution, even though cross-sectionally it will appear that incomes are being redistributed from the affluent to the poor.

The final group of papers, those under the heading "Redistribution and the Public Choice Process," explores some of the questions touching income redistribution that go beyond the usual economic models. In a paper that bridges economics and political science, Otto Davis and John Jackson attempt to interpret the voting of members of representative assemblies on distributional issues. The question they address is the one that occupied Edmund Burke: whether representatives of the people, once voting in assembly, reflect the will of their electorate or exercise independent judgment. Davis and Jackson dissect in some detail the votes of members of the U.S. Senate on three roll calls relating to the Family Assistance Plan and relate these to the political party of the legislator, his geographic region, and to an index of the sympathy for such a program among each legislator's constituency. Survey data, which differentiate among the attitudes of individuals by income, race, region and rural or urban place of residence, are used in constructing the measure of constituency support. In the aggregate, Davis and Jackson find that legislators tend to vote in accord with constituent desires on distributional issues. However, their results show that constituents' desires regarding distribution themselves fail to accord fully with self-interest. Both Southern constituents and Southern Senators appear to have been unfavorably disposed toward family assistance legislation, despite the fact that Southern states, in terms of fiscal flows, stood to gain most from it.

In contrast to Davis and Jackson, who envision legislators as politicians acting as proxies for their constituents, Julius Margolis traces out the implications of a more complex model of the politician and the political process. As Margolis describes him, the politician or government official, like many other actors in the social process, is a profit maximizer who interacts on various levels with the households and firms that demand government favor. Within this context, responsiveness to constituents is, as Margolis points out, but one means of obtaining the private returns that the politician seeks. He may equally well trade favors with special-interest groups, or provide services for those who can best finance them, either legally through campaign contributions or illegally through bribes. Any analysis that focuses solely on political "representation" of voters' desires fails to take into account the goals that motivate men to run for office in the first place, which Margolis argues often can be reduced to personal profit or power maximization.

The final paper by Harold Hochman considers the dilemma posed by policy attempts to correct inefficient or inequitable economic arrangements. Developing the notion of "fair" economic rules, as introduced by John Rawls, Hochman shows that these define endstates which rational men would agree are just. In fact, all men might agree that if society were to start *de novo,* one set of economic arrangements (say, free economic competition) would be "fairer" than another (say, monopolistic control of certain industries). However, we do not have the option of starting anew. And in trying to remove those inequitable arrangements that already exist policy-makers may work new injustices. Is the owner of a taxi license, who paid $20,000 for the right to operate his vehicle, to see the value of his license destroyed, because society now decides to legislate free competition? By its very nature a question like this about what constitutes a "fair" means of effecting a "fair" economic outcome does not permit a final answer. But Hochman examines the real-world political and economic mechanisms that are used to cope with the problems of transitional equity and offers grounds for choosing among them.

It may be appropriate, at this point, to mention two objections to the papers in this book that emerged during discussion at The Urban Institute conference. First, it was objected that the papers dealt almost exclusively with redistribution of income in favor of the poor, whereas in reality most redistribution that occurs in the United States is from middle-class taxpayers generally to some specific group of the middle class that has managed to carve out for itself a privileged niche in the country's tax and subsidy system. A recent study of tax incentives and subsidies conducted by the Joint Economic Committee of the Congress confirmed that the amount of money that the federal government disburses as price subsidies to agricultural producers, or to owners of capital in the form of reduced rates of taxation on capital gains, dwarfs in magnitude the transfers to the poor that occur in welfare programs.[3] Although these facts are incontrovertible, redistributive transfers in the United States on balance are equalizing, and it is this net redistribution in the direction of equality which emerges from the compromises and vicissitudes of the political process that this book is about.

As a second criticism, it was noted that all of the papers display signs of an exceedingly uneasy truce between theory and the real world. Economic models are discussed and policy implications are drawn from the models, without much effort to discuss the circumstances of the people—the "poor"—who are most affected by these policies. Whether it makes sense to hold a conference on income distribution, in an academic setting, without the presence of the poor or their interest groups, is a question that troubled many of those who attended the conference. The fact that government policies often are formulated in just this manner only points up the apparent incongruity of theorizing about—or legislating with regard to—poverty, while maintaining the poor at arm's length.

Finally, it would undoubtedly help the reader make his way through this book, if we could provide him with some idea as to what the total amount of income redistribution from rich to poor is in the

United States. Several ambitious attempts have been made to calculate the incidence, by income class, of all government benefits and to calculate the incidence, by income class, of all taxes, whether levied by state and local or federal governments.[4] Similar attempts have been made to catalog the magnitude of private transfers. However, the problems involved in this kind of calculation are so acute that it seems fruitless to reproduce the conclusions these papers have reached. Who shall we say benefits from price subsidies for agricultural products—the farmer or the consumer? How is the value of public schooling to be computed—by the amount expended, by the academic results achieved, or by the increments to pupils' lifetime earnings? Who benefits from the money spent on national defense, which alone accounts for a substantial portion of the national budget? Any calculation of the net distributive effect of governmental programs is extraordinarily sensitive to the assumptions that are made regarding consumer valuation of the program benefits, so much so that a defensible allocation of benefits from governmental programs can be no more than an urgent objective.

Even the calculation of tax payments is fraught with difficulty. Whether the burden of property-tax payments, the principal instrument of local taxation, falls upon the consumer of housing services or upon the owners of the housing stock is a matter of theoretical debate that remains unresolved. One author has gone so far as to argue that by far the most progressive element of the property tax derives from the deadweight loss that it imposes on the owners of capital. That is to say, the principal cost of the tax payment to wealthy families is taken to be the curtailment of profit opportunities that otherwise would exist rather than the actual payment of taxes. It should be clear that estimating the profits that would be reaped from investments that, in fact, are not undertaken is almost as speculative an enterprise as guessing who ought to be credited with the benefits from national-defense spending. Determining the ultimate incidence of other tax instruments, such as the corporate income tax, is almost equally difficult.

However, one example may suffice to show that the net redistribution accomplished by governmental intervention is less than many people believe. The most progressive of the tax instruments in the United States commonly is thought to be the personal-income tax. Good records are available as to the personal income of taxpayers, before and after payment of the federal income tax. Table 1 illus-

TABLE 1

Comparison of Percentage Shares of Family Personal Income Received by Fifths and Top 5 Percent Before and After Federal Individual Income Tax, 1962

Families ranked from lowest to highest income	Before Tax	After Tax
Poorest fifth	4.6%	4.9%
Second fifth	10.9	11.5
Middle fifth	16.3	16.8
Fourth fifth	22.7	23.1
Richest fifth	45.5	43.7
Total	100.0	100.0
Top 5 percent	19.6	17.7

Source: Edward C. Budd, ed., *Inequality and Poverty*. (New York: Norton, 1967) pp xiii, xvi.

trates that although income taxation does indeed reduce the inequality of incomes to some extent, by most standards the diminution of income inequality would be regarded as small.

We end this introduction where we began it, by noting that despite their urgency, many of the most basic questions about income distribution and redistribution remain unanswered. They remain unanswered in part because data are lacking, but more importantly because it has not been until recently that distributional questions have received the same thoughtful consideration among economists, political scientists, and others that has been accorded to the more standard academic topics. This book will have achieved its purpose if it encourages a more systematic application of social science theory to distributional issues.

NOTES

[1] J. S. Mill, *Principles of Political Economy*, J. M. Robson, ed. (Toronto: University of Toronto Press, 1965).

[2] J. Rawls, *A Theory of Justice* (Cambridge, Mass.: Harvard University Press, 1971).

[3] *The Economics of Federal Subsidy Programs*, Papers Submitted to the Joint Economic Committee (Washington, D.C.: Government Printing Office, 1972). See also G. Tullock, "The Charity of the Uncharitable," *Western Economic Journal* (December 1971).

[4] For example, W. I. Gillespie, "Effect of Public Expenditures on the Distribution of Income," in R. A. Musgrave, ed., *Essays in Fiscal Federalism* (Washington, D.C.: Brookings Institution, 1965). For a critical examination of the assumptions involved in such estimates, see Henry Aaron and Martin C. McGuire, "Public Goods and Income Distribution," *Econometrica* (December, 1970) .

Redistribution through Public Choice

I

The Institutional Setting for Distributional Questions

1

Income Redistribution
and Efficiency Norms

WILLIAM BREIT

The distinction between "efficiency" and "equity" has became a main staple of the literature of welfare economics. It is most often tied up with the question of judgments concerning the distribution of income and goes back at least to John Stuart Mill's famous distinction between the scientific and the "natural" laws of production contrasted with the institutionally determined laws of distribution.

In his now classic work, *Welfare and Competition,* published in 1951, Professor Tibor Scitovsky warned that the economist must always be prepared to judge economic organization and policies by the double criteria of efficiency and equity. But he soon relents. The economist cannot set up standards of equity since he has only one of the two yardsticks by which economic policy can be judged.[1] In discussing the problem of the distribution of income, Scitovsky concedes that only "common sense" and not economic science can justify "taking $100 from a millionaire and giving it to a beggar."[2] And he concludes that in regard to the distribution of income, "[i]t seems advisable... to keep objective and provable statements meticulously apart from argument based on subjective feeling alone. This is the basis of our distinction between efficiency and equity. We regard all arguments based on subjective judgment as matters of equity and use the term efficiency only in connection with statements that can be proved."[3]

William Breit is Professor of Economics at the University of Virginia. He wishes to express his indebtedness to William P. Culbertson. Jr., for his many trenchant suggestions. Others who must be named, but not implicated, are Edgar K. Browning, Kenneth G. Elzinga, Roland N. McKean, Donald L. Martin, John H. Moore, Laurence S. Moss, Edgar O. Olsen, and Roger Sherman. At a later stage James M. Buchanan and Martin Bronfenbrenner made penetrating criticisms.

In his long-awaited revised edition, published in 1971, Scitovsky added a chapter called "Equity and the Distribution of Income." He had, however, little to add to the subject as he had left it in 1951. "Equity," we are told solemnly, "is a matter of conscience, not of economics.... As long as total or virtually total ignorance persists on this subject the toleration of income inequalities must necessarily remain a matter of individual conscience."[4]

This is surely an unduly pessimistic judgment. From Adam Smith on, economists have had much to say about the effects of alternative distributional arrangements on welfare as defined in some sense that economists have believed would be given wide assent. Classical economics was concerned largely with the impact of various distributional possibilities on long-run annual per capita income. To Smith, of course, income inequality was a *sine qua non* of capital formation, the hiring of productive labor, and the maximization of annual income. In Malthus's treatment any redistribution of income in favor of the laboring class would lead to a higher birth rate among workers that would drive down the wage rate until the margin beyond the survival level disappeared. Hence no permanent improvement in laborers' living standards was possible, and it was folly for others to sacrifice their welfare in the vain attempt to improve the living conditions of the working class. The classical economists' policy recommendations were made on the basis of what they must have understood to be "weak" value judgments, judgments that most educated persons would accept once the implications of various distributional arrangements were understood. Of course they did not explicitly make a distinction between normative and positive analysis. But they at least vaguely sensed that recommendations concerning the appropriate distribution of income were necessary if the fledgling "moral science" of political economy was to be taken seriously as a discipline worthy of study.

The point being made is not the meek one that economists from time to time have advocated certain distributional policies, but the bolder assertion that they have traditionally done so in what they understood to be their role as economists. It is true that until the latter part of the nineteenth century precise economic reasoning seemed to indicate that inequality in the distribution of income was consistent with maximization of welfare as that term might have been understood. For this reason classical economic thought seemed to later writers to have "conservative" implications. Herbert J. Davenport, for example, writing in 1913, accused economics of being "a system of apologetics, the creed of the reactionary, a defence of privilege, a social soothing sirup—a smug pronouncement of the righteousness of whatever is—with the still more disastrous corollary of the unrighteousness of whatever is not."[5] In fact, at the time that Davenport wrote these words of indictment (no doubt under the charismatic spell of his colleague at the University of Missouri, Thorstein Veblen) economists could hardly be charged with "the painting of utopias and the capitalizing of dreams."[6] For by then the emphasis had decidedly shifted from the defense of inequality to a much more egalitarian stance. Economists were using the most powerful tools of their science in ways that indicated that efficiency in the distribution of income required a great degree of redistribution.

In 1883 the English utilitarian, Henry Sidgwick, had sounded a clarion call to reform in the name of economic science: "The more society approximates to equality in the distribution of wealth among its members, the greater on the whole is the aggregate of satisfactions which the society in question derives from the wealth that it possesses."[7] Sidgwick referred to Bentham as his authority for the notion that "aggregate satisfactions" are the best benchmark of welfare. But it was the development of Jevons's tool of diminishing marginal utility that gave to such recommendations a degree of precision and force unparalleled in the history of the subject.

In 1902 Edwin Cannan read a paper in which he explicitly referred to the contributions of Jevons on marginal utility and stated: "Moralists and Statesmen have long seen the evils of great inequality of wealth, and now, thanks to modern discoveries in economic theory, the economist is able to explain that it is wasteful."[8] Not long after this, Cannan explained the change from the classical emphasis on inequality to the neoclassical stress on greater equality as being a result of a change in the analytical equipment of economics, not a change in values. "This change is due in great measure to... the doctrine of marginal utility, which stamps as economical many things which could formerly be recommended only on 'sentimental' or non-economic grounds."[9] Pigou carried the argument further than anyone else in his book *Wealth and Welfare* and in later editions of his *The Economics of Welfare*. He stated unequivocally: "[I]t is evident that any transference of income from a relatively rich man to a relatively poor man of similar temperament, since it enables more intense wants to be satisfied at the expense of less intense wants, must increase the aggregate sum of satisfaction. The... 'law of diminishing utility' thus leads securely to the proposition: any cause which increases the absolute share of real income in the hands of the poor, provided that it does not lead to a contraction in the size of the national dividend from any point of view, will, in general, increase economic welfare."[10]

In 1920 Hugh Dalton, a Member of Parliament and Reader in Economics at the University of London, and later Chancellor of the Exchequer, published his book, *Some Aspects of the Inequality of Incomes in Modern Communities*. Dalton minced no words in asserting the scientific foundations of his policy recommendations. He said categorically: "An unequal distribution of a given amount of purchasing power among a given number of people is, therefore, likely to be a wasteful distribution from the point of view of economic welfare, and the more unequal the distribution the greater the waste. This is merely an application of the economists' law of diminishing marginal utility...."[11] In his later works on public finance he made use of this doctrine to justify progressive taxation.[12] In 1929 Josiah Wedgwood, at the beginning of his book, *The Economics of Inheritance*, stated that when "the full implication[s] of the theory of diminishing utility of successive additions to income are realized,... it becomes obvious that great inequalities in the division of the product of industry among the individuals concerned are not only socially deplorable but an *economic* defect in the social system."[13]

Unluckily for egalitarians, the authority with which economists could offer redistributional advice was severely shaken in 1932, when Lionel Robbins published his *An Essay on the Nature and Significance of Economic Science*. Among the many contributions of that book was the disheartening suggestion that economic science could not establish a basis for income redistribution using the utilitarian efficiency norm and the principle of diminishing marginal utility. Although the great majority of English economists had accepted the principle of redistribution as following ineluctably from economic science, Robbins ventured to suggest that the idea was "entirely unwarranted by any doctrine of scientific economics...."[14] Amazingly, from the vantage point of hindsight, economists had overlooked the "great metaphysical question" of the comparability of different individual experiences. As every sophomore in economics learns almost immediately, interpersonal comparisons of utility cannot be made since there is no means of testing the magnitude of one person's satisfaction as compared to another's.

Robbins's earthquake (although anticipated on the continent by Pareto) hit the economists of the twentieth century almost as hard as Jevons's tornado had hit their predecessors. The idea that redistribution of income was a scientifically grounded policy lingered on only in the economic underworld. In the depths of the Great Depression, when inadequate demand was, by wide agreement, the cause of the debacle, redistribution doctrines found a warm and agreeable shelter in the house of underconsumptionists of both institutionalist and Marxist varieties. But the justification for such policies was no longer based on neoclassical utility theory and the utilitarian ethic.[15]

One valiant and ingenious last attempt to salvage something from Lionel Robbins's wreck was made by one of his former students, Abba P. Lerner. In 1944, in his *The Economics of Control,* Lerner argued that it was still possible to give advice on income redistribution even when it is admitted that we are agnostics on any individual's utility function. In Lerner's words: "If it is impossible, on any division of income, to discover which of any two individuals has a higher marginal utility of income, the probable value of total satisfactions is maximized by dividing income evenly."[16] In arguing his case Lerner relied upon the following five assumptions.

1. [I]t is not meaningless to say that a satisfaction one individual gets is greater or less than a satisfaction enjoyed by someone else.

2. There is no way of discovering with certainty whether any individual's marginal utility of income is greater than, equal to or less than that of any other individual.

3. The principle of diminishing marginal utility of money income holds generally.

4. [S]atisfaction is received only from one's own income.

5. [The analysis is presented as] the solution to the problem of maximizing the probable satisfactions that can be attained by the member of society from a given income.

Because Lerner's analysis is one of the most remarkable analytical feats in economic science, it will be instructive to review his argument here.[17]

Let us refer to Figure 1 for an illustration of this argument. By assumption 3 we know that the marginal utilities of income schedules correspond to those illustrated in Figure 1. But by assumption 2 we cannot know to which individual to assign each schedule. Thus we have no way of knowing the division of income that will maximize total satisfactions. In effect then, we know that starting from any unequal division of income and given a movement to an equal (or more equal) division of income, we are just as likely to have diminished total satisfactions as to have increased them. For example, in Figure 1 suppose person A to have a money income of $120 and person B to have a money income of $80. This unequal division of income may correspond to point X in Figure 1, where Schedule I will be that of person A and Schedule II will be that of person B. If we were now to transfer $20 from A to B (that is, in Figure 1 a movement from point X to point E) we would increase B's satisfactions by area H but diminish A's satisfactions by area H plus area G. There would be a net loss of satisfactions equal to area G. But it is equally likely by assumption 2 that the initial division of income (A=$120, B=$80) corresponds to point X' where Schedule II is that of A and Schedule I that of B. Under these equally likely circumstances, the transfer of $20 from A to B (that is, a movement from point X' to point E in Figure 1) would diminish A's satisfactions by area J but increase B's satisfactions by area J plus area K. There would be a net gain in satisfactions equal to area K. Since either result (net loss of G or net gain of K) is equally likely and since the gain exceeds the net loss (K > G) the maximization of the probable total value of satisfactions requires that income be divided evenly.

Some of the initial excitement generated by this model is inevita-

FIGURE 1

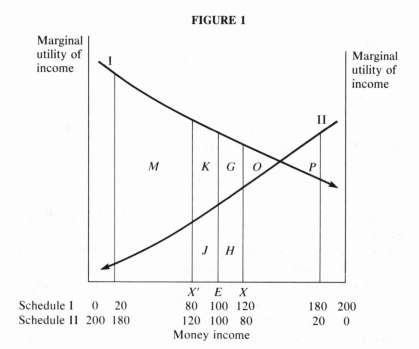

Schedule I	0 20	80 100 120	180 200
Schedule II	200 180	120 100 80	20 0

Money income

bly reduced when it is realized that the analysis rests on the implausible idea that incentives are not affected by the redistribution; that the income being divided has been received by chance and is in no way related to functional distribution. Futhermore Lerner created some confusion by switching his analysis from his rather mild probabilistic assertion to a much stronger proposition regarding actual satisfactions. The latter proposition he has since disclaimed.[18]

During the 1950's the question of income redistribution generally disappeared from economic discussion. With the overwhelming emphasis on economic growth and its ubiquitous benefits, the size of the pie was of greater interest than the distribution of the slices. In the latter part of the 1960's events once again brought the distribution question to the attention of economic theorists.

The recent contributions have eschewed the older approach based on the maximization of satisfactions. Instead, an individualistic approach is taken in which Pareto optimality becomes the welfare criterion. These economists have dispensed with counting noses and summing satisfactions. The optimum is not defined as a maximization of aggregate satisfactions but rather in terms of movements to positions where no one can be made better off without making someone else worse off. There have been two basic variants of this approach. One is based on a voting model analysis in which it is argued that redistribution schemes would be voted in unanimously at the constitutional level of choice. If we assume that each individual is a risk averter and that he is completely ignorant about the income he will receive in the future, the individual, rather than take a chance on getting too low an income, would prudently vote for equality.[19]

One of the chief weaknesses of this approach is the strong assumption that individuals know nothing about their future income. They are, in a sense, imagined to be voting from the womb, without any knowledge concerning whose womb they are in. Since it is likely to be impossible to achieve unanimity, even at the constitutional level, something short of unanimity is necessary. But this removes the analysis from the realm of pure Pareto optimality and places it into the category of "honorary" Pareto optimality.[20] Any movement without compensation payments to the losers must inevitably involve interpersonal comparisons of utility and we are face to face once again with Lionel Robbins's objections, which have never been successfully answered.

The other approach entails the assumption of interdependent utility functions combined with the theory of externalities and public goods. The interdependent utilities approach was given its initial impetus by James M. Buchanan's assertion that in the purely individualistic model confined to a single period choice some net redistribution would tend to be carried out by the fiscal system. But, unlike the voting model approach for multiperiod choice, "this transfer would depend on the fact that individuals include the utility of others than themselves as arguments in their own utility functions."[21]

This suggestion of Buchanan's was followed up by Hochman and Rodgers in an important paper published in 1969.[22] In their model it is assumed that individuals are motivated by benevolence in the sense that one man's welfare is assumed to enter in a positive and marginally relevant way into another's preferences. Their argument, in essence, takes the following form. If A gets pleasure from seeing B with a higher money income and if, indeed, B is better off when he receives the money (as evidenced by his not rejecting the transfer), it is Pareto optimal for A to transfer money income to B. At this point, Hochman and Rogers introduce the notion of the "free rider," which turns the analysis into a case for collectivization of the transfer because charity is seen to be a public good. That is, A expects that another person, C, whose well-being is also interdependent with B's welfare, will be motivated to transfer money income to B. But C has similar expectations with regard to A and would prefer to "free ride" off A's generosity. It follows that, just as in the case of national defense and lighthouses, an optimal amount of private charity does not emerge. Coercive taxation to finance the transfers is called for in order to achieve Pareto optimality. In short, the interdependent utility assumption means that externalities exist that can be internalized by the state, and the standard public goods argument is adduced as an "explanation" and justification of collective redistribution schemes.

Hochman and Rodgers claim that one advantage of their approach is that it allows us to analyze the motives behind redistribution. In other words, the assumption of interdependence allows us to "get behind" the utility function and see why people are dissatisfied with the laissez-faire distribution of income. If benevolence is the explanation of redistribution, that is worth knowing, and the interdependent utility assumption allows a technical examination of the full implications of such motivation.

This alluring prospect held out by the utility interdependence approach is vitiated, however, when we realize that we cannot learn much about motives when we use it. The truth is that the Hochman and Rodgers utility function in which benevolence is the explanation of redistribution has the same implications for equality as the motive of malevolent concern with the incomes of the rich, in which envy drives the poor to "level down" the incomes of the rich.[23] But if the same evidence can be adduced to support precisely opposite explanations of individual motivation, this must mean that, even when we

step behind the utility function to peer at motives, we still are looking through a glass darkly. And it should be noted that no amount of
rationalization could support the proposition that redistribution that
follows from malevolent concerns is Pareto optimal, since the whole
point of a malevolent impulse must be the desire to see at least one
other person worse off.

Moreover, it is not clear why the motives behind an individual giving to charity or voting taxes to coerce himself and others to redistribute income to the poor should require more scrutiny than the
forces motivating the same individual to purchase private goods. An
individual buys an ordinary commodity because he has a preference
for it; it enters as an argument into his utility function. Why cannot
charity and the fiscal residuals that indicate redistribution be
explained on the basis of an individual's having preference for
greater equality? In short, it can be hypothesized that the distribution
of income itself enters as an argument into the individual's utility
function. If such a model is used, redistribution will be seen to be a
collectively supplied public good in which the actual degree of
equality in the distribution of income is arrived at through a majority
voting process generating an outcome to which all must adjust. This
approach, using the conventional assumption of utility independence, will overcome the chief defects of the recent formulations
while, in some measure, retaining the individualistic approach.[24]

In order to clarify the issues involved in the theory of income redistribution it will be useful to refer to a geometrical artifact. Along
the horizontal axis in Figure 2 we measure the degree of inequality
in the distribution of money income. This is expressed in terms of a
Gini coefficient of concentration, which is derived from the area between the Lorenz curve for an economy and the diagonal of perfect
equality stated as a proportion of the total area under the diagonal.
This coefficient has a range between 0 (for complete equality) and 1
(for extreme inequality).

Along the vertical axis we measure the real output of the
economy, and we shall make the simplifying assumption that the
economy produces only two physical commodities, A and B, and
there are no externalities present. Now we shall assume that there is
a unique income distribution consistent with the maximum level of

FIGURE 2

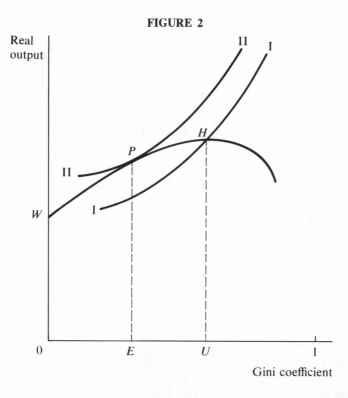

real output. This maximum output is attained when the rate of substitution of final products in purchase on the market is equal to the rate at which it is technically possible to substitute final products in production. In other words, each factor is paid in accordance with its marginal product. As long as each factor is paid in accordance with its marginal product it has an incentive to seek employment where its product is highest. Similarly the buyer of resources has an incentive to use the resources most efficiently, if he is being paid in accordance with his marginal productivity. Hence total output is maximized. In our diagram this point is representend by *H*. Perhaps it is not necessary to add that this payment in accordance with marginal productivity secures the most efficient allocation of resources by setting the rates per unit of resource. It does not, however, determine the distribution of income to each individual in society, since total income of any individual depends not only on the rate but also on the amount of resources that he owns. Since there are inequalities in the ownership of resources, the resulting Gini coefficient will not be consistent with an equal distribution of income. On our diagram the resulting Gini coefficient churned out by payment of all factors in accordance with marginal productivity is U.

Since H represents maximum real output, all points to the left and right of H will be lower than H. That is, the redistribution of money income from Gini coefficient U to achieve any Gini coefficient to the left or right of U will adversely affect the efficient allocation of resources, making for lower real output. This must be true because redistribution cannot be accomplished by magic. Taxes must be imposed and payments made to individuals without regard to marginal productivity. Since lump sum taxes are impossible and some uses of resources, such as leisure, are untaxable, there are no taxes that do not entail damage to output by inducing resources to be shifted to less efficient uses. Thus the attempt to change the Gini coefficient from U to any other distribution of income will, by altering incentives, lower real output.[25]

We can now draw a curve connecting all points to maximum output associated with each distribution of income. It is assumed that there is only one redistributive program consistent with some maximum level of real output and that each Gini coefficient is associated with a *unique* distribution of income and real output. This curve cuts the vertical axis at W, indicating that complete equality of income distribution will be associated with some maximum positive level of real output. The curve rises over a range of Gini coefficients until it reaches point H—the output generated when all the marginal conditions are properly satisfied—and then declines. Each point along this "output possibilities" curve associated with a unique Gini coefficient represents the most efficient point along some corresponding and unique production possibilities curve for commodities A and B.

In order to "explain" the income distribution that will be uniquely determined in our society, it will be useful to make the fairly strong assumption that each individual in society knows the Gini coefficient and has a preference as to what he would like it to be. In other words, we explicitly introduce the distribution of income itself (along with real output) as an argument in the individal's utility function. We can then draw an indifference map for such an individual in which each curve shows the trade-offs between real output and the alternative Gini coefficients consistent with that output.[26]

What will the slope of such a curve look like? It seems plausible that most people would be indifferent in choosing between alternative combinations of greater equality and lower real output. That is, the indifference curve would be convex from below, and it is represented in Figure 2 as curve I. It should be noted that indifference curve I cuts the real output possibilities curve at *H*, indicating that the market process leading to the most efficient output of commodities A and B does not generate a Gini coefficient allowing this individual to maximize his satisfactions. In order to reach his highest indifference curve it is necessary that redistribution take place in such a manner as to generate Gini coefficient *E*. At this point the individual reaches his highest indifference curve II, which is tangent to the output possibilities curve at *P*. If this is a plausible psychology to assume for most persons, it follows that individuals will reach their position of maximum satisfaction in regard to their choice between real output and the desired income distribution at some point to the left of *H*. In other words individuals will attempt to maximize their satisfactions by choosing a Gini coefficient of greater equality than that determined by strict adherence to marginal productivity rules.

Perhaps it would be useful to explore briefly the properties of an individual's psychology different from that described above. Specifically, what would the indifference curve of an individual who was satisfied with the Gini coefficient *U* be like? In other words, what is implied by saying that an individual accepts the marginal productivity distribution as the appropriate distribution or that an individual accepts completely the ethical proposition that people deserve—and only deserve—what is produced by the resources they own?

As everybody knows, this is the principle enunciated by John Bates Clark: "If each production function is paid for according to the amount of its product, then each man gets what he himself produces.... If wages, interest and profits, in themselves considered, are fixed according to a sound principle, then the different classes of men who combine their forces in industry have no grievances against each other. If functions are paid according to their products, men are also. Hence, while rights are personal, the issue of rights that is involved in distribution is settled by a functional study."[27] More recently, Robert Strotz has maintained that "income should be distributed so that total income is a maximum."[28]

To take Clark and Strotz seriously would imply an indifference curve that is tangent to the output possibilities curve at H. For an individual's indifference curve to be tangent to the output possibilities curve at H would require that it be either horizontal, bell shaped, or V shaped. Since our usual conception of an indifference curve conflicts with this construction, such a psychology seems strange and unrealistic (assuming, of course, that the Gini coefficient is an argument in the utility function).

We can conclude, therefore, that the distribution of income resulting from the marginal productivity rule is unlikely to be acceptable to most individuals in society. Moreover, by including the Gini coefficient as an argument in the individual's utility function, we have, in effect, said that redistribution is a "collective good." For we must all live with one uniquely determined Gini coefficient. Each person cannot adjust to his optimally preferred quantities, since redistribution is a good supplied collectively. It is probable that some individuals will prefer a Gini coefficient to the right of E in Figure 2 and some will prefer it to be to the left. But only individuals with indifference curves identical with that representing the median preferences of society will achieve the desired distributional arrangement, under a simple majority voting scheme, since median preferences remain controlling under majority voting.[29]

It might be objected that any individual who is unhappy with the outcome of the democratic process and prefers more equality to the amount represented by the collectively supplied Gini coefficient can himself affect the Gini coefficient through private charity. But the "free rider" argument blunts the thrust of this assertion. Since the number of persons with whom any individual interacts is large, the individual will consider his own behavior to have little effect on others. In other words, "utility-maximizing behavior does not dictate that voluntary action toward common ends be independently or privately taken."[30] Therefore the individual reacts by adjusting to the behavior of "others." Moreover it can be seen that preferences for redistribution as expressed in some Gini coefficient lead to the classic public-goods problem on both the demand and the supply side. On the demand side, the individual may dissemble his preferences in order to "free ride" on the charitable inclinations of others. On the supply side, as already noted, individuals must adjust to the same collectively supplied Gini coefficient.

It should be noted that although we have asserted the public-goods character of redistribution, we have maintained an independent utility methodology. Indeed the analysis is consistent in spirit with that of Henry Simons, who asserted candidly that "the case for drastic progression in taxation must be rested on the case against inequality—on the ethical or aesthetic judgment that the prevailng distribution of wealth and income reveals a degree ... of inequality which is distinctly evil or unlovely."[31] Our argument is that the aesthetic judgment of Henry Simons reveals a preference that "makes sense" in the light of what we know about the ordinary properties of indifference curves. But if Simons-type preferences for equality are typical, there are evident externalities to be internalized by collectivizing the consumption of this good. One could, of course, make this voting model consistent with Pareto optimality by alleging that such a rule might be determined unanimously at the constitutional level of choice. However, the cost involved in achieving unanimity, even at the constitutional level, are probably so great that we would have to settle for something short of unanimity and therefore short of Pareto optimality in justification of the redistribution decision.[32]

It might be tempting to conclude that our actual government policies in respect to redistribution do not support the insurance-voting model approach, the utility interdependence approach, or the approach taken in this paper. For example, it has been alleged by George Stigler that actual redistributive expenditures follow Director's law: "Redistributive expenditures are primarily for the middle classes, and financed with taxes imposed on the poor and the rich."[33]

The evidence, however, is not consistent with the assertion. The middle income classes, the dominant group that can secure control of the coercive machinery of the state, employ this machinery to tax the rich and give to the poor. The most comprehensive empirical study of the total effects of both government taxation and expenditures at all levels of government concludes that net "redistribution occurs from the upper income brackets to the lower income brackets, but not in the middle income brackets,"[34] Although there are serious problems involved in any attempt to quantify either benefits received or tax costs paid, by income class, this evidence is consistent with a theory that argues that the resulting Gini coefficient is the one desired by the class in society with median preferences that achieves the desired redistributional arrangement through a simple majority voting scheme. Voters impose taxes on the rich and redistribute the proceeds to the poor in order to satisfy their own preferences for a greater degree of equality. The desire on the part of middle-income classes to redistribute, through the fiscal system, from rich to poor might be based on a desire for greater social stability. The fear of the middle-income groups that rioting, looting, burning, and other crimes are a result of relative poverty induces them to prefer greater equality than the laissez-faire solution to the distribution problem brings about. Thus a narrow self-interest motive is completely consistent with egalitarian preferences. The middle-income classes simply take advantage of the majority voting rule to achieve the desired Gini coefficient at the expense of the rich. To this arrangement everybody in society adjusts. It is possible to hold to this theory without any claim of interdependence in utility functions, or even to a voting model in which greater equality is the prudent risk averter's way to insure against unforeseen contingencies in his future income. One bonus that comes from the acceptance of this theory is that it dispenses with Pareto optimality as a justification for coercive redistributive schemes. The repeal of Director's law has left a void. I suggest that its place be filled by Mencken's law, which states all that needs to be said on the subject of alleged utility interdependence as justification for income redistribution: "Whenever A annoys or injures B on the pretense of saving or improving X , A is a scoundrel."[35]

NOTES

[1]Tibor Scitovsky, *Welfare and Competition* (Homewood: Richard D. Irwin, 1951), p. 59.

[2]*Ibid.,* p. 60.

[3]*Ibid.*

[4]Tibor Scitovsky, *Welfare and Competition,* rev. ed. (Homewood: Richard D. Irwin, 1971) pp. 287-88.

[5]Herbert J. Davenport, *The Economics of Enterprise* (New York: Augustus M. Kelley, 1968), p. 528. First published in 1913.

[6]*Ibid.,* p. 530.

[7]Henry Sidgwick, *The Principles of Political Economy* (London: Macmillan, 1883), p. 519.

[8]Edwin Cannan, *The Economic Outlook* (London: P.S. King, 1912), p. 178.

[9]Edwin Cannan, *Theories of Production and Distribution of Classical Political Economy* (London: Staples Press, 1953), pp. 405-7.

[10]A.C. Pigou, *The Economics of Welfare,* 4th ed. (London: Macmillan, 1932), p. 89.

[11]Hugh Dalton, *Some Aspects of the Inequality of Incomes in Modern Communities* (London: Routledge, 1920), p. 10.

[12]Walter J. Blum and Harry Kalven, Jr. *The Uneasy Case for Progressive Taxation* (Chicago: University of Chicago Press, 1963), pp. 39-45, 74-80.

[13]Josiah Wedgwood, *The Economics of Inheritance* (London: Routledge, 1929), p. 3.

[14]Lionel Robbins, *An Essay on the Nature and Significance of Economic Science,* 2d ed. (London: Macmillan, 1935), p. 137.

[15]Two of the major underconsumptionists making a case for redistribution were H. Gordon Hayes and C.E. Ayres. An exposition of the maldistributionist case for redistribution and some statistical skepticism with regard to such arguments can be found in Martin Bronfenbrenner, *Income Distribution Theory* (Chicago and New York: Aldine Atherton, 1971), pp. 104-12.

[16]Abba P. Lerner, *The Economics of Control* (London: Macmillan, 1944), p. 29.

[17]The following paragraph is taken, without substantial change, from William Breit and William P. Culbertson, Jr., "Distributional Equality and Aggregate Utility," *American Economic Review* (June, 1970), p. 436.

[18]*Ibid.,* pp. 435-41. See also Abba P. Lerner, "Distributional Equality and Aggregate Utility: Reply," *American Economic Review* (June, 1970), pp. 442-43.

[19]James M. Buchanan and Gordon Tullock, *The Calculus of Consent* (Ann Arbor: University of Michigan Press, 1962), ch. 13.

[20]I am indebted to my colleague, Leland B. Yeager, for suggesting this term to me.

[21]James M. Buchanan, *Public Finance in Democratic Process* (Chapel Hill: University of North Carolina Press, 1967), p. 296. Buchanan's first suggestion of the public-goods character of redistribution is contained in his review article devoted to Musgrave's "Theory of Public Finance" in *Southern Economic Journal* (January, 1960), pp. 234-38, especially p. 236.

[22]Harold M. Hochman and James D. Rodgers, "Pareto Optimal Redistribution," *American Economic Review* (September, 1969), pp. 542-57.

20   William Breit

[23]Bronfenbrenner has noted this symmetry without drawing the implications. See Martin Bronfenbrenner, *Income Distribution Theory*, p. 101n.

[24]Lester C. Thurow also treats redistribution as a public good and dispenses with the assumption of interdependent utility functions. Both Thurow and I draw similar conclusions using such a model. However, my approach has the advantage of a simpler geometrical construction than that employed by Thurow and, I believe, brings out the issues more sharply. For one thing, Thurow does not seem to realize that a public goods problem arises in the case of interdependent utility functions as well as when the distribution of income per se enters as an argument into the utility function. See Lester C. Thurow, "The Income Distribution as a Pure Public Good," *Quarterly Journal of Economics* (May, 1971), pp. 327-36.

[25]For a review and restatement of this proposition, see Abba P. Lerner, "On Optimal Taxes With an Untaxable Sector," *American Economic Review* (June, 1970), pp. 284-94.

[26]Charles Goetz has pointed out to me that since some items valued by persons are not priced in ordinary measures of output (e.g., leisure), the dimensions along both the abscissa and ordinate in Figure 2, for purposes of logical rigor, should be considered to be measured in terms of some utility dimension. However, for purposes of objective measurement, the Gini coefficient is taken with respect to money income distribution, and the money value of output, as measured, is used as the dimension on the ordinate.

[27]John Bates Clark, *The Distribution of Wealth* (New York: Kelley & Millman 1956), pp. 7-8.

[28]Robert Strotz, "How Income Ought to Be Distributed: A Paradox in Distributive Ethics," *Journal of Political Economy* (June, 1958), p. 197.

[29]The issues involved in majority voting and the demand for collectively supplied goods are discussed in detail in James M. Buchanan, *Public Finance in Democratic Process,* especially chs. 9, 11, 12. It should be noted that the model employed in this paper is not necessary to "explain" the observed departures from pure productivity distribution. Under the latter, we know that average income would be higher than median income. If the recipients of the redistribution are franchised, and everyone votes purely in terms of his own self-interest, the median voter would control the outcome, and departures from pure productivity distribution would be observed. Neither interpendence nor public good assumptions are necessary for this result. However, the model employed in this paper leads to the prediction that, even if recipients of the transfers could not vote, there would be observed departures from the pure productivity distribution. But the above consideration is particularly damaging to Hochman-Rodgers and all other Pareto optimal redistribution arguments, since genuine Pareto optimal redistribution cannot be convincingly claimed unless recipients are eliminated from franchise.

[30]*Ibid.,* p. 114.

[31]Henry Simons, *Personal Income Taxation* (Chicago: University of Chicago Press, 1938), pp. 18-19.

[32]It is worth noting that the mere demonstration of the public goods character of any commodity (and hence of "market failure") does not necessarily imply that its collective provision financed through coercive taxation would involve Pareto-optimal moves. For if one person objects to the collective provision of this good and is not

compensated to achieve his approval when the action is taken, then the move violates the Pareto criterion. It is unlikely that most decisions to provide public goods in cases of "market failure" ever involve Pareto-optimal moves. This is not to imply that the goods ought not to be provided collectively, only that the Pareto-optimality criterion alone is an unsatisfactory guide to public policy.

[33]George J. Stigler, "Director's Law of Public Income Redistribution" *The Journal of Law and Economics* (April, 1970), pp. 1-9.

[34]W. Irwin Gillespie, "Effect of Public Expenditures on the Distribution of Income" in Richard A. Musgrave, ed., *Essays in Fiscal Federalism* (Washington, D.C., The Brookings Institution, 1965), pp. 122-86. Quote on page 166.

[35]H.L. Mencken, *Newspaper Days 1899-1906* (New York: Knopf, 1941), p. 38. After stating his law. Mencken went on to lament, "The moral theologians, unhappily, have paid no heed to this contribution to their science; and so Mencken's law must wait for recognition until the dawn of a more enlightened age." I am indebted to Miss Betty Adler, curator of the Mencken Room at the Enoch Pratt Free Library in Baltimore, for kindly supplying me with this reference.

2

Who Should Distribute What in a Federal System?

JAMES M. BUCHANAN

It is frequently asserted that redistribution, as a governmental function, can be properly assigned only to the central or national government.[1] The remaining half of this assertion implies that allocative functions can, by contrast, be performed by local governmental units if the appropriately defined "publicness" ranges are spatially limited and if interjurisdictional spillovers are not significant. I want to examine this "principle" of modern public finance theory in some detail and in some depth.

It is difficult to separate positive and normative strands in the orthodox discussion of this principle. If redistribution is interpreted exclusively in terms of coercively-imposed transfers of income and wealth from some persons to others, dicussion concerning the possibility of carrying out this activity at various levels of government reduces to a single positive proposition. The ability of any person, agency, or governmental unit to coerce another depends on the range of alternatives open to the one to be coerced. If an individual has available to him multiple options that offer substantially the same utility prospects, no other person exerts much power over him. In the limit, the perfectly competitive market minimizes man's power over man or, conversely, maximizes man's freedom from coercion by other men. It should be evident that the power of any government to extract income and wealth coercively from a person is related inversely to the locational alternatives that are available to

James M. Buchanan is University Professor of Economics and General Director, Center for Public Choice, at Virginia Polytechnic Institute and State University. He is indebted to his colleague, Charles Goetz, for helpful comments.

that person. For this reason alone, a local governmental unit in a national economy is severely limited in its strictly zero-sum redistributive activity. It is constrained by the ability of individuals to shift among alternative locationally separated jurisdictions, and this constraining influence operates even when the existence of relevant and sometimes significant decision thresholds is acknowledged. Since persons do not have comparable abilities to shift readily across national boundaries, the power of a central or national government to enforce imposed redistribution policies is clearly greater than that possessed by local authorities.

If this is all there is to the "principle" that the redistributive function must be performed centrally, extended discussion would hardly seem to be warranted. In what follows I assume that those who advance the principle have something more than this in mind, and especially that attention is not exclusively focused on the strictly zero-sum redistributive activities of governments. In Section I, I discuss the sharing of gains-from-trade from the provision of collective consumption of public goods at the various governmental levels, In Section II the related but analytically separate category that is commonly called "Pareto optimal redistribution" is examined. In this setting income-wealth redistribution is itself treated as a public good. In Section III the Pareto optimality approach is extended to apply to the whole set of institutions or processes that generate specific distributional outcomes. As will become evident, the discussion in this section is most closely related to the explicitly normative or value-laden treatment that is accorded distribution by many scholars. In both Sections II and III an attempt is made to restrict discussion to those aspects of the analysis that bear directly on the functional location of redistribution in a hierarchical governmental system, that is, in a federal polity.

I. DISTRIBUTION OF GAINS-FROM-TRADE

Gains-from-Trade in Private Goods

Modern economic theory is somewhat misleading in its distributive implications. Given an initial set of individual resource endowments, including capacities or skills, this theory implies that there is a uniquely determinate position on the utility-possibility frontier that tends to be produced through the operation of the market process. The final distribution of the gross gains-from-trade seems to be determined independently of the path or process through which it is reached. In one sense this suggests first the solving of the simultaneous equations of the whole complex system and second the inference from solution to that unique set of initial endowments that might have been required to generate it. This has always seemed to me to turn things around. The market process tends to generate an equilibrium, but the location of this equilibrium on the "social utility surface," that is, its distributional characteristics, depends on the path through which it is approached. It seems unreal to postulate the perfect recontracting that is required to produce a one-for-one correspondence between an initial set of endowments and a final distribution of utility or welfare among individuals. Any plausibly realistic model must allow exchange to be made, and implemented, before equilibrium is finally, if ever, attained. Trading at prices that are different from those that might characterize the potentially attainable final general equilibrium solution must be allowed to take place. Once this is done, however, the path toward the utility-possibility frontier delineates the set of positions attainable on the frontier.[2]

Markets do not work perfectly, and there are numerous constraints on the freedom of trading among individuals and groups. If we drop the formalism of modern general-equilibrium theory, we can discuss the market process within any given set of externally imposed constraints. It becomes meaningful to talk about the characteristics of the equilibrium that will tend to emerge within the set of institutional limits postulated, and we can utilize the concept of a feasible or attainable utility-possibility frontier, the location of which will be dependent on such limits.

I can illustrate this point geometrically and in such a way as to introduce the central elements of this paper. Figure 1 is drawn in a two-man utility space. I want to use this two-man construction, however, both here and later, to depict situations faced by individuals in many-person settings. Hence, to each person in the construction, the "other person" is conceived to be the whole environment

FIGURE 1

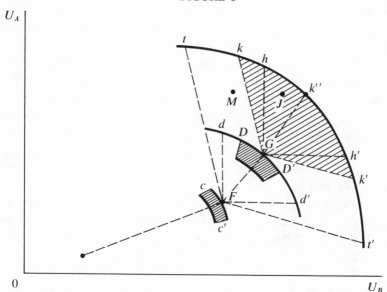

that he confronts, including the behavior of many other persons, an environment that he considers to be beyond his own power of control or influence, at least in any direct sense.

In a Hobbesian world, where life is indeed "nasty, brutish, and short," and where neither property rights nor trade exists, the utility positions attained by the two persons, A and B, are shown at *E* in Figure 1. This position depicts reaction-curve equilibrium in the savage and anarchistic "society." The distribution of utility, which reflects the instrumental distribution of real goods, depends strictly on the relative abilities of persons to survive and prosper in the hostile environment of potential conflict.

Once property rights are defined and legally protected, market-type exchanges become possible, and these allow dramatic gains to be secured by all parties. Modern microeconomic theory implies that movement takes place along a unique price vector, which could be indirectly represented in Figure 1 by the heavily dotted line extending from *E* to point *F*, a position on a utility-possibility frontier under the institutional structure that allows voluntary exchange. As noted above, the one-to-one relationship between E and F exists only in a regime of perfect recontracting, which requires, in its turn, the presence of a large number of traders on both sides of all markets, along with an absence of all barriers to the consummation of trade. If we drop any of these requirements, the one-to-one correspondence vanishes and the initial position, E, along with a practically workable market order may produce a position along or near a finite and narrowly defined segment of a frontier. The shaded area between and below the points c and c' depicts this set of positions. Regardless of the particulars of the institutional process, we can think of the market or exchange system as insuring that one position in this set will be attained.

It is important to understand the basic reason for the relatively narrow limits within which the final distribution of the gains-from-trade is bounded. These limits are a direct consequence of the ability of single traders to select among alternatives. In the extreme and formal model each trader is a pure price taker in all markets. There is no room for bargaining, as such, despite the presence of mutual gains in each two-party contract. We need not impose the severe restrictions of the formal model, however, to confine the utility or welfare distribution within relatively narrow limits, as shown.

Gains-from-Trade in Local Public Goods

We may now introduce localized collective-consumption or public goods and services. Suppose that the existing technology along with existing individual preference functions makes possible the efficient joint consumption of certain goods and services that are spatially limited and that are nonexcludable among beneficiaries. Local governmental units emerge to finance and to provide these goods and services. We assume, as before, that the central government exists only to enforce property rights, to insure against fraudulent contracts, and to guarantee freedom of resource flows throughout the national economy.

If there are efficiency gains to be secured from the provision and consumption of such localized public goods, the utility-possibility frontier is shifted outward from that which is attainable in the setting that allows only for the provision of purely private goods.[3] In Figure

1 the introduction of these goods allows positions to the northeast of the set bounded by c and c' to be attained.

How are the gains-from-trade in localized public goods to be distributed? If we assume that private-goods equilibrium is attained at F, any position within the inclusive limits defined by F, d, and d' would reflect mutual gains, or in the many-person setting, gains to all parties. In a regime of spatially competitive governments, however, we should predict that the range of attainable utility or welfare distributions would be considerably more confined than the set indicated. The reason is identical with that shown to impose bounds on the distributions of the gains from private-goods trade. If there are alternative sellers and buyers, the power of any one to impose terms of trade on market participants is restricted. This principle applies directly to the competition among local governmental units. Consider a single local government that provides a public good to its citizens. Can this unit extract from an individual citizen-taxpayer-beneficiary all the fiscal surplus that the enjoyment of this public good represents? It can do so only if and to the extent that he has no alternatives available to him, if there are no better "deals" in other locations, taking into account the costs of making a move. But it seems clear that the prospects of "voting with the feet" that individuals face in a regime of spatially competitive local governments in a federal system insure results that are broadly comparable in kind to the operation of effectively competitive markets.

This process of adjustment involves both distributional and efficiency dimensions. The distribution of the gross gains-from-trade in local public goods is restricted. At the same time these gains tend to be fully exploited, insuring that the equilibrium finally attained will fall along or near the utility-possibility frontier itself rather than inside it. The results are comparable in kind to those produced by workably competitive markets, but this is not to suggest that either the distributional or the efficiency constraints are nearly so confining as those that open-ended market adjustment tends to guarantee. The Tiebout adjustment mechanism does not offer a wholly satisfactory analogue to market competition, despite its directional effects.[4]

For purposes of illustration in Figure 1, the provision of local public goods through a regime of spatially competitive local governmental units tends to narrow the set of attainable outcomes to the shaded area between and below the segment DD'. As drawn, this set is not so narrowly confined as that shown to be attainable from trade in purely private goods, although outcomes are still restricted to a subset of those positions that exhibit nothing more than mutual gains to all parties.

It is important to emphasize that these results do not depend in any way on the collective decision-making rules in local governments. These rules may range all the way from Wicksellian unanimity or quasi-unanimity, through the direct democracy of the New England town, the representative democracy of a city council, to the effective dictatorship of Boss Crump. Within any specific jurisdiction, the rule or institutions for reaching local fiscal decisions and the levy of taxes, along with the selection of the size and mix of the expenditure budget, will determine the final distributive outcomes, although these will rarely be unique. Conceptually, we can think of the distributional position attained by an individual, say A, as ranging over the whole set of possibilities represented by the shaded area between and below D and D' as this person shifts from one local jurisdiction to another and/or as the decision rules vary. If A should be dictator, a position at or near D might be secured, and if B replaces him, A might find himself at D'. But the point to be stressed here is that, regardless of the decision rules, the migrational or locational alternatives that are potentially available to all citizens in the federalism insure that the distributional set of outcomes attainable within any single local unit is narrowly bounded.

Gains-from-Trade in National Public Goods

Assume that a position, shown by G in Figure 1, is attained through the operation of market competition in supplying private goods and through spatially competitive local governments in supplying localized public goods. But we now assume further that there remain new welfare or efficiency gains to be exploited through the allocation of some resources to the production-provision of collective-consumption goods that are not confined geographically, at least not within the boundaries of the national government's jurisdiction. For purposes of analysis, we assume that neither local governments nor market institutions will devote resources to the provision of such goods.[5] Furthermore, we assume that all collective-consumption goods and services fall into one or the other of the two distinct categories examined here, the strictly local or the strictly national.[6] The effect of introducing the existence of national public goods is to shift the utility-possibility frontier outward.

If the central or national government in the federalism accepts the responsibility for organizing the provision of these goods, how will the gross gains-from-trade be distributed, and how efficient will the production-provision be? There is a major difference between this and the two earlier models examined, a difference in kind and one that should be immediately apparent. Since there are no competing "sellers" of the national public goods, there are no effective constraints on the range of distributional outcomes that are comparable to those demonstrated to be present both under private-goods market process and under localized public-goods provision through local governments. Alternatives always exist, and these will define the extremes of potential distributive outcomes. The individual can migrate across international boundaries and he can join others in revolutionary uprising against the national government. In the United States in the 1970's, however, these can scarcely be considered effective alternatives, and especially for individuals who are "representative" members of the national citizenry. And such extreme limits surely will not confine the distributional outcomes even within the set of positions that dominate the initial or no-trade position (G in Figure 1) in the standard sense. There is no external constraint that insures against central government distributions of gains-from-trade that fall outside the set of positions that exhibit gains to all parties, that is, outside the area bounded by h, h', and G. One, some, or even many persons in the economy could be made worse off with than without central-government provision of national public goods.

It seems plausible, however, to postulate some broad limits on central-government or federal-government fiscal power. Constitutional restrictions do exist, despite Supreme Court confusion between constitutional order and "social justice." Elements of a fiscal constitution remain in being, and these prevent arbitrary and discriminatory exercise of the taxing power by the federal government.

Although the extension to the spending side of the budget is not symmetrical, there are also some legal limitations on overt discrimination in the allocation of governmental benefits. Within existing constitutional constraints, and so long as the model is restricted to one where the central government supplies and finances only genuinely national public goods and services, as reasonably classified, we can talk meaningfully about some bounded set of distributional outcomes. In terms of our illustration in Figure 1, we postulate that such constraints will insure outcomes within the shaded area defined by G, k, and k'. Note that this allows for some positions outside the set that dominates G for all persons in the group (the set Ghh') but that these nonintersecting positions are restricted in range. In the real world, of course, there are no necessary restrictions of the sort depicted in the construction.

The broader range of possible outcomes here than in the two earlier models is apparent, but a second feature should also be noted. In both earlier models the existence of effective alternatives serves to insure not only the limited range of distributional possibilities but also the approximate achievement of the utility-possibility frontier. That is to say, alternatives also generate pressures toward efficiency. The absence of effective alternatives to national public-goods provision eliminates such pressures. There is no force tending to push the system to positions along or near the kk' boundaries, and final positions well within the shaded area seem equally if not more likely to emerge.[7] The implications of the analysis for the relative efficiencies of local and central government are clear. It is directly predictable that central or national government will be less efficient than local units.[8]

In order to bound the set at all, we have found it necessary to resort to constitutional-legal constraints, a step that was not required in the discussion of local governmental provision of public goods. Within the set, as now bounded, the position actually attained will depend on the particular operation of the decision-making process at the central-government level. Since the set is relatively more inclusive, and by a wide margin, than the comparable one in the earlier or local-government model, the analysis suggests that the structure of collective decision-making rules is much more important in central-government or federal-government affairs, more important for individual participants, than in local-government matters or in the market. The reason, of course, is, again the relative absence of effective alternatives. Without alternatives, the individual is a necessary party to the outcome collectively selected even if he, personally, remains strongly opposed or is even harmed in the process.[9] At the central-government level, alternatives remain, at best, potential. In working democracies significant departures by governments from outcomes desired by majorities or even by intense minorities will, of course, provide incentives to nonincumbent parties and politicians to offer more efficient and more preferred alternatives.

The construction of Figure 1 allows us to depict the distributional consequences of a transfer of local government functions to the central government. Suppose that local units are abolished and that the central government assumes the responsibility for providing localized public goods throughout the area of what becomes a unitary political system. The range of possible outcomes, under the same constitutional-legal constraints, is expanded to the area bounded by F, t, and t' in Figure 1. Clearly, opportunities now exist for sharing the total gains from "public-goods trade" that were not present under the genuinely federal system. The central government may now, under certain decision-making processes, produce an outcome such as that shown at M, which lies wholly outside the set that was previously attainable. Furthermore, this position becomes attainable under the same rules. Note, also, that the new position, M, might lie farther inside the utility-possibility locus than J, which we may assume to have been the position attained under the federal organization. This reflects the reduced pressure toward efficiency in the structure characterized by less effective alternatives for individual choice.

The effects of shifting the dividing line between local and central government are clear. Centralization tends to widen the set of possible distributional outcomes and, simultaneously, to reduce the institutional pressures for efficiency in public-goods provision. In the analysis to this point we have assumed that there is a clear-cut distinction between localized and central public goods and services, that the efficient jointness-nonexcludability ranges are sharply delineated. As we know, however, these ranges are nearly always fuzzy, and intergovernmental spillovers exist for almost all localized public goods. The argument for central-government takeover often hinges on the relative significance of these spillover effects. Centralization allows for the internalization of the intergovernmental externalities that these spillovers represent; this, considered in isolation, can increase overall efficiency in public-goods supply. Against this must be placed the offsetting efficiency drain that centralization makes possible through its elimination of effective alternatives. The accompanying widening of the range of distributional possibilities may or may not be considered a desirable attribute in its own right.

As indicated earlier, to place any plausible restrictions on the set of outcomes produced by central-government action we found it necessary to resort to constitutional-legal constraints. In this context, and as the construction of Figure 1 suggests, central-government takeover of local functions becomes equivalent to a relaxation of such constitutional limits. The elementary point developed in this and preceding paragraphs should not be excessively belabored. Perhaps it is obvious to everyone that the amount of redistribution of welfare that the federal government can accomplish under a budget of, say 50 billion dollars is significantly less than that which becomes possible with a budget of 250 billion dollars. Even with extreme progressivity in rate structure, with the general tax base, and with accompanying redistributive elements in spending patterns, the distributional possibilities in the former case may fall far short of those in the latter, even if, in shifting to the larger budget, the tax base is seriously eroded, the rate structure is made less progressive, and if the pattern of spending becomes, in itself, somewhat less redistributive.

II. PARETO OPTIMAL REDISTRIBUTION

In the discussion of Section I, individual utility functions were implicitly assumed not to contain arguments for either the income-wealth characteristics of others (flows or stocks) or for their specific commodity and service characteristics (flows or stocks). If this assumption is dropped, and interdependence among persons in any or in all of these respects is introduced, redistribution may emerge as a specifically chosen objective in an idealized voluntaristic choice process. In the terminology of welfare economics, redistribution may involve Pareto shifts to the Pareto-welfare surface. This surface may be unattainable without redistributional activity. And this activity may be, but need not be, over and above the results forthcoming from the sharing of the gross gains-from-trade in private and in orthodox public goods and services.

Redistribution as a Private Good

I shall use a threefold classification and examine redistribution as (1) a purely private good, (2) a local public good, and (3) a national public good. If interpersonal interdependence exists, itself an empirical question, the form of this interdependence must be empirically ascertained since these alternative descriptive categories embody differing implications.

If an individual secures utility from the act of making income transfers to other persons but secures no utility from increases in the income or wealth levels of others apart from his own act of giving, or secures no utility from other's acts of giving, redistribution becomes analogous to the consumption of a purely divisible or private good.[10] There are no "public" properties; neither nonexcludability nor joint-consumption efficiency is present. We should observe this sort of redistribution to take place in the wholly voluntary sector. In the construction of Figure 1 this purely private redistribution would be embodied in the attainment of the market equilibrium somewhere in the set bounded by c and c'.

Redistribution as a Local Public Good[11]

Our emphasis now shifts to those situations where individual utility functions include arguments for the income-wealth characteristics of others, as such, but where these "others" are residents of spatially defined local communities or jurisdictions. Individuals are wholly uninterested in the incomes of those beyond the confines of the local community. Furthermore, we assume that, for those potential transfer recipients within the local jurisdictions, specific identification is either not possible or not relevant for choice. That is to say, potential taxpayers in the local community are interested in the income level of the "local poor," but they make no identification of the members of this group, as such.[12]

Initially, we may examine a submodel in which taxpayers in the separate localities are immobile; they do not shift among communities in response to differential fiscal pressures. The potential welfare recipients are, by contrast, assumed to be fully mobile as among localities, and they respond directly to the level of welfare payments or income transfers.[13] If we ignore costs of migration, one condition for equilibrium in this model is that the transfer payments per person be equal in all localities. The potential recipients will distribute themselves among the communities to insure that this condition is fulfilled. The system of interaction between welfare or transfer recipients on the one hand and local taxpayers on the other generates an equilibrium that is Pareto optimal, despite the interdependence between the level of "bad" in a given community and the community's own efforts at eliminating this.

The interaction becomes more complex when we allow a Tiebout-like adjustment among potential taxpayers to accompany the migrational adjustments of welfare recipients. The equilibrium that will be produced retains Pareto optimality characteristics, however, since persons will tend to locate themselves among the spatially competitive local governments in accordance with their own preferences for redistributive activity. Although the migrational adjustments of potential recipients insure that transfers per person are equal in all localities, the net transfers away from taxpayers may differ among separate communities, with the trade-off being made in terms of the number of recipients.

In the geometry of Figure 1 local-government action in providing income-wealth redistribution that can be classified as a strictly local public good becomes no different from the action involved in supplying any other local public good. The utility-possibility frontier is shifted outward, and the equilibrium will tend to fall in the area bounded by D and D', as before.

Redistribution as a National Public Good

If individual utility functions include arguments for the income-wealth positions of other persons throughout the national economy without spatial distinctions, local governments find themselves in what appears to be the familiar public-good dilemma. Since the single unit cannot exclude others from the benefit of its own action, investment in the activity of redistribution will be suboptimal. There are, however, differences between this and the standard public-good case. To an extent, redistribution, as an activity that generates utility, is divisible. The local community that carries out redistribution transfers income to specific local residents; it cannot, by the nature of the production process here, generate benefits that spill over equally to all persons in the nation. Hence, despite the assumed national scope of the utility interdependence that motivates the activity, the "production divisibility" restores at least elements of excludability. Local communities find themselves in a reciprocal-externalities interaction. This suggests that the suboptimality in result will be less than that indicated to be present in the pure public-good interaction and may, under some conditions, vanish.[14]

If a case for federal-government or national-government redistributive activity is to be based on the grounds of strict utility interdependence, evidence should be available to indicate that the sociocultural environment is such that the effective limits are, indeed, those determined by national boundaries rather than those more limited in space on the one hand and those more extensive on the other.

III. "CONSTITUTIONAL" REDISTRIBUTION

Those who have advanced the "principle" that the redistribution function must be performed at the central-government level in a federal system need not accept either of the models developed above. In rejecting such models many scholars have, however, been too quick to resort to externally derived ethical norms. This step tends to remove the discussion from the realm of scientific discourse with predictable results.

To a partial extent the analysis of redistribution can be shifted to another plane, and without explicit value commitment, by examining what I have called "constitutional" redistribution.[15] This approach begins with the empirically valid proposition that explicit distributions of income are not, in fact, objects of choice for collectivities at any level. The relevant choices to be made are those among rules or institutions that, in turn, operate to generate probability distributions of distributive outcomes or allocations. At the stage of genuine "constitutional" choice, it is not appropriate to include the standard arguments in individual utility functions, nor is it at all appropriate to introduce explicit utility interdependence in the sense discussed in the preceding section. Conceptually at least, individuals engaged in "constitutional" choice remain uncertain about their own income-wealth positions in subsequent periods during which the rules to be adopted will remain in force.[16]

To clarify the argument here, it will be useful to compare and contrast allocation and distribution. At the "constitutional" stage market institutions may be chosen along with a decision to enforce contracts made under these institutions. Resources will be allocated, and it becomes meaningful to discuss the process under the "constitutional" rule that insures that these market institutions will remain in being. In the allocative process final products will be distributed in accordance with the rules. To this extent, distribution accompanies allocation. But the distributive pattern that accompanies market process, the distribution of the gross gains-from-trade, may not embody characteristics that are fully acceptable at the "constitutional" level of decision. The "game" may not seem "fair," quite independently of identification of particular recipients during specific market periods. If this is generally accepted, attempts may emerge, at the "constitutional" level, to introduce what we may call redistributive institutions, which are aimed to modify the distributive outcomes of market process.

This elementary logical derivation is not substantially changed when we allow for public-sector allocation, either at the central-government or local-government level. Constitutionally, a set of institutions may be established that determines the appropriate functions for the market, for local government, and for central government. Operating within these limits, the separate units allocate resources and distribute final goods and services. Over and beyond this pattern of results, however, explicitly redistributive institutions may also be constitutionally introduced.

The advantage of the "constitutional" approach is that it allows for a conceptual derivation of redistributive institutions in terms of Wicksellian efficiency, without resort to explicit value norms. Once redistributive institutions are constitutionally adopted, and as these operate, the actual redistribution that they produce must be zero-sum. Hence, at this stage, it becomes conceptually impossible to derive the unanimous support required for Wicksellian efficiency without introducing the utility interdependence of the type discussed in Section II.

Whether or not such explicitly redistributive institutions will emerge constitutionally, for any of the several reasons that might be adduced,[17] is an empirical question. Also, even if these do emerge the criteria for efficiency may or may not be satisfied. These questions are not directly relevant to my purpose in this paper. The "principle" that redistribution must be performed at the central-government level may be restated as follows: If redistributive institutions or rules are to be selected at the "constitutional" level, these can be enforced only by the authority of the central or national government because of the zero-sum characteristics of the actual redistributions attempted during subsequent periods of application of these rules.

We may use an elementary example to demonstrate the validity of the principle as interpreted. For expositional simplicity only, assume that no public goods exist, and that the market has been constitutionally selected as the allocating process over a well-defined national economy, which includes local-government as well as central-governmental jurisdiction. Suppose that those persons living within a geographically defined subarea of the national economy should decide, again at some constitutional stage of deliberation, to modify the market-determined distributive pattern toward greater equality. Such rules are put into being for the single subarea government. As the rules are applied, however, individuals who are subjected to net taxes will find it advantageous to shift to other local jurisdictions, and potential recipients of net transfers will find it advantageous to shift into the redistributive jurisdiction. The Tiebout adjustment, by both groups, will make accomplishment of the intended distributive results impossible for the local community. This analysis is relevant even if it is acknowledged that those very persons who might have supported the imposition of the redistributive rules at the constitutional stage will themselves shift location when these rules come into operation. Effective enforcement of redistributive rules or institutions that are aimed at modifying the distributive outcomes in the market, or in the combined market-public sector process, must be carried out by the governmental jurisdiction that is itself coincident with the market in the geographical area.

There is, of course, nothing inconsistent in the combined presence of redistributive institutions, in the constitutional sense, and Pareto-optimal transfers, as chosen in the operational working of political process. A "constitutional" decision may be made to finance a major portion of central-government budgets with a progressive income tax, quite independently of and in advance of knowledge about the public-good mixes that describe such budgets. As these budgetary-mix choices are made, however, one of the components may well be the transfers of income designed for poverty relief.

As the analysis of Section I demonstrated, there is more range of variation in the distribution of the gross gains-from-trade in the central government's provision of public goods and services than there is in the distribution of such gains from the provision of goods either through the market or through local governments. When this is recognized, and if a sizable central-government sector exists, the institutionalization of redistribution may be limited largely if not wholly to tax-side constraints on central-government fiscal structure. If a "fiscal constitution" is designed to insure a substantial role for progressive taxation, regardless of the demand pattern for publicly supplied goods, marginally or inframarginally, the final distribution of welfare may be constrained to fall within specific limits. (In Figure 1 such constitutional restriction may insure that the final distributional outcome falls between, say, the rays terminating at k and k''.) The institutionalization of redistribution in this manner will, necessarily, distort the in-sector allocative process of the central government. The satisfaction of the necessary marginal conditions for optimality in the provision of goods and services becomes more difficult and, in practical reality, may become impossible. These allocative inefficiencies may be offset against the distributional "efficiencies" that progression in the fiscal structure is predicted to generate.

IV. CONCLUSIONS

Methodologically, this paper contains one tautological proposition and two sets of predictive hypotheses in political economy. The proposition states, quite straightforwardly, that zero-sum transfers, defined in utility dimensions, are limited by the extent of individual alternatives. The first set of hypotheses concerns the existence and the importance of utility interdependence as among specifically definable persons and groups, within the context of an operative political process. Individuals are observed to perform private charities, to join voluntary groups with charitable objectives, and to support redistributive transfers at local, central, and international governmental levels. The overall divison of distributional responsibility among these separate institutional structures that might be required to meet Pareto criteria for optimality can be determined only empirically. The second set of hypotheses concerns the existence, actual or potential, of consensus among individuals on the establishment and maintenance, constitutionally, of rules of fiscal structure that embody income-wealth redistribution.

It is important to emphasize that nowhere in the discussion has it been necessary to introduce external ethical norms, either my own or those arbitrarily derived from some fanciful "social welfare function." In this sense, I have not answered the "should" question posed in the paper's title. Indirectly, my answer is: *The redistribution that "should" be performed at various levels of government is that which individuals, acting through their collective entities, local and central, expressly prefer.* Idealized outcomes that reflect some "true" amalgamation of individuals' preferences are not, of course, possible to attain. Political outcomes emerge from the workings of institutions, themselves imperfect, that exhibit stochastic variety and, on occasion, internal inconsistency. This makes the task of the political economist especially difficult; he cannot "read" the genuine preferences of individuals from the revealed political outcomes that he observes. The empirical testing of the hypotheses derivable from either of the two analytical models requires sophisticated and highly imaginative research. The potential for the central government to effect zero-sum transfers, derivable from no plausible model of consensus, and reflecting the will of a dominant political coalition, breaks any direct connection between observed governmental behavior and the Pareto conditions for efficiency, at the operational or constitutional level. Within certain carefully drawn limits, this obstacle could be handled in the simpler of the two models, that of straightforward Pareto-optimal transfers. For genuine constitutional choice, however, observed opposition to the actual operation of redistributive institutions cannot, in itself, provide evidence of an absence of "efficiency" in the more comprehensive choice of social institutions.

Despite such problems, the discussion of what we may call the "political economy of redistribution" has been substantially advanced in recent years.[18] There is no cause for retreat into obscurantist ethics, which does little more than embroil us, one with another, over just whose personal set of values "should" be selected by that nonexistent yet subservient elite through which too many of us seek in unconscious willingness to subvert ordinary democratic process.

NOTES

[1]For a statement to this effect, see R.A. Musgrave, "Economics of Fiscal Federalism," *Nebraska Journal of Economics and Business* (Autumn, 1971), p. 10.

[2]For a sophisticated critique of modern general-equilibrium theory that expresses much of my own, and largely intuitive, dissatisfaction, see Maurice Allais, "Les théories de l'équilibre économique général et de l'efficacité maximale," *Revue d'Économie Politique* (May, 1971), pp. 331-409.

[3]For purposes of discussion here, I assume that local public goods will not be provided through ordinary market processes. This is not a realistic assumption. In the absence of local government, entrepreneurs would find it profitable to organize arrangements through which local public goods would be provided, even those that are nonexcludable. In some circumstances, and especially where tie-in arrangements can be introduced that effectively reinstate excludability, market organization may prove even more efficient than local governmental units. In other circumstances, where exclusion cannot be introduced even indirectly, market arrangements may emerge, but these may remain seriously inefficient in supplying the local collective goods.

[4]The now-classic paper here is Charles M. Tiebout, "A Pure Theory of Local Ex-

penditures," *Journal of Political Economy* (October, 1956), pp. 416-24. For a critical assessment of the Tiebout adjustment process, under its most favorable assumptions, and in terms of efficiency-optimality criteria, see James M. Buchanan and Charles J. Goetz, "Efficiency Limits to Fiscal Mobility," *Public Economics* (April, 1972), pp. 25-44.

[5]As noted with reference to the market supply of local public goods, this is an unrealistic assumption. It is made here only for the purpose of simplifying the exposition.

[6]Much the same applies here as in the preceding footnote, although genuine problems emerge when we allow for the existence of public goods whose efficiency jointness-nonexcludability ranges are geographically limited but not sufficiently to allow for effective competition among spatially defined collective bodies.

[7]William Niskanen has presented plausible arguments to the effect that central-government bureaus, possessing monopoly powers in the provision of particular public goods and services, "sell" these services, in effect, at all-or-none terms to "buyers," that is, to legislatures. In this case, all the fiscal surplus is squeezed out as bureaucratic waste, at least in the limit, and net gains-from-trade vanish. In terms of our model, the Niskanen hypothesis suggests that, with many central-government goods, the actually attainable utility-possibility frontier does not extend beyond G. See William A. Niskanen, *Bureaucracy and Representative Government* (Chicago: Aldine, 1971).

[8]This prediction may seem bizarre in the face of popular mythology about local-government corruption. Local governments have their own equivalents of Bobby Baker and the Rayburn Building, but governments at this level cannot, by the nature of their situations, have their own Tulsa ship canals, Florida barge canals, maritime and farm subsidies, HEW bureaucracy, F-111 airplanes, or, even, their own Vietnam wars.

[9]In the market, the individual need not be at all interested in the "decision rules." In fact, these are rarely discussed. He does not "vote" on the prices that he confronts in the marketplace. He has no need to do so because his protection is provided, ideally and conceptually, in the presence of alternative sellers and buyers. The individual in a local government may vote, directly or indirectly, on tax and budget matters, but the possible increments or decrements to his utility that such choices can produce are confined in value by his migrational prospects. The basic difference between the importance of decision rules at the central-government and local-government levels seems to have been wholly ignored in the Supreme Court reapportionment decisions, which were apparently based on bad economics as well as naive political science.

[10]This motivation may, of course, be mixed with others. For a discussion that emphasizes this aspect, see Thomas Ireland, "Charity Budgeting," in Thomas Ireland and David B. Johnson, *The Economics of Charity* (Blacksburg: Center for Study of Public Choice, 1971).

[11]This subject has recently been discussed in some detail by Mark Pauly. My discussion is confined to only a few of the models that he develops. At certain points, however, my results diverge from those suggested by Pauly. See Mark V. Pauly, "Redistribution as a Local Public Good," paper presented at COUPE meeting, Cambridge, October 1971.

[12]In this model the making of income transfers becomes analogous to the removal of a "bad" rather than the purchase of a "good." In some respects, these two acts are

behaviorally equivalent, but here it seems useful to make a conceptual separation between them.

[13]This model seems realistic because nonfiscal elements may well dominate the fiscal in taxpayer locational decisions.

[14]The "distribution of redistribution" among separate local units may be nonoptimal while at the same time the total amount of redistribution may be larger than that which would be generated under fully centralized redistribution by the central government. For a discussion of the general model, see James M. Buchanan and Milton Z. Kafoglis, "A Note on Public-Goods Supply." *American Economic Review* (June, 1963).

[15]In more general terms, the shift to "constitutional" levels of choice or decison making, and especially when collective alternatives are involved, allows many of the standard tools of welfare economics to be used in what would otherwise seem value-laden territory. On this, see my, "The Relevance of Pareto Optimality." *Journal of Conflict Resolution* (December, 1962), pp. 341-54, and also James M. Buchanan and Gordon Tullock, *The Calculus of Consent* (Ann Arbor: University of Michigan Press, 1962).

[16]The similarity between this approach and that of John Rawls should be apparent. See John Rawls, *A Theory of Justice* (Cambridge. Mass.: Harvard University Press, 1971).

[17]I have, in earlier works, discussed some of these. See Buchanan and Tullock, *The Calculus of Consent,* and also my *Public Finance in Democatic Process* (Chapel Hill: University of North Carolina Press, 1967). For further discussion, see Richard E. Wagner, *The Fiscal Organization of American Federalism* (Chicago: Markham, 1971), pp. 4-6. Also, see paper 9, by Mitchell Polinsky, in this book.

[18]For a paper that summarizes much of this discussion, see Harold M. Hochman, "Individual Preferences and Distributional Adjustment," presented at the New Orleans meeting of the American Economic Association, December, 1971.

3

Suburban Exploitation
of Central Cities and
Governmental Structure

DAVID F. BRADFORD AND
WALLACE E. OATES

The fiscal difficulties of the central cities and, in fact, the whole host of social and economic problems that contribute to our so-called urban crisis are largely the result, according to some observers, of a systematic "exploitation" of the cities by residents of suburban municipalities. The precise form this exploitation takes is often not made explicit, but at any rate the assertion is that the suburbanites are in large measure to blame for the deterioration in the quality of life in the cities.

The term "exploitation" typically refers to an "unjust relationship" between one individual (or group of individuals) and another. It is therefore a normative concept and can take on a precise operational meaning only when a just relationship is defined. Unfortunately, there seems to be no generally accepted definition of such a relationship between residents of cities and suburbs, with the result that exploitation of central cities by their suburbs has been given a number of different interpretations.

In some of the public-finance literature, for example, the term has been used to describe a process in which suburban commuters utilize the public services provided by the cities but then return home to their residential communities to pay (at least the bulk of)

David F. Bradford and Wallace E. Oates are members of the Department of Economics at Princeton University. They are grateful to Robert Aten, Theodore Bergstrom, Lester Chandler, Bruce Hamilton, and Daniel Hamermesh for a number of extremely helpful comments on an earlier draft of this paper.

their local taxes. The suburbanites thus exploit the central-city residents who must, willy-nilly, support public services for the commuters in order to have any themselves. This we shall call the "narrow" public-finance version of the exploitation thesis.

In the writings of more popular commentators on the plight of American cities, however, quite another set of issues dominates the discussion. Here the sin of the suburbanites is said to be their clustering in homogeneous settlements from which the poor are "walled-out" by zoning and other devices, there to enjoy public-service standards higher than those maintained in the central city while paying less in local taxes. This situation describes exploitation of the central city, and more generally of the poor, in a rather odd sense. It appears that the tax instruments available to local governments, taken together with the package of services normally provided by them and with the rules for local political procedures, tend to produce local public budgets that are somewhat redistributive toward the poorer residents of the jurisdiction.[1] A local governmental system that allows formation of jurisdictions uniform in income composition thus allows the upper-income families of a metropolitan area to avoid "exploitation" by the poorer families of the area. By taking away their ability to exploit the rich through the local fiscal system, the suburban governmental system exploits the poor!

Whichever of these notions of exploitation is accepted, there is little doubt that the system wherein public services are provided by relatively small and autonomous local-government jurisdictions in the suburbs has important implications for the distribution of welfare when compared to the obvious alternative of a unified metropolitan jurisdiction or the transfer of public functions to even higher (state or federal) levels of government. Particularly in view of the California and New Jersey court decisions that the finance of public schools through local property taxes is incompatible with the equal service provisions of the state constitutions, there is a pressing need for analyses of the distributive and allocative effects of the enlargement of fiscal jurisdictions.

The latter issue of the economic effects of fiscal consolidation is the central concern of this study. Rather than attempting to provide a definition and an examination of exploitation in some particular sense, we prefer to study the effects of alternative forms of governmental and fiscal structure on the distribution of income and uses of resources in metropolitan areas and to leave the reader to draw his own conclusions about the forms and extent of exploitation implied by these alternatives.

Before turning to our central issue, however, we shall in Section I examine the current state of knowledge about what we have termed the narrow public-finance view of exploitation. In Section II we review the way the current system of local public finance operates. In preparation for the analysis to follow, we lay particular stress here on the pressure toward the formation of income-homogeneous fiscal units. In the next two sections (Sections III and IV), which contain the most important material in the paper, we attempt to analyze the implications for the distribution of welfare of the choice between the current, fragmented system of local government and a unified metropolitan-wide government of some sort. Section III contains an analysis of the long-run equilibrium differences we might expect, and Section IV an analysis of the redistribution resulting from the transition from the current system to our model of a unified system. Section V presents a brief summary and some concluding remarks. Throughout we have tried, wherever possible, to provide quantitative, as well as qualitative, evidence and conclusions.

I. THE NARROW PUBLIC-FINANCE
EXPLOITATION THESIS

Some twenty years ago Amos Hawley found that local public spending per capita in 76 cities, each with a population in excess of 100,000, showed a positive correlation to the proportion of the population in the metropolitan area living outside the central city. From this finding Hawley concluded that central cities were being exploited by the suburbs in the sense that residents of the cities "...are carrying the financial burden of an elaborate and costly service installation, i.e., the central city, which is used daily by a non-contributing population in some instances more than twice the size of the contributing population."[2] Hawley used 1940 data for his study. A number of later studies using more recent fiscal and population figures, notably studies by Harvey Brazer and Julius Margolis, found this same type of empirical relationship, but these authors were far more cautious about drawing the type of inference Hawley drew from this phenomenon.[3] In particular, it is clear that suburban commuters do make some positive contributions to the fiscal well-being of the city. Many cities, such as Philadelphia, Detroit, and New York, have local income or wage taxes levied on income earned in the city. In addition, most cities levy sales taxes and, in some cases, a variety of user charges, including such things as tolls on bridges and tunnels leading into the city. Less directly, but perhaps at least as important, the use of city facilities by a greater number of suburban residents may increase the level of economic activity in the city and thereby enhance city property values with a corresponding stimulus to city receipts from property taxation. In fact, residential suburbs have been known to claim that the cities take advantage of them by reaping the tax benefits from a high concentration of commercial-industrial property, whereas the suburbs must service the population (particularly the heavy expense of providing public education). The existence of a positive correlation between central-city expenditures per capita and the fraction of the population living in the suburbs is not convincing evidence for the exploitation thesis. The suburban commuters may even more than pay for the extra costs of the public services that the city must provide.

A few studies have been undertaken to attempt to settle this issue by measuring both the fiscal contribution and the fiscal costs that suburban residents bring to the city. The approach has typically been to allocate the costs of city services on a per capita basis between city and suburban users of city services and to estimate the fiscal receipts to the city that come from the pockets of suburban residents. The difference between costs imposed and revenues generated by suburban users of city services is then calculated. Such studies have generally found little in the way of fiscal exploitation one way or the other. William Neenan, for example, notes the findings of James Banovetz in a study of the Twin Cities metropolitan area. Banovetz's results indicate that "...no conclusive evidence can be found to support charges that either the core cities of Minneapolis and St. Paul or their suburbs in Hennepin or Ramsey Counties, respectively, are subsidizing the other to any appreciable extent."[4]

Neenan himself is the author of a recent study of suburban exploitation in the Detroit metropolitan area.[5] In comprehensiveness of services included and in the care with which measurements of service flows are carried out, Neenan's analysis probably represents about the best that can be done. We shall therefore review briefly his procedures and findings.

Neenan's approach differs from that of earlier studies. Rather than simply allocating costs on a per capita basis, he develops indices of "willingness-to-pay." Assuming the benefits (that is, the willingness to pay) to vary proportionately with income, Neenan allocates the benefits from city services among city and suburban residents according to their relative income levels. An example may be helpful here. Suppose that the cost per visit (total cost per number of visits) of operating the city's museum is one dollar. If a suburban resident has twice the level of income as that of a city resident, Neenan would attribute a benefit of two dollars per visit to the suburban user of the city museum and a benefit of only one dollar to a city resident. Since, in Neenan's sample of seven suburban communities, income levels in the suburbs are generally higher than those of city residents, this approach naturally has the effect of placing a relatively high value on city services consumed by suburbanites.

Neenan's procedure is biased in two ways toward a finding of positive exploitation. First, because of higher suburban incomes, his technique generates a value of city services to all users that exceeds their cost; thus a suburbanite may well pay the costs he imposes on city residents and yet realize a "consumer surplus" when these costs are compared to his willingness-to-pay. But Neenan assumes that the suburban resident "exploits" the city if he does not contribute to the city treasury the full benefits from any city services he consumes. This is somewhat like saying that the purchaser of a commodity exploits the seller because he gets more in satisfaction than he gives up in terms of his payment (that is, he realizes a consumer surplus). Now surely an ethical question exists as to how these "gains-from-trade" should be allocated between city dwellers and suburbanites, but it does seem somewhat questionable to insist, as Neenan in effect does, that they should all accrue to the residents of the city.[6] It would seem to make just as much sense to argue that city residents should be fully compensated for the costs imposed by suburban users of city services, but that there is no compelling reason why they should receive payments in excess of these costs. At any rate, Neenan's approach is surely favorable to obtaining results indicating suburban exploitation of the city.

Second, it should be noted that the particular assumption made by Neenan, namely, valuation proportional to income, does not seem to be derivable from any more fundamental assumptions about the underlying demand functions. Figure 1 illustrates what happens to the total valuation of a given output as income varies for the simple case where demand is linear and unit income elastic.[7] At output G_1, a doubling of income leads to considerably less than a doubling of total valuation (as measured by the areas under the demand curves). As a little experimentation should convince the reader, as long as we are operating in a region in which the lower-income citizen positively values increments in G (that is, to the left of G_2), no income elasticity would be large enough to produce a doubling of total valuation with a doubling of income, if the underlying demand curves are linear. All this says is that it is difficult to know whether Neenan's particular assumption is reasonable or not; we suspect that his willingness-to-pay factor is high.[8]

In spite of these procedures, which favor the exploitation thesis, Neenan finds it to be of minor quantitative significance. The net subsidy from Detroit to the seven suburban communities ranges from $1.73 per capita to $12.58 per capita, with a median value of only $6.78. This compares with an average level of local spending per capita in the United States in 1966 (the year of Neenan's data) of roughly $200. Neenan's study, like the others, thus suggests that the narrow public-finance version of the suburban exploitation thesis is of little moment.

Moreover, it seems to us that these types of studies do not confront directly certain far more fundamental and important issues

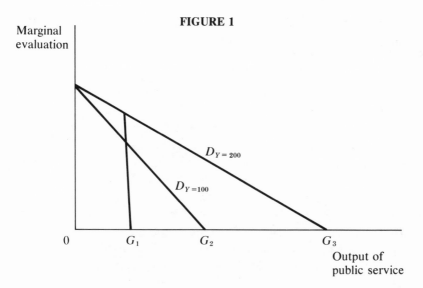

FIGURE 1

Marginal evaluation

$D_{Y=200}$

$D_{Y=100}$

0   G_1 G_2 G_3

Output of public service

concerning the fiscal structure of metropolitan areas. In particular, we see three broad sorts of questions that specialists in public finance would want to ask about urban fiscal organization:

1. How does the efficiency of the provision of public services and the allocation of activities in metropolitan areas vary with alternative governmental structures?

2. If the residents of one jurisdiction within the area (say, the current residents of the central city) were interested simply in maximizing their own real wealth, what expenditure and taxing or pricing policies should the government of that particular jurisdiction adopt?

3. How does the distribution of wealth or welfare (or, more conventionally, the distribution of income) observed within urban areas under current governmental structures compare with that which would exist under alternative organizations of the local public sector?

One might think that the existence of measured exploitation, such as that found by Neenan, provides *prima facie* evidence that the allocation of resources to public activity in the metropolitan area is inefficient, at least relative to some sort of ideal organization. Unfortunately, this conclusion is not valid. Once a zoo has been constructed, the cost of allowing extra visitors is sure to be less than the average of all costs, including capital costs. If it is priced at marginal cost, the jurisdiction operating the zoo will be shown on Neenan's analysis to be exploited by visitors from outside that jurisdiction, who cover the marginal, but not the average, cost they "impose." This would be the result even if the zoo were constructed to efficient scale and in the presence of efficiency in every aspect of the urban economy. It is true, of course, that if any facility is used to a significant degree by individuals from outside the sponsoring jurisdiction, and if increases in capacity benefit all (for example, by reducing congestion) in a way that cannot be effectively priced, there is a presumption that "too little" capacity will be purchased. However, measured exploitation tells us nothing about the presence of such inefficiencies or about the extent of possible gains from eliminating them, even judged against a nonoperational ideal standard.

A more practical issue is whether central cities, or other jurisdictions viewed as selfish collectives, are doing all they can for their members. James Buchanan has pointed out that it may make sense for a central city to adopt apparently regressive policies in order to retain *some* of the surplus generated by upper-income residents in the provision of a public good.[9] One can generalize this and ask what policies will maximize the welfare of the existing citizens (or of some specified subgroup of citizens), taking into account the possibility of exploiting the residents of other jurisdictions (à la the optimal tariff). An obviously interesting further question is how the equilibrium of a system of such competing jurisdictions is likely to look when judged by efficiency criteria (and again the analogy of tariff wars in international trade is suggestive). In any case, the existence of measured exploitation tells us nothing about where to look for "profitable" policy changes from the point of view of the central city, nor can it even be taken as evidence that the central city is not already following an optimal strategy.

It appears that studies of suburban exploitation are fundamentally concerned with issues of income distribution. Ultimately the studies seem to say, not that the metropolitan area's organization is inefficient, not that the central city is doing less well by its citizens than it might, but simply that too big a piece of the benefits is going to the rich suburbs. Our reservations regarding these studies viewed in this light are, first, that they do not specify the alternative system against which outcomes in the existing urban structure are to be tested and, second, that they have focused on only one aspect, and probably a quantitatively insignificant one, of the way in which metropolitan governmental structure influences both the city-suburb and the rich-poor income distribution. As we indicated in the introductory section, local public budgets appear to have a redistributive potential, the force of which is much muted by the availability of a suburban structure permitting "specialization" by income class. In the following sections we begin to explore the ways in which the income distribution that results differs from that which would obtain if metropolitan areas were unified fiscal jurisdictions.

II. REVIEW OF THE OPERATION
OF THE CURRENT SYSTEM

Let us define the Current System as an institutional structure for providing a substantial portion of public services in metropolitan areas by autonomous local fiscal units, each with taxing and zoning powers.[10] What we wish to stress here is the pressure in the Current System toward a set of jurisdictions uniform in income or wealth composition. This stems in part from the tendency, already noted, for local public budgets to be somewhat redistributive from wealthier to poorer members of the fiscal unit.

We should perhaps be somewhat more precise. What appears to be the case is that wealthier members of a large mixed-wealth population can gain by forming a separate fiscal unit. There are *two* sorts of economic reasons for this, only one of them having to do with the redistributive character of public budgets; the other stems from systematic variations in demand for public services with levels of income. Charles Tiebout was the first to explore systematically the way the availability of many alternative local governmental units allowed for diversity of tastes for publicly provided services.[11] Tiebout argued that an equilibrum residential location pattern in such a system would be efficient in the sense that it would not be possible to change the assignment of people to communities, the mix of services provided in any community, or the distribution of private goods in such a way as to make someone better off, with no one worse off.

Among the various aspects of the Current System that did not receive explicit treatment in Tiebout's analysis is the available set of financng instruments and institutions for political choice. When one recognizes that the taxes available to local governments tend to be strongly wealth correlated and, more particularly, tend to assign higher shares of tax burdens to those with the *relatively* higher wealth within communities, it is clear that there is added to the taste-variation element (which itself tends to produce income-homogeneous jurisdictions in response to higher demands for various public services from higher-income households) a further, possibly quite significant, pecuniary force toward income homogenization of suburban communities.

In the absence of control over entry to the community, however, this would appear to be a recipe for musical chairs, with the well-to-do coalescing into units that then become extremely attractive to anyone less wealthy, who would fall toward the bottom of the income distribution in the wealthy community and hence bear a relatively small tax burden. Add to this picture the political choice mechanism of majority rule within communities so that the composition of the public-service package cannot be controlled by the original members of the group, and one has a set of strong forces working against the stability of equilibria characterized by highly income-homogeneous suburban communities.

In an ingenious analysis Bruce W. Hamilton has shown how local zoning power can bring order to this system.[12] The predominant source of local governmental revenues is the property tax. By requiring minimum purchases of housing services, communities can essentially confine entrants to the community to those who will generate at least as much incremental tax revenue as they do incremental costs in the public budget. Taking the ideal case, Hamilton assumes local governments can put a precise floor under the value of real estate owned, and hence the taxes paid, by any net additional members. Since those purchasing more than the minimum amount of housing pay more taxes than those at the floor, there is a pressure toward the formation of differentiated communities until, "in the limit," one observes a set of communities homogeneous in housing consumption. The remarkable attribute of this solution noted by Hamilton is that it converts the property tax into an ideal benefit tax. A family wishing to consume its desired level of housing, but more public services, moves to another community with the same zoning requirement but providing the higher service level. The increment in the family's tax bill will just equal the increment in costs imposed on the new community. Moreover, in this situation the tax on housing services is free of deadweight loss. Because of the diversity of housing-public service combinations available, it is possible for a family (by moving, it must be noted) to buy more housing without paying more tax, while continuing to receive a given bundle of public services. Furthermore, the outcome may be expected to be stable. There is no possibility for migrants to increase their public services without paying more in taxes, and no reason to expect shifts in majorities that will alter the bundle offered by a given community, since those with different preferences will have no incentive to enter in the first place.

There are, of course, many differences between the model sketched out above and the actual suburban governmental system. However, much the most important element not yet introduced (it is introduced by Hamilton) is the presence in the system of one, large, jurisdiction that, in the nature of things, cannot become an income-uniform unit: the central city. By virtue of its history, size, and economic function, it can hardly be imagined to be composed of any uniform income group.

In the model described there will be in any jurisdiction with a wide spread of income levels a steady pressure on those at the upper end of the distribution to emigrate to income-homogeneous suburbs. In the logic of the model the central city is the odd man out, and one would expect, in the absence of compensating advantages to the upper-income families, to find the central city inhabited only by the poorest families in the metropolitan area.

The idea of central cities as "holders of the bag" is, of course, not a new one and may be found, for example, in the description by Edgar Hoover and Raymond Vernon of the process of migration of middle-income and upper-income classes and of industry and jobs from the central cities to increasingly accessible surrounding suburban communities.[13] Certainly consistent with this picture are the data contained in the various government censuses conducted over the last thirty years. Especially in the older metropolitan areas, one typically finds absolute losses in population in the central city, rapid growth in the population of suburban communities, growing disparities in relative levels of income between central city and suburban residents, a shift in the racial composition of the central city with a growing proportion of economically disadvantaged minority groups, rising tax rates in the cities relative to those in the suburbs, and a continuing shift of the relative share of economic activity to the suburbs. All this is well known and empirically substantiated.

The relationship between this process and the governmental structure of urbanized areas has not, however, been carefully spelled out. The Current System tends to reinforce the other pressures toward suburbanization of upper-income families and toward income homogenization of the suburbs. It may be asked whether these phenomena, and the role of the Current System in generating them, are necessarily a bad thing. There are two important reasons, one widely recognized the other hardly discussed at all, for thinking they might be.

The first reason is that income segregation is a force perpetuating income differences in the sense that a person's being born into a poor community seems to increase his chance of being a poor adult. This in itself is likely to be seen as offensive. In addition, as will be argued below, income segregation not only influences who will be poor but also probably increases the variance of the income distribution.

The second reason concerns the pressure toward suburbanization in the Current System. Cities presumably increase productivity as the result of economies of agglomeration; an excessive centrifugal force thus leads to a reduction in wealth. Taken by itself, the Current System appears to generate such an effect. Whether one must be concerned about this depends upon whether there would be too little or just the right amount of agglomeration were the influences of the governmental structure neutralized, and upon whether those influences are quantatively significant. What is involved here is a second-best situation. The suburban sector in the idealized version of the Current System operates with perfect efficiency, whereas the central city is seen as inherently incapable of the sort of benefit taxation that would enable it to be efficient in the same sense. Much as the presence of an incurable monopoly may require deviations from competitive behavior in other sectors to achieve second-best efficiency, the presence of an incurable central city may require interference with an apparently efficiency-enhancing suburban system.

The quantitative importance of the suggested ill effects of income segregation and of excessive suburbanization of upper-income families as well as the quantitative significance of the governmental structure in inducing these outcomes are far from clear. Nor is it obvious how valuable, on the other hand, are the efficiency advantages of the Current System. In the next section we discuss these issues further and attempt to pull together such quantitative evidence as is now available.

III. THE LONG-RUN DISTRIBUTION
OF WELFARE UNDER A UNIFIED
FISCAL STRUCTURE

In this section we want to investigate how the distribution of welfare in a system in which public services of entire metropolitan areas are administered and financed by single authorities (be they metropolitan governments or, perhaps, state governments) would compare with that under the Current System. For this purpose we assume that the Unified System (by which we shall mean a consolidated fiscal jurisdiction encompassing at least the whole metropolitan area) is in long-run equilibrium in the sense that all adjustments of location, composition of public services, etc., have been made. In this context there is obviously no reason to be concerned with the distribution of welfare between central city and suburban residents per se. Rather, we shall ask the following kinds of questions: Which classes of individuals, in terms of personal characteristics of productivity, taste, etc., will be better off and which worse off (and by how much) under the Unified System as compared to the Current System? How might the overall size distribution of income vary with governmental structure? And finally, in terms of economic efficiency, in which system is the "potential welfare" greater? That is, if we had the proverbial lump-sum, optimal redistribution taking place, which system would make people better off?

To reach any sort of reasonably precise conclusions we must make some specific assumptions concerning the fiscal structure under the Current and Unified Systems. To facilitate the analysis both in this section and in the next, we shall postulate that the federal government carries on the same set of redistributive programs and other activities in both systems. As outlined in the preceding section, we take the Current System to be one in which local public services are financed primarily by local real property taxes with levels of expenditures and tax rates determined in the main by each jurisdiction within the metropolitan area. In contrast, under the Unified System we assume that decisions concerning levels of spendng on public services are determined on (at least) a metropolitan-wide basis and are financed by a tax system with a uniform set of rates applicable to the entire area. For much of the analysis, we shall assume a central role for a metropolitan-area property tax. This obviously need not be the case. In fact, one of the attractions of a Unified System is presumably the potential for a greater reliance on other (possibly more progressive and efficient) forms of taxation. We shall offer a few observations on this, but the reader should have little difficulty in modifying the analysis to account for alternative revenue structures under the Unified System.

Income Redistribution from Rich to Poor

We look first at the differences in the size distribution of real income under the Current and Unified Systems. The difficulties inherent in locating the incidence of taxes and imputing the benefits of public-expenditure programs can give us little confidence in any precise calculations of fiscal incidence. However, it is possible, we think, to reach some qualitative (and a few rough quantitative) judgments on the basis of what we see as a shortcoming in most existing studies of fiscal incidence. In one of the best-known and most comprehensive of these studies W. Irwin Gillespie allocated both the fiscal benefits and the tax costs of public programs among income classes for public programs at all levels of government in the United States for 1960.[14] For state-local fiscal programs Gillespie found a redistribution in favor of those families with incomes under \$5,000 (increasing their money incomes by roughly 30 percent) and little or no redistribution among families with incomes in excess of this figure.[15] What is interesting for our purposes is that these estimates were generated largely by applying general assumptions about the incidence of various taxes and expenditures to state and local aggregates. Gillespie reasons, for example, that the benefits from expenditures on primary and secondary education can be allocated among students by simply dividing aggregate spending by the number of pupils. But this fails to recognize (as we shall see in the next section) that expenditure per pupil is typically significantly higher in richer than in poorer areas under the Current System.

In fact, Gillespie's estimates may come closer to approximating fiscal incidence under our Unified System than under the Current System. Consider, for example, the extreme case in which all public services are provided locally and complete income segregation has taken place. Then, clearly, there will be no redistributive effects generated by the state-local fiscal system. The other extreme is the Unified System with similar expenditure patterns and tax rates across the whole metropolitan area; here "average" fiscal incidence by income class (which seems to be closer to what Gillespie is measuring) would presumably be a reasonable measure of actual patterns. The Current System lies somewhere between the two polar cases. There has been some, probably substantial, income segregation. However, its extent has been limited by, among other forces, the necessarily income-integrated character of central cities. Furthermore, state governments do provide a substantial portion of public services and raise even more of the revenue within their boundaries.

Taken together these observations suggest that, as far as redistribution through the fiscal system is concerned, changing from the Current to a Unified System will result in a redistribution of income from the wealthy to the poor. However, the resulting pattern of fiscal incidence may resemble more closely Gillespie's measurements for the existing system, rather than more pronounced pro-poor fiscal effects. The potential for redistribution is, of course, greater in the Unified System should political forces favor more progressive tax-expenditure packages.

Possibly more important than the change in income distribution via the fiscal system could be the change resulting from reduced income segregation. We have no quantitative evidence to offer on this issue, however, and raise it mainly in the hope of encouraging empirical work. The influence of income segregation on the variance of the income distribution may be illustrated by a simple, if admittedly extreme, example. Imagine that an adult's productivity is purely a function of the average productivity of those in the community of his birth. In this case, equalizing the average productivity in communities would lead in one generation to fully equalized productivities of individuals.

Efficiency Differences Favoring the Current System

The thrust of the Tiebout analysis is that the Current System has some desirable efficiency properties, and, as we discussed earlier, Hamilton's extension of this theory to include the property tax and residential zoning reinforces these characteristics. An equilibrium in this idealized version of the Current System is efficient, not only in the sense that a Pareto-optimal amount of public services is offered in each community and no reshuffling of families among communities (possibly accompanied by side payments) could make everyone better off but also in having a tax system with no deadweight losses.

The latter advantage may not be trivial. A real-estate tax rate of 3.0 percent amounts to an excise tax on housing of roughly 25 percent. A wedge of this magnitude between the marginal cost and marginal valuation of housing could well have a substantial influence on housing choices and leave a significant opportunity for gain from the purchase of additional housing at the existing equilibrium. Assume, for example, that the price elasticity of demand for housing is unity.[16] The elimination of a 25 percent excise tax on a commodity with a unit price elasticity of demand and consuming 25 percent of the household's budget generates a net gain equal to roughly 1 percent of the household's income. The ability of the Current System to neutralize the deadweight loss of the real property tax as applied to residential housing would thus appear to be a significant advantage.

However, some factors tend to work against the importance of this characteristic of the Current System. First, the variety and number of suburban communities are small compared to the magnitudes that would be required to reach the level of efficiency implied by complete elimination of the deadweight loss. There is still substantial variation in income and housing consumption within communities, and we can safely presume that there are many property owners confronting decisions to enlarge or otherwise alter their properties, a margin at which the deadweight loss of the property tax remains. Second, several policies of the federal government, especially the freedom from income tax of the implicit rent from owner-occupied housing and the deductibility from taxable income of local property taxes, tend to offset the distorting effects of the property tax, particularly in the suburbs and particularly as applied to wealthier households with relatively high marginal tax rates under the federal income tax. Third, as we have pointed out, the Current System does not eliminate the deadweight loss associated with the real property tax in central cities, where, incidentally, the tax rates tend to be substantially higher than in the suburbs. Thus the potential welfare advantage of the Current System in terms of reducing the deadweight loss due to the property tax in housing must be regarded, we would judge, as small. Moreover, we should again note the possibility under a Unified System of a tax structure relying less heavily on property taxes and, as a result, perhaps generating less in deadweight losses.

A more serious matter may be the sacrifice of the other sort of efficiency in a Tiebout world. The choice of public services by a community in this model amounts to exactly the same thing as the choice of a consumption bundle by an individual household. We take it that under a Unified System there will be strong pressure to provide, in some sense, the same public services to all households, whereas under the Current System households make a choice between private and public expenditure and among compositions thereof by choosing their residential community appropriately. The efficiency advantage of the Current System is similar to that of a market system over a system involving equal division of some set of private commodities among all households. The quantitative extent of this efficiency gain depends upon the degree of difference in the demands for public services among communities in the Current System and the price elasticity of demand (or, more precisely, the elasticity of the marginal valuation of those services with respect to changes in their levels).[17]

To develop a feeling for the potential quantitative importance of this welfare gain from the Current System, we have chosen to examine local public expenditures for primary and secondary education. This choice was dictated by the relatively large magnitude of these expenditures in local public budgets, by the availability of reasonably good data, and, especially, by the current importance for public policy of the issue of equalizing educational expenditures.

For purposes of empirical estimates (both in this section and later), we have chosen a group of central cities and suburban communities in New Jersey. With its extremely heavy emphasis on local finance, high degree of fiscal fragmentation, and preponderant reliance on local property taxes, New Jersey appears to represent about as good an approximation to our Current System as we are likely to find. Our sample includes the five central cities and a group of fifty-three residential communities in the eight counties in Northeastern New Jersey that are included in the Census definition of the New York Standard Consolidated Area.[18] This area encompasses three Standard Metropolitan Statistical Areas (SMSAs): Newark, Jersey City, and Paterson-Clifton-Passaic, and two additional counties: Middlesex and Somerset, an area that in 1960 had a population of almost 4 million. Let us call this empirical counterpart to the Current System the New Jersey Metropolitan Area (NJMA), and its government as a Unified System the New Jersey Metropolitan Government (NJMG). For the most part we rely on 1960 data, for which we have comprehensive demographic and fiscal information, but we also have available for some categories roughly comparable figures for 1970.

The public service that we examine here is measured by expenditure per pupil in public schools; in fact, we shall assume that "expenditure per pupil" is a public good in the Samuelson sense within each community.[19] Within our sample, expenditure per pupil in the school year 1959-1960 varied from $295 to $547, with an average value of $413 over the whole set of communities. There is thus a substantial variation among communities in the chosen level of provision of this public good, a matter that we shall examine further in Section IV.

Our procedure will be to estimate the loss in efficiency that would have resulted from enforcing a uniform level of expenditure per pupil of $413 (the mean value of spending across the sample) throughout the NJMA in 1959-1960.[20] To make this estimate, we require a marginal valuation function for expenditure per pupil. Specifically, let us assume that each individual has the demand function

$$(1) \qquad E = AY^\alpha P^\beta$$

where E is expenditure per pupil, Y is his family income, P is the "price" of an additional dollar of spending per student, and A, α, and β are constants. Then, for given values of E and Y, P is the value to that family of a one-dollar increase in per pupil expenditure. Solving (1) for P yields

$$(2) \qquad P = \left(\frac{E}{A} Y^{-\alpha}\right)^{1/\beta}$$

This relationship is of the form

$$(3) \qquad P = BE^{1/\beta}Y^\gamma$$

where

$$B = \left(\frac{1}{A}\right)^{1/\beta}, \ \gamma = -\frac{\alpha}{\beta}$$

If we assume these parameters in the demand function to be the same for everyone, the aggregate marginal value of a one-dollar change in per pupil expenditure for the n members of the community is

$$(4) \qquad \sum_{i=1}^{n} P_i = \sum_{i=1}^{n} BE^{1/\beta} Y_i^{\gamma}$$

The marginal cost of expenditure per pupil is simply n_s, the number of pupils in the community.[21] If the community undertakes the efficient level of spending per pupil, we would thus have that

$$(5) \qquad \sum_{i=1}^{n} P_i = BE^{1/\beta} \left(\sum_{i=1}^{n} Y_i^{\gamma} \right) = n_s$$

We can greatly simplify our procedure with one final assumption that each community is homogeneous in income so that every family in a given community in 1960 possessed the median family income for that community. Then (5) becomes

$$(6) \qquad nBE^{1/\beta} Y^{\gamma} = n_s$$

where Y is the median family income for the community in 1960. If we solve (6) for E and put the equation in log form, we get:

$$(7) \qquad \log E = -\beta \log B + \beta \log \left(\frac{n_s}{n} \right) - \gamma\beta \log Y$$

Using our cross-section of 53 suburban communities, we estimated equation (7) by ordinary least squares and obtained:

$$(8) \qquad \log E = 4.0 - 0.36 \log \left(\frac{n_s}{n} \right) + 0.65 \log Y$$
$$\quad\;\; (16.0)\;\;(5.6) \qquad\qquad\quad (7.7)$$

where the numbers in parentheses are the absolute values of the t-statistics for the respective coefficients and where $R^2 = .57$.[22] The estimated coefficients of the variables are all significantly different from zero at a 99 percent level of confidence and possess the anticipated signs. Using these regression results, we can go back and compute estimated values for our key parameters where we find that:

$$\beta = -0.36 \qquad\qquad \log B = -\frac{1}{\beta}(4.0) = 11.10$$

$$\gamma = -\frac{1}{\beta}(0.65) = 1.80 \qquad\qquad B = 65{,}840$$

$$\alpha = -(\beta\gamma) = 0.65 \qquad\qquad A = 55.5$$

We recall from equation (1) that β and α can be interpreted respectively as the price and income elasticities of demand for per-pupil expenditure.[23] Note how small is the price elasticity, implying the potential for substantial efficiency losses in the Unified System.

Using these estimated values for our parameters, along with our information on expenditure levels and changes in expenditure per pupil, we can calculate the valuations of changes in per pupil expenditure in each of our fifty-three suburban communities. If we take a linear approximation to the change in marginal valuation (that is, a linear approximation to the demand curves over the relevant range), we can substantially simplify our calculations. The value at the margin to the community of an additional dollar devoted to increasing the educational expenditure is exactly one dollar. The value of such a marginal dollar at a level of expenditure per pupil differing from the initial level by an amount ΔE is thus

$$(9) \qquad\qquad \frac{P'}{n_s} \approx \left(n_s + \frac{\partial P}{\partial E} \cdot \Delta E\right)/n_s$$

where P is interpreted as the community marginal evaluation of expenditure per pupil (6), and P' is the community marginal evaluation after the change, ΔE. Differentiating the left-hand side of (6) and making use of the equilibrium condition, $P = n_s$, we have

$$(10) \qquad\qquad \frac{\partial P}{\partial E} = \frac{P}{\beta E} = \frac{1}{\beta}\left(\frac{n_s}{E}\right)$$

so that the value of a marginal dollar of expenditure at the new level is

$$(11) \qquad\qquad \frac{P'}{n_s} \approx 1 + \frac{1}{\beta}\left(\frac{\Delta E}{E}\right)$$

By the usual consumers' surplus arguments, the approximate value per dollar of a sum used to bring about a change ΔE in per pupil expenditure is

$$(12) \qquad \frac{1}{2}\left(\frac{P'+P}{n_s}\right) \approx \left[1 + \frac{1}{2\beta}\left(\frac{\Delta E}{E}\right)\right]$$

We used this expression to obtain an estimate of the deadweight loss that would occur if the total amount spent on education in our sample of communities was so redistributed as to equalize the expenditure per pupil at the average level of $413. Given the range of initial spending levels, this implied increases ranging up to 40 percent and decreases to 25 percent for the communities in our sample.

After calculating the change in educational spending for each community, we used (12) to compute the value of these sums as viewed by the members of communities themselves. Since, by assumption, marginal valuation equaled marginal cost at the original level of expenditure per pupil, communities in which per pupil expenditure increased valued the amounts gained at less than the dollar amounts involved, whereas communities suffering a reduction in expenditure per pupil valued the loss in spending in excess of the actual dollar amount. The absolute values of these differences are the deadweight losses. Finally, we compared the mean value of these aggregate losses across communities to the mean of the absolute value of the change in educational expenditures. In short, this is the average deadweight loss as a percentage of the average change in expenditures.

For those communities that would have realized an increase in expenditure per pupil, this figure is about 35 percent. This figure indicates that each additional dollar of expenditure received by those jurisdictions that were net gainers was valued, on average, at only about $0.65; conversely, the computations indicate that dollars transferred away from the school budgets of communities were valued at an average of about $1.15 each. These estimates are obviously quite large; they suggest that, subject to our assumptions, the transfer of a dollar of school spending from one community to another under our hypothetical 1960 program for NJMA would have involved a mean deadweight loss of $0.15 for the contributor and $0.35 for the recipient, or a total deadweight loss of roughly $0.50.

Such large estimates suggest that losses of efficiency in this form should be carefully considered in any choice between the Current System and a Unified System. However, we would urge caution in the interpretation of these particular findings. We have made highly simplifying assumptions to estimate the price elasticity of demand for expenditure per pupil and to calculate our measure of inefficiency. Furthermore, the particular service under study, education, is one that might well be used to argue in favor of a Unified System, since it is believed by many to involve substantial spillover benefits.[24] Several recent court decisions, for instance, could be interpreted as taking this point of view. It is interesting that other local services, including garbage collection, recreational facilities, and fire protection, are not so frequently cited as generating spillover benefits, although, in a highly mobile society, almost any local service clearly has some external effects and for certain services, such as police protection, they may be quite important.

*Efficiency-Enhancing Characteristics
of the Unified System*

The most obvious advantage in terms of economic efficiency of a Unified System is its potential for internalizing the spillover effects associated with public budgetary decisions of the many independent communities in the Current System. However, to give a reasonable assessment of the Unified System as an internalizer is a difficult task, particularly since there exist alternative techniques (involving communication and negotiations among communities) to achieve this objective. To attempt to evaluate this source of increased efficiency seemed to lead us too far afield so that we will do no more here than simply note its possible importance.

There is, however, another respect in which the Unified System may promote economic efficiency relative to the Current System. In our discussion of the operation of the Current System, we stressed its tendency toward "excessive" income segregation and especially the "excessive" incentives to suburbanization resulting from the central city's necessarily income-integrated character. In this section we want to investigate whether, in the complex of forces producing the suburbanization of upper-income families, those arising from the governmental structure are of measurable significance. The answer to this question is obviously of great importance, for it has direct implications for the potential of alterations in local fiscal organization or policies to influence decisions of households and business firms and thus the economic characteristics of metropolitan areas.

Evidence that would enable us to answer this question is scarce, although there is some. Richard Muth, for example, notes that the tendency for cities to spread out as they increase in population size is stronger than can be accounted for by the differential housing-supply response predicted by his estimated relationships.[25] Although he offers some other possible explanations, it is certainly conceivable that this could result from an increase in the number of local jurisdictions from which to choose as the absolute population of the metropolitan area grows; this would presumably strengthen the centrifugal force we have described. Muth finds in addition that "the lower the average income level of the central city relative to its suburbs, the smaller is the central city's population and the larger is the land area occupied by the urbanized area," a result that can be explained in terms of the local fiscal structure.[26]

Bruce Hamilton has also found some corroboration of his model of choice of community. We have already described the implication of his analysis that the real property tax in the suburbs does not impose any deadweight loss. In the central city, however, this deadweight loss will remain. Put another way, the property tax is, in effect, ignored in choosing the amount of housing to consume in the suburbs (since the tax depends only on the amount of public service the household chooses to buy, a choice it makes by its selection of community), but it will influence the housing choice in the central city. This implies an observable difference in housing demand functions between central city and suburbs, a difference that Hamilton finds supported by econometric evidence.[27]

More direct evidence is presented by Bradford and Kelejian, who estimate relationships predicting the residential division of poor and rich families between the central city and suburbs.[28] Their econometric model includes variables designed to measure the net benefit of the central-city fiscal system relative to that of the alternative suburban fiscal system to the middle class and poor. Although the presumptive bias in this case is against the variables used, they are found to have statistically significant explanatory power. In an illustrative calculation of the influence of these variables, an "average" city was constructed and its government given an increase of transfers from higher levels of government from 20 to 50 percent of the city's total expenditure. The result was an increase of the fraction of the imaginary urbanized area's middle-class families living in the central city from 60 to 72 percent.

This result actually understates the impact of the illustrative policy on the structure of the urbanized area implied by the Bradford-Kelejian model. They find the income distribution of the central city itself to be a very important determinant of the location of middle-class residents, who show a marked tendency to flee poverty in the central city. This influence is found to operate with a much longer lag than the "direct" fiscal effect, and hence it did not affect the outcome of the example. Over a longer period, however, the "favorable" effect on the central-city income distribution would reinforce the shift of middle-class families back to the central city.

Feedback phenomena such as this seem bound to magnify, perhaps greatly, the dispersive effect of the current fiscal structure of urban areas. As upper-income families move out, the incentive increases for their employers to move out. Central-city amenities involving increasing returns to scale and catering to wealthier families —theaters, clubs, etc. — become uneconomical, reducing the city's attraction. The story could be spun out at length, although that would be a weak substitute for some solid quantitative knowledge (little of which is available) about these phenomena. The point to be emphasized is that it seems possible in principle that relatively small direct effects working against the central city could cause very large shifts in outcomes, and it may be very difficult to distinguish between a high income elasticity of demand for suburban space and a large systemic response in reduced urban amenity to a small initial shift in the relative fiscal surplus of middle-class families in the central city. It thus seems plausible that the fiscal organization under the Current System has played an important role in the process of suburbanization, although the extent of its effect is still not very clear.

Income Segregation under the Unified System

Although we have stressed the fiscal inducements for the formation of income-homogenized communities under the Current System, it by no means follows that such tendencies would be entirely absent under a Unified System. In fact, there is little doubt that, even if our metropolitan areas had been consolidated fiscal jurisdictions throughout their history, we would still observe a substantial degree of residential segregation by income class. This view is supported by an examination of the large fiscal units with which we have been familiar—the central cities themselves.

Here one is struck by the fact that, in spite of fiscal unification, the quality of the public services (particularly schools, cleanliness, and protection from crime) vary widely in different sections of the same city. Certain public schools are known in most cities to be better than others and some areas safer in which to walk. The quality of amenities varies considerably even within these unified fiscal districts.

This phenomenon can be better understood if we make a careful distinction between inputs and outputs of public services. For this purpose we draw upon a conceptual framework (similar to that used by others) that R. A. Malt and we developed in an earlier paper.[29] There we differentiated between what we called "D-output," or services directly produced, and "C-output," the level (or quality) of public services actually consumed by individuals.

To be more systematic, let I be a vector of inputs in the production of public services. In the case of schools, for example, this vector might consist of number of teachers, schoolrooms, or books. The vector I maps through a production function into a vector D of "directly produced" services. To return to education, D could consist of providing a given number of students with instruction of a specified kind (for example, a certain number of "standard" mathematics lessons). If we were concerned with protection from criminal acts, we might associate D with certain levels of surveillance, such as traffic control activity, resulting from an input I of men, cars, communications systems, and so on.

An individual, however, is presumably interested in the level of services consumed; he is interested in the quality of the schools his and other children attend and in the degree of protection from crime he actually receives. And these are determined only in part by D. They depend also on a number of other variables that describe the "environment" in which the direct outputs are provided. A specified degree of surveillance, for example, will provide a higher level of protection from crime in an area where there are few prone to commit criminal acts than in an area where this "propensity" is much higher. Likewise, as we have learned from the Coleman Report and other studies, the education a student receives depends largely on a number of variables, such as the characteristics of his schoolmates, that have little to do with the vector of public inputs into the school system.

More formally, the argument is that we can express an individual's utility function in the form

$$(13) \qquad U = U(C_1, C_2, \ldots C_n, Z)$$

where Z is a vector representing the level of his private-goods consumption and C_i is his level of consumption of the ith public service. In turn, we have

$$(14) \qquad C_i = f_i(D_i, E)$$

which indicates that the level of public services consumed depends both on D_i, the level of services produced (a function of inputs), and on E, a vector indicating the environmental characteristics of the area in which the service is provided.

With this background, let us return to our observation of the considerable variation in the quality of public services within cities themselves. This stems largely, we would guess, from the fact that fiscal unification tends to generate pressures more for uniformity in inputs than for outputs of public services. With the same set of tax rates applicable to the jurisdiction as a whole, one area, for example, is likely to protest loudly if the level of expenditure per pupil in the schools serving its children falls significantly below that in another part of the city. The discussion surrounding some of the recent court decisions has also been largely "input-oriented." In the California case, for example, the central point seems to have been that variations in the size of the tax base per pupil led to lower spending and hence inferior schools in poorer districts. There remains, however, the further issue, admittedly a difficult one to handle, that equality in expenditure per pupil by no means implies an equal quality of schools.

As a rough approximation, let us then visualize a city with a uniform tax structure and an identical vector of inputs for all public services in all sections of the city. It seems clear that we would expect to find in such a city variations in the quality of services consumed, the C-vector, because of differences in the environmental characteristics in the various parts of the city. More specifically, we would expect a clustering of the relatively wealthy in more costly residences, serving to provide an environment (an E-vector) favorable to a higher-quality package of public services. Wealthier neighborhoods will have better schools, even with the same expenditure per pupil, because of the characteristics of the pupils themselves and their families. Likewise, such sections will generally be cleaner and safer places to live than poorer areas of the city. Thus, in spite of the same tax structures and service inputs, we find that the quality of public services is likely to be significantly higher in wealthy than in poor parts of the city.

An interesting implication of this result would seem to be that the "tax price" of public services would actually be lower in these wealthier sections of the city because the same tax rate yields a higher quality of public services consumed, a "bigger" C-vector. This, however, need not be the case. Local services have typically been financed by income-related taxes, like the property tax, so that those living in higher-valued dwellings pay more in taxes. Moreover, to the extent that any favorable "fiscal" differential remains, it will tend to be capitalized into higher rents.

What we have here is an example of an economy of agglomeration analytically identical to that which occurs when, say, garment makers locate near one another. The mechanism sustaining this configuration is the willingness of those benefiting from the agglomeration to outbid others for the site. A curious question arises here, however. What is it that prevents poor people from outbidding rich people for sites near other rich people? The sheer price of the real estate is not a fully adequate explanation, as there are many examples of poor people occupying, in high density, expensive sites. The answer to the question may be that the consumption services involved typically are demanded with a high-income elasticity. We may here have the principle underlying the fact that rich people tend to form suburban communities, and garment-makers do not.) Or it may be that formal or informal zoning techniques are used, or "gentlemen's" agreements of one sort or another.[30]

In addition, as Wilbur Thompson has pointed out: "The wealthier urban households tend to cluster for many reasons unrelated to local public finance .... More commonly, income segragation is socially based as families choose their neighbors by using income as an index of desirable personal and social characteristics, and housing value as the surrogate for the unknown income."[31]

The thrust of these arguments, then, is to weaken somewhat the expectation of gains in economies of integration in a Unified System. The "natural" forces of relatively cheap housing inducing concentrations of poor people in central cities and of the tendency of wealthier families to reside in income-specialized neighborhoods even within a fiscal jurisdiction make it likely that in a Unified System, as in the Current System, cities would still have become sites of serious social and fiscal problems. But fiscal consolidation should have made these problems somewhat less intense and have provided a framework better suited to coping with them.

IV. IN THE LONG RUN WE ARE ALL DEAD

In the previous section we were primarily concerned with the long-run equilibrium properties of two structures for providing public services in urban areas: the Current System and the Unified System. Of equal interest, however, is the nature of the redistribution of welfare that would take place as a consequence of a shift from the Current System to the Unified System.

As before, we must make some simplifying assumptions about the existing system and some specifications concerning the sort of Unified System to which the hypothetical transition is to be made. For purposes of our analysis, we shall assume that under the Current System all local public services are financed by local real property taxes with levels of expenditures and tax rates determined independently by each jurisdiction within the metropolitan area. With the shift to a Unified Jurisdiction, we assume that all financing becomes centralized with revenues still raised by a tax on real property but with a uniform rate applicable to all property in the jurisdiction. Within this framework, we shall initially perform two sets of conceptual experiments. First, we postulate that expenditures per capita throughout the metropolitan area remain unchanged and examine the redistributive effects of substituting an area-wide property tax for the differing tax rates existing under the Current System. Incidentally, once this "baseline" analysis is established, the reader should have little difficulty in analyzing the implications of alternative financing schemes, such as a shift away from property taxation to increased reliance on an income tax. In our second group of experiments we shall hold constant the aggregate level of revenues and expenditures for the metropolitan area as a whole, but assume that, under the Unified Jurisdiction, expenditures per capita (or per pupil in the schools) are equalized across all sections of the metropolitan area. This will allow us to examine the redistributive effects of shifts in expenditure patterns as we move from the Current System to our hypothesized Unified Jurisdiction. We shall, in this part of the study, place a special emphasis on expenditures for public education in view both of their relatively large magnitude and their current importance for public policy. The analysis will consider the effects of this shift in the short run in which the stock of housing and structures is assumed fixed and, to a lesser extent, some of the longer-run changes that we might expect.

The most obvious shortcoming of this approach is the failure to integrate the tax and expenditure sides of the budget in the context of the new governmental system so as to take account of the effects of

TABLE 1

Equalized Tax Rates for Central Cities (1960)

Newark	4.94%
Jersey City	5.85
Paterson	3.91
Clifton	2.03
Passaic	3.53

Source: Morris Beck, *Property Taxation and Urban Land Use in Northeastern New Jersey* (Washington, D.C.: Urban Land Institute, 1963), Appendix B.

this change in fiscal structure on the aggregate levels of expenditures and receipts themselves. We shall, however, offer some observations later on this matter, where we shall argue that this should not alter greatly the general character of the results we obtain from our earlier experiments.

To generate empirical estimates of the various redistributive effects, we shall use the same sample of five central cities and fifty-three suburban municipalities in Northeastern New Jersey that we described and used for estimation purposes in the preceding section. Our procedure will thus be to take the New Jersey Metropolitan Area (NJMA) and study the patterns of income redistribution associated with a shift from the Current System to "the" New Jersey Metropolitan Government (NJMG). As earlier, we shall rely heavily on 1960 data, but will in most cases be able to provide some at least roughly comparable estimates for 1970.

Turning to our first experiment, we take the equalized or "true" value of taxable property in 1960 for the NJMA as a whole and simply divide it into the property-tax revenues collected by all local jurisdictions in the area for that year to determine what uniform metropolitan rate would have generated this aggregate level of receipts.[32] This rate for the Unified Jurisdiction is 3.03 percent. It is apparent from Table 1 that aside from Clifton this would have implied a substantial reduction in property-tax rates for the central cities. In particular, for the two largest cities — Newark and Jersey City — the reduction in tax rates would have been close to 40 and 50 percent, respectively. In contrast, the mean tax rate in 1960 for our sample of suburban communities was 2.53 percent. A shift to a Unified Jurisdiction would thus have raised the tax rate on the property of a "typical" suburbanite in the NJMA from 2.53 to 3.03 percent, or an increase of about 20 percent.

What can we say about the redistributive implications of these results? In the short run, the most important point to note is that this shift consists of a redistribution of wealth among property owners. The preceding calculations would therefore suggest, on average, a redistribution away from suburban property owners to those in the central cities. If we assume that the typical suburbanite owns his own home and use the mean value of an owner-occupied home in our sample of suburban communities of $19,000, a first approximation would be that his property-tax bill for 1960 would haven risen from about $475 to 570.[33]

However, this calculation overlooks an important effect: the impact of the change in the tax rate on the value of the property. The amount of wealth redistribution away from a landlord is simply the capitalized value of the change in his annual taxes or, in income dimensions, the annual tax change itself. The most obvious manner of estimating the latter is simply to multiply the original value of the property by the increase in the property-tax rate, as we have just done above. However, this is presumably an overestimate, since the increase in tax rate (holding government services constant) will tend to reduce the market price of the property. If we consider the market value, V, of a property generating a before-tax net rental flow of R dollars annually to be $V = R/(i + t)$, where i is the appropriate discount rate and t the property-tax rate, then the value of the property after a (ceteris paribus) change in the tax rate to t^* will be $V(i + t) / (i + t^*)$. The naive method of estimating the change in taxes ignores this fact. However, it is not difficult to show that the naive estimate need only be multiplied by a correction factor of $i/(i + t^*)$ to yield an estimate that incorporates the capitalization of the change in the tax rate.[34]

To apply this result, we must make a guess as to the correct rate of discount. Since the above argument treats gross rents as constant, a defensible procedure probably only in real terms, the discount rate we should use is a real rate, say, something between 4 and 8 percent. Since t^* in our case is 3 percent, this corresponds to a range in

$i/(i + t^*)$ from 0.57 to 0.73. For purposes of our rough calculations we have taken $i = 6$ percent, so that the estimated tax changes used in the remainder of this section are obtained by multiplying the naive version by 0.67. The reader with other ideas about the discount rate will have little difficulty readjusting our results.

The data presented earlier on changes in tax rates indicate that a shift to a Unified System would induce a redistribution on average from owners of suburban property to owners of property in the central cities. Taking $19,000 as the value of our typical suburban residence, we find, under the assumption of full capitalization at 6 percent, that an increase in the property-tax rate from $2\frac{1}{2}$ to 3 percent would reduce the value of this typical property to slightly more than $18,000. This represents a transfer of wealth away from the suburban property owner to owners of central-city property of approximately $1,000 in the form of an increase in the annual tax bill from $475 ($0.025 \times 19,000$) to roughly $540 ($0.03 \times 18,000$).

In the city, where a much larger fraction of the housing stock consists of rental units, the short-run benefits from reduced tax receipts would accrue primarily to landlords; this would presumably do little for the poor in the cities since they are predominantly renters. On the other hand, a significant fall in tax rates in the cities should make some contribution in the long run both to the construction of new rental units and the maintenance of existing ones with resulting reductions in levels of rents; it should also encourage business firms to locate (or at least remain) in the city, thereby creating more jobs easily accessible to the city poor. To get a very rough idea of the possible long-run impact on city rents, we took the median rent in each of our five central cities for 1960, estimated the reduction in the property-tax payment on that unit after the creation of the NJMG (using the figures from Table 1), and then simply assumed this reduction to be passed forward fully in terms of lower rents to occupants.[35] The results are presented in Table 2. At least for Newark and Jersey City, the fall in rents would have been substantial (respectively, roughly $100 and $130 annually); they are somewhat more modest for the others. However, these are no doubt overestimates, since they assume full shifting to tenants and make no allowance for the loss in deductions under the federal-income tax;

TABLE 2

Median Rents in Central Cities (1960)

	Actual	*Under NJMG with Shifting*
Newark	$77	$69
Jersey City	71	60
Paterson	75	72
Clifton	84	89
Passaic	69	67

moreover, for the city poor, the change is exaggerated since their initial level of rent would typically be less than the median rent for the city as a whole.

What turned out to be at least as interesting and somewhat more surprising was an analysis of the redistributive effects of the introduction of NJMG among the suburban communities themselves. The variation among these municipalities is quite striking and, moreover, bears little relationship to levels of income. The effective tax rates within this sample vary all the way from 1.59 to 5.45 percent so that the introduction of a uniform metropolitan tax rate would in many instances generate large changes in local tax bills. To see by how much these changes would redistribute income from richer to poorer communities, we first simply regressed the change in the tax rate for each community (that is, 3.03 percent minus the actual 1960 rate in the community) against median family income (1959) and found

$$(15) \qquad \Delta t = 0.05 + 0.07Y \qquad R^2 = 0.03$$
$$(0.1) \quad (1.3)$$

where Δt = change in tax rate ($\overline{\Delta t} = 0.5$)

Y = median family income (in thousands of dollars, $\overline{Y} = \$8.3$)

N = 53 (number of observations)

and where the numbers in parentheses are the absolute values of the t-statistics for the respective coefficients.[36] We see that, although the sign of the income variable is positive as expected, it is not significantly different from zero, which is reflected in the equation's ability to explain only a minute fraction of the change in tax rates.

To pursue this matter a bit further, we also examined the relationship between the change in the size of the typical tax bill in each community and median family income. To facilitate this calculation, we simply assumed that the median-income family in each community lived in the median-valued, owner-occupied dwelling. The naive estimate of the change in the tax payment, T_i', for the typical resident in the ith community, therefore is

(16) $$\Delta T_i' = (\Delta t_i)V_i$$

where V_i is the median value of an owner-occupied dwelling in municipality i.[37] Applying our correction factor to obtain $\Delta T_i = 0.67 \Delta T_i'$ and regressing the change in tax bill on median income we get

(17) $$\Delta T = 58 + 15Y \qquad R^2 = 0.12$$
$$(1.1) \quad (2.6)$$

In equation (17) the income variable is statistically significant and suggests that, on average, an increase of $1,000 in median family income is associated with a rise of about $15 in property-tax payments. The relationship, however, is extremely weak. This is evident when we examine some of the communities in the sample. There were, for instance, seven communities in the group of fifty-three with median family incomes in excess of $10,000. Of these seven "richest" communities, two had tax rates under the Current System of 3.01 and 3.02, respectively, and hence experienced virtually no change in tax rates and hence tax bills after our creation of the NJMG. A third community in this group experienced an increase in tax rate slightly less than the mean change for the sample as a whole. This means that, of the seven communities with the highest median family income, three would have had rises in their tax rates and two increases in their tax bills far less than the average for the sample as a whole.

In summary, the results of our tax experiment under the creation of NJMG suggest a redistribution of income in the short run away from property owners in the suburbs as a group to owners of property in the cities with some longer-run effects probably filtering down to renters in the city. In addition, the shift to the NJMG would generate a considerable redistribution of income among residents of the suburbs, ranging from changes in tax payments for a typical resident in each of our sample of municipalities from +$226 to −$226. And this does not allow for redistributive effects within communities. These redistributive effects among suburbs would seem at best to be only very weakly income related. It thus appears that, at least in the short run, the introduction of a metropolitan-wide tax on real property would redistribute income in nontrivial sums but in a rather haphazard way.

We turn now to our second set of experiments involving equalizing expenditures across the NJMA. We examine first spending on public schools. Our procedure here (similar to that earlier) is to assume that aggregate expenditures on public education are the same under the Current System and under NJMG. However, we postulate that, with the creation of NJMG, expenditure per pupil is equated in all school districts and shall examine the shifts in spending per pupil that such an equalization would imply.

If we take total current spending on public elementary and high-school education in NJMG in the school year 1959–1960 and divide by the weighted enrollment, we find that expenditure per student under NJMG would have been $413. Table 3 indicates actual expenditure per weighted pupil in 1959-1960 in the five central cities in the sample. We find that the introduction of NJMG would have generated some increase in educational spending in three cities. However, the changes would appear, on the whole, to be fairly modest. In the two largest cities, expenditure per pupil would have remained unchanged in Jersey City and would have risen by less than 10 percent in Newark. For our sample of suburbs as a whole, the mean value of expenditure per student was $418; there would thus have taken place, on average, only a very small shift in educational spending from the suburbs to the cities.

Once again the most striking effect is to be found in the redistribution of expenditures among the suburban municipalities. Expenditure per pupil within our sample varied from $295 to $547, which implies a change in spending per student ranging from +$118 (an

TABLE 3

Current Expenditure Per Weighted
Pupil (1959–1960)

Newark	$381
Jersey City	413
Paterson	377
Clifton	360
Passaic	414

increase of 40 percent) to -$134 (a reduction of about 25 percent). Aside from these extremes, an inspection of the results reveals tht there would be quite significant changes in spending on schools for a large number of communities within the sample. In contrast to our tax changes, these alterations in expenditure per pupil are strongly related to income. The regression equation (18) indicates that, for

$$(18) \qquad E = 174 + 22Y \qquad R^2 = 0.34$$
$$ (4.9) \quad (5.1)$$

each increment of $1,000 to median family income, a "typical" community spends an additional $22 annually per pupil. Equalizing current spending per pupil in the NJMA would thus have tended to raise this figure in poorer municipalities and lower it in high-income jurisdictions.

Turning to spending for functions other than education, we find that it is by no means clear that consolidation would have worked in favor of the cities. One of the reasons that cities have higher tax rates than suburban communities is that they provide a wider range of public services. In an important study of the Milwaukee metropolitan area, H. Schmandt and G. Stephens found that larger jurisdictions in terms of population provided a far greater number of services in the public sector than did smaller jurisdictions.[38] It is frequently the case, for example, that smaller suburban communities leave the job of trash and garbage removal to private firms or that fire protection is provided by a volunteer fire department. In contrast, if metropolitan areas were unified fiscal districts, we should expect pressures to assure that services provided publicly in one part of the metropolitan area would generally be provided publicly elsewhere; in all likelihood, there would thus be more public services provided in the suburbs, part of the cost of which would fall on city residents. This would not necessarily be true for all services. It might still make sense, for example, to have a single publicly provided zoo in the central city that would serve the residents of all the metropolitan area. Nevertheless, we should expect some narrowing in the range of services provided publicly between cities and suburbs relative to that existing under the Current System.

Substantial city-suburb expenditure differentials for noneducational functions do in fact exist in the NJMA. Table 4 shows current municipal spending per capita on all functions other than schools and debt service for our five central cities in 1960. At least for the two largest central cities, current expenditure on nonschool functions greatly exceeds $52, which is the mean value of this variable for our sample of suburban municipalities. The difference, incidentally, is only in small part attributable to higher welfare payments in Newark and Jersey City. A far larger part of the differential reflects higher spending on such things as police, fire protection, and hospital services.[39] Among the suburbs themselves, we find that spending on these functions bears a small, but significant, positive relationship to income so that a leveling of spending across suburban municipalities would be, on average, modestly income equalizing. There would, however, be numerous exceptions to this.[40]

The overall picture that emerges from our study is that the replacement of the Current System in the NJMA by a Unified Jurisdiction in 1960 would have resulted in a fall in property-tax rates in the central cities and a rise in the average tax rate in the suburbs. However, we found wide variations in the changes among the suburbs and no strong indication that, on the whole, these changes would systematically benefit either the rich or the poor. On the expenditure side, equalizing current expenditure per pupil would have resulted in modest increases in spending in most cities but a more radical alteration among the suburbs, with expenditure per pupil typically rising in low-income communities and falling in higher-income municipalities. Spending on noneducational functions would, in contrast, have fallen significantly in the cities and risen somewhat

TABLE 4

Expenditure per Capita on Municipal Functions
Other than Schools and Debt Service (1960)

Newark	$110
Jersey City	128
Paterson	65
Clifton	50
Passaic	75

Source: *Twenty-Third Annual Report of the Division
of Local Government*, State of New Jersey, 1960.

in the suburbs, with the distribution of the increase among suburban
communities varying inversely, in most cases, with income.

It is appropriate at this point to re-examine briefly our rather
unrealistic assumption of unchanged spending and revenues with the
introduction of a Unified Jurisdiction. In our judgment, aggregate
spending on most functions would probably rise. It is difficult to
believe, for example, that with existing commitments a large number
of suburban communities would be able to make substantial cuts in
their school budgets. Rather, we should expect to see a "leveling
upward" in expenditure per pupil so that increases in spending
would significantly outweigh reductions. This in fact appears to have
taken place in Toronto. In a study of the effects of introducing a metropolitan government on educational spending, Gail Cook found
that "Before federation (1951) there was no significant difference between the expenditures of the Toronto municipalities and the control municipalities.... After federation (1961) the Toronto municipalities expenditures on education were significantly higher than those
of the control municipalities."[41] Similarly for noneducational functions, we should predict rising expenditures, in part as we have
noted, because of the increase in the range of services provided
publicly in the suburbs. This would mean higher tax rates and spending than envisioned in our experiments, but note that the pattern of
relative changes between city and suburbs and among the suburbs
themselves would still be essentially the same as described in the
preceding analysis.

TABLE 5

Equalized Tax Rates for Central Cities (1970)

Newark	6.39%
Jersey City	6.40
Paterson	5.23
Clifton	2.38
Passaic	4.00

Source: Robinson V. Cahill, et al., Superior Court of New Jersey Law Division, Hudson County Docket No. L-18704-69 (Jan. 28, 1972), Appendix A.

The empirical study in this section has been based upon data for 1960. This raises the question of how the metropolitan finances have changed over the last decade. On the basis of the information we have been able to assemble, we find that the general picture is much the same as in 1960 except that some of the differentials we noted earlier seem to have increased in magnitude. Table 5, for example, indicates that effective property-tax rates in the central cities (with the exception of Clifton) have risen to extremely high levels. However, tax rates in suburban municipalities have also increased dramatically; the mean of the county averages of municipal tax rates for our eight counties had reached 3.67 percent by 1970.[42] This no doubt overstates somewhat the increase in suburban tax rates since the cities are included in these averages, but it is clear that rates in the suburbs have risen rapidly, perhaps proportionately almost as much as those in the cities. Even if this is true, however, the absolute gap between property-tax rates in the cities and those in the suburbs in NJMA has almost certainly widened substantially over the past decade. The institution of a NJMG would thus appear, on the tax side, to have a somewhat greater redistributive effect in favor of the cities than in 1960.

On the expenditure side, we find that spending on schools also increased rapidly over the decade. Table 6 shows the current expense per pupil for 1971-1972 for our five cities.[43] These figures compare with an unweighted average of current expenses per pupil in the eight counties of $1,084.[44] As in 1960, expenditure per pupil

TABLE 6

Current Expense Per Pupil (1971–1972)

Newark	$1121
Jersey City	897
Paterson	857
Clifton	961
Passaic	928

Source: Same as Table 5.

in the cities (with the notable exception of Newark) is somewhat below that for the suburban communities as a whole. A perusal of the data indicates, however, that, as in 1960, there are wide variations in school spending among suburban districts, with many districts spending considerably less per pupil than the cities.

Likewise, spending on (noneducational) municipal functions has increased greatly since 1960. Table 7 (as compared to Table 4) indicates that nonschool spending per capita more than doubled over the decade in our five central cities. However, expenditure per capita on these functions also more than doubled, on average, in our sample of suburban municipalities, rising from a mean value of $52 in 1960 to a mean of $134 in 1970.[45] Thus the relative levels of expenditure between the cities and suburbs remained roughly the same, although the absolute differential obviously increased substantially. There is again a wide variation in expenditure per capita among the suburbs, although no suburban community in the sample spent as much as either Newark or Jersey City.

TABLE 7

Expenditure per Capita on Municipal Functions (1970)

Newark	$279
Jersey City	292
Paterson	184
Clifton	146
Passaic	160

Source: *Third-Annual Report of the Division of Local Finance*, 1970, State of New Jersey, September, 1971.

V. SUMMARY AND CONCLUDING REMARKS

Our reading of the evidence suggests that suburban exploitation of central cities interpreted as the failure of suburbanites to bear their fair share of the costs of city services is typically of minor quantitative importance. What is of greater significance and interest for the distribution and levels of welfare among residents of metropolitan areas is the choice of governmental structure. The Current System of providing public services relies heavily on independent fiscal decisions by a multitude of small jurisdictions using the property tax as a primary source of revenues. Alternatively, we can envision a Unified System encompassing (at least) the entire metropolitan area with expenditure decisions being made on an area-wide basis to be financed by a property (or other form of) tax(es), where a single rate structure would apply to the entire jurisdiction.[46] We may distinguish two sets of issues: those having to do with the long-run equilibrium differences between the Current System and a unified metropolitan government, and those concerned with the transition from one system to the other.

In the long run we should expect a somewhat more egalitarian distribution of income under a unified fiscal structure than under the Current System. We are not, however, convinced that the difference would be very great unless the Unified System involved a basic shift away from property taxes to more progressive forms of taxation, or unless the secondary effects of reduced income segregation on individual productivity differences proved important.

On efficiency grounds there are arguments in favor of both alternatives. The Current System offers families a wider scope of choice in terms of combinations of private and public services. For education, our evidence suggests that this choice is widely exercised and highly valued. Arguing against the Current System (in addition to interjurisdictional externalities) is its excessive pressure toward the formation of wealth- or income-homogeneous communities, and correspondingly its excessive tendency for suburbanization of upper-income families. Just how different the two systems would look in this respect is difficult to predict, since there are "natural" forces favoring income segregation (genuine or perceived economies of agglo-meration) as well as the "artificial" fiscal forces. However, the central city would almost certainly have a significantly higher proportion of wealthy families under a Unified System. Empirical evidence on the social value of this difference is badly needed.

Turning to the transition from the Current System to a plausible sort of Unified System, we found, for our sample of New Jersey cities and suburban communities, that this would redistribute wealth in some unexpected and rather haphazard ways. On the tax side, the effect of shifting to an area-wide real property tax would redistribute wealth principally among landlords with the effects on others, via changes in the supply of housing and other structures, being difficult to predict and occurring only after the rather long lags involved in such supply changes. We do not know much about the wealth distribution of landlords in the central city, where a large proportion of families are renters. In the suburbs we know a little about landlord wealth, since we know median family income and the median value of owner-occupied homes in each community. Within the suburbs there would be substantial redistribution, but the change in tax bills would be only weakly and nonprogressively related to income. Since, in addition, there is presumably nontrivial income variation within suburban communities, the redistribution may be even more erratic than our estimates suggest.

On the expenditure side, in the case of a shift to a uniform level of expenditure per pupil in public schools, the redistribution would tend more clearly to be from rich to poor, although hardly at all from suburb to city residents. Shifting to a uniform expenditure per capita on noneducational functions would be slightly redistributive from rich to poor in the suburbs. It is most unlikely that equalization would be carried this far between city and suburb, but to the extent it was carried, and to the extent that unification meant the extension of central-city services to the suburbs, this equalization would work very much to the disadvantage of central-city residents.

It is rather difficult to draw any sweeping conclusions from all this. The picture is cloudy, and its features as presently discernible do not point to a clearly superior governmental structure for urban areas. Of course we cannot expect empirical evidence alone to dictate the choice, but it is obvious that more and better quantitative studies of the sorts of phenomena discussed in this paper would be extremely valuable.

NOTES

[1]In his comprehensive study of the redistributive effects of governmental budgets, W. Irwin Gillespie found that, in the United States for 1960, state-local budgets were redistributive in favor of families with incomes under $5,000. See his "Effect of Public Expenditures on the Distribution of Income," in R. A. Musgrave, ed., *Essays in Fiscal Federalism* (Washington, D.C.: Brookings Institution, 1965), pp. 164-66.

[2]Amos Hawley, "Metropolitan Population and Municipal Government Expenditures in Central Cities," *Journal of Social Issues* (1951), p. 107.

[3]Harvey Brazer, *City Expenditures in the Unites States* (New York: National Bureau of Economic Research, 1959); Julius Margolis, "Metropolitan Finance Problems: Territories, Functions, and Growth," in James Buchanan, ed., *Public Finances: Needs, Sources, and Utilization* (Princeton: Princeton University Press, 1961), pp. 229-93.

[4]William Neenan, "Suburban-Central City Exploitation Thesis: One City's Tale," *National Tax Journal* (June, 1970), p. 119.

[5]*Ibid.*, pp. 117-39.

[6]In one Detroit suburb, Grosse Point Park, Neenan in fact finds that the residents contribute more in revenues to Detroit than they impose on the city in terms of costs, but yet "exploit" the city because these payments fall short of their measured willingness-to-pay.

[7]We assume here that these are "income-compensated" demand curves, so they indicate the marginal valuation of each additional unit of output.

[8]It may be objected that linear compensated demand curves are too special a case to cast doubt on Neenan's weighting. Let us examine a more transparent example: the case of homothetic individual preferences defined over alternative bundles of a private good X and a public good G, which we represent by the utility function $U(X, G)$. Consider a particular bundle of the two goods: (X_0, G_0); this would generate a level of utility $U(X_0, G_0)$. We determine next an increment to the quantity of X, which would precisely compensate the individual for the loss of G_0. We would thus have

$$U(X_0 + \Delta X, 0) = U(X_0, G_0)$$

Let us define the total valuation of the public good, $V_g(X_0, G_0)$, as equal to ΔX. We can then write:

$$U[X_0 + V_g(X_0, G_0), 0] = U(X_0, G_0)$$

Homothetic preferences imply that, for positive t,

$$U[t(X_0 + V_g(X_0, G_0)), 0] = U(tX_0, tG_0)$$

from which it is clear that $V_g(tX,tG) = tV_g(X,G)$; total valuation is a linear homogeneous function. Thus, for this case total valuation is doubled by doubling the quantities of both the private and public goods. Doubling the quantity of the private good alone less than doubles the total valuation of the public good.

[9]James M. Buchanan, "Principles of Urban Fiscal Strategy," *Public Choice* (Fall, 1971), pp. 1-16.

[10]For an insightful overview of the characteristics of this system see Julius Margolis,"Metropolitan Finance Problems."

[11]Charles Tiebout, "A Pure Theory of Local Expenditures," *Journal of Political Economy* (October, 1956), pp. 416-24.

[12]Bruce W. Hamilton, "The Impact of Zoning and Property Taxes on Urban Structure and Housing Markets," Ph.D. dissertation, Princeton University, 1972.

[13]Edgar Hoover and Raymond Vernon, *Anatomy of a Metropolis* (Cambridge: Harvard University Press, 1959).

[14]W. Irwin Gillespie, "Effect of Public Expenditures."

[15]The redistribution toward the poor, incidentally, resulted from a "sharply 'pro-poor' expedenture schedule [which] outweighs a 'pro-rich' tax schedule," *ibid.*, p. 165.

[16]This seems a reasonable estimate. See Richard Muth, *Cities and Housing* (Chicago: University of Chicago Press, 1969), p. 69, and Frank deLeeuw, "The Demand for Housing: A Review of Cross-Section Evidence," *Review of Economics and Statistics* (February, 1971), pp. 1-10.

[17]For a detailed theoretical treatment of this issue, including a discussion of the measurement of such efficiency losses, see Wallace E. Oates, *Fiscal Federalism* (New York: Harcourt Brace Jovanovich, 1972), ch. 2.

[18]For a listing and description of the suburban communities in the sample and the sources of data, see Oates, "The Effects of Property Taxes and Local Public Spending on Property Values: An Empirical Study of Tax Capitalization and the Tiebout Hypothesis," *Journal of Political Economy* (November-December 1969), pp. 957-71

[19]To allow for the increased cost associated with education at higher grade levels, the figures used are expenditure per weighted pupil. For a description of the weighting scheme, see Oates, "The Effects of Property Taxes," p. 962. This procedure, incidentally, typically results in a figure for expenditure per pupil that is slightly less than that where no weighting is employed.

[20]We are ignoring at this point the important possibility of inter-jurisdictional external effects associated with local education, a matter to which we shall return later.

[21]We shall assume that this cost is borne by the residents of the community. With financing by a local property tax, this would imply either an absence of commercial-industrial property or that such property is owned by residents of the community. The bulk of the real property in most of the suburban communities in our sample is residential.

[22]We have not attempted here to be very thorough or rigorous in setting forth our conceptual structure. For a very careful investigation of sufficient conditions to assure the appropriateness of our approach, and for further empirical results, see the paper by Theodore Bergstrom and Robert Goodman, "Private Demands for Public Goods," *The American Economic Review* (June, 1973), pp. 280-96.

88   *David F. Bradford and Wallace E. Oates*

[23]These price and income elasticities are, incidentally, remarkably close to those used by Robin Barlow. Barlow used estimates of -0.34 and 0.64, respectively, which he took from a cross-section study of Detroit communities by Gensemer. The price variable in the Gensemer study, defined somewhat differently from ours, was the percentage of taxable property classified as nonindustrial. See Barlow, "Efficiency Aspects of Local School Finance," *Journal of Political Economy* (September-October 1970), pp. 1028-40.

[24]See, for example, Burton Weisbrod, *External Benefits of Public Education* (Princeton, N.J.: Industrial Relations Section, 1964). Even in the absence of external effects, local collective-decision procedures may result in subefficient levels of spending on education as suggested by Robin Barlow's study, "Efficiency Aspects of Local School Finance." Finally, from another viewpoint, some might object that this whole approach is inappropriate, since education is a kind of Musgrave "merit good."

[25]Richard Muth, *Cities and Housing,* pp. 317-18.

[26]*Ibid.,* p. 329.

[27]To the extent that the "tax-price" for public services among suburban communities with similar housing opportunities does vary, the differences are likely to become capitalized so as to equalize the attractiveness of the alternative communities of residence. Some empirical work seems to support this contention; see, for example, Oates, "The Effect of Property Taxes."

[28]David F. Bradford and Harry H. Kelejian. "An Econometric Model of the Flight to the Suburbs," *Journal of Political Economy* (May/June 1973), pp. 566-89.

[29]See Bradford, Malt, and Oates, "The Rising Cost of Local Public Services: Some Evidence and Reflections," *National Tax Journal* (June, 1969), 185-202.

[30]Fiscal consolidation, incidentally, does not necessarily imply the absence of local zoning authority. In some central cities, such as Baltimore, for example, particular sections of the city are empowered to enact regulations (e.g., minimum lot sizes) concerning land-use patterns within their districts.

[31]*A Preface to Urban Economics* (Baltimore: Johns Hopkins Press, 1965), p. 128.

[32]The data required for this calculation were taken from the *Annual Report of the Division of Taxation, 1960,* Department of the Treasury, State of New Jersey, p. 52.

[33]The great bulk of housing units among this group of communities was, incidentally, owner occupied. Also, to be a bit more precise, our estimated value of a "typical" suburban property is the mean value of the median values of owner-occupied dwellings in the 53 suburban municipalities rounded off to the nearest thousand; the actual mean was $19,200.

[34]Assuming complete capitalization of property taxes, the market value of a property yielding a gross annual rent of R (forever) is

$$V = \frac{R}{(i + t)}$$

where the notation is the same as in the text. The annual tax bill is, of course, tV. When the tax rate is increased to t^*, we took as our naive estimate of the increase in the tax bill ($\Delta T'$) simply

$$\Delta T' = (t^* - t)\, V = (t^* - t)\frac{R}{(i + t)}$$

If, however, we take account of the fall in the value of the property we have

$$\Delta T = t^*V^* - tV$$

where V^* is market value following the capitalization of the tax increase. We can express this as

$$\Delta T = t^* \left[\frac{R}{(i + t^*)} \right] - t \left[\frac{R}{(i + t)} \right]$$

$$= R \left[\frac{i(t^* - t)}{(i + t^*)(i + t)} \right]$$

We can convert the naive estimate, $\Delta T'$, into ΔT by simply multiplying the former by the correction factor $[i/(i + t^*)]$.

[35]These estimates were constructed by using (like Muth, *Cities and Housing*, p. 137), a gross-rent multiplier of 100. The rent was multiplied by 100 to obtain an estimate of the market value of the unit to which the change in the tax rate was applied to generate our naive estimate of the alteration in the tax bill. This was then multiplied by 0.67 to take account of the increase in property values generated by the decrease in the tax rate.

[36]There is, incidentally, substantial variation in median family income among this group of municipalities ranging from $5,900 to over $14,000.

[37]This is probably not too bad an assumption for our purposes. Most dwelling units in these communities are, as noted earlier, owner occupied. Moreover, the simple correlation coefficient between Y and V is in excess of 0.9, and, in regressions of V on Y, the addition of variables reflecting the distribution of income did not significantly affect the outcome.

[38]H. Schmandt and G. Stephens, "Measuring Municipal Output," *National Tax Journal* (December, 1960), pp. 369-375.

[39]Although some of this differential reflects a larger number of services provided in the cities, it may also result in part from the fact that a higher level of spending (or inputs) per capita may be necessary in the cities to obtain a given quality of output. In terms of our analytic framework, the E-vector in the city relative to that in the suburbs may require a larger input of directly produced services (the D-vector) in order, for example, to provide a given level of protection from criminal acts. As Norton Long observes about the cities, "The direct dollar cost of law enforcement is large, but not nearly so large as the cost of its failure to produce the product—security—which is its manifest function." See his "The City as Reservation," *The Public Interest* (Fall, 1971), p. 31.

[40]A regression of spending for noneducational functions on median family income in our sample of 53 suburban communities indicated that a rise of $1,000 in family income was associated, on average, with an increase of $3.40 per capita in expenditure.

[41]Gail Cook, "Effect of Metropolitan Government on Resource Allocation: The Case of Education in Toronto," Institute for the Quantitative Analysis of Social and Economic Policy, University of Toronto, Working Paper 7207 (April, 1972), p. 10.

[42]Robinson V. Cahill et al., Superior Court of New Jersey Law Division, Hudson County Docket No. L-18704-69 (Jan. 28, 1972), Appendix A.

[43]The figures in Table 6 are not based on weighted enrollments but are simply current expenditure divided by the total number of students in grades kindergarten through twelve in the public schools. This should not, we judge, affect the comparability of these figures within our set of jurisdictions very significantly.

[44]To be precise, this figure was derived by taking a simple average of the eight county averages of current expense per pupil. The source is the same as that for Tables 5 and 6.

[45]*Third-Annual Report of the Division of Local Finance, 1970*, State of New Jersey, September, 1971.

[46]We have in this paper limited the analysis essentially to two alternatives: extreme fragmentation or complete unification. Obviously, there is a myriad of other possible organizations of the public sector, and no doubt an optimal structure would involve differing size jurisdictions for providing various public services. However, at least for an initial exploration of the effects of governmental structure on resource allocation and the distribution of income, we think it has probably been more useful to see how much we can say about these polar cases.

II

Redistributive Aspects of
Resource Allocation Policies

4

Environmental Protection
and Income Distribution

————◆●◆————

WILLIAM J. BAUMOL

It is difficult, at least from a reading of the newspapers, to avoid the impression that concern over environmental externalities varies significantly with income class.[1] The poor and the wealthy seem to assign different priorities to environmental protection. The proposed construction of an oil refinery produces anguished cries from middle- and upper-income groups nearby but is welcomed as a source of better jobs by groups that are less affluent. Proposals to ban DDT seem to have been received with rather less enthusiasm in the underdeveloped countries than in the wealthier nations. This should, of course, come as little surprise to an economist. Assuming environmental quality to be a normal good, we should expect that wealthier individuals would want "buy" more of it.

Obviously, distribution is also affected because the costs of a policy of environmental protection may not be shared proportionately among income classes. It is difficult to predict in advance how these costs will generally be divided since the methods that will be used to finance such programs are unsettled. Yet even here some pertinent observations can be offered. Moreover, it is possible to judge in a very preliminary manner what would be the distributive effects of one proposed program—the imposition of taxes (subsidies) upon activities that generate externalities.

To deal with these issues at all, I have been forced to adopt several

William J. Baumol is Professor of Economics at Princeton University and New York University. He wishes to express his gratitude to the National Science Foundation for its generous support, which made possible the completion of this paper, and to W. E. Oates for his contributions to its substance.

drastic simplifications. The world is taken to consist of two distinct income groups—the rich and the poor, with the middle classes either nonexistent or subsumed under the first category. Only two types of communities are considered—those in which wealthy and impecunious live side by side and are affected equally by pollution and by the supply of public goods, and communities that are completely segregated, with the rich living in protected enclaves while environmental damage is at its worst in the areas inhabited by the poor.

Despite these and other simplifications our conclusions are hardly unambiguous. Yet the discussion will suggest that there is some reason to expect the supply of public goods often to be excessive in the eyes of the poor and inadequate in the opinion of the wealthy.[2] Moreover, it will be argued that environmental measures, unlike other public services, may tend to reduce job opportunities, at least in the short run, and so their cost may fall most heavily on those who can least afford them. Finally, the available evidence will be shown to imply that Pigouvian taxes are likely to be rather regressive.

Thus there seems to be some basis for the view that environment "is not the poor man's game." Yet, since there is strong evidence that health and longevity are affected substantially by pollution and by other types of environmental damage, the interests of society, including its less affluent members, undoubtedly require some sort of relatively efficient environmental program, even taking into account its distributive consequences. But the pious hope that the "distributive branch" of the fiscal authority can be trusted to compensate for the regressive effects of a new set of taxes also carries little conviction. At the end of this paper a few comments will be offered on this subject.

I. RICH, POOR, AND SUBSTITUTION BETWEEN PRIVATE AND PUBLIC GOODS[3]

We begin our discussion by considering the benefits side of an environmental program. In the next several sections we assume that an effective program for the protection of the environment has somehow been instituted, using Pigouvian taxes or some other instrument. We then investigate how the resulting reallocation of resources is likely to be regarded by the rich and by the poor (paying no attention to the method by which it has been achieved). The arguments with which the discussion begins hold for any public good, not just for environmental protection, and that part of the discussion will therefore be framed in terms of the more general public goods concept. Later, however, it will be argued that whereas public goods generally may well be regressive in the distribution of their net benefits, there are special reasons why this is even more plausible for environmental programs.

Elementary consumer theory leads us to expect that, so long as commodity prices are fixed and the same for everyone,[4] the marginal rate of substitution (MRS) between any two goods will be the same for any two persons. A may be wealthy and B may be impecunious but if A's MRS of strawberries for gin is 1.73, the same will be true for B. The poor man's equilibrium point naturally lies on a far lower budget line than the rich man's, and their indifference curves may differ considerably in shape. But since their budget lines are parallel, at the point of tangency the two indifference curves must have the same slope.

There is, however, something counterintuitive about this result. It does not seem plausible that the affluent and the impoverished will typically have the same subjective substitution ratio between potatoes and box-seat tickets to the opera. Intuition tells us that the poor are likely to give higher priority to "the necessities" or, at the very least, that the types of luxuries to which a high value is assigned will differ markedly by income class.

In part, the conflict between these observations and the arguments from consumer theory is, of course, illusory, stemming from the distinction between marginal and average relationships. Despite the equality of their equilibrium MRS's, the proportions between the quantities of the various commodities bought by different individuals can vary substantially. A poor man simply may be expected to consume relatively fewer units of luxury than a wealthy person before its marginal rate of substitution for necessities is brought into equality with the ratio of prices. This is just a slight variant on the marginalists' explanation of the diamond-water paradox.

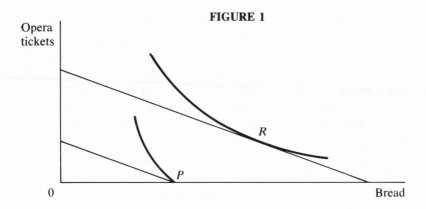

FIGURE 1

Opera tickets

0

Bread

But there is more to the matter. In at least two significant cases it simply is not true, in general, that the MRS's of rich and poor will be equal in equilibrium. The first involves commodities that are, characteristically, not consumed by one or the other of the income classes. This, I suspect, is the main source of our intuitive reluctance to accept the proposition about equality of MRS's. The second case is that of the public goods, which is our main concern in this paper.

The unpurchased commodity case is easily disposed of. We know it occurs, and occurs frequently. The rich do not usually purchase second-hand clothing, and the poor do not often buy yachts. When one defines two similar goods differing in quality to be different items, the number of such cases obviously grows enormously. As Figure 1 illustrates, where commodities are not usually bought by members of both income groups the MRS's of rich and poor may be expected to be unequal. If the impecunious consumer never buys box seats at the opera, at his equilibrium point, P, the slope of his indifference curve between opera tickets and bread must equal or exceed that of his price line; that is, we must have $(MU_{bp}/MU_{op}) \geq (p_b/p_o)$, where MU_{bp} and p_b are, respectively, the poor man's marginal utility and price of bread (at the equilibrium point), etc. Thus the poor man's relative marginal valuation of lower-class consumption goods will, characteristically, be higher than that of the rich man, just as our intuition leads us to suspect.

FIGURE 2

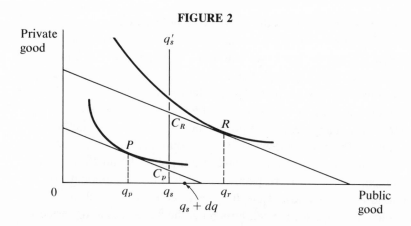

The accepted explanation of the diamond-water paradox may, then, sometimes be a bit too pat. Here is obviously a case in which the amendments to the standard models introduced by the ability of activity analysis to deal with the possibility of corner maxima do contribute insight and do add significantly to the realism of the analysis.

Just as the non-negativity constraints can be a source of inequalities in MRS's in the unconsumed goods case, the constraint that serves as Samuelson's definition of the pure public good can also produce such inequalities.[5] A pure public good is defined to be one that is necessarily supplied in equal amounts to all persons who consume it.[6] In any event, as McGuire and Aaron, Barzel, Buchanan, Tullock and others have emphasized, the public supply of public goods generally leads to a uniformity of supply of public goods that does not adapt itself readily to the differing desires of different groups in the community.[7]

This means (Figure 2), that if the rich man's and the poor man's indifference maps are superimposed as before, every individual's consumption point must lie somewhere on the vertical line above q_s (points C_p and C_R), where q_s is the quantity of the public good supplied. It is obvious that with consumers of neither type free to decide for themselves how much of the public good they wish to consume, their MRS's between public and private goods need no longer be equal. This is the source of the deadweight loss from uniform provision of public services, which was discussed in quite a different context by Bradford and Oates in paper 3 of this book.

Suppose, as a standard of comparison, that a perfect substitute for the public good were available on the open market at a fixed price (which it is perhaps convenient to think of as equal to MC/n, where MC is the marginal cost of producing the public good and n is the number of persons who will purchase some of it at that price.[8] Then we obtain two hypothetical equilibrium points R and P for the rich and poor consumer, respectively, indicating the amounts of the public good they would ideally like to consume if each individual could determine for himself how much he purchases at the price indicated.

On plausibility grounds we can go further than this. If we assume that a public good such as environmental protection is not an inferior good, and that the indifference maps of the typical wealthy and impecunious individuals are not greatly dissimilar,[9] it seems reasonable that the rich man will want more of the commodity than the poor man typically does. The quantity of the public good supplied by the government may then very well fall between these two levels.

For convenience in our subsequent discussion let us employ an artificial device to make the preceding assertions a bit more specific. The assumptions of the preceding paragraph imply that point R must lie above and to the right of P and that the vertical line at q_s lies between points P and R. Now, at tangency points R and P the MRS between the public and private goods would be the same for rich and for poor. But C_R, the actual consumption point for the representative rich man, lies to the left of R along the same budget line. We may therefore take it on the usual grounds that the absolute slope of his indifference curve at C_R is greater than it is at R. The reverse holds for the less wealthy individual, for the corresponding points C_P and P. It follows that if the slope of the price line represents the ratio of marginal costs of public and private goods, a move along the production possibility frontier in the direction of a reduced output of public goods will be beneficial in terms of the preferences of the poor but disadvantageous when measured against the MRS of the rich.

This is precisely in accord with the impressions one has from public reactions to environmental protection measures. It is the wealthier part of the population that seems to want more effective public policies in this area, whereas, as we have already noted, the poor do not generally seem quite so anxious to see this done.

II. DIFFERENCES IN PUBLIC-GOOD PRICES FOR RICH AND POOR

So far the argument has assumed that rich and poor pay the same prices for their public goods. In fact that is not generally true. The most obvious exception is the result of progressivity in the tax structure that may mean that a given outlay on environmental protection costs more for the rich than it does for the poor. Strictly speaking, for there to be such difference in price, progressivity is neither necessary nor sufficient. Even a somewhat regressive tax structure is compatible with a higher absolute cost to the wealthy. All that is required is that when public outlays increase by x dollars, the increase in tax paid by a wealthy individual be somewhat more than x/n (where n is the number of potential taxpayers) and that the tax paid by a poorer person increase somewhat less than this amount. That is, for the price of a public good to be relatively high for the rich man, his corresponding tax payment need just be higher absolutely than the poor man's, and this is quite compatible with a regressive tax.

Moreover, what is relevant here is not the progressivity of the initial tax structure but that of the incremental tax that can be attributed to a rise in outlays on environmental protection. Paradoxically, it may be that the sharper the progressivity of taxes currently in force, the more difficult it is to achieve a given degree of progressivity in an incremental tax. Suppose that taxes on upper income groups are already very high—close to 100 percent or, at least, close to levels at which significant incentive effects are feared. Then when an overall increase in taxes is legislated it will not be easy to assign more of the rise in tax payment to a wealthy than to a poor taxpayer.

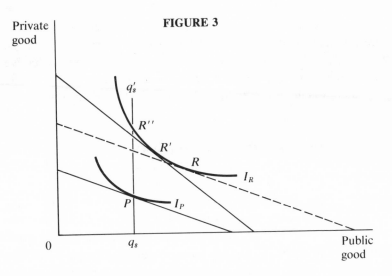

FIGURE 3

In sum, progressivity of taxes need by no means imply that the tax price of a given increase in environmental protection need be greater for the rich than it is for the poor.

Nevertheless, it is plausible that at least a mild degree of price discrimination of this sort does characterize many tax systems. If this were the only source of difference in the cost of environmental protection for the rich and the poor it might indeed decrease the difference between the levels of protection desired by the two income groups. In Figure 3 the budget lines for the poor and the rich are now shown to differ in slope, that of the rich being the steeper of the two (the relative price of the public good is higher for them). Even if there were compensation for any income effect, it is plausible that the quantity of public good that would be demanded at these prices by representative members of the two income groups would be closer than if the prices for the two classes had been the same. Thus, in the figure we see that point R', the equilibrium point of the representative wealthy individual, lies to the left of R, his equilibrium point if he were to face the same relative prices as the less affluent purchaser.

But this is surely not how things work out in practice. The degree of progressivity of the incremental tax system is not very clearly known even to professional economists. Certainly, the typical individual is unlikely to have more than the vaguest idea of the connection between a particular piece of environmental legislation and his prospective tax bill. The notion that variation in the degree of progressivity of the incremental tax can influence significantly the relative demands of rich and poor for public goods is rather implausible.

III. VISIBLE DIFFERENCES IN
COSTS FOR RICH AND POOR

The preceding discussion, then, questions the significance of the progressivity of the tax rates for the relative demands for environmental protection by rich and poor. However, it is not meant to imply that all cost differences are unimportant. On the contrary, it will now be argued that there are cost differences that are likely to seem of critical importance to the public and that for the first time in our discussion lead us to differentiate sharply between environmental protection and other public goods.

Most activities of the public sector make a very visible contribution to job opportunities. The construction of a dam or of a plant producing military equipment makes directly for increased employment. The popularity among legislators of such projects when located in their own constituencies confirms that this is often taken to be true.

On the other hand, it seems widely believed that environmental protection measures inhibit industrial activity. A tax that discourages effectively the demand for a polluting commodity is obviously deliberately designed, at least in part, to restrict the output of the industry that produces it. Marginal analysis does indeed confirm that the tax will tend to reduce the output of the product, although we know that it need not produce a decrease in overall employment since it may stimulate the volume of pollution-control activities.

Any employment-restricting effects of environmental measures may be increased by the fact that such policies are not instituted in all countries or in all areas within a country simultaneously. The region that imposes them unilaterally will find itself at a competitive disadvantage in the production of the polluting items. Whether or not this will reduce its overall level of employment it will certainly make for a decrease in the demand for labor in the industries directly affected.

Direct controls may have employment effects that are even more immediate. When a community bans a proposed oil refinery or projected airport, residents will find that their job opportunities are limited immediately. In a number of cases attempts to ban polluting activities have led to massive protests apparently for just this reason.

There is, therefore, a critical difference between environmental programs and other types of public activity, the latter tending at least in the short run to stimulate the supply of jobs whereas the former work to inhibit them. Obviously, there are some automatic offsets and some that are optional. Measures that penalize the emission of pollutants will stimulate the manufacture of recycling and purification equipment. Moreover, appropriate monetary and fiscal programs can be used to offset any loss in employment entailed in an environmental protection policy. But unless Professor Musgrave's stabilization branch of the public sector acts promptly and effectively it seems hard to deny that such a policy can contribute to employment problems.

In principle, this burden need not inevitably fall more heavily on the poor. A new refining plant may offer an unusually high proportion of jobs to executives and technicians. This comment is particularly pertinent for an economy in which a stable level of employment is maintained, for there the contraction of polluting activities will merely produce a reshuffling of labor, and the effects on income distribution will then depend on the relative change in demand for high-income and low-income employees.

However, where environmental protection does restrict job opportunities, it seems difficult to deny that the unemployed themselves are those who are hurt most. And these will, of course, tend to be in the lowest-income stratum. Here the poor certainly have more to lose than the wealthy. This would appear to be how they themselves view the matter. When one reads newspaper accounts of a local controversy over some proposed polluting plant, the invariable rallying cry of its proponents (who are usually reported to be drawn largely from the community's lower-income groups) is that prohibition of the enterprise will mean a loss of jobs that are "badly needed."[10]

This discussion has a direct bearing on the diagrammatic analysis of the preceding section. At least in the eyes of the poor themselves, and, very likely, in fact as well, the opportunity costs of environmental measures may be much higher for the poor than they are for the wealthy. This very visible difference in cost undoubtedly swamps any cost advantage to the poor resulting from progressivity of the tax system (an advantage that, as we have seen, is in any event rather questionable).

Thus the relative slopes of both the perceived (and possibly the real) budget lines for rich and poor may well be the reverse of those depicted in Figure 3. It is for the poor that this type of public good is more costly in terms of private outputs forgone. Although those public goods that stimulate employment may indeed be cheaper for the impecunious, the reverse may well be true of environmental programs. Thus relative prices may actually increase the difference between the degree of environmental protection desired by the upper and lower income groups, rather than bringing them closer together in the manner suggested by Figure 3.

IV. GEOGRAPHIC SPECIALIZATION IN ENVIRONMENTAL QUALITY

The public goods argument exaggerates the regressive effects of environmental programs in at least one important way. The world is not composed of a single homogeneous community in which the quantity of a public good (the quality of the environment) is the same for everyone.

As the classic Tiebout model emphasizes, different communities do supply different quantities of public goods, and land values and taxes do act as part of a market mechanism allocating environmental quality and other public services in accord with consumer preferences. One can imagine an ideal model in which there exists a large number of communities offering the individual virtually any degree of environmental quality he may wish to consider, each with its associated tax rates representing the cost of maintaining that quality level. In such a case, if the conjectures of the preceding sections are valid, the poor might generally be expected to settle in relatively polluted communities and the wealthy to live predominantly in clean neighborhoods.

This picture does not completely misrepresent reality. Indeed the preceding observations have been used to suggest that the poor in fact suffer *more* from externalities than the rich and that,[11] consequently, they are likely to benefit more from measures that improve the quality of the environment. But that conclusion would appear to go too far. First, it assumes that separation of rich and poor is quite complete and corresponds very closely to the level of pollution and other types of environmental damage. Second, it assumes that environmental protection policies will always assign priority to the cleansing of the dirtiest areas and this, too, need not always be the case. To examine the possibilities more systematically we shall therefore consider briefly two polar types of situation: first, the Tiebout world in which everyone has complete choice of neighborhood and, at an appropriate price, can find one that is perfectly suited to his preferences and, second, the Samuelson world in which everyone lives in the same area and so is offered precisely the same benefits from environmental protection taken as a pure public good.[12] These two worlds will be used to examine the distribution of benefits of three prototype sorts of environmental improvement measures: (1) uniform expenditures per community, (2) uniform standards for all communities, (3) the establishment of protected areas of high environmental quality.

Assume first that expenditures on cleansing of the environment are determined locally by the community and that none of the three policies to be considered has been imposed. We then can easily represent the Tiebout and Samuelson equilibria with the aid of Figure 2. In the Tiebout world, a community that is poor will make it possible for each of its residents to end up at point P at which his indifference curve is tangent to the price line given by the tax cost of the public good and the price of his market basket of private goods. For, by assumption, there is a community perfectly suited to every taste and every resident will select it for himself so that q_p, the quantity of public good supplied in the area in which he settles, happens to suit his preferences perfectly. Similarly, the public-good supply in the rich community in the Tiebout world will be q_r. If we assume constant costs for the buyer of public and private goods, as they would be if both were obtained from competitive suppliers, the price lines in the two communities will be equal in slope so that the same will be true of the indifference curves at points P and R. By contrast, in the Samuelson world, if we assume equal costs of public goods to rich and poor, the quantity provided will be the intermediate amount q_s, which is perfectly adapted to neither rich nor poor,[13] and where we may expect the rich man's indifference curve to be steeper in absolute value than the poor man's.

We turn to our three prototype policies.

(1) Uniform Increased Expenditures

As before, in the Samuelson world, with prices equal for everyone, an increase in public-goods supply can be expected to benefit the rich more than the poor.

On the other hand, in the Tiebout world the policy will lead to an equal rightward move in both communities. But since in our Tiebout case the indifference curves in both communities were equal in slope at their initial equilibrium points, the change (at least for minor displacements from equilibrium) should benefit rich and poor equally. In other words, the distributive effects of minor changes should be neutral. Actually, in this case no one benefits; there is a net loss to everyone since he is forced away from his optimal point. Only if the supply of the incremental public good is somehow financed from outside is there a net gain. In a perfect Tiebout world no intervention is needed to deal with externalities. For more substantial deviations from the Tiebout equilibrium it is easy to show that as long as the utility functions of rich and poor are homothetic, equal increments in public expenditure, beyond the Tiebout optimum, will exact more welfare costs from the poor than from the rich. This is true because the same absolute excess spending of public goods creates a greater proportional distribution of the poor man's budget than of the rich man's.

Thus a policy of equal expenditure seems never to favor the poor disproportionately in its distribution of benefits, At worst, in the Samuelson world, the rich benefit disproportionately, and, at best, for minor changes in the Tiebout world, neither gains more than the other.

(2) Uniform Standards

Suppose now that a law is imposed requiring all communities to provide the public good up to level $q_s + d_q$, where d_q is some positive increment. Then, as before, in the Samuelson community the rightward move from q_s can be expected to benefit the wealthy more than it does the poor.

In the Tiebout case, however, the results may be reversed. The wealthy community, since the quality of its environment already exceeds the adopted standard, will be totally unaffected. Its public-good supply will remain at q_r. On the other hand, the poor community will find its public-good supply increased from q_p to $q_s + dq$. The change is obviously substantial, but whether it is a benefit is by no means clear. If it is financed from outside obviously it will constitute a substantial gain to the poor. However, if the community is forced to finance the program itself (as often seems to be true in reality, as for example, in the case of municipal treatment plants) *then the poor will in fact have had a substantial net loss imposed upon them.* They will have been forced to lay out for the public good more than they want to.

Thus, while uniform standards may favor the poor in a Tiebout model, even this is by no means certain. Even this case, which seems to come about as close as any to what Mishan had in mind, may still not turn out to be to the advantage of the impecunious.

(3) Sanctuaries of Cleanliness

It is quite possible that universal and uniform standards may produce results that are unacceptable to society. For they may simply result in uniformity of environmental degradation. An alternative policy, which may have much to recommend it, involves the isolation of heavily polluting activities—inducements to confine them to relatively limited areas with other places serving as sanctuaries for environmental quality. Such a result can be obtained in a rather inefficient manner by zoning devices, or more efficiently by some variety of tax device, for example, one in which taxes on emissions of fumes vary directly with the initial purity of the atmosphere in the area.

However, it is easy to show that such an arrangement is virtually certain to be detrimental to the poor in a Tiebout economy.[14] Since they may be assumed to inhabit the dirty areas to begin with, the imposition of these policies is likely to make their communities dirtier still as polluting activities are driven there from the protected areas. Moreover, rents in the dirty regions may be expected to increase as well, as more polluters are induced to locate there.[15] Thus the poor will find themselves living in less attractive areas and receiving less rent advantage relative to the cleaner areas than they would in the absence of the program.

Clearly, none of this is conclusive. One can think of cases in which matters work out otherwise.[16] Yet none of the preceding cases suggests that the poor are likely to obtain the larger share of the gains from a program of environmental protection. This seems particularly plausible because reality does not permit the complete range of geographic choices, each offering its distinctive menu of public goods. The rich and the poor cannot afford to live too far apart; the rich offer jobs to the poor and obtain their services in return. Separation imposes time and travel costs on both parties so that in practice we find slum areas cheek by jowl with the homes of the wealthy. But such areas are Samuelsonain communities in which foul air or its purification affects both rich and poor, and in such locations it would seem from the preceding discussion that the benefits of environmental protection may well flow disproportionately to the wealthy.

V. REGRESSIVITY OF PIGOUVIAN TAXES?

So far the discussion has dealt with environmental programs in general, with no attempt made to differentiate among them. For a program based on direct controls or governmental investment or moral suasion we may have gone about as far as one can, *a priori,* in discussing its probable effects on income distribution. However, Pigouvian taxes raise an additional distributive issue, for these taxes will almost certainly affect the income distribution directly.

In principle, examination of their distributive effect seems to be a straightforward exercise. Pigouvian taxes are simply excise taxes that differ from other excise taxes only in the choice of commodities on which they are levied. One therefore should be able to investigate the issue by determining which goods are likely to be subjected to Pigouvian taxes and then searching the public finance literature for evidence on the incidence and degree of regressivity of taxes on this set of commodities.

The first task turns out to be rather more simple than the second. At least the superficial evidence indicates that the prime candidates for such taxes include petroleum products, electricity generation, other fuels, chemicals, pulp and paper, motor vehicles, aviation, mining, and processing of metals. No doubt other items can be added to the priority list, but this seems at least to be a reasonable beginning.

A search of writing in public finance for evidence on the distributive effects of taxes on these items is, however, disappointing. The bulk of the evidence deals with excise taxes as a class rather than the taxes on individual products, and much of the aggregative material is too superficial for our purposes. Usually, an excise tax is taken to be borne by different classes of taxpayer in proportion to their expenditures on the taxed items. But this ignores all the lessons of the theory of tax incidence and general equilibrium analysis. For example, as is the case with many of the commodities on our list, if the taxed commodities themselves are inputs to other production processes, the outputs of those processes may also be expected to rise in price. Moreover, if any of those processes is subject to declining average costs it is easy to show that its product's price may well rise by more than its increased tax cost. To determine who pays how much as a result one would, ideally, need to know the relative elasticities of demand for the taxed item, for items that use it as an input, for outputs using inputs substitutable for and complementary to the taxed item, and cost functions for each of these. It would, of course, be absurd to criticize empirical studies for failing to implement such an analytic process in all its complexity. However, where, as in the case of the fuels and the metals, an increase in the price of a commodity is likely to have significant effects on prices throughout the economy, some attempt to take these consequences into account would appear to be essential.[17]

Even if we are willing to accept oversimplification, it has so far proved possible to find only one set of studies sufficiently disaggregated to provide any indication of the probable progressivity or regressivity of Pigouvian taxes.[18] This is a piece of research carried out at Rutgers University by J. M. Schaeffer.[19] His study does not conclude that all excise taxes are regressive in their net effects. For example, it indicates, somewhat surprisingly, that a tax on the sale of clothing is likely to increase the progressivity of the tax system in the state of New Jersey. However, it does indicate that taxes on all utility expenditures, and on gas and electricity, in particular, would be highly regressive. Taxes on water and sewage would also be regressive, though considerably less so than those on gas and electricity. Specifically, the elasticity of the sales tax base with respect to income level (Schaeffer's measure of progressivity), with income classes weighted by population size, is 0.99 for the sales tax base in New Jersey as a whole, 0.47 for all utility expenditures, 0.44 for gas and electricity, and 0.71 for water and sewage. All the corresponding measures recalculated by other methods show similar patterns.

These figures are. of course, far from conclusive. They deal with only a subset of polluting activities and treat only one locality for a limited period (1960-1961). Above all, they make no attempt to take into account repercussions elsewhere in the economy. Yet they certainly do nothing to dissuade us from the fear that Pigouvian taxes are likely to contribute substantially to the regressivity of the tax system.

VI. IMPLICATIONS FOR POLICY

The analysis of this paper then seems to lend support to the view that environmental protection measures do tend to aggravate the inequality of the distribution of real income. They lead to a reallocation of resources more closely in accord with the desires of the rich than with those of the poor. Moreover, their most visible cost, the tangible real income they force individuals and the community to forego, is also likely to fall most heavily on the lower-income groups.

There are two obvious polar reactions to these observations. An oversimplication of the reaction of the pure economist might assert that resource allocation and income distribution are two separate issues and that one should not be permitted to interfere with a rational resolution of the other. No matter what their distributive implications, one should seek to institute policies that make for efficiency in resource utilization, leaving it to some other (unclearly identified) branch of government to take the steps required to achieve a more just distribution of income.

The other extreme view, again one that is probably rarely held in its most naked form, asserts that the elimination of poverty is a matter of much higher priority than the (primarily aesthetic) issue of environmental protection. If the latter interferes with the former, so much the worse for it; it is a luxury whose attainment must at the very least be postponed until the more pressing problem of inequality is reduced to reasonable proportions.

To me neither of these views is really acceptable. The vague hope that the "distribution branch" of government will somehow undo any incidental mischief caused by environmental policy is just not good enough. The past performance of redistributive policy does not really make us confident that further aggravation of inequality will somehow be offset.

On the other hand, postponement of environmental protection measures is not an appealing notion. If the measures are vital matter of public health and perhaps even of survival, even the poorest citizen may not have much reason to thank the legislator who resists effective action on these matters, even if it is apparently done for his sake.

Similarly, distributive considerations need not justify the neglect of efficiency in the regulation of externalities. For example, if it is true that the achievement of a given degree of environmental improvement will be far more costly if carried out through direct controls rather than by fiscal means, the standard of living of the poor may be affected significantly and adversely by the adoption of the former in preference to the latter. It is true here as elsewhere that a larger share of a much smaller pie is not always an advantage.

To me it would seem, rather, that the moral of the analysis is that environmental legislation should ideally be paired with measures designed explicitly to offset its undesired distributive consequences. Rather than simply relying on pious hopes for the eventual rectification of any resulting inequities, I think a coupling of environmental and redistributive measures will enable us to increase their political acceptability and to deal more appropriately with the social priorities.[20] By acting simultaneously and explicitly on both issues we can have some assurance that environmental policy does not become yet another influence that makes the rich richer and the poor poorer.

NOTES

[1]The professional literature on this subject is rather sparse. However, see A. Myrick Freeman, "The Distribution of Environmental Quality," in Allen V. Kneese and Blair T. Bower, eds., *Environmental Quality Analysis: Theory and Method in the Social Sciences* (Baltimore: Johns Hopkins Press, 1972).

[2]In other words, this implies that, typically, an increase in the supply of a pure or near-pure public good will yield a regressive distribution of benefits. This assertion should not be confused with the equally plausible hypothesis that governmental subsidy (or supply at low cost) of largely private goods, such as medical care, is apt to be

progressive in its distribution of benefits, increasing the relative well-being of the poor.

³The discussion in this section bears some structural similarity to that in Michael S. Koleda, "A Public Good Model of Government Consolidation," *Urban Studies* (June, 1971), pp. 103-10.

⁴It is often suggested that prices paid for items of given quality do differ markedly by income class; i.e., that the poor pay more because prices in their neighborhoods are typically higher. Since the argument here depends on equality of relative prices such a phenomenon need not affect it seriously. In any event, several careful studies by persons whose biases would lead us to expect them to look carefully for evidence that the poor and the members of minority groups are exploited, found no statistically significant differences between prices inside and outside the ghettos, even for standard items obviously fixed in quality. The studies did suggest that the poor purchase more frequently at small retail shops where they can obtain credit, rather than at lower-priced supermarkets. However, the small neighborhood shops offered similar prices in rich and poor neighborhoods, and the same was true of the supermarkets. See, e.g., Roger Alcaly and A. K. Klevorick, "Food Prices in Relation to Income Levels in New York City," *Journal of Business* (October, 1971).

⁵Paul A. Samuelson, "The Pure Theory of Public Expenditure," *Review of Economics and Statistics* (November, 1954).

⁶Of course, this does not mean that all persons need derive the same "utility" from it. If the sulphur content of the atmosphere is reduced by a given percentage this affects equally the rich and the poor who live or work near one another. But the relative valuation of the improvement cannot be assumed *a priori* to be equal. In fact, this valuation is just what we are about to discuss.

⁷See M. McGuire and H. Aaron, "Efficiency and Equity in the Optimal Supply of a Public Good," *Review of Economics and Statistics* (February, 1969), pp. 31-39; Y. Barzel, "Two Propositions on the Optimum Level of Producing Collective Goods," *Public Choice* (Spring, 1969), pp. 31-38; J. M. Buchanan, "Notes for an Economic Theory fo Socialism," *Public Choice* (Spring, 1970), pp. 29-43; G. Tullock, "Social Cost and Governmental Action," *American Economic Review* (May, 1969), pp. 189-97.

⁸In the figure the hypothetical budget lines for the rich and poor persons have been drawn to go respectively through points C_R and C_p. This is necessarily valid only on the assumption that the private good is a composite commodity including all items other than the public good used by the consumer, saving being one of these items. In addition to this Hicksian premise it requires the assumption that the incremental tax payment of the individual resulting from the supply of the public good is equivalent to MC/n, the market price for the artificial substitute commodity. As we shall see in the next section, progression of taxes may violate this assumption for we may then be unable to assign to everyone the same hypothetical price for the substitute public good and yet have that price equivalent to his incremental tax payment.

⁹This premise attributes differences in consumption by income class entirely to their income disparities, rather than to variations in tastes. The validity of this assumption is not entirely obvious. The education and home environment of the different income groups undoubtedly influence their consumption patterns. Thus witness the celebrated differences between the consumption patterns of the *nouveaux riches* and those whose wealth goes back several generations. Even if these dif-

ferences disappear over the very long run it is conceivable that differences in tastes are inherited and that some of these differences (e.g., in attitudes toward labor and saving) in turn produce systematic differences in income.

[10]Even if employment is not hurt by environmental protection measures, real output, conventionally measured, will tend to be reduced since a given set of inputs will yield a smaller bundle of outputs than before. In many cases this cost, too, will probably fall most heavily on the poor. If a ban on DDT undermines the "green revolution" with its spectacular contribution to grain outputs in underdeveloped areas, can there be any serious doubt about the income group that will suffer the resulting malnutrition or starvation?

[11]See, e.g., E. J. Mishan, "The Postwar Literature on Externalities: An Interpretive Essay," *Journal of Economic Literature* (March, 1971), pp. 1-28.

[12]C. Tiebout, "A Pure Theory of Local Expenditures," *Journal of Political Economy* (October, 1956), pp. 416-24; P. A. Samuelson, "The Pure Theory of Public Expenditure," *Review of Economics and Statistics* (November, 1954), pp. 381-87.

[13]This assumes that some compromise arrangement is agreed on by a method other than simple majority vote among the poor and wealthy. Otherwise, the majority group would simply supply the public good at its optimal level.

[14]The Samuelson model is not relevant to this case, which requires as one of its premises differentiation in the environmental quality of different communities.

[15]Actually, this is not inevitable. For example, the imposition of a differential tax that falls more heavily on polluting activities in protected areas may reduce output in both areas if the tax differential is sufficiently small. Thus, let a firm produce in two areas, A, which is unprotected, and B, which is protected, and let x_a and x_b be its outputs in the two locations that are produced at respective costs $c_a(x_a)$ and $c_b(x_b)$, let its total revenue be $r(x_a + x_b)$, and let the tax rate on production in the two locations be t and kt, where $k > 1$. Then if the firm's objective is to maximize profits its problem is to

$$\text{Max } \pi = r (x_a + x_b) - c_a(x_a) - c_b(x_b) - tx_a - ktx_b$$

yielding the first order conditions

$$r' - c_a' - t = 0$$
$$r' - c_b' - kt = 0$$

Differentiating totally with respect to t, x_a, and x_b, we obtain

$$(r'' - c_a'') \, dx_a + r'' \, dx_b = dt$$
$$r'' \, dx_a + (r'' - c_b'') \, dx_b = kdt$$

or solving, and letting D represent the determinant of the system,

$$\frac{dx_a}{dt} = [(1 - k)r'' - c''] / D$$

Thus if $r'' < 0$ and $c'' > 0$, dx_a/dt will be negative with k sufficiently close to unity, i.e., if the tax differential is not great enough, x_a, the firm's output in the unprotected area, may be reduced by the tax.

[16]Perhaps the most obvious pro-poor result would be achieved if public policy called for alleviating pollution where it presently is most severe, while financing this

improvement out of general revenues. This would be the reverse of a policy of "sanctuaries of cleanliness" with the reverse distributive effects.

[17]Professor Leontief's work on input-output analysis of pollution may well provide an important component of the requisite analysis.

[18]For a typical discussion of the evidence of regressivity of excise taxes generally, see Joseph A. Pechman, *Federal Tax Policy*, rev. ed. (New York: Norton, 1971), pp. 156-58 and G. A. Bishop, "The Tax Burden by Income class, 1958" *National Tax Journal* (March, 1961), pp. 41-59.

[19]Schaeffer defines this elasticity as the percentage change in the group's expenditure on the item (the amount subject to tax) resulting from a small percentage change in its income. See J. M. Schaeffer, "Sales Tax Regressivity under Alternative Tax Bases and Income Concepts," *National Tax Journal* (December, 1969), pp. 516-27.

[20]For example, it might be desirable, in the design of a negative income tax to tie the values of its parameters (the basic support level and the marginal "tax" rate) to the regressivity of the remainder of the tax system. Then an increase in tax rates would automatically bring with it an increase in the progressivity of the negative income tax that would preserve the relative financial position of the poorer members of the community.

5

The Distributional Impact of Performance Contracting in Schools

GEORGE E. PETERSON

Nineteenth-century liberalism held that every public supplier of services must be less efficient and less solicitous of consumer wants than its private counterpart. From this it concluded that the citizenry would best be served if municipalities left the important business of service provision in private hands. Subsequent generations, as we know, failed to heed the liberals' advice, but of late the view that public services could better be provided by private firms has enjoyed a sort of second coming among those dismayed by the apparent deterioration of local service quality. The last few years have brought numerous proposals to return municipal-service functions to the private sector. This paper examines one of those mechanisms, performance contracting in the public schools.

Like the other market devices that have been proposed, performance contracts originally were drawn up to demonstrate that a wise use of profit incentives could increase productive efficiency. Their success in that respect can best be described as "mixed to poor." Preliminary studies show that students in schools that have been operated by private firms under performance contracts have performed about as well, or as poorly, in terms of standard test results, as students at similar schools operated on traditional principles.[1] Of

George E. Peterson is Economic Studies Director of the Land Use Center of The Urban Institute.

course it is too soon to form a final judgment of the effectiveness of performance contracting as an organizational technique. The Office of Economic Opportunity (OEO) experiments tried to test so many variables, in such a short time, that the principle of using financial incentives to emphasize educational priorities may well have been lost in the shuffle.[2]

For a time it seemed that of the performance contract schools the best record belonged to the Banneker School of Gary, Indiana. Whereas pupils in the second, third, and sixth grades, in the experimental programs operated by OEO contractors, scored an average gain of 0.4 grade equivalents on reading tests and 0.5 on mathematics tests, elementary students at the Banneker School in their first year registered average gains of 0.7 and 1.1 years, respectively. Behavioral Research Laboratories (BRL), which conducted the Banneker School experiment, enjoyed two advantages that were not available to other performance contract firms. First, the company was given responsibility for operating an entire school. Second, it was originally guraranteed that the experiment would last three years, a guarantee that seemed to free it from the temptation to contrive spectacular results in the first year of operation.

Just how successful the Banneker School experiment really was probably never will be known. During the second year of the experiment (the school year 1971-1972) one of the longest teacher strikes in United States history took place in Gary. As a consequence, the standard tests scheduled for the spring of 1972, upon which payment to BRL was to be based, could not be administered. In December of 1972, six months ahead of schedule, Gary's performance contracting experiment was terminated. Although the interested parties offered different accounts of the reasons for this decision, it was clear that Gary school officials were dissatisfied with the results that had been achieved.

For the moment, the specific idea of utilizing private firms to give public school instruction appears to be dead. It is unlikely, however, that we have seen the last of efforts to harness profit incentives to the provision of public services. In fact, variants of the performance contracting device currently are being used to pay private firms to provide other municipal services, such as trash collection. In Detroit, the school board's insistence that teachers' salaries should be adjusted to reflect the improvement in standardized achievement test results of the pupils in their classrooms—a slightly different form of profit inducement—recently led to another prolonged teachers' strike.

In this paper we want to consider the redistributive effects of attaching prices to public sector outputs by means of incentive contracts. That these redistributive effects may be large, compared to any efficiency gains, is illustrated by the Banneker School's experience. The contract between BRL and the Gary school system called for the firm to receive $800 per year for each pupil who, after three years under its tutelage, surpassed grade norms in reading and mathematics on standard Metropolitan Achievement Tests. The first evaluation carried out at Banneker revealed that, in response to this structuring of profit opportunities, the contractor had drastically shifted classroom resources toward instruction in reading and mathematics, the two subjects that determined the firm's remuneration, and away from such subjects as science and social studies, where success was not to be rewarded financially.[3] This skewing of instructional effort may prove to be the most important lesson of the Banneker experiment for performance contracting generally. The introduction of a new pricing system, or a new market, never has efficiency effects alone. The same profit incentives designed to increase efficiency also have distributional implications. In the case of performance contracting in schools, where the "outputs" are embodied in children, fixing the price system may also have strong distributional implications by determining which children benefit most from the firm's educational efforts.

Our concentration in this paper on the distributional implications of the Banneker School's performance contract serves principally to keep us in touch with reality, for the analysis applies equally well to any performance contract which provides that the contractor will be remunerated according to the number of subjects that perform above a specified norm. The paper is divided into five sections. The first and second sections develop the theory of profit-maximizing behavior for a firm interested only in expected profits; the third section considers the modifications to be expected in the firm's behavior if it is risk averse; and the fourth section tests the distributional implications of the model against the first year's experience at the Banneker School.[4] The fifth section provides a concluding account of the effects of performance contracting.

I. PROFIT-MAXIMIZING BEHAVIOR
FOR THE EDUCATIONAL ENTREPRENEUR

We start with a simple model in which education, or rather test scores, are produced in linear fashion:

$$y^i = \text{test score of individual } i$$

$$(1) \quad y^i = aX_1^i + bX_2^i + e \begin{cases} X_1^i = \text{previous year's test score of} \\ \quad\quad \text{individual } i \\ X_2^i = \text{firm's dollar expenditure in} \\ \quad\quad \text{current year on individual } i \end{cases}$$

$$e = \text{error term}$$

Function (1) is a summary function. Behind it, we can assume, stands a production function that states that the expected increment in test scores, due to the school's instruction, is a linear homogeneous function of variable educational inputs, such as skilled teacher time, unskilled teacher time, and use of instructional materials. Or

$$(2) \quad y_i - aX_1^i = F(q_1 \ldots q_n) \begin{cases} F = \text{linear homogeneous function} \\ q_j = \text{amount of educational input } j \end{cases}$$

It is well known that a profit-maximizing firm, which operates with a linear homogeneous production function and faces fixed input and output prices, will stay on a fixed proportions production ray, regardless of the magnitude of its output. In our case we can assume that the market prices of inputs — principally teachers' wages and prices of school materials — are beyond the power of a single school to alter, whereas "output" prices are fixed by the terms of the performance contract itself. This means that the school in our model always will employ its educational inputs in the same proportion, however much attention it devotes to a particular pupil. If student A receives twice as much teacher time as student B, he will, for example, also get twice as much attention from teachers' aides and make twice as intensive use of programmed materials. Furthermore, under these assumptions each dollar that the firm expends on inputs will buy the same expected increment in test results since (2) implies constant returns to scale. The constant returns feature accounts for the fact that in (1) test results can be represented as a linear function of school expenditures.

We should admit at once that the formulation above has been chosen for its simplicity, not its realism. Equation (1) carries the unfortunate implication that, if only enough money is spent, any pupil can reach any level of test achievement. Despite this implication, expression (1) is considerably more plausible than the linear production function often used in educational studies, for although (1) implies that marginal output per dollar optimally spent remains constant, it does not imply (as a linear production function does) that there are no diminishing returns to a school's factors of production. Expression (1) is perfectly consistent with a world where the marginal product of individual factors, such as instruction by teachers' aides, declines with increasing dosages; it requires only that there be no diminishing returns to the optimal combination of productive inputs.

It may be objected that the voluminous research on educational production functions has failed to turn up any reliable relation between achievement test scores and per pupil expenditures,[5] and that an analysis placing this relation at the center of its theory must be off to a bad start, however much allowance is made for the advantages of simplicity. Fortunately, the evidence from cross-sectional studies is not relevant here. What cross-sectional studies show, in effect, is that as among different schools, higher teachers' salaries and lower pupil-teacher ratios do not make for higher achievement test scores, in any regular sense. The "production function" we are considering is quite different. It applies only to a single school, or classroom, and implies that, given the quality of teachers and materials available and given teachers' salaries, the more attention devoted to an individual pupil, the more progress he is likely to show. Of course it is possible that a pupil's performance is quite unrelated to efforts to instruct him; but, if so, that is quite a different (and much more serious) matter from saying that dollar expenditures, by school, are unrelated to average pupil performance. All performance contracting and all education as well seem to be based on the presumption that by exerting more effort, in terms of teachers' time, aides' time, and use of materials, a school can help children to learn.

Now national achievement tests are normed in such a way that grade level standards, $\bar{y}$, are known before application of the test in a given year. These norms also are independent of current year test results in Gary. The entrepreneur's revenue function for individual i then is:[6]

$$(3) \qquad\qquad R = \begin{cases} 800 \text{ if } y^i > \bar{y} \\ 0 \quad \text{ if } y^i < \bar{y} \end{cases}$$

and the total profit function is

$$(4) \qquad\qquad \Pi = \sum_i R^i - \sum_i X_2^i$$

We can assume that the error term in the output function (1) is distributed normally as $e \sim n(0, \sigma^2)$ and that under the optimal production methods the error terms for individual pupils are identically and independently distributed. This last assumption does not deny that children often learn as a group in such a way that an extraordinary improvement registered by one child is likely to be associated with significant improvement by others. It only implies that unpredictable deviations in pupil performance about their expected values will not be correlated. The assumption that the error terms are identically distributed implies that the predictability of the production relationship does not vary with the child's performance level or with the magnitude of the educational resources expended on him.

Given this assumption of independence, the entrepreneur's total revenue function can be considered as the sum of n Bernoulli trials, each of which pays $800 if successful (the pupil surpasses the national average on the standard test) and nothing if unsuccessful, with a different probability of success at each trial. The probability of individual success is distributed as a cumulative normal function.

(5) $\qquad p^i = \text{Prob}(y^i > \bar{y}) = N(aX_1^i + bX_2^i - \bar{y}_i \; ; \; \sigma^2)$

and where $\hat{y} = Ey^i = aX^i + bX_2^i$

Suppose the entrepreneur behaves as a maximizer of expected profits. Then,

(6) $$E\Pi = 800\sum_i p^i - \sum_i X_2^i$$

which has as its first-order condition

(7) $$\frac{\partial(E\Pi)}{\partial X_2^i} = 800\,\frac{\partial p^i}{\partial X_2^i} - 1 = 0$$

or

(7′) $$800\,\frac{b}{\sigma}\,\frac{dp^i}{dZ^i} = 1$$

where Z^i represents the number of standard deviations by which pupil i's expected test score exceeds the national norm,

$$Z^i = \frac{aX^i + bX_2^i - \bar{y}}{\sigma}$$

and second-order condition

(7″) $$\frac{d^2p}{dZ^2} < 0$$

What can we conclude from these optimality conditions? First of all, we find, as we should expect, that the greater the increments in expected test achievement that the firm can buy with each dollar it expends on instruction, the higher the levels of expected test performance to which the firm will educate its pupils. That is,

$$\frac{dy^i}{db} = \frac{\sigma}{Z} > 0$$

Since the "production function" for education is notoriously uncertain, it is also of interest to determine how the firm will respond to changes in the degree of predictability in the production relationship, as measured by σ. Totally differentiating (7) with respect to σ and simplifying, we find

(8)
$$\frac{d\hat{y}}{d\sigma} = \frac{1}{Z}(Z^2 - 1) \begin{cases} <0 \text{ for } Z < 1 \\ >0 \text{ for } Z > 1 \end{cases}$$

(8′)
$$\frac{dZ}{d\sigma} = \frac{\partial Z}{\partial \sigma} + \frac{\partial \sigma}{\partial y}\frac{d\hat{y}}{d\sigma} = \frac{-1}{\sigma} < 0$$

In terms of the firm's behavior, (8′) implies that reductions in the random component of the production function will always lead to higher probabilities that the pupils educated by the firm will surpass the national test average. However, once $Z > 1$ the firm will also use any increase in the precision of the production function to reduce the pupils' expected achievement levels. This result merits a bit of elaboration. The firm is paid for having pupils' results exceed $\bar{y}$. As long as the production function for education contains a good deal of random error, in order to be reasonably certain that his pupils will exceed the national average, the educational entrepreneur must educate them to a high level of expected test performance. On the other hand, if the educational production is highly predictable, with little random error, the firm can get away with educating its pupils to a lower expected test performance, while maintaining the same probability that $y^i > \bar{y}$. Conditions (8) and (8′) together imply that the point $Z = 1$ represents a sort of cut-off point. Under the cumulative normal distribution, $Z = 1$ corresponds to a probability of 84 percent that the student will exceed the national average. If the firm originally finds it optimal to give pupils this much preparation, it will capitalize on any reduction in uncertainty of preparation by doing two things: increasing the *probability* that $y^i > \bar{y}$, thereby increasing its expected revenue, but simultaneously decreasing the expected value of pupils' achievement by cutting back on instructional costs. Both moves, of course, increase the firm's expected profit. If, on the other hand, originally the firm's optimal point had $Z < 1$, the firm will take all the increased profit potential that comes from increased precision in the production function in the form of expected revenue gains. In fact, it will reinforce the reduction in σ, by increasing its investment in the pupils and raising their expected test scores.

II. DISTRIBUTIONAL IMPLICATIONS

The first important distribution consequence of the performance contract follows immediately from (7'). Note that the variable X_1, that is, the pupil's past test score, does not appear in the optimality condition. This means that if the optimal solution is an interior solution, an individual's optimal expected score on this year's test is independent of his past test performance. *In other words, given the production assumptions, the expected test scores of all students in whom the entrepreneur invests resources will be the same, regardless of their previous record of accomplishment.*

The significance of this result for resource distribution deserves emphasis. The italicized sentence does not imply that the educational entrepreneur will expend the same amount of resources on each pupil. Quite the contrary. The entrepreneur will spend however much is needed to bring each pupil's expected test performance, $\hat{y}$, up to the optimal level, y^*,

$$\text{where } \frac{dp}{dZ} = \frac{1}{800} \frac{\sigma}{b}$$

This level is determined purely by the production function and is independent of the student's past record. Given that the firm invests in a pupil, the poorer the pupil's past test results are, the more the firm will have to spend on him to bring him up to the optimal level of expected test performance. However, as long as the firm is a strict maximizer of expected profits, the student's past record will also determine whether the firm chooses to teach him at all. Some pupils will be so bright that, even without further instruction, their expected test scores exceed the optimal level, y^*. These pupils will find that no resources whatsoever are spent on them.

Figure 1 illustrates the situation. The diagram presents a cumulative normal curve, giving for each expected test score, $\hat{y}$, the probability that the actual test score, y^i, exceeds the national average, thereby permitting the entrepreneur to collect his $800.

In Figure 1, y^* represents the optimal point at which $dp/dZ = 1/800\ \sigma/b$. Let us think of y^o as pupil i's expected test results before he receives any instruction in the current year. That is, $y^o = aX_1^i$. If the firm spends any resources at all on pupil i, it will invest enough in him to bring his expected test performance up to the optimal level. The student originally at y^o, for instance, will receive enough instruction to be transported along the cumulative normal curve to point y^*. The resource expenditure this requires is $y^* - y^o/_b$. If even without instruction a pupil's expected test score lies to the right of y^*, the probability of his exceeding the national average, when the test is administered, is so great that it does not pay the entrepreneur to educate him further. A strict profit maximizer would tell the child to spend the day in the public library.

Are there also pupils whose past record of test achievement is so poor that a profit-maximizing entrepreneur will not find it worthwhile to give them instruction? Yes. An entrepreneur bent on maximizing expected profits will invest only in those pupils for whom the average increase in p^i per dollar spent, when investment is carried to its optimal point, exceeds the *marginal* return available to him at y^*. In other words, the entrepreneur will invest in a pupil if and only if

$$(9) \qquad \frac{p(y^*) - p(y^o)}{y^* - y^o} > \frac{\sigma}{800b}$$

The lower cut-off point for the entrepreneur is shown as y^{**} in Figure 1. Note that the marginal return to investment at y^{**} is negative. Despite this, it pays the entrepreneur to invest in pupils who start at this point, because further investment in them will bring increasing returns. The terms of the performance contract have converted the assumedly linear production function into a nonlinear revenue function that has increasing returns to scale up to the point $\hat{y}$, which represents the national test norm. The entrepreneur is willing to accept marginal losses between y^{**} and y^{***} because, by moving the pupil

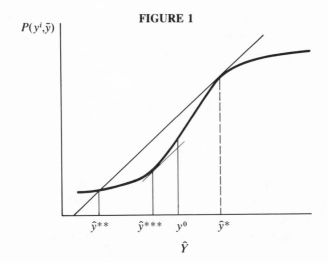

FIGURE 1

$P(y^i, \bar{y})$

$\hat{y}^{**}$ $\hat{y}^{***}$ y^0 $\hat{y}^*$

$\hat{Y}$

to y^{***}, he is able to generate surplus profits on all investments between there and the optimal point.

In summary, the entrepreneur who maximizes expected profits
under a performance contract of the kind we are discussing will treat
the school population in radically different ways. Let $\bar{g}$ represent the
value, $\sigma/800b$, which is determined by the production function
alone. The entrepreneur will then divide the school population into
three groups:

(a) Those at the upper tail of the ability distribution, for whom

$$\frac{dp_o^i}{dZ_o^i} < \bar{g} \text{ and } Z_o^i > 0$$

These pupils will have no resources spent on them. They are too
able.

(b) Those in the middle of the distribution, for whom either

(i) $$\frac{dp_o^i}{dZ^i} > \bar{g} \text{ and } Z_o^i > 0$$

or (ii) $$\frac{p(y^*) - p(y^o)}{y^* - y} > \bar{g} \text{ and } Z_o^i < 0$$

These pupils will be the object of the firm's expenditures. For this group, the lower a pupil's expected test results are at the outset, the more educational resources he will have lavished on him.

(c) Those at the lower tail of the distribution, for whom

$$\frac{dp_o^i}{dZ_o^i} < \bar{g} \text{ and } Z_o^i < 0$$

These pupils will have no resources spent on them. They are not able enough.

In actuality, the firm has one other decision to make: whether it will operate as a "school" at all. If the production function contains a large amount of random error, the firm may figure it can maximize profits by shutting down. Even if the firm gives no instruction, chance fluctuations will see to it that some students score above the national average on the standard achievement tests. For each of these successful students, the firm will collect $800, cost-free. The basic optimality condition obtained previously was

$$(8') \qquad\qquad C\frac{b}{\sigma}\frac{dp^i}{dZ^i} = 1$$

where C is the payment the firm receives for each pupil who exceeds the grade norm. This figure previously was taken to be $800. We recall that dp^i/dZ^i is simply the standardized normal density function, which has a maximum value of $1/\sqrt{2\pi} = 0.4$. For (8') to hold, then, it must be true that $\sigma < 2.5Cb$. If the error term, σ, is larger than this, relative to C and b, no solution to the optimality condition is possible. In this case, the productive relationship between the firm's expenditures and pupils' test scores is so unpredictable that the firm maximizes profit by making no expenditures at all, on any of its pupils. Evidently, the less productive are educational expenditures, as indicated by the coefficient b, or the less the firm gets paid per successful pupil, as indicated by C, the more likely it becomes that the firm will maximize profits by never opening the schoolhouse door.

Of course we should not expect to walk into a school building and find a company, operating under performance contract, that literally provides no instruction for its most able and least able students or that has sent the entire student body home for the year. There are implicit constraints on the behavior of a firm that operates a public school, one of which surely prevents it from refusing to educate its pupils. But in parceling out the time of teachers and teachers' aides, in fixing the size of reading groups, and in many other ways, schools have considerable flexibility regarding the amount of resources they spend on each pupil. Our results predict that these expenditures and —what is perhaps more measurable—pupils' test improvements will be systematically skewed by the incentive system.

III. RISK AVERSION

Up to now, we have assumed that the educational entrepreneur maximizes expected profits. Operating a school for profit, however, is a risky undertaking, as the contractors in the OEO experiment discovered to their loss. We should consider, then, if risk aversion on the part of the entrepreneur will alter the distributional impact of a performance contract of the kind we are considering.

The entrepreneur's total revenue function in our model is simply the sum of several hundred independent revenue functions, or Bernoulli trials, one for each pupil in the school. The stochastic element in each of these revenue functions is a cumulative normal variable giving the probabiliy that the pupil's test results will exceed the national average. The Central Limit Theorem applies here. To a very good approximation, the entrepeneur's total revenue stream can be treated as normally distributed, with mean $800 \sum_i P_i$ and variance $800^2 \sum_i P_i(1 - P_i)$. As is well known, when an uncertain income stream is normally distributed, the entrepreneur's preferences regarding it can be fully expressed as a function of the expected income and its variance.

We then have a system:

(10) $U = U(E\Pi, \text{Var }\Pi)$ $\dfrac{\partial U}{\partial E} > 0$ $\dfrac{\partial U}{\partial \text{ Var}} < 0$

(11) $E\,\Pi = 800 \sum_i p^i - \sum X_2^i$

(12) $\text{Var }\Pi = 800^2 \sum_i p^i (1 - p^i)$

The first-order condition for utility maximization now is

(13) $\dfrac{\partial U}{\partial E}\left[800\,\dfrac{b}{\sigma}\,\dfrac{dp}{dZ} - 1 \right] + \dfrac{\partial U}{\partial \text{ Var}}\,800^2 \left[1 - 2P^i \right]\dfrac{b}{\sigma}\,\dfrac{dp}{dZ} = 0$

If the entrepreneur should be risk neutral, $\partial U/\partial \text{ Var} = 0$ and (13) reduces to $800\,\dfrac{b}{\sigma}\,\dfrac{dp}{dZ} - 1$, which, of course, is the same as the optimality condition given in the previous section.

Sandmo has shown that under ordinary pricing systems, where uncertainty attaches to the final sale price, a risk-averse firm will always produce less than a risk-neutral firm.[7] Expression (13) shows that the terms of our performance contract alter that general result. The second term on the left-hand side of (13) is always positive, since $P > 1/2$ by the second-order condition. This implies that for a risk-averse producer it is always true that at the optimal point $800\,\dfrac{b}{\sigma}\,\dfrac{dp}{dZ} < 1$. Consequently, the optimal prob $(y_i > \bar{y})$ must be greater for the risk-averse producer than for the risk-neutral one, which means that the risk-averse producer will always provide the pupil with more instruction than a producer who maximizes expected profits. At the margin, the risk-averse entrepreneur will deliberately reduce his expected profit by "overpreparing" his pupils so as to cut down the risk that they will fail to meet the national grade average and thereby generate no revenue at all for him.

The risk-averse entrepreneur also will provide instructions for more of the school's superior students. As we have shown, the risk-averse firm will carry its investment in pupils to an optimal point that lies to the right of y^*, the optimal point for maximization of expected profits. Those pupils whose original expected test scores lie between the two optimal points will receive instruction only if the school is operated by the risk averter. At the other end, the risk-averse entrepreneur will not undertake investment in as many low-achievement pupils. The investor who maximizes expected profits finds it profitable to carry investment to the point of zero return. But the marginal investment that he undertakes increases the variance of his profit. This can be seen in Figure 1. The point y^{***}, which represents the lowermost test score in which the entrepreneur will invest, has a variance $p(1-p)$, which, by the symmetry of the cumulative normal curve, is less than the variance at the optimal point, y^*. For this reason, the risk-averse entrepreneur will not want to duplicate the risk-neutral producer's marginal investment; the gain in expected profit is zero and (what is indifferent to the maximizer of expected profits) the variance of profit is made greater.

IV. EMPIRICAL RESULTS

It is with misgivings that we propose to test the implications of the foregoing model against data from the Banneker School. Anyone who has seen the teachers in the Banneker School knows that to represent them as single-minded profit maximizers is a caricature. To suggest, as our model does, that entrepreneurial acquisitiveness might lead teachers to neglect altogether the most able and least able children in the school is plausible only if one shuts his eyes to the commitment that teachers obviously feel to the children in their care. Nevertheless, the principal purpose of performance contracting has been to induce school personnel to respond to profit incentives. The distributional implications of the profit incentives in our case are clear. It seems appropriate, then, to inquire whether educational "production" has been skewed in the way profit-mazimizing theory would predict.

The model developed in this paper predicts that the performance contractor will divide his school population into three groups: a

TABLE 1

Test Gains in Mathematics for National Sample and Banneker School Pupils

| | *Pupil Performance at Beginning of Year Distance above (below) Grade Norm* | | | | |
	−40% or more	*−20% to −40%*	*0 to −20%*	*0 to +20%*	*+20% or more*
National Sample	0.68	0.73	0.92	1.10	1.15
Banneker School	0.80	1.15	1.20	1.14	1.04
Net Superiority (lag) of Banneker School	+0.12	+0.42	+0.28	+ 0.04	−0.11

Source: 4,000 pupil sample from Metropolitan Achievement Test; Banneker School results.

high-ability group, which receives no instruction, a low-ability group, which receives no instruction, and a middle-ability group, within which instruction is apportioned in inverse relation to achievement levels. Tables 1 and 2 have been drawn up to determine if the empirical data corroborate, in any degree, this theoretical implication.

The first row in both tables represents what we might call average test gains under standard production conditions. We have assembled data for 4,000 pupils who took the Metropolitan Achievement Test in the school year, 1970-1971. The first row of the two tables presents the average test increment as a function of the pupils' starting point relative to their grade norm. For instance, the first column on the left applies to pupils who started the school year more than 40 percent behind their grade norm. For sixth-grade pupils this would mean they were at least 2.4 years behind. A multiplicative relationship of this sort, in which a two-year lag in fourth grade is equivalent to a three-year lag in sixth grade, is implied by the basic production relation as given in expression (1).

TABLE 2

Test Gains in Reading for National Sample
and Banneker School Pupils

*Pupil Performance at Beginning of Year
Distance above (below) Grade Norm*

	−40% *or* *more*	*−20%* *to* *−40%*	*0* *to* *−20%*	*0* *to* *+20%*	*+20%* *or* *more*
National Sample	0.75	+0.77	+0.95	+1.06	+1.17
Banneker School	0.68	+0.76	+0.82	+0.85	+0.74
Net Superiority (lag) of Banneker School	−0.07	−0.01	−0.13	−0.21	−0.43

Source: 4,000 pupil sample from Metropolitan Achievement Test; Banneker School results.

The second row of Tables 1 and 2 presents the actual gains in the Metropolitan Achievement Test scored by the third- through sixth-grade pupils at the Banneker School. The third row represents the net superiority (lag) of gains at the Banneker School, compared to the national average. The achievement levels across the columns of Tables 1 and 2 have been chosen to represent the distribution of test results actually found at Banneker School.

As can be seen at once, the pattern that emerges in the third row of Tables 1 and 2 coincides rather well with the theoretical relationship predicted from the incentive structure of the performance contract. Students at the upper tail of the Banneker distribution performed least well, compared to the national average, in both mathematics and reading. In mathematics students at the lower tail also performed less well than the Banneker pupils as a whole.[8] For those in the middle range there is some tendency for students with lower achievement levels to improve more than those with better achievement levels. Of course differential incentive effects are not the only possible explanation of this result. It may be that ordinary public school instruction is especially laggard or ineffective in preparing students who start out in the lower-middle range of achievement. Thus any firm that made an all-out effort to improve instruction might find that it automatically produced the greatest test improvement for students in this range.

Table 3, however, provides independent evidence that tends to confirm the incentive interpretation. Gary school officials decided at the outset that they would not force any families to participate in the Banneker School experiment who did not want to do so. Therefore, they adopted a policy of permitting any family who wished to transfer their child to another school. This free exit policy presents a unique chance to infer directly family satisfaction with the school program. The first row of Table 3 presents the distribution of achievement levels among the original Banneker pupil enrollment. The second row presents the distribution of starting achievement levels among the children who transferred out of the school after the completion of the first year of the experiment. Some of these children's families left the school district altogether, so that their action cannot be interpreted as a judgment on the quality of education at the school. For the most part, however, transfers were made by families who remained resident in the Banneker School District.

If the profit-incentive model is correct, we should predict that transfers out of the Banneker school would be most frequent among pupils at both tails of the ability distribution, because these are the students whom, according to the model, the educational entrepreneur will find it profitable not to instruct. As one can see, the actual rates of transfer coincide with this theoretical prediction.

Once again, alternative interpretations are possible, It may well be that children at both tails of the ability distribution have the greatest difficulties in any public school. If so, a policy of free exit might always result in a concentration of transfers in these ability groupings, whatever the organization of the school. However, a deliberate choice of another public school in Gary in preference to the Banneker school would seem to imply more than plain dissatisfaction. It seems to imply that the family believes instruction at the other school is, for their child, better.[9] In any event, without wishing to inflate claims to empirical verification, we may safely conclude that Tables

TABLE 3

Distribution of All Banneker Pupils and Out-Transfers

Percentage above (below) Grade
Norm at Beginning of Year

	−40% or more	−20% to −40%	0 to −20%	0 to +20%	+20% or more
Proportion of all Banneker Pupils	19.0	31.1	30.4	13.0	6.5
Proportion of Out-Transfers	24.5	25.2	23.4	11.8	15.1

Source: Banneker School Pupil Enrollment Rolls

1, 2, and 3 tend to substantiate the hypothesis that the educational entrepreneur has skewed his instructional efforts in the direction that profit maximizing theory would suggest.

V. CONCLUSION

In one sense the results reported in this paper may be encouraging to those who advocate a greater role for profit incentives in the public sector. The evidence indicates that a firm's response to profit signals can be rapid, even in a field like public schooling where there is no tradition of pricing. However, the conclusion we have drawn for Banneker is that the profits to be gained from shifting resources from one "output" to another were considerably greater than the profits to be had from pure efficiency gains. This is likely to be true of almost all public services. When a public output, like schooling or trash collection, consists of a number of quality dimensions, attaching a price to a limited number of the output dimensions is bound to direct an entrepreneur's resources to producing these aspects of the service, to the neglect of others.

As long as the public authorities are able to take into account all of the output dimensions, and place a realistic price tag on each, the shifting of resources in response to profit incentives need not pose a problem. Far from it. Pricing may then prove to be an effective means of steering energies away from traditional but unproductive activities into new ones. However, if, as seems more likely, the outputs of a school or other public service are too numerous and too difficult to measure to make pricing of each dimension feasible, then by resorting to performance contracts the public authority may create large-scale shifts in resources that it does not intend. On a truly free market, the price of each aspect of the public-service bundle would be determined implicitly by consumers' willingness-to-pay for variations in the service mix, so that in the end whatever shifts occurred would be those the consumers wanted. It is the combination of a bureaucratically fixed set of prices with the likelihood that several quality dimensions that consumers value have been left unpriced that creates the problem of misleading price signals. On balance, the evidence suggests that the introduction of explicit prices into the public sector is likely to cause far more output shifting than efficiency gains.

NOTES

[1] The principal performance contracting experiment, conducted by the Office of Economic Opportunity, involved students in grades 1, 2, 3, 7, 8, and 9, at eighteen different sites. At all grade levels the mean achievement gains of experimental and control students were virtually identical. Only one group, the eighth-grade control students, advanced as much as one full grade level. Office of Economic Opportunity, *An Experiment in Performance Contracting: Summary of Preliminary Results*, OEO Pamphlet 3400-5, (February, 1972). See also Battelle Memorial Institute, *Interim Report on the OEO Experiment in Performance Contracting* (1972); and Rand Corporation, *Case Studies in Educational Performance Contracting*, Six Volumes, R-900/1-6 (1971). A smaller OEO experiment tested the effectiveness of salary incentives paid through teachers' organizations, instead of profit incentives earned by private firms. The results of this experiment were equally discouraging. See Office of Economic Opportunity, *A Demonstration of Incentives in Education*, OEO Pamphlet 3400-F (February, 1972).

[2] OEO had contracts with six different firms. In addition to the common arrangement of scaling the firms' remuneration, in part, according to pupils' test score gains, the experiment tested numerous different educational "technologies": i.e., different combinations of programmed learning materials, widely different pupil/teacher ratios, several different degrees of paraprofessional participation, and a wide variety of material incentives used to reward pupils.

[3]The allocation of instruction time became a matter of considerable dispute between the Gary Teachers Union and the Banneker authorities. According to a report by Indiana Assistant Superintendent for Instructional Services, John J. Hand, from September to December, 1970, the Banneker curriculum allotted no time to science and very little time to social studies. For the year as a whole, Hand reported that mathematics instruction at Banneker received from one third more to twice as much time as recommended in *The Administrative Handbook for Indiana Schools.*

[4]Previous theoretical analyses of the economics of performance contracting have been restricted chiefly to contracts written for defense procurement. See J. J. McCall, "The Simple Economics of Performance Contracting," *American Economic Review* (December, 1970), pp. 837-46, and F. M. Scherer, "The Theory of Contractual Incentives for Cost Reduction," *Quarterly Journal of Economics* (May, 1964), pp. 257-80.

[5]Reviews of this research are contained in H. Averch et al., *How Effective Is Schooling? A Critical Review and Synthesis of Research Findings* (Rand Corporation, 1972); in Frederick Mosteller and Daniel P. Moynihan, eds., *On Equality of Educational Opportunity* (New York: Random House, 1972); and in Christopher Jencks et al., *Inequality: A Reassessment of the Effect of Family and Schooling in America* (New York: Basic Books, 1972).

[6]We abstract from the provision of the Banneker contract that made payment contingent upon student performance after three years, rather than after one year.

[7]Agmar Sandmo, "On the Theory of the Competitive Firm under Price Uncertainty," *American Economic Review* (March, 1971), pp. 65-73.

[8]The absence of a sharp pattern at the lower tail may be partially attributable to the fact that the Banneker payments were to be based on three-year results. Thus the firm had an incentive to work with students who had little likelihood of reaching grade norms right away.

[9]This interpretation is borne out by some of the Rand interviews with parents who removed their children from the Banneker School. These interviews, as well as interviews with other parents and teachers, led the Rand evaluation team to conclude that "the major criticism we heard was a lack of challenge for students who were highly proficient in the skill areas. At the start of the year there were not enough enrichment and other materials for students who had topped-out. . . ."

George E. Peterson is a member of the Senior Research Staff, Urban Institute.

6

Distributional Preferences in Public Expenditure Analysis

MARTIN S. FELDSTEIN

The purpose of public expenditure evaluation is to provide information useful to the politically responsible decision makers. More specifically, the economists' role is to estimate the economic effects of a project and then to summarize or aggregate these effects in a way consistent with economic theory. Only by such aggregation can the information about a project be reduced to a usable form. This is why, despite the obvious simplifications and approximations, we generally aggregate benefits and costs at different times into a present value by the simple device of discounting at some constant rate.

The problem of aggregating the benefits and costs that accrue to families in different income classes is the subject of this paper. In general, cost-benefit analyses have ignored this problem and given the same "weight" to all benefits and costs, The value of a project has been measured as the increase in national income, adjusted for any positive or negative externalities that are not reflected in income changes and for any differences between aggregate consumer surplus and market payments that are due to indivisibilities. For simplicity I call this the "national-income approach."

I believe that the national-income approach often fails to provide sufficient relevant information. Politically responsible decision

Martin S. Feldstein is Professor of Economics at Harvard University. The current version of the paper is essentially the same as the one presented at the conference. A few footnotes have been added to deal with some of the issues raised by Professor A. M. Freeman, III.

makers do have distributional preferences that are not reflected in the summary national-income measure and that do not seem capable of integration with it. Those responsible for public-expenditure choices have the options of ignoring their distributional preferences and selecting the project with the highest national-income benefit, of ignoring the economists' national-income calculations and selecting the project that appeals on distributional grounds, or of attempting to balance the national-income benefit measures against the seemingly incommensurate and generally unquantified distributional preferences. I suspect that the result of this is that the advice of economists is often ignored and, even more often, is simply not sought. Because economists have preached "efficiency only" and have used an arbitrary national-income measure, actual decisions have probably given too little weight to economic considerations and to systematic analysis in general. In many cases the result may be smaller national-income benefits than would have been achieved by a systematic balancing of equity and efficiency in project choice.

My aim in this paper is to contribute to the development of a method of integrating distributional equity and national-income efficiency in the planning of public expenditure. I am not advocating that decision makers should replace the national-income approach by their own criterion. Rather, I start from the premise that decision makers often do reject the national-income measure and wish to substitute their own distributional preferences.[1] I want to develop a method of summarizing the economic effects of alternative projects that allows decision makers to apply their preferences after the technical analysis is complete.

More specifically, I shall offer a new metric for summarizing the effects of a project. Instead of the ordinary contribution to national income, I suggest that we evaluate projects in terms of the "uniformly distributed dollar" (UDD) equivalent of benefits and costs. A UDD is a dollar distributed uniformly over all the families in the population; a benefit of sixty million UDD's is equivalent in value to giving a dollar to each family. The UDD value of any actual distribution of benefits and costs reflects the decision maker's distributional preferences. A primary purpose of this paper is to present an operational method of representing the decision maker's preferences by a single parameter and then to use that method to approximate the UDD value of different benefit and tax distributions. I think of this analysis as a type of applied econometrics rather than as an exercise in economic theory. I use specific parametric forms to represent the basic relationships in order to provide operational procedures and simple summary measures.[2]

In Section I, I discuss a number of arguments that have been made in favor of ignoring distributional preferences. In the second section I discuss the use of the uniformly distributed dollar (UDD) measure and suggest approximations that permit an operational method of representing alternative UDD values of benefits and financing. The emphasis, as I have already indicated, is on extending the information that economic analysis provides to the responsible decision maker. In Section III I consider the nature of the relative marginal value weights that are used in the UDD measure and the related problem of the excess burdens of redistributive-expenditure programs. I also suggest there that previous attempts by economists to estimate the distributional weights by studying past political decisions were inappropriate. Section IV is a brief concluding summary.

I. SHOULD ECONOMISTS IGNORE DISTRIBUTIONAL PREFERENCES?

Before developing a more specific analysis, I want to deal with the arguments that have been used in advocating that economists should ignore distributional considerations and use equal weights, that is, should adopt the national-income measure. I begin with what I believe to be the least compelling arguments. First, it is occasionally suggested that the national-income approach is justified by the compensation tests of Kaldor and of Hicks.[3] By now the strictures of Little[4] and others against this criterion when compensation is not actually paid are so familiar that no further comment is necessary. Similarly, although the use of equal weights might seem "ethically neutral," there is no real basis for favoring equal weights over any other set of weights. Finally, the national-income approach is often invoked in the name of "efficiency," thus suggesting that it is value free. Unfortunately, this obscures its very strong distributional assumption and confuses equal weighting with the very much weaker Paretian definition of efficiency.

I turn now to a stronger and more common argument. It is frequently asserted that the tax and transfer process can be used to achieve the desired income distribution and that public-expenditure decisions should be made on efficiency grounds only. Even at a purely theoretical level this is wrong. It is in effect an extension of Hotelling's appealing but incorrect case for marginal-cost pricing,[5] for the avoidance of excise taxes, and for the raising of all government revenue by the income tax. More than twenty years ago Ian Little showed that the income tax is necessarily superior to selective-excise taxes only if the supply of labor is constant.[6] The basic point is that if "one time" lump-sum taxes are not possible and the supplies of labor and capital are not fixed, any tax, including the income tax, disturbs the first-order conditions for allocative efficiency. The theory of the second best tells us that if all the households' first-order conditions cannot be satisfied, it is generally desirable to violate all those conditions. In the current context this implies that it is theoretically better to use a complete set of "inefficient" excise taxes and "inefficient" public-expenditure programs. To use only an income tax and to exclude inefficient projects would further reduce the welfare attainable in the second-best economy. So much for the theoretical case against inefficient expenditure.

At a practical level economists should recognize that if politically responsible decision makers believe that income has not and will not be adequately redistributed through the tax-transfer process, they will use their expenditure decisions to influence the distribution of real income. If expenditure decisions are going to reflect distributional preferences, I think that economists should help to see that this is done in a systematic and consistent way.

Arnold Harberger has argued along quite different lines that applied welfare economics should ignore distribution and merely add the gains and losses to different individuals without distributional weights.[7] His first reason is that a cost-benefit analysis should be capable of being checked by others and therefore should not reflect the economist's personal distributional preferences. This mixes two quite separate issues. I agree with Harberger that the economist's personal preferences should not be reflected in the analysis. This does not imply, however, that economists should provide neither a framework for using the decision maker's weights nor, as I suggest in the next section, a parametric approximation to represent different values and use this to calculate the values of each project according to the different weighting schemes. Cost-benefit analysis can be informative about the implications of distributional preferences without embodying the preferences of the decision maker.

Harberger's second argument is that national-income accounting ignores distribution. Presumably consistency then justifies our doing so for project evaluation. I do not find this at all persuasive. First, the purpose of national-income accounting is quite different from the purpose of individual-project evaluation. The evaluations of individual projects are designed as a guide for choice. National-income accounts are used to direct choice only in the area of stabilization where the accounts measure aggregate demand and not well-being. Although national income is used as a crude measure of long-run changes in economic well-being, this is primarily because the aggregate distribution of income has been so relatively stable. Moreover, I doubt that outside the realm of stabilization any decisions (for example, a major tax change) would be made without considering the distributional effects just because national income is predicted to increase. Second, although it would no doubt be useful to have a measure of national welfare that reflected the distribution as well as the total of income, the problems of developing such a measure are much greater than they are in the evaluation of the marginal changes that result from public-expenditure choices.[8] Finally, I cannot avoid noting that the national-income convention is to value public services in national income at factor cost. If we adopted this convention as well as the "no weighting" rule, no public project would be worth doing!

II. THE UDD VALUE OF BENEFITS
AND FINANCING

The uniformly distributed dollar (UDD) provides a useful numéraire for reflecting distributional preferences in stating the aggregate value of the benefits and taxes that result from an expenditure program.[9] In concept, a UDD is a single dollar divided equally among all the families in the nation. A project that yields exactly one dollar in net benefits to each family produces total benefits of some 60 million UDD's.

To illustrate the use of the UDD metric, let $f(y)$ be the relative frequency of families with annual income y,[10] let $w(y)$ be the relative weight that the decision maker gives to an incremental dollar given to or taken from a family at income level y,"[11] and let $v(y)$ be the average net benefit per household with income y.[12] I shall assume for now that $v(y)$ is sufficiently small that it does not change the relative weight given to a household. I shall also assume that the benefits of the project are known with certainty, occur only in the current period, and are provided without user charges.

The welfare value (measured in a "utility" or "welfare" numéraire) of a uniformly distributed dollar is then $\int w(y) f(y)\, dy$. The corresponding welfare value of the benefits is $N \int w(y)\, v(y)\, f(y)\, dy$, where N is the total number of families in the population. The value of the net benefits, expressed in terms of UDD's is therefore

$$(1) \qquad V_{\text{UDD}} = \frac{N \int w(y)\, v(y) f(y)\, dy}{\int w(y) f(y)\, dy}$$

Note of course that the value of V_{UDD} corresponding to $w(y) = 1$ for all y is the usual measure of unweighted aggregate benefits.

A convenient and intuitively natural form for the relative weight relation, $w(y)$, is the constant elasticity function[13]

$$(2) \qquad w(y) = y^{-\eta}, \ \eta > 0$$

The single parameter η provides a measure of how egalitarian the decision maker's preferences are. A one percent increase in family income implies an η percent decrease in the relative weight given to a dollar of benefits and costs. This parametric approximation permits the value of V_{UDD} for each project to be calculated for a wide range of η's. The economist provides information that allows the decision maker to introduce his own distributional preferences after the technical analysis is complete.[14] Since the decision maker may find it difficult to specify his distributional preferences precisely, calculating the V_{UDD} value for each project as a function of η makes it possible to see whether the choice among projects is sensitive to the value of η.[15]

Consider, for example, the choice between two projects, A and B. Project A makes the greater contribution to unweighted national income and would therefore be preferred by the traditional cost-benefit criterion. A higher fraction of the benefits of project B goes to lower-income families. Figure 1 shows the two V_{UDD} functions for these projects. Both V_{UDD} curves increase with η, indicating that for both projects the per capita net benefits are greater among lower-income families, that is, the distribution of net benefits departs from being uniform with respect to income in favor of lower-income families. Project A is preferable at $\eta = 0$, that is, when benefits are unweighted, and remains preferable until the quite high value of more than $\eta = 2.5$, that is, until a 20 percent increase in income leads to a more than 50 percent decrease in the relative weight given to incremental benefits and costs.

It is now useful to consider the benefits and financing of a project separately. I shall assume that all incremental projects are financed by a proportional increase in the personal-income tax and that the tax collected from each family causes an equal change in its net income.[16] Let $t(y)$ be the amount collected from each family at income level y per dollar of total tax collected. By analogy with equation 1, the UDD value of one dollar of tax revenue is

(3)
$$t_{UDD}(\eta) = \frac{\int y^{-\eta} t(y) f(y)\, dy}{\int y^{-\eta} f(y)\, dy}$$

Since the income tax is progressive, $t_{UDD}(\eta)$ is less than one for all positive values of η. The higher the weighting elasticity η, the lower the UDD value of a dollar of income tax. To illustrate this calcula-

FIGURE 1
Distributional Preferences and Project Choice

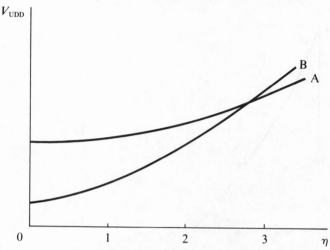

tion, $t_{UDD}(\eta)$ has been evaluated for the 1969 income tax.[17] Figure 2 presents the resulting $t_{UDD}(\eta)$ function. Note that $t_{UDD}(0) = 1$ is implied by the definition. Even for the relatively low value of $\eta = 0.5$ the UDD value of a tax dollar falls to 0.62, reflecting the implied progessivity of the income tax. If the total tax cost of a project is T dollars, the UDD value of this financing is T times $t_{UDD}(\eta)$.[18]

I turn now to the more challenging problem of assessing the UDD value of a project's benefits. Let $b(y)$ describe the average value of benefits per family with income y, N the total number of families, and $B_{UDD}(\eta)$ the UDD value of a project's benefits associated with weighting elasticity η:

$$(4) \qquad B_{UDD}(\eta) = \frac{N \int y^{-\eta} b(y) f(y) \, dy}{\int y^{-\eta} f(y) \, dy}$$

If the benefit distribution of a project $[b(y)]$ is known precisely, the values of $B_{UDD}(\eta)$ can be calculated from equation 4. Often, however, the general properties of the benefit distribution may be known approximately even though $b(y)$ cannot be specified exactly.[19] How can equation 4 be implemented best if the benefit function $b(y)$ can

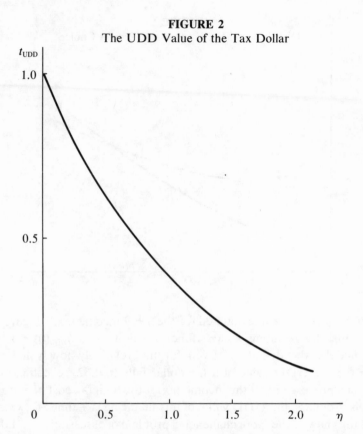

FIGURE 2
The UDD Value of the Tax Dollar

be estimated only approximately? Even if $b(y)$ is known exactly, can an approximation simplify the calculation of $B_{\text{UDD}}(\eta)$? Two alternative parametric specifications are appealing: the constant-elasticity benefit function $b(y) = by^\beta$ and the polynomial function $b(y) = b_0 + b_1 y + b_2 y^2 + \ldots$. Because both of these are quite natural approximations and because both lead to particularly simple expressions for B_{UDD} both will now be examined in more detail.

Consider first the constant elasticity-benefit function $b(y) = by^\beta$.[20] Equation 4 can then be written as

(5)
$$B_{\text{UDD}}(\eta) = \frac{Nb \int y^{\beta-\eta} f(y)\, dy}{\int y^{-\eta} f(y)\, dy}$$

This can be restated as

$$(6) \qquad B_{\text{UDD}}(\eta) = \frac{Nb \int e^{(\beta-\eta)\ln y} f(y)\, dy}{\int e^{-\eta \ln y}\, f(y)\, dy}$$

The integrals on the right-hand side of equation 6 are equivalent to moment generating functions of the variable $\ln y$, the logarithms of family income, with "dummy parameters" $\beta\text{-}\eta$ and $-\eta$.[21]

Since the distribution of family income $f(y)$ can be well represented by the log normal density, equation 6 implies:

$$(7) \qquad B_{\text{UDD}}(\eta) = \frac{Nb \cdot \exp\{(\beta-\eta)\bar{Y} + 0.5(\beta-\eta)^2 \sigma_Y^2\}}{\exp\{-\eta\bar{Y} + 0.5\eta^2 \sigma_Y^2\}}$$

$$\sigma^2_Y \qquad = Nb \cdot \exp\{\bar{Y} + 0.5\beta\,(\beta - 2\eta)\,\sigma_Y^2\}$$

where $\bar{Y}$ is the mean of the logarithm of income and σ_Y^2 is the variance of the logarithm of income. For the log normal distribution there is a one-to-one correspondence between the first two moments of the logarithm of the variable ($\bar{Y}$ and σ_Y^2) and the first two moments of the variable itself ($\bar{Y}$ and σ_Y^2):

$$(8a) \qquad \bar{Y} = \ln \bar{y} - 0.5 \ln (1 + \sigma_y^2/\bar{y}^2)$$

$$(8b) \qquad \sigma_Y^2 = \ln (1 + \sigma_y^2/\bar{y}^2)$$

Equation 7 can therefore be rewritten as

$$(9) \qquad B_{\text{UDD}}(\eta) = Nb\bar{y}^\beta\,(1 + R)^{0.5\beta(\beta-1)\,-\,\eta\beta}$$

where $R = \sigma_y^2/\bar{y}^2$, the relative variance of income.

Recall that the traditional "unweighted" sum of benefits corresponds to the B_{UDD} value for $\eta = 0$:

$$(10) \qquad B_{\text{UDD}}(0) = \frac{N \int b(y) f(y)\, dy}{\int f(y)\, dy} = N \int b(y) f(y)\, dy$$

For the constant elasticity-benefit function,

$$B_{\text{UDD}}(0) = Nb\bar{y}^\beta(1 + R)^{0.5\beta(\beta-1)}$$

The entire B_{UDD} function of equation 9 can therefore be rewritten

$$(11) \qquad B_{\text{UDD}}(\eta) = B_{\text{UDD}}(0) \cdot (1 + R)^{-\eta\beta}$$

FIGURE 3
Effect of β and η on the Relative UDD Value of Benefits

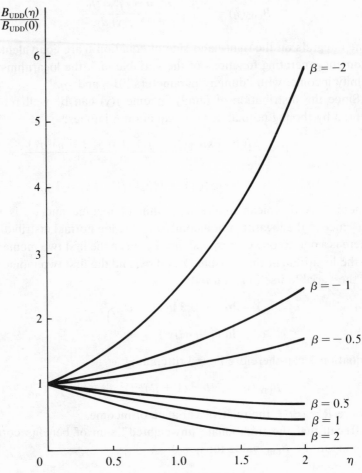

For a given unweighted total benefit $[B_{\text{UDD}}(0)]$, the $B_{\text{UDD}}(\eta)$ value is a function of the relative dispersion of income (R), the weighting elasticity (η), and the income elasticity of benefits (β). If the income elasticity of benefits is positive (negative), the B_{UDD} value of a project is a decreasing (increasing) function of both R and η. For any value of R and any $\eta > 0$, the B_{UDD} value of a project is a decreasing func-

FIGURE 4
Effect of β and η on the Relative UDD Value of Benefits

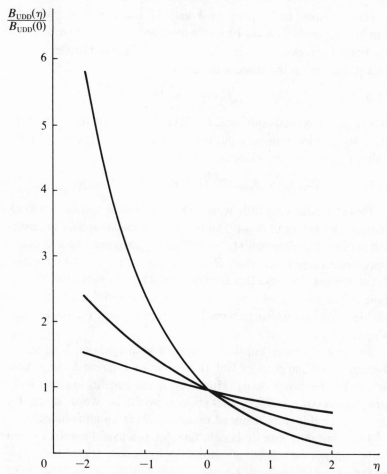

tion of the income elasticity β. Moreover, the higher the values of R and η, the greater the proportional decrease in B_{UDD} as β increases. These relationships are illustrated in Figures 3 and 4, using a value of $R = 0.55$ for the relative variance of income.[22] Figure 3 shows the ratio of $B_{\text{UDD}}(\eta)$ to the traditional total value $B_{\text{UDD}}(0)$ as a function of η for different values of the benefit elasticity β. Figure 4 shows that ratio as a function of β for different values of the relative weight elasticity η.

These figures and equations 3 and 11 indicate how the usual benefit cost analysis could be easily modified to reflect distribution if the benefit function has constant elasticity. The traditional net value of a project is, in the current notation,

$$(12) \qquad V_{\text{UDD}}(0) = B_{\text{UDD}}(0) - T$$

where T is the total additional tax levied to pay for the costs.[23] To take distribution into account, the economist provides not a single value $V_{\text{UDD}}(0)$ but the values of a function:

$$(13) \qquad V_{\text{UDD}}(\eta) = B_{\text{UDD}}(0) \cdot (1 + R)^{-\beta\eta} - T \cdot t_{\text{UDD}}(\eta)$$

This step adds very little work to the traditional cost-benefit evaluation. The values of $B_{\text{UDD}}(0)$ and T must be calculated for the usual evaluation. The function $(1 + R)^{-\beta\eta}$ and $t_{UDD}(\eta)$ need be calculated only once each year, when R and the structure of taxes change. Nevertheless, I believe that the economist who presents the $V_{\text{UDD}}(\eta)$ function of equation 13 provides much more useful information to the decision maker than he would by presenting only the single value $V_{\text{UDD}}(0)$.[24]

As an illustration, consider a project with traditional aggregate benefits of 80 and costs of 100. If distribution is ignored, the project would not be worth doing. However, if the benefits are relatively progressive ($\beta = -0.25$), the project would be worth doing for $\eta \geq 2$ even if it were financed by an equal tax on all families.[25]

The constant elasticity-benefit function is a useful approximation if the benefits are related monotonically to income. It obviously cannot be used if the value of benefits is at first an increasing function of income and later a decreasing function of income. This will often be the case. Even if the use of some public service decreases monotonically with income, the dollar value per unit is likely to be an increasing function of income over at least some range. A polynomial-benefit function is a potentially useful approximation in such cases. Moreover, it is easy to derive a simple way of calculating the B_{UDD} function from the parameters of the polynomial.

Let the actual benefit function be approximated by[26]

(14)
$$b(y) = \sum_{k=0}^{K} b_k y^k$$

This implies

(15)
$$B_{\text{UDD}}(\eta) = \frac{N \int y^{-\eta} \cdot \sum_{k=0}^{K} b_k y^k \cdot f(y)\, dy}{\int y^{-\eta} f(y)\, dy}$$

or

(16)
$$B_{\text{UDD}}(\eta) = N \sum_{k=0}^{K} b_k \frac{\int y^{k-\eta} f(y)\, dy}{\int y^{-\eta} f(y)\, dy}$$

Each of the terms in the sum is of the same form as in equation 5, that is, $B_{\text{UDD}}(\eta)$ is now a weighted sum of the ratio of moment-generating functions, with the polynomial parameters (b_k) as weights. The right-hand side of equation 16 can therefore be evaluated to yield

(17)
$$B_{\text{UDD}}(\eta) = N \sum_{k=0}^{K} b_k \bar{y}^k (1 + R)^{0.5k(k-1)-\eta k}$$

The value of benefits can therefore be calculated as a weighted sum of terms of the form $\bar{y}^k (1 + R)^{0.5k(k-1)-\eta k}$ that are not specific to the individual project. Figure 5 presents these values for k from 1 through 4. The information in Figure 5 permits evaluating $B_{\text{UDD}}(\eta)$ for any polynomial benefit function not exceeding a fourth order.

It is clear from equation 17 that $B_{\text{UDD}}(\eta)$ is related to the traditional benefit $B_{\text{UDD}}(0)$ by multiplying each term in its polynomial approximation by $(1 + R)^{-\eta k}$. Since these terms may vary in sign, nothing general can be said about the qualitative effects of incorporating distribution.

The discussion throughout this section has focused on describing the V_{UDD} function of each alternative project. In some situations the economist may be able to do more than this. For an investment

FIGURE 5
Polynomial Benefit Function Factors

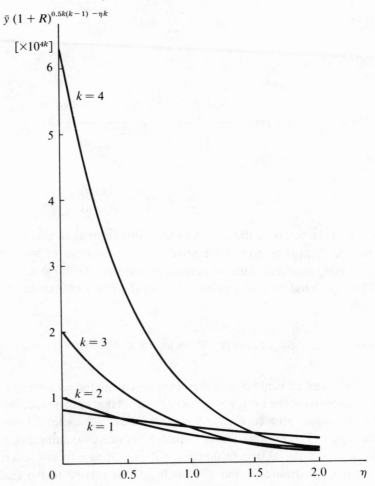

$\bar{y}\,(1+R)^{0.5k(k-1)\,-\eta k}$

$[\times 10^{4k}]$

$k=4$

$k=3$

$k=2$

$k=1$

decision that requires choosing among a set of mutually incompatible alternatives, for example, alternative techniques or sizes or locations, the economist may be able to reject some alternatives as clearly dominated (that is, inferior to some other alternative at every value of η) and present only the undominated set to the decision maker. Such an undominated set might be described as "efficient in the broad sense" to distinguish it from the single project that is "efficient in the narrow sense," that is, when distribution is ignored. When there is a budget constraint or other specific resource constraints, the economist can use the V_{UDD} function to find the set of projects that is optimal at each value of η.[27] The final choice of projects must, however, reflect the preferences of the responsible decision maker. It is to the specification of this that I now turn.

III. DEFINING THE $w(y)$ FUNCTION

Previous proposals to reflect distribution in public expenditure have identified the $w(y)$ function with the relative values to be given to an incremental dollar of consumption at each income level. In conventional terms, this $w(y)$ is the derivative of the social-welfare function. It is, I am afraid, inappropriate to assess the decision maker's $w(y)$ function defined in this way and then apply it to aggregating incremental benefits and taxes in the way described in Section II. I hope in this section to clarify the nature of the difficulty and to suggest an approach to its solution.

The problem of using a marginal social welfare function in the framework of Section II can be seen most clearly by considering the following hypothetical argument that might be made by someone who is opposed to the use of any unequal weights:

"I understand and accept the view that the marginal social welfare of income is higher among lower-income families than among higher income families. Nevertheless, I believe that an incremental dollar of benefits or of taxes should be given equal weight. The democratic political process has already used the tax system to maximize social welfare. This optimization takes into account the effects of taxes and transfers on individual factor supply (such as work effort, saving, risk taking). The optimum does not imply equal marginal social welfare for all families as Edgeworth naively assumed.[28] That would be true only if we could have once-for-all lump sum taxes and transfers. The optimum is characterized by the condition that there would be no net gain in social welfare from additional taxes and transfers because the deadweight losses would just offset the pure distributional gains.

As the studies by Mirrlees and by Fair have shown,[29] an optimal tax structure may not be very progressive and the differences among the marginal social welfares of different individuals may be quite large. Nevertheless it is an optimum, and further attempts to change it through public expenditure decisions should be avoided."

This argument is extreme. It assumes that the political process has successfully and consistently optimized a welfare function and that the current decision maker has the same distributional preferences as those expressed in the tax optimization. Moreover, and this is the point that I now wish to emphasize, it treats public-project benefits and incremental cash transfers as equivalent. I think it is important to realize that there is a qualitative similarity but a quantitative difference between taxes and public benefits.

As the argument above indicates, selecting a $w(y)$ function to use in the framework of Section I is similar to selecting an income-tax schedule. Both imply a relationship between earned income and "total disposable real income" (including public services). But the income-tax schedule is relatively clear and precise whereas the effects of selecting a $w(y)$ function are quite ambiguous. In particular, the effect of a $w(y)$ function on individuals' total real incomes depends on the set of projects that are later considered. For this reason, even if the $w(y)$ function were publicly known, its distorting incentive effects would probably be less than for a tax function with the same redistributive impact. Moreover, whereas the income-tax function is actually known, the $w(y)$ function could only be inferred by the public through observing the projects that are undertaken. Individuals know more about the public programs that affect themselves than about the benefits that others receive. Even if they were aware of all the benefits provided to families at different income levels, such as housing, transportation services, manpower training, and health insurance, they would not know the value of these benefits to the recipients. The result is likely to be an underestimate of the progressivity implied by the $w(y)$ function.

What are the implications of all this? It suggests that there are two approaches that could be used in dealing with the disincentive effects that follow from allowing distributional preferences to affect public expenditure. First, one might adopt the methods of optimal tax theory and, starting with an explicit social welfare function, derive an optimal $w(y)$ function. To the extent that the choice of a $w(y)$ function is similar to the choice of an income-tax function, this could in principle be done along the lines suggested by Mirrlees.[30] If the marginal social welfare of incremental income decreases as family income increases, the optimal $w(y)$ function would also decrease but at a slower rate than marginal social welfare because of the disincentive effects of progressivity. The interesting papers by Mirrlees and by Fair (cited in footnote 29) indicate that it is not possible to obtain anything more precise without quite strong parametric assumptions. Moreover, the current context has the additional problems that the $w(y)$ function is imperfectly related to the distribution of benefits and that the public's perceptions of different programs with the same actual progressivity may not be the same.

The alternative approach is to identify $w(y)$ with the marginal social-welfare function and to adjust the benefit and tax functions [$b(y)$ and $t(y)$] for the estimated deadweight losses due to distorting incentive effects. For the reasons that I have given above, these adjustments are likely to be more important for taxes than for benefits. The adjustment to the value of benefits will also vary from program to program. At one extreme, if the decision maker believed that Congress was optimizing and accepted the distributional preferences used in that optimization, a dollar of tax revenue would have the same adjusted UDD value regardless of the family from which it was taken (see footnote 25). This is likely to provide a bound on the adjustments. The adjustments should be less if the decision maker has more egalitarian preferences than are implied in the income-tax structure or if the distorting incentive effects of the benefits are expected to be less than for an equivalent redistribution through taxes and transfers. For many applications, when the public does not perceive that different benefits are being given to persons at different income levels, no adjustment of the $b(y)$ function need be made. Corrections for the deadweight burdens can then be limited to the $t(y)$ function. As shown in Section II, evaluating the UDD value per dollar of tax need not be repeated for each project.[31]

Nevertheless, it is unfortunate that economists have given little attention to the excess burden due to distorting factor supply by public-expenditure programs. Information on such excess burdens is relevant even if distributional considerations are to be ignored, that is, even if the net benefits are evaluated with equal weights. If it is not taken into account in project evaluation, decisions will be biased in favor of too much public spending and too much redistribution through spending rather than through taxes and transfers.

Before concluding this section, I want to comment on the previous attempts to infer the appropriate distributional weights by examining past political behavior. The discussion above suggests that the implicit assumptions in this estimation procedure are inconsistent and the resulting weights are therefore inappropriate.

Eckstein (1961) was the first to propose this general approach.[32] He suggested that the "government's notion of marginal utilities of income" might be derived from the marginal rates of personal income tax by assuming that the government acts on the principle of equimarginal sacrifice. Haveman developed the same approach.[33] Our tax structure can be interpreted as consistent with equimarginal sacrifice if, but only if, it is assumed that income taxes do have distorting effects on factor supply and therefore create a deadweight loss. But if there are distorting effects, the rates reflect both the marginal utilities of income and the deadweight losses from increased progressivity. Any attempt to recover the implicit marginal utility function would require solving Mirrlees'[34] problem in reverse: Given an "optimal" tax function and an assumption about individual behavior, what is the underlying maximand? Because I believe that our tax structure does not reflect such sophisticated optimization, I do not think this difficult question is actually worth answering.

Mera (1969) rejected the Eckstein suggestion on the incorrect premise that equimarginal sacrifice required the extreme progressivity of taxing all income above a certain level,[35] i.e., Mera ignored the excess burden effects. He suggested instead that taxes were set according to the principle of either equal absolute sacrifice or equal proportional sacrifice. Mera then estimated the utility of income functions implied by these two tax principles, again ignoring the excess burden problem. Thus, even if one accepted the assumption that taxes are set to imply equal absolute sacrifice, Mera's calculations would still be incorrect. Moreover, if one really wanted to believe that Congress has optimized the income-tax structure according to some criterion, there would be no reason to reject the utilitarian principle of equimarginal sacrifice.[36]

Although the assumption of a welfare maximizing structure cannot be used to infer marginal utilities of income, it does have the important implication that the welfare value of an additional dollar of tax from any family is equal.[37] But as the discussion of this section has indicated, it does not imply that the welfare value of an additional dollar's worth of benefits is equal for all families. That depends on the extent to which those benefits alter the factor supply incentives.

Weisbrod suggested that previous Congressional behavior in the selection of projects, rather than in the setting of tax rates, should be used to infer distributional weights.[38] Haveman and Mack have already noted a number of important conceptual and practical problems connected with this proposal.[39] The current analysis presents the further problem that, even in principle, a unique set of marginal social welfare weights could be inferred only if the benefits associated with each project were first adjusted for the expected excess burdens associated with it.

These brief comments should indicate the futility of attempts to estimate "the" approriate set of distributional weights by studying past political decisions. Moreover, the economist's use of any such $w(y)$ function deprives new decision makers of the opportunity to reflect their own distributional preferences. It would be better if we turned our attention to the problems of estimating the distributional impact and corresponding excess burdens of alternative public expenditure programs.

IV. SUMMARY

Public expenditure analysis is a process of aggregation. The detailed information about each possible project must be summarized in a measure that allows projects to be ranked and an optimal set of projects to be selected. All practical aggregation involves a loss of information. Designing a method of public expenditure analysis requires a balancing of the gains and losses of different aggregation procedures.

It is a primary contention of this paper that project evaluations should not submerge distributional implications by weighting all benefits equally. Politically responsible decision makers are likely to want to give more weight to benefits in some income classes than in others. Because lump-sum taxes and transfers are impossible, it is appropriate to use public expenditure programs as one means of redistribution. If project evaluations do not reflect distributional preferences, they will often be dismissed as irrelevant to the actual problem of choice.

The practical problem is to incorporate distributional information in the project evaluation without also embodying the preferences of the economic analyst. Section II develops an operational method of doing this in terms of a uniformly distributed dollar (UDD) *numéraire*. If the decision maker's preferences can be approximated by a constant elasticity function, the UDD value of a project can be expressed as a function of that elasticity. The economic analysis thus reflects distribution while permitting decision makers to introduce their own preferences *after* the technical analysis is complete. More specific parametric methods of revising the traditional "national income" measures to reflect distributional preferences are developed for use when the benefit distribution can be approximated by either a constant elasticity function or a low-order polynomial.

In Section III I discuss the difference between the marginal social welfare of incremental consumption at different income levels and the corresponding marginal social welfare of incremental taxes and benefits. Taxes and benefits that are related to income have incentive effects and therefore create excess burdens. These excess burdens should be taken into account in public expenditure evaluation even by the decision maker who would give equal weight to incremental consumption at every income level.

In concluding I should note that throughout this paper a particular notion of equity has been assumed. In particular, distributional equity is expressed as relative weights on incremental consumption at different income levels. The source of these weights is irrelevant; it does not matter whether or not they reflect interpersonal altruism, that is, utility interdependence. But the framework of this paper does not permit the distribution of some goods (for example, health or education) to be more important than the distribution of others. Only the money value of the benefits to the recipient is relevant in assessing $b(y)$. This excludes both "specific altruism" (that is, utility interdependence with respect to some goods but not others) and "paternalistic preferences" (that is, merit goods). Since such specific aspects of equity are often important in practice, it would obviously be worthwhile to consider ways of extending the framework of this paper to deal with this problem.

NOTES

[1]The analysis is limited to preferences defined in terms of income classes. Other characteristics (e.g., age, color, and region) are ignored.

[2]The econometric policy models of Tinbergen and Theil are thus similar in spirit although very different in actual structure. See J. Tinbergen. *On the Theory of Economic Policy* (Amsterdam: North-Holland, 1963; and H. Theil, *Optimal Decision Rules for Government and Industry* (Amsterdam: North-Holland, 1964).

[3]N. Kaldor, "Welfare Propositions and Interpersonal Comparisons of Utility," *Economic Journal* (1939), pp. 549-52; J. R. Hicks, "The Valuation of Social Income," *Economica* (1940), pp. 105-24.

[4]I. M. D. Little, *A Critique of Welfare Economics* (Oxford: Oxford University Press, 1950).

[5]H. Hotelling, "The General Welfare in Relation fo Problems of Taxation and of Railway and Utility Rates," *Econometrica* (July, 1938), pp. 242-69.

[6]The requirement is actually much stronger. The *compensated* supply of labor must not be price sensitive, i.e., the indifference curve must have a kink at the optimum. See I. M. D. Little, "Direct versus Indirect Taxes," *Economic Journal* (September, 1951), pp. 577-84.

[7]A. C. Harberger, "Three Basic Postulates for Applied Welfare Economics," *Journal of Economic Literature* (September, 1971).

[8]Papers by Fleming and Harsanyi indicate the strong types of assumptions needed to measure total welfare as a weighted sum of functions of individual incomes. Regardless of the form of the welfare function, linear aggregation with fixed weights is appropriate for project evaluation if the effects on each individual are sufficiently small. See J. M. Fleming, "A Cardinal Concept of Welfare." *Quarterly Journal of Economics* (August, 1952), pp. 366-84; and J. C. Harsanyi, "Cardinal Welfare, Individualistic Ethics and Comparisons of Utility," *Journal of Political Economy* (1955), pp. 309-21.

[9]The distributional effects of a project include not only the benefits received and taxes paid but also the effects through changes in factor prices that result from a shift in net factor demands. These factor price effects could in principle be valued in the same way as the direct effects of taxes and benefits and then added to the total UDD value of the project. The problems of implementing this which arise in estimating the changes in factor prices are the subject for a future paper. The current discussion follows the tradition in tax incidence analysis of ignoring expenditure effects on factor demand. See, e.g., A. C. Harberger, "The Incidence of the Corporation Income Tax," *Journal of Political Economy* (June, 1967).

[10]Describing the income distribution as a continuous function is only for notational convenience and should be regarded as an approximation to the actual discrete distribution.

[11]These weights may now be interpreted as the relative marginal social welfare of income as viewed by the decision maker. Section II provides a detailed discussion of their meaning. The income distribution and corresponding weights could of course be adjusted to differences in family size and composition as in, e.g., B. Bridges, Jr., "Family Need Differences and Family Tax Burden Estimates," *National Tax Journal* (December, 1971).

[12]The quantity $v(y)$ is the average dollar value of the benefits minus the additional taxes per family with income y; it is in effect a net consumer surplus measure. Families at income level y may differ in their valuation of the specific benefits. Since a dollar of benefits to any family at the same income level is treated as equivalent, the average value provides sufficient information.

[13]For previous applications of this form in the context of public expenditure, see: O. Eckstein, "A Survey of the Theory of Public Expenditure Criteria," in *Public Finances: Needs, Sources, and Utilization*, James M. Buchanan, ed., (Princeton: Princeton University Press, 1961); M. S. Feldstein, "The Derivation of Social Time Preference Rates," *Kyklos* (1965), pp. 277-86; Feldstein, "Equity and Efficiency in Public Sector Pricing; the Optimal Two-Part Tariff," *Quarterly Journal of Economics* (May, 1972); Feldstein, "Distributional Equity and the Optimal Structure of Public Prices," *American Economic Review* (March, 1972); Feldstein, "The Pricing of Public Intermediate Goods," *Journal of Public Economics* (March, 1972); A. M. Freeman, III, "Income Distribution and Planning for Public Investment," *American Economic Review* (June, 1967), pp. 495-508; and M. McGuire and H. Garn, "The Integration of Equity and Efficiency in Public Project Selection," *Economic Journal* (December, 1969), pp. 882-93. F. P. Ramsey used this form in the study of optimal growth; see his "A Mathematical Theory of Saving," *Economic Journal* (December, 1928), pp. 543-59. For later uses see T. Koopmans, "Objectives, Constraints and Outcomes in Optimal Growth Models," *Econometrica* (January, 1967), pp. 1-16; see also K. J. Arrow and M. Kurz, *Public Investment, the Rate of Return and Optimal Fiscal Policy* (Baltimore: John Hopkins University Press, 1970). The constant elasticity function is also prominent in representing von Neumann-Morgenstern utilities. In that context it is refered to as implying constant proportional risk aversion: see J. W. Pratt, "Risk Aversion in the Small and in the Large," *Econometrica* (January-April, 1964), pp. 122-36, and K. J. Arrow, *Aspects of the Theory of Risk Bearing*, Yrjo Jahnsson Lectures (Helsinki: Yrjo Jahnsson Foundation, 1965).

[14]It is an important advantage of this approach that the economist's analysis can be done without eliciting the decision makers' preferences in advance. The analysis is therefore useful when there are several decision makers whose identities may not even be known in advance. Unlike the iterative procedure suggested by S. A. Marglin, the economist's task is therefore completely separated from the political decision. Marglin, *Public Investment Criteria* (London: Allen and Unwin, 1967).

[15]Note that the use of a constant elasticity weighting function for aggregating benefits over individuals is in some ways similar to the simplification of using a constant discount rate for aggregating benefits over time; see Feldstein, "The Derivation of Social Time Preference Rates."

A. B. Atkinson discusses the special implications of using a constant elasticity function to reflect distributional preferences. See Atkinson, "On the Measurement of Inequality," *Journal of Economic Theory*, Vol. 2 (1970), pp. 244-63. I learned of this interesting paper after I had adopted the constant elasticity form for the UDD given in my articles: "Equity and Efficiency in Public Sector Pricing; the Optimal Two-Part Tariff"; "Distributional Equity and the Optimal Structure of Public Prices"; "The Pricing of Public Intermediate Goods."

[16]This implies that no part of the tax is shifted and that there is no excess burden. Both these simplifications could be relaxed in a more thorough analysis; see in particular the comments in Section III.

[17]The data for this calculation are taken from the U. S. Internal Revenue Service, *Preliminary Report, Statistics of Income — 1969 Individual Income Tax Returns,* Publication 198 (February, 1971), (Washington: Government Printing Office, 1971). Two quite crude assumptions are made in this calculation: the taxpaying unit is treated as a family, and y is measured by adjusted gross income. A calculation of t_{UDD} (η) using more appropriate measures would be quite worthwhile.

[18]It should be emphasized that this ignores the excess burden problem; see Section III below. See also footnote 19.

[19]Recall that the benefits are assumed to be distributed without charge. Using a price to allocate the output of a project provides information about the value of benefits. On the problems of optimal pricing, see P. A. Diamond and J. A. Mirrlees, "Optimal Taxation and Public Production, II," *American Economic Review* (June, 1971); and M. S. Feldstein, "Distributional Equity and the Optimal Structure of Public Prices."

[20]Note that this function is implied if all families receive the same physical quantity of the good (as with a Samuelsonian pure public good) and the individual demand functions for the good have constant income elasticity. More generally, if the quantity of the good received is a constant elasticity function of income, say $x(y) = x \cdot y^{\alpha1}$, and the value per unit is some other constant elasticity function of income, say $p(y) = p \cdot y^{\alpha2}$, then the benefit function has constant income elasticity: $b(y) = x(y) \cdot p(y) = x \cdot p \cdot y^{\alpha1 + \alpha2} = by^{\beta}$.

[21]The expression $f(y)\ dy$ can be readily transformed to $g(\ln y) \cdot d(\ln y)$ by the usual change of variable method without altering the value of the integral.

[22]The value of $R = 0.55$ is based on a mean of \$8,168 and a standard deviation of \$6,070 for disposable family income. The basic data for pretax incomes [U. S. Bureau of the Census (1970)] was transformed to disposable income, using effective tax rates

estimated by Pechman. See U. S. Bureau of the Census, *Current Population Reports: Consumer Income,* Series P60, No. 70 (July 16, 1979). See also J. A. Pechman, *Federal Tax Policy,* 2d ed. (Washington: Brookings Institution, 1970). The $t_{UDD}(\eta)$ function should be recalculated for this type of income distribution.

[23]This ignores the complication of costs not equal to government expenditures and the role of sales revenues to finance costs. If the social cost of resources is not equal to the government's expenditure, the difference can be included among the benefits; e.g., hiring unemployed labor provides a benefit to those workers.

[24]If there is uncertainty about the value of β, alternative $V_{UDD}(\eta)$ functions could be calculated for different β values that are assumed to bracket the unknown true β.

[25]This financing corresponds to $t(\eta) = 1$ for all η. As is indicated in Section III, even with income-tax finance, the appropriate value of $t(\eta)$ may be close to 1.

[26]This might be based on examination of a complete estimated $b(y)$ function or may be derived from assumed quantity and value relations. For example, if the average quantity used per family is a decreasing linear function of income $[x(y) = x_0 - x_1 y]$ and the value per unit is an increasing linear function of income $[p(y) = p_0 + p_1 y]$, the benefit function is a quadratic, $b(y) = x_0 p_0 + (x_0 p_1 - x_1 p_0) y - x_1 p_1 y^2$.

[27]The ability of the economist to eliminate projects that are not "efficient in the broad sense" is an important advantage over the purely descriptive "tableau" method discussed by McKean and Weisbrod. The tableau method also has the disadvantage of providing the decision maker with too much undigested information. It is too difficult to be consistent without a formal procedure for aggregation. See R. N. McKean, *Efficiency in Government through Systems Analysis* (New York: Wiley, 1958); and B. Weisbrod, "Income Redistribution Effects and Benefit-Cost Analysis," in S. B. Chase, ed., *Problems in Public Expenditure Analysis* (Washington: Brookings Institution, 1968).

[28]F. Y. Edgeworth, "The Pure Theory of Taxation," *Economic Journal* (1897), pp. 46-70, 226-38, 550-71.

[29]J. A. Mirrlees, "An Exploration in the Theory of Optimum Income Taxation," *Review of Economic Studies* (April, 1971), pp. 175-208; R. C. Fair, "The Optimal Distribution of Income," *Quarterly Journal of Economics* (November, 1971), pp. 551-79; M. S. Feldstein, "On the Optimal Progressivity of the Income Tax," *Journal of Public Economics* (1973), forthcoming.

[30]Note that the problem is different from the one considered in Diamond and Mirrlees in two important ways. First, a complete set of optimal indirect taxes, as derived by Diamond and Mirrlees, cannot be assumed to exist. Second, the function for an optimal progressive income tax is not developed in their analysis. See Mirrlees, "An Exploration in the Theory of Optimum Income" and Diamond and Mirrlees, "Optimal Taxation and Public Production."

[31]Calculating the adjustments to the $t(y)$ function is related to but not identical with the type of excess burden calculation in Harberger. In the current context $t(y)$ is an incremental tax. See A. C. Harberger, "Taxation, Resource Allocation and Welfare," in J. Duesenberry, ed., *The Role of Direct and Indirect Taxes in the Federal Revenue System* (New York: National Bureau of Economic Research, 1964).

[32]O. Eckstein, "A Survey of the Theory of Public Expenditure Criteria."

[33]R. H. Haveman, *Water Resources Investment and the Public Interest* (Nashville: Vanderbilt University Press, 1965).

[34]Mirrlees, "An Exploration in the Theory of Optimum Income Taxation."

[35]K. Mera, "Experimental Determination of Relative Marginal Utilities," *Quarterly Journal of Economics* (August, 1969), pp. 464-77.

[36]Mr. Charles Brown has pointed out to me that even if Mera's calculations were accepted at face value, they could not be used as he suggests for project evaluation. If taxes are designed to imply equal absolute sacrifice, there is no reason to select projects to maximize the sum of additional utility; if Congress is not "ultilitarian" in designing its tax structure, there is no reason for being so in project selection.

[37]If the distributional preferences of Congress are accepted.

[38]B. Weisbrod, "Income Redistribution Effects and Benefit-Cost Analysis."

[39]R. H. Haveman, "Comment (on Weisbrod)," and R. Mack, "Comment (on Weisbrod)," both in S. Chase, ed., *Problems in Public Expenditure Analysis* (Washington, D.C.: Brookings Institution, 1968).

III

The Behavioral Basis of Redistribution

7

Explaining Income
Redistribution

JAMES D. RODGERS

The need is for some grasp of the infinitely complex, intangible
and downright contradictory character of men's interests, conscious and unconscious, and their interaction with equally in-
tricate mechanical, biological, neural and mental processes in
forming the pattern of behavior. The great vice is oversimplification, and the leadership which gets attention is as
much addicted to it as the inarticulate public. As between such
conceptions as universal love, will-to-power, and economic interest, the only question is whether any one can be more absurd
than another as a theory or as an ideal of social life.
                    Frank Knight, *Risk, Uncertainty and Profit*

The purpose of this paper is to examine the theories (or fragments of
theories) offered by economists to account for income redistribution
and to assess how well these models "work" in describing the income redistribution that is actually observed. The objective is not to
explain how the redistribution that occurs through particular public
programs varies in dollar amount year by year, but rather to explain
in a more fundamental sense why redistribution occurs at all and
why redistributive programs have the characteristics they do. Attention is confined largely to income redistribution achieved by governmental action rather than by the action of single individuals or
private groups. In Section I, the theories are discussed. In Section II

James D. Rodgers is Associate Professor of Economics at Pennsylvania State University.

we evaluate the usefulness of the theories in explaining the existence and nature of redistributive programs designed to alleviate poverty. Some conclusions are given in Section III.

I. THE THEORIES

It is useful to distinguish three distinct models that have been offered to explain redistributive activity. The first model (1) involves a democratic structure in which all persons (taxpayers and nontaxpayers alike) have one vote, and the preferences of voters are assumed to be independent. Coalitions are formed that use the state to undertake programs of actions that benefit the members and disperse cost either generally or to voters not in the coalition. In this model of narrow self-interested behavior, voters in the coalition exercise their political power to take income from everyone else; and the voters outside the coalition, having independent preferences, are unequivocally injured, although few individuals are losers on all collective decisions in a sequence. The second and the third models in their initial formulations assume a different framework for making collective decisions. The framework is one in which only taxpayers have the vote and in which voting decisions are made by the unanimity rule. In both models transfers are made willingly. In model 2 people use the state as an insurance agent to provide coverage against risks that the private market cannot insure. "Premium" payments are made to the state in the form of taxes in return for protection against hazards that would temporarily or permanently interrupt the flow of current income to citizens. Model 3 assumes that individual utility functions are interdependent in the sense that the distribution of income or the existence of poverty has effects on individual welfare that are not priced in the market. Since improvements in the welfare of the poor benefit any nonpoor person, whether he contributes anything himself or not, voluntary contributions by the nonpoor will lead to insufficient redistribution. Hence the nonpoor choose to collectivize redistribution, taxing themselves to make transfer payments to those having low incomes. Each of these models is now examined in more detail.

Model 1. Narrow Self-Interest

The narrow self-interest model has been formulated in two variants, one highly simplified and one more sophisticated. These variants will be discussed in turn.

The Downs Model. The simplified version is represented by Anthony Downs,[1] but it appears also, for example, in the writings of Stigler,[2] Breit,[3] and Davis.[4] In these models, the crucial variable is the income levels of voters (as opposed to other variables such as age, sex, and occupation). In the Downs model of the behavior of political parties, redistribution from those with high incomes to those with low incomes is a device used by parties to obtain votes. If votes are distributed equally (everyone has one) but incomes are distributed unequally, the support of many low-income voters can be bought at the expense of a few wealthy voters. More precisely, if two parties are in competition and if a simple majority is required to gain (or to remain in) office, the party that offers a platform of redistribution to the bottom 51 percent of the population from the top 49 percent (in terms of income) will gain office. The bottom 51 percent of the population is the winning coalition. A platform proposing redistribution to any group other than the bottom 51 percent can be defeated by one that proposes redistribution to this group alone.

Whether equal sharing of gains among the bottom 51 percent is a stable solution to this "game" is uncertain. As Tullock has noted,[5] the median voter and other voters composing the top 1 percent or so of the coalition have a good position in that, if this group receives any less than an equal share, it can form a coalition with the 49 percent not in the coalition and improve its own position. Yet this might also be said for any member of the coalition who gets a smaller share of the gains than other members get. Perhaps all that can be said is that, since the total amount of receipts obtainable by the coalition of the bottom 51 percent of voters is larger than the receipts obtainable by any other coalition of 51 percent, a force is present that is conductive to the maintenance of such a coalition if formed or to the return to such a coalition if it is initially formed but then dissolves.

A number of qualifications to this theory immediately arise. As Downs noted in his original presentation, there are several reasons why the amount of redistribution may stop short of that necessary to achieve complete leveling of incomes at the top of the distribution. First, those in the bottom 51 percent may find that the impairment to work incentives from complete equalization of incomes at the top would reduce total income by so much that they would prefer less-than-proportional shares of the initial national income to their shares of the smaller total available when incomes are leveled at the top.

A second effect working in the same direction is the expectation by coalition members that they may be in the upper brackets some day themselves. The importance of this effect would depend on many factors that this simple model leaves out of account but which are important in determining the degree of upward economic mobility. One plausible assertion, however, is that the coalition members may well differ in their expectations for being wealthy, and these expectations are likely to be directly related to their incomes.

Although the degree of mobility of individuals within the actual distribution of income is unknown, many individuals who are poor share one or more demographic or social characteristics that serve to reduce their chances of assuming a position in the top half of the distribution. Of the 29 million Americans in 1966 who were classified as poor by the Social Security Administration, 5,3 million were persons over 65 years of age. Another 2.6 million persons in the poverty group who were between 18 and 64 years of age were "severely" disabled (unable to work regularly at any gainful occupation). Of the total of 29 million in poverty, approximately 15 million were under 18. This leaves about 14 million voters in poverty, at least half of whom were past retirement age or severely disabled. A large number of the remaining 6 million voters in poverty are persons with low levels of educational attainment.[6] Since the mobility of this group is severely restricted, the pressure within a coalition of the bottom 51 percent of voters to restrain the extent of the leveling of the top of the distribution would come mostly from those voters above the poverty line.

A final qualification is the presumed positive relationship that exists between economic position and political power. Individuals having great wealth have more of the wherewithal to persuade others. As Downs notes: "Usually voters with the highest incomes also have the most political power, since in an uncertain world they can use their financial resources to create influence for themselves. [This] sets up a counterforce that may completely overshadow... the natural 'Robin Hood' tendency of a democratic government.... If it does, rational government action may even redistribute income from the poor to the rich."[7] In the simple model with which we have been dealing, people may be uncertain about two things: their future position in the distribution and the disincentive effects that redistribution will produce.[8] Wealthy individuals may be able to reduce the amount of income they would be required to transfer to the poor by devoting resources to convincing the low-income coalition that the disincentive and economic-growth deterrent effects of redistribution would be substantial.

A More Sophisticated Narrow Self-interest Model. One of the weaknesses of the Downs model and other models (for example, Stigler's model of Director's Law)[9] is the assumption that income is the strategic basis for the formation of voter coalitions and that, as a consequence, redistribution takes place along a one-dimensional continuum. The primary difficulty with this assumption is that empirically most of the redistribution that is observed is not obviously vertical in nature. The people who pay and those who receive are determined in only a very few cases by income position exclusively, and in many cases income position is only tenuously related to a determination of who pays and who receives. In certain cases extremely wealthy people pay no tax at all; and, in general, simply being poor is not enough to guarantee receipt of an income transfer.[10]

These facts of actual redistribution cast doubt on the Downs model and others like it. An important element of the Downs model, however, is retained in the more sophisticated models. This is the idea that people seek to use the government either to gain general benefits and disperse cost via tax loopholes to others or to gain special benefits and disperse cost generally to other persons.

This more general model was first developed in a paper by Gordon Tullock,[11] in which he dealt with the problem of resource allocation under majority rule with vote trading. The essence of the model is that, when collective decisions are made by majority rule, each voter will exchange his vote with the minimum number of other voters necessary to insure passage of a piece of legislation beneficial to him, so long as the gains he receives from this legislation are not outweighed by his share of the tax costs of the projects benefiting those with whom he trades his votes. Since the individual voter excludes from his calculation the tax cost imposed on others not in the coalition formed by vote trading, a misallocation of resources tends to result. The private tax cost to voters in the coalition is less than the social cost, since the taxes paid by those not in the coalition are not taken into account by coalition members.

Although the allocative implications of majority rule are important, the redistributive effects are under consideration here. It is clear that redistribution goes hand in hand with the misallocation of resources. Income flows from those not in the coalition to coalition members, who get benefits without paying the full resource cost.

In the more nearly complete version of this model, in Buchanan and Tullock's book,[12] redistribution is the result of the operation of a decision rule requiring less than consensus. From the individual's point of view, this is the external cost imposed upon him by the operation of a decision rule not requiring unanimity. The operation of a less than 100 percent rule implies a considerable amount of redistribution in the form either of providing special benefits to a particular group at general taxpayer expense or of providing general benefits while giving special tax breaks to particular groups. Over a series of issues an individual will find himself in the minority on some decisions, in which case he will be assessed tax payments but receive no benefits, and in the majority on others, in which case he receives benefits partly or entirely at the expense of others. How he does over a series of decisions is uncertain. Particular individuals may do very well, and others may fare very badly.[13]

This model differs from the Downs model in two respects. First, any government decision may involve redistribution; explicit income transfers are not the only means by which redistribution takes place. Second, redistribution does not necessarily, or even primarily, take place in vertical manner from those persons in one income bracket to those in another. Domestic sugar producers may induce representatives from "sugar states" to introduce legislation to restrict imports of foreign sugar. The representatives trade votes on other bills, which other representatives (who have little preference one way or another about sugar quotas) desire in exchange for their support on the import quota bill. Income is redistributed from all consumers of sugar to domestic sugar producers, since the domestic price of sugar is higher than if the import quota bill had not been passed. The resulting redistribution does not necessarily have a vertical pattern, particularly if all the increased monopoly rents do not go to the owners of the sugar-producing firms but go partly to labor employed by the firms. Even if the owners get the entire increase in rents, stock ownership may be either widely dispersed or narrowly concentrated; and the position of the stockholders in the income distribution is not certain.

The pattern of redistribution in the Buchanan-Tullock model is, therefore, not specified. It depends on which groups of individuals organize to obtain transfers or differential benefits and how successful the representatives of such groups are in the congressional log-rolling process. To be more precise about the pattern of redistribution that will emerge, one needs a theory telling what groups will organize for the purpose of lobbying for benefits and what will be the chances of success of the lobbying effort.

While no well-developed theory of this sort exists, there are a number of considerations which help explain why characteristics *other than income* most frequently provide the basis for coalitions seeking to use the machinery of government to gain income at others' expense. Consider a particular income class, say the bottom 50 percent of income recipients as in the Downs model, or even the bottom 10 percent. The costs of organizing such a group would be enormous for several reasons. First, of course, there is the mere size of the group. In addition, there is no reason to expect the members of the class to know one another personally nor to have even impersonal dealings with more than a small fraction of the other members. Nor will the identity of the members of an income class necessarily remain stable over time. Finally, for any coalition the passage of beneficial legislation is a public good, in that benefits flow to a member of the group whether or not he helps bear the cost of the lobbying effort. For some coalitions it is possible to offer selective incentives in the form of some private good (or the threat of some private bad) to induce each member to bear his share of the cost. It would seem to be difficult, however, to do this for a large diverse group having nothing more in common than being in the same income bracket.

In sharp contrast is the relative lack of impediments to government aid to particular economic units having something in common other than, or in addition to, income. Perhaps governmental assistance to particular industries provides the best example. In his paper, "The Theory of Economic Regulation," George Stigler has argued that, "As a rule, regulation is acquired by the industry and is designed and operated primarily for its benefit" (p. 3).[14] Among the advantages possessed by the economic units in a particular industry (as compared with the economic units in an income class) are: (1) the small size of the group, along with the ease of identifying the group's members and the stability of the group's membership over time; (2) the presence of an existing organization (usually a trade association) that provides to each member of the group services that can be used as an incentive to induce members to contribute to the cost of activities (such as lobbying), designed to induce the government to enact legislation benefiting all members of the group;[15] (3) the "hidden" nature of the redistribution effected and the very small cost it imposes on the persons, for example, the consumers of the industry's product, from whom income is being taken. This third advantage is important because it implies that the group harmed may not even be aware of the redistribution that is occurring. The hidden nature of the income transfers and the high cost of organizing buyers to resist it imply, in turn, that a representative introducing such industry legislation in Congress will find logrolling comparatively easy since the other members of Congress will not be intensely opposed to such legislation. None will find it particularly advantageous to represent unorganized consumers. As Stigler has observed, "A representative cannot win and keep office with the support of the sum of those who are opposed to: oil import quotas, farm subsidies, airport subsidies, hospital subsidies, unnecessary navy shipyards, an inequitable public housing program, and rural electrification subsidies" (p. 11).[16]

Another advantage (4) of industry groups over income groups is the ability of the former to provide seemingly convincing reasons why everyone will benefit from government aid. For example, they claim that oil import quotas are necessary to assure an adequate supply of petroleum in the event of war; and that licensing of tree surgeons is necessary to protect the public against tree quacks, shysters, and inexperienced persons. Outright government aid to persons in a particular income class may be more difficult to justify as being socially beneficial.

To sum up this brief discussion of narrow self-interest models, it must be concluded that they fail (in their present form at least) to offer clear-cut predictions about the pattern of redistribution in democracies operating under majority rule. Accordingly, they do not necessarily predict the emergence of redistribution to low-income persons. There does seem to be an ample supply of real-world counterparts to the coalitions in the Buchanan-Tullock model, as represented, among other examples, by government aid to industries. Here, the self-interest explanation seems wholly sufficient to account for the redistribution that occurs. Also, since small groups are involved, votes are few, and representatives would be expected to want financial aid (such as campaign contributions) if they are to make a deal to support a program beneficial to the group. All this seems to square with experience. On the other hand, since an income class would find organization more difficult, the political party (as in the Downs model) or congressional representatives must assume the entrepreneurial function of providing favorable legislation. With a large block of voters involved, one might expect this to occur. But the qualifications pointed out by Downs may work against what would otherwise be the income class most likely to be singled out by politicians to favor with legislation—the bottom 50 percent. In addition to these qualifications, lower voter participation rates among the poor also reduce the returns from providing them with benefits—so long as we abstract from the benefits such programs may provide to nonrecipients. Even at this stage, therefore, there are grounds for asserting that self-interested demands by the recipient poor do not necessarily appear to be sufficient to explain the existence of transfers for their benefit. Before considering other evidence for this position, we first look at two other theories of redistribution to the poor, each of which considers benefits to nonrecipients.

Model 2: The Insurance Model

Within any given year in the United States a large amount of redistribution takes place in the private sector of the economy as a result of the operations of private insurance plans, as a large proportion of the population pays insurance premiums and a smaller segment receives benefit payments. In 1969 United States life insurance companies paid out 7,162 million dollars in death benefits; and health insurance benefits amounted to 7,575 million dollars.[17]

The theory of individual participation in private sector insurance plans has been developed extensively.[18] The basic model specifies that when risk-averse individuals find that each of them is subject to the same risk, they have an incentive to develop a way to hedge against it. By regularly contributing a portion of their incomes to a common pool out of which payments to those who experience the misfortune can be made, all of the individuals can be made better off. The operation of such arrangements produces redistribution at any point in time. The payments contributed by some members of the community go to the insured individuals who suffer the misfortune.

More recently, it has been emphasized that private markets, providing some types of insurance that individuals desire, may fail to emerge.[19] In such circumstances individuals may find that by acting collectively (via government action) they can obtain for themselves such coverage as the private market cannot provide. As a consequence, everyone can reach a preferred position. This view is given in the two following quotations:

> ...a good part of the preference for redistribution expressed in government taxation and expenditure policies and private charity can be reinterpreted as a desire for insurance. It is noteworthy that virtually nowhere is there a system of subsidies that has as its aim simply an equalization of income. The subsidies or other governmental help go to those who are disadvantaged in life by events the incidence of which are popularly regarded as unpredictable; the blind, dependent children, the medically indigent. Thus, optimality, in a context which includes risk-bearing, includes much that appears to be motivated by distributional value judgements when looked at in a narrower context.[20]

An individual who is a risk-averter might reasonably support ... welfare programs, even if he were philosophically opposed to income redistribution. There is always the possibility that anyone might have a streak of bad luck and be pleased to take advantage of programs designed to palliate the effect of that luck. In a sense, welfare programs provide a kind of "income insurance." Individuals pay taxes as premiums, in the expectation that if, by chance, they should experience a significant decrease in income, they would be able to collect from that "insurance." But the problem of the incentives is also analogous to a problem in insurance called "moral hazard." Ideally, an event to be insurable should be completely random. If an individual can alter his behavior in such a way as to make an event more likely to happen (by starting a fire, for instance), then the event may not be completely insurable. Since individual incomes are subject not only to random disturbances arising from events over which they have no control but also depend on the individual's supply of work effort, incomes may well not be strictly insurable.[21]

Buchanan and Tullock offer another reason (in addition to moral hazard) for failure of a private income insurance plan to emerge:

... since income is the primary economic magnitude to be considered in his over-all life planning, the individual will rarely have sufficient wealth at the outset of his life to purchase the "income insurance" that utility-maximizing considerations would dictate to be rational. Nor will potential sellers of such insurance be in a position to enforce the sort of contracts that might be required to implement such a program in the real world.[22]

Although they do not mention it explicitly, these authors presumably have in mind here the imperfections in the capital market that prevent the individual from borrowing the funds to purchase such insurance at the beginning of his earning years (imperfections due to legal prohibitions on indentured servitude) and legal restrictions and transactions costs faced by insurance sellers.[23] (See paper 9, by A. Mitchell Polinsky.)

The model, then, is basically this: If individuals are risk averse, smoothing of income fluctuations is beneficial. The desire for income smoothing is not adequately met by private insurance plans because of moral hazard and imperfections in the capital market. Collective provision of the redistribution carried out by government can be interpreted as a mechanism for achieving citizens' desires for greater stability in the flow of income.

An aspect of this model that is not entirely clear, however, is whether a "fiscal club" composed of all persons in the community would unanimously decide to institute a compulsory income-insurance program. Clearly it would if the provision of this kind of collective service provided net benefits to everyone, but whether all would be made better off is unclear without considering the circumstances of choice and the severity of the moral-hazard problem.

Consider first the circumstances of choice. The different circumstances of choice by members of the community can be distinguished sharply for purposes of contrast, even though individuals in the real world actually will find themselves somewhere on the continuum of possible circumstances between these two extremes. At one extreme individuals know their incomes and their places in the distribution of income with certainty for as long as they live, as well as the incomes of their children, grandchildren, and so on. With these circumstances of choice, the purpose of income insurance —risk reduction—is absent; and the group would not choose an insurance program by unanimous consent unless there was at least some degree of mobility of individuals within the distribution. The reason is perhaps obvious, but a bit more elaboration will prove useful. Suppose that an income insurance program were proposed that would prevent the income of any person from falling below a given level, say $\bar{y}$. Given the certainty of the income streams of all persons, the operation of this program would clearly impose burdens on those whose incomes never drop below $\bar{y}$ and benefits on those whose incomes were always to be less than $\bar{y}$. The net benefits or burdens imposed on other individuals could also be calculated. Clearly, with perfect certainty, each person could calculate how he would fare under the program, and some would be made worse off and would vote against it. With a unanimity decision rule, the program would not be adopted.

At the other extreme from perfect certainty is the situation where individuals do not know what position in the distribution they will occupy. If this is taken literally to mean that a given person does not possess subjective probability estimates, there is no way for him to make a rational decision about whether to vote for an income-insurance plan. However, let us suppose that complete uncertainty means that each person thinks he has the same chance of being in any position in the distribution. Each person faces a situation

FIGURE 1

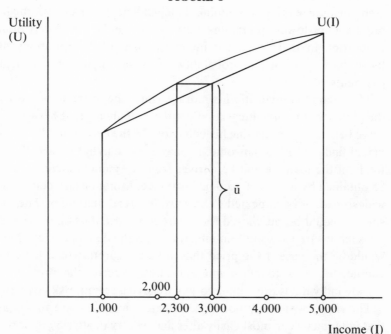

depicted in Figure 1. The utility of each person is $\bar{U}$, which corresponds to the utility of an expected income of $3,000 or a certain income of $2,300. An individual would then be willing to pay as much as $700 for an insurance policy that guaranteed him an income of $3,000.

Any government insurance program that can provide this security with operating costs of less than $700 per person could make all citizens better off. A real world situation of this sort is difficult to imagine, however, for it assumes that individuals possess no information at all as to what their position in the income distribution will be. To make the model more realistic, many complications could be introduced; but only two need be examined for our purposes. The first is that individuals use their current incomes to estimate what their future incomes will be. Those at the bottom and the middle of the income distribution may, therefore, have a much greater direct interest in income insurance than those at the top of the distribution. To induce upper-income groups to agree to participate in a collective income-insurance plan (assuming independent preferences) might require much lower "premium contributions," either absolutely or in proportion to their expected incomes, than the contributions of those having a higher probability of being eligible for benefit payments.

The second complication is moral hazard, the problem posed by the ability of the individual to affect the probability that he will receive benefits by modifying his behavior. To the extent that the individual finds work burdensome, he may seek to avoid it partially or totally if the main benefit he derives from it—money, income—can be obtained by means of income insurance. Moral hazard can be so widespread, or be expected to be so widespread, that no private insurance could be purchased for a particular risk. The supply price for such insurance would, in effect, exceed the demand price. This would be the case if the price that private insurers would have to charge, taking account of moral hazard, exceeds the price that private individuals are willing to pay to have a certain risk covered.

The risks most likely not to be privately insurable are those (a) that individuals can most easily alter and will try to alter by their behavior once they are insured, (b) that are random over only a small subset of the population (limiting thereby the amount of total risk reduction due to the law of large numbers), and (c) that individuals have the least risk aversion toward.[24]

It is instructive to consider how likely it would be for a private insurer to provide insurance against the risk of having a low income. Clearly, such a risk, because it is appropriately characterized by both (a) and (b) above, is not likely to be insurable. The premium payments would likely be so high as to choke off all demand for such insurance by those who otherwise might desire it. Both the moral-hazard problem and the fact that poverty is not a random variable over the entire population would serve to preclude a market.

The types of insurance that are available privately help to guard against being impoverished by providing a hedge against selective events that could make one poor. But insurance against poverty itself is not purchasable privately because this would involve insuring a whole basket of risks, and over some of these the individual exerts substantial control.

Two important observations are in order in the light of the foregoing. First, it is by no means certain that a governmental "poverty-insurance" program would command the support of high-income groups, since those persons might not find it a "good buy" in the sense that other insurance policies are a "good buy." Second, the moral-hazard problem suggests that the risk that a public-poverty program would be designed to reduce would be those for which moral hazard was not considered to be a significant problem. The resulting welfare programs would be expected to be, as Arrow has indicated, categorical in nature.[25] Having a low income would not be enough to get public welfare. Rather, one would have to be blind, disabled, or too young or too old to be in the labor force, or otherwise have some "good reason" beyond his control (as judged by those paying taxes to finance the program) for not being able to work to be eligible. These restrictions serve, in effect, to separate high and low moral-hazard risks. Pauly has shown that moral hazard may make the collective provision of certain types of insurance not provided by the market undesirable,[26] in the sense that it would make people worse off than they would be with no insurance. Although his analysis specifically dealt with medical insurance, it clearly has applicability here.

Presumably, government would have open to it no alternatives in terms of behavioral restrictions that are not available to private insurance firms.[27] It might, however, have lower administrative, especially selling, costs because the government program could be made compulsory. This cost saving might reduce costs by an amount sufficient to make the program beneficial to all, or it might not. All depends on the size of the cost reduction made possible by a shift in the method by which the insurance is provided. If such cost savings are very small in relation to the costs due to moral hazard, the program will make individuals worse off in the expected utility sense and will not emerge by unanimous consent of a fiscal club.

There is also a redistributive problem that arises from the ability to separate people into different risk classes. Incomplete separation causes a redistribution of income from lower-risk to higher-risk persons, if both groups are lumped together and made to pay the same premium for insurance. One would expect this classification of individuals into various risk classes to be somewhat easier for an income-insurance program. Not only would this task be easier for the government, but individuals would also tend to be aware of risk differences for different groups. If all persons were lumped together and required to pay the same premiums, wealthier persons might well find such insurance a very bad bargain from a self-interested viewpoint and refuse to vote for the program. Poorer groups would, conversely, find the insurance a very good buy.

The income-insurance model then carries the following implications about redistribution: (1) Since the purpose of the program is to protect persons against having a low income, it would necessarily result, at any point in time, in vertical redistribution. (2) If each person has independent preferences, unanimous support of an income-insurance program would probably require placing persons in different risk classes with lower charges for the upper-income groups. Putting everyone in the same risk class might make the premiums paid by high-income persons so high that they would be made worse off by participation in the program. And (3) attempts would likely be made to base eligibility for benefit payments on other factors in addition to low money income in order to reduce the significance of moral hazard. The cause of a person's poverty would be considered important, with considerable effort devoted to distinguishing those causes beyound the persons's control from those causes that are within his control. Attempts would be made to develop criteria of employability. All these efforts would be designed to reduce the cost of insurance by reducing moral hazard. Many poor persons might be eligible for no benefits.

Model 3. Interdependent Preferences

In the last few years, a number of papers have developed a theory of redistribution based on the assumption of interdependent preferences.[28] In the broadest sense, utility interdependence refers to a situation where one or more commodities relevant to individual utilities are not priced in the market. In the recent models of redistribution it is assumed that the persons giving up income have included as an argument in their utility functions either some activity, attribute, or variable pertaining to recipients, which the transferors hope to alter by redistribution, or some measure of inequality that the transferor desires to alter. The externality postulated is different from such usual examples as these involving smoke, noise, or attractive gardens by the assumption that if the potential recipients' incomes were much higher (or income more evenly distributed), the externality would cease to be marginally relevant.[29]

It is useful to classify the models in two broad categories, those in which the motive for the redistribution is direct and those in which the redistribution is viewed as part of a process to achieve some other objective. The models of direct motivation have taken three forms in the literature, each of which can be specified by the particular variable that appears in the transferor's utility function. These three forms are

(1) $$U_e = f_I (X_{eI}, \ldots, X_{en}; T)$$

(2) $$U_e = f_I (X_{eI}, \ldots, X_{en}; Y_a)$$

(3) $$U_e = f_I (X_{eI}, \ldots, X_{en}; X_{aI})$$

where U_e is the utility function of man E and $X_{ei}, \ldots, X_{en}$ are the private goods in his utility function. In all three formulations it is assumed that prior to any transfer made by E,

$$\partial U_e/\partial T, \ \partial U_e/\partial Y_a, \text{ and } \partial U_e/X_{aI} > 0$$

The first manner of specifying the interdependence, that is, letting the amount transferred, T, be an argument in the E's utility function, suggests that the act of making transfers is the source of the transferor's satisfaction and not the effect of his gift.[30] This type of interdependence presumably could motivate only voluntary transfers. E would gain no satisfaction from transfers that he was forced to make nor from those made by others.[31] The utility he derives comes from the very act of giving, and he is concerned about the effect of his gift only insofar as there exists simultaneously an interdependence of another kind involving what he thinks other people think of him as a result of his giving (or of his *not* giving). Giving money indiscriminately probably gains a person less esteem in the eyes of others than giving to what are generally regarded as "worthy causes." In biblical times E would be the Pharisee. His transfers, if not actually made out of vanity, are self-seeking in the narrowest sense.

If everyone had preferences of this kind, transfers would have no public good characteristics, and there would be no benefits from collectivizing redistribution from the standpoint of transferors.[32] If only the latter group had the vote or decisions were made by unanimous consent, any public redistribution of income observed would have to be explained in another manner. Only private transfers could be explained by this type of preference.

The second type of interdependence, as specified in equation (2), reflects a concern on the part of E with the income level of A. As used in the Hochman-Rodgers model,[33] this is taken as an empirical proxy for A's welfare or utility level. With $Y_e > Y_a$ and only two persons involved, E simply makes A a gift (provided that the marginal rate of substitution between A's income and his own exceeds the rate at which A's income can be increased by reductions in Y_e).[34] If we assume that his own income and A's income are normal goods to E, two propositions follow. First, if E's initial income rose with A's held constant, the transfer E would make to A would rise. Second, if A's initial income rose with E's held constant, the transfer E would make to A would decline.[35] If we shift from a model having one benefactor and one recipient to one having many benefactors and one recipient, these two results imply two others: (1) the "price" faced by any one giver will rise enormously, and (2) the givers who will make the largest transfers, if any transfers are made at all, will be those with the highest incomes. Result (1) follows because, as one benefactor makes a transfer to A, his income rises and the desired transfers of all other benefactors fall. Hence A's income may rise by only a dime for every dollar a particular benefactor transfers to him. Result (2) follows directly from the assumption that A's income is a normal good.

The private market equilibrium level of transfers will, therefore, be suboptimal since the summed marginal rates of substitution of the benefactors will exceed the rate at which the benefactor group's income can be "transformed" into recipient income, which, with no transactions costs, equals unity. That is,

(4) $$\Sigma \, (\partial U_i / \partial Y_a)/(\partial U_i / \partial Y_i) > 1$$

where there are N benefactors. Collectivizing redistribution, therefore, can make everyone better off.

If only the benefactors participate in approving the collective redistributive arrangements and if a unanimity rule is used to make decisions, then, with zero bargaining costs, the outcome that emerges would be such as to make (1) an equality and everyone would benefit. If all benefactors plus the recipients participate in the decision making and if the unanimity rule is employed, it is conceivable that a Pareto optimum will be attained at which the inequality in equation (5) is *reversed*,[36] although with the unanimity rule in operation no benefactor would be any worse off in this equilibrium than if no transfers at all were made. Finally, with a majority rule for making decisions, a coalition of $(n + 1)/2$ benefactors may form and force the benefactors not in the coalition to finance most or all of the transfers to A, leaving them worse off than with no redistribution.

In extending this model to include more than one recipient, one approach is simply to increase the number of public goods. If we let each recipient's income represent an additional public good, the market failure problem and the optimality conditions (one for each recipient) can be discussed in much the same manner as above. However, much simplification is possible if a plausible assumption is made about benefactor preferences. This is that any nonpoor person desires to see the largest transfers go to the poorest people and will adjust transfers until all poor recipients have the same income.[37] In this manner, poor individuals can be aggregated, and the nonpoor can be viewed as deciding how much to transfer for purposes of poverty alleviation, with the stipulation that whatever amount occurs will be distributed among the poor in much the same way as water would fill a lake with an uneven bottom. A rigorous development of this model, as a fiscal application of Pareto-optimal redistribution, is found in Von Furstenberg and Mueller.[38] Assuming that tastes for transfers are uniform within income classes and that the income elasticity of demand for transfers is a constant across income classes, these authors calculate the pattern of redistributive taxes and transfers under alternative assumptions about the level of the guaranteed minimum income.

Unfortunately, the transfers having a vertical and equalizing pattern in the real world do not fit the predictions of this model in several respects. Existing transfer programs are not of the minimum-income type in structure. Persons with higher market incomes than others obtain larger transfers; and some persons, although poor, are ineligible for transfers. Characteristics, in addition to having a low income, are used to determine eligibility. Furthermore, many transfer programs that are vertical and equalizing are in-kind rather than cash programs.

Two explanations of why the kind of transfers we actually see do not fit the predictions of this model could be offered. One is that the preference pattern assumed is correct but that the collective decision process actually in operation in the real world is different from that implicitly assumed in the model. The preferences of those financing the transfers simply are not reflected properly. The other explanation is that the political process generates programs that reflect preferences of taxpayer-donors correctly, but the preferences specified in the model are not an accurate description of these actual preferences. Or divergence between the model's predictions and reality could be explained as the joint effect of these causes.

The decision-making process underlying the interdependence model is one of a franchise limited to the taxpayer-donors. The decision rule must be one of unanimity with full side payments possible at zero transactions costs. The results that emerge would be Pareto optimal, although the results might differ from those obtained by Von Furstenberg and Mueller since they require the Lindahl solution, an outcome that will not necessarily emerge under the decision-making arrangements postulated. Clearly, there is plenty of room for the model's predictions to deviate from reality because of the difference between actual collective decision making and the idealized sort represented here. We shall return to this problem in Section II, and in the remainder of this section we shall consider the possible alterations that have been suggested for the basic preference assumptions of the model.

Some economists have argued that this model does indeed incorrectly represent preferences implying that the outcome of the political process is a fairly good approximation to the results that would emerge from the idealized process assumed by the model. Buchanan, for example, has argued that there

> ... is a lack of interest on the part of the public in real income distribution as such. One must search diligently to find much "social" concern expressed for the prudent poor whose lives are well-ordered and stable. The evidence seems to indicate that general redistribution of purchasing power is not widely desired. Instead, members of the public want, and express through their behavior patterns, relief for specific spending patterns.[39]

This criticism of the type of interdependence assumption made in equation (2) has generated a number of efforts[40] in which the type of interdependence assumed is like that specified in equation (3), where some particular commodity consumed by A enters the utility function of E. The analysis is much the same, and it is possible by this alteration in assumptions to explain the existence of the in-kind redistribution of such necessities as food, medical care, and housing. Indeed, since recipients always would prefer the cash equivalent of any in-kind subsidy, it would seem at first glance difficult to reconcile the existence of such programs in any other manner. Yet to the extent retrading (between recipients and nonrecipients) of the subsidized goods can be prohibited, these subsidies would also be beneficial to suppliers of these goods; and this could constitute either a competing explanation or simply add to the support of such in-kind programs provided by others (both taxpayers and recipients). An additional problem is that not all redistributive programs aimed at the poor are in-kind in nature. It would seem that if either the interdependence as specified in equation (2) or that specified in equation (3) explained transfers to the poor, then either all the transfers would be in cash or they would all be made in-kind, with no mixture of the two.

A second modification of the assumption about interdependence specified in equation (2) has been suggested. In this modification, Y_a is regarded as only one argument in A's utility function, the other being leisure, L_a, which is assumed either not to enter equation (2) or to enter and be valued separately by E.[41] The rationale for this modification has been primarily stimulated by results of public-opinion polls and by the discussion in Congress about how to reform the existing welfare program with the primary issue being how to (a) minimize the work disincentive effects of a welfare program and (b) separate those who are not expected to be able to work from those persons who are capable of working. The result of excluding L_2 for equation (2) implies that taxpayers with this type of preference would desire that a welfare program take the form of providing wage bonuses for the poor since this type of transfer, by enlisting the aid of a substitution effect toward more work effort, enables the taxpayer to "purchase" a given increase in Y_a for a smaller tax cost than through either a lump-sum transfer program or, *a fortiori*, a transfer program that made the size of payments inversely related to income. This model also implies that taxpayers would desire a separate program for those individuals who could not work at all, since for this group a wage bonus program would be unable to raise money incomes. Nor would taxpayers have to worry about unwanted substitution effects for this group.

A second class of interdependence models, although not formally developed by anyone as yet, is suggested by discussions of the many indirect benefits from having poverty alleviated. Lyndon Johnson, in a presidential message on poverty, put much emphasis on the benefits of a successful "war on poverty" for the nonpoor.

> Our fight against poverty will be an investment in the most valuable of our resources—the skills and strength of our people.
> And in the future, as in the past, this investment will return its cost many fold to our entire economy.
> If we can raise the annual earnings of 10 million among the poor by only $1,000 we will have added 14 billion dollars a year to our national output. In addition, we can make important reductions in public assistance payments which now cost 4 billion dollars a year, and in the large costs of fighting crime and delinquency, disease and hunger.

This is only part of the story.

Our history has proved that each time we broaden the base of abundance, giving more people the chance to produce and consume, we create new industry, higher production, increased earnings, and better income for all.

Giving new opportunity to those who have little will enrich the lives of all the rest.[42]

Taxpayer preferences may indeed be specified to incorporate income transfers as a kind of capital input into a production process yielding several "products" of direct utility to households. Although not precluding direct interest by the nonpoor in the welfare or consumption levels of the poor, altruistic concern is unnecessary. Raising the income level of recipients represents a course of action that the transferor believes will produce some other result in which he is ultimately interested. One goal might be a reduction in the crime rate or the probability that he or his property will be damaged by violence. To carry the production analogy further, the income transfer is merely one input into a production process; another would be expenditures on law enforcement activities, which the transferor's taxes help to finance. This situation is representable by the following utility and "production" functions:

$$(5) \qquad\qquad U_E = f(Z_1, \ldots, Z_n)$$

$$(6) \qquad\qquad Z_i = g_i(X_1, \ldots, X_m) \ (i = 1, \ldots, m)$$

Here the "ultimate" goods appearing in equation (5) are produced by a process defined by equation (6),[43] the production rule used to produce the Z_i. Suppose Z_1 represents the safety of streets at night in the area where E lives, or, more precisely, $Z = 1 - p$, where p is the probability of E's being personally injured or of having his property stolen or destroyed by violence. One of the inputs that it would be worthwhile employing to "produce" more Z_1 could well be poverty-alleviating income transfers, since criminal activities of various kinds tend to be more likely where there is extreme poverty.[44] This kind of interrelationship could then be a motivation for making income transfers.[45]

There is, of course, likely to be considerable uncertainty in the mind of the individual about the precise nature of the production function. This implies that the marginal productivity of the various "inputs" is uncertain. Still, if we start from an initial position in which a certain ratio of, say, income transfers and expenditures on law enforcement is being "used," the standard theory of production would predict that a reduction in the effective "price" of income transfers (brought about by, say, a reduction in administration costs of welfare programs and/or by a change in the structure of the program so that more of the program's funds go to the very poor) would be expected to induce a substitution of income transfers for expenditures on law enforcement, provided those in charge of governmental expenditures were sensitive to this shift in what constitutes desire. Similar alterations would occur if improved knowledge of the determinants of crime established a more precise and significant link between poverty and crime, so that everyone came to believe that the "marginal productivity" of income transfers is much greater than existing previous evidence had indicated.

This discussion raises a related question that should be asked more explicitly. Given that a person is concerned about alleviating poverty because of a self-interested desire to reduce some of its manifestations and effects, or because of a genuine concern for the plight of the poor, what type of poverty program would he desire to see adopted so that he would feel that he is getting the most for his tax dollar? Or, to put the question in a more illuminating way, what type of program would he prefer if he wanted to minimize the present value of future tax payments made to finance a poverty program, knowing that such tax payments would continue or be reinstituted if at some point discontinued, as long as anyone's income was below the "poverty line"? The individual with this objective would probably seek a program that put considerable emphasis on human capital formation, so that the marginal productivity of the poor would be raised sufficiently to allow their market incomes to rise above the "poverty line." At this time his tax payments for poverty relief, except those made on behalf of the untrainable poor, would cease. Since our knowledge is too limited to determine the optimal mix of transfers earmarked for various types of human capital investment and other in-kind transfers that minimize the present value of poverty taxes, various people, if each has the same objective, may well disagree about what the size and composition of the optimal poverty program should be. Yet one would expect considerable emphasis on human-resource development programs in any poverty program that drew its political support from the individual taxpayers desiring to minimize the present value of future poverty-tax payments. Although one might question whether taxpayers view the question of poverty in such a sophisticated manner, the emphasis frequently placed on getting people off the welfare roles suggests that preferences may well be consistent with this formulation.

II. EXPLAINING ACTUAL REDISTRIBUTIVE PROGRAMS

Although discussions of redistribution sometimes suggest that a "vast" amount of redistribution occurs in the United States in any given year because of government action, no one seems to know exactly how much this represents in dollars. Primarily, the difficulty resides in the general equilibrium nature of the problem of expenditure and tax incidence. As Aaron and McGuire have noted in an important although nihilistic paper:

> Authors of studies of the distributional effects of governmental fiscal operations are driven into countless compromises in order to obtain any results at all since the comparison of the actual distribution of income with that which would prevail under substantially different government policies is the general equilibrium problem *par excellence*.[46]

That no very reliable estimates of the change in distribution of income caused by all governmental activities combined are available is not particularly important for our purpose, however. The government does not have one single redistributive program designed explicitly to alter the distribution of income in a particular way. Rather, there are a host of different fiscal operations with differing objectives, and it is these individual programs that must be examined to assess how well the models reviewed in Section I explain them. Estimates of aggregate fiscal residuals combine phenomena that it would be preferable to separate.[47] Looking at the residuals as a whole creates too great a temptation to try to explain the entire aggregate by a single theory. Although this might be justifiable if there were but one government program with the purpose of achieving the degree of redistribution indicated by the residuals, such is not in fact the case, and attempting to apply a single theory to the aggregate pattern seems more likely to mislead than to illumine.

In what follows attention is confined primarily to public-welfare programs. An assessment of which of the previous models seems best able to account for these programs will be attempted, using two kinds of information. The first kind is the nature and characteristics of the programs, such as eligibility requirements and the form in which transfers are made. The second kind of information is that supplied by voting behavior and opinion polls.

Inferences from the Nature of Welfare Programs

Before the relevant characteristics of current welfare programs are reviewed, it is instructive to consider briefly the nature of the first public-welfare programs in this country.

The first public-welfare programs in operation in America were modeled after the Elizabethan Poor Law of 1601. Under the terms of this law, if an individual could not provide for himself, his family was legally liable for his support. If he had no family or if they could not support him, he was supported by a public program financed and administered locally. Recipients were classified into two broad classes, adults and children; and the adults were subclassified according to whether they could work. Children were given apprenticeship training, disabled adults were assigned to the almshouse, and able-bodied adults were forced to work in the community (or be sent to prison if they refused) until they could find other work in the labor market. This welfare system was supplemented by settlement laws requiring evidence of property ownership and proof of ability to remain off the pauper roles to gain settlement in a particular locality.[48]

If we judge by the disdain shown those on public relief and the humiliating experiences they often suffered,[49] the early public-welfare programs were apparently controlled by those paying the taxes to finance relief. It seems unlikely that the poor would have made it so humiliating and so difficult for themselves to obtain transfers if they had had any power of decision in the matter. Rather, the pauper program apparently was operated to provide benefits to (or reduce costs imposed on) the nonpoor. Reflected in the program was a mixture of two desires by taxpayer-donors, a desire to help the poor who could not be blamed for their own deprivation and a desire to punish those who were able bodied and who apparently were trying to get "something for nothing" rather than work as others did to earn their living. These two desires resulted in attempts to distinguish between persons who were thought to be poor because of their own moral weakness, shiftlessness, and improvidence and those who were poor because of some condition beyond their control.

Current public assistance and in-kind welfare programs are composed of Old Age Assistance (OAA), Aid to Families with Dependent Children (AFDC), Aid to the Blind (AB), Aid to the Permanently and Totally Disabled (APTD), the Food Stamp Program (and other nutrition programs), housing subsidies, and higher education aid to disadvantaged students. The first four programs, authorized under the Social Security Act, contain remnants of the English Poor Law. Under current law, employable recipient adults must register for and accept training or work. If they do not, benefit payments are reduced.[50] Residency requirements exist in most states, and most states require support by relatives where this is possible.[51]

Two features of the current programs are of particular importance for our purposes. The first is that whereas need as established by a means test is an eligibility requirement in all programs, it is the sole requirement only for the recently established programs to give aid in kind. Each of those programs that are part of the Social Security Act requires recipients to meet other criteria that serve in a rough way to separate those who can work from those who cannot. The second characteristic is that some of the benefits are payable in kind rather than in cash.

The first feature can be explained as an expression of the preferences of those financing the program or as an expression of recipient preferences. The former explanation would be that taxpayers are sympathetic to the plight of those who are poor as a result of some chance event that could make anyone (even an upper-income taxpayer) poor. Such poverty is easy to understand. Along with the possibility of empathy, the taxpayer recognizes that for this type of program he is a potential recipient himself. In contrast, it is apparently less easy for many persons to sympathize with those poor who are not blind, disabled, very old, or very young. Many persons today, as in the past, seem to feel that the poverty of this latter group is the result of undesirable characteristics within the control of the individuals. In a 1964 Gallup poll persons were asked, "In your opinion, which is more often to blame if a person is poor—lack of effort on his own part or circumstances beyond his control?" Among persons with an income of $10,000 and over, more blamed lack of effort than blamed circumstances. Among persons with incomes under $3,000, more cited circumstances as the cause of poverty than lack of effort. The nationwide findings for all respondents and for the subset of respondents with a definite opinion are shown here.[52]

All Respondents

Lack of effort	33%
Circumstances	29
Equal	32
No opinion	6

Subset of Respondents

Lack of effort	54%
Circumstances	46

Many persons, then, may feel that providing aid to this group promotes a "something for nothing" attitude and encourages a natural propensity to avoid work if a livelihood can be obtained without it. Moreover, the taxpayer may view himself as extremely unlikely ever to be made poor unless he becomes blind, disabled, or old. Hence a program extending benefits to those who are poor but who do not also have one of these other characteristics is not viewed as a source of potential benefit. In sum then, separation of persons into various categories to determine eligibility can be explained as a combination of selective sympathy and a desire for insurance on the part of taxpayers. Both Models 2 and 3 have applicability in explaining this feature of current welfare programs.

An alternative explanation for the categorical nature of welfare programs providing cash benefits is that existing recipients, having gained the payments they receive by exercising their political power, desire to exclude would-be entrants into their "industry" in order to maintain higher payment levels for themselves. If the separate groups eligible for benefits under OAA, AB, AFDC, and ATPD were highly organized coalitions of the minimal effective size, however, it is not clear why a sizable fraction of such groups do not claim the benefits for which they are eligible and for which they have ostensibly contributed time and resources to obtain.[53] That a sizable fraction of those eligible do not claim benefits to which they are legally entitled casts doubt on the coalition hypothesis. Although actual recipients may be better off under categorical programs, it does not seem likely that this feature of the existing welfare system is primarily a result of their organized political power.

The fact that some programs provide benefits in kind rather than in cash is an additional feature apparently damaging to the self-interest model as an explanation of welfare programs. As pointed out earlier, in-kind transfers are consistent with a model of redistribution in which taxpayers have the poor's consumption levels or particular commodities as an argument in their utility functions. Since recipients would be better off with cash—assuming that transfers of the same dollar magnitude are made—the existence of in-kind programs is in conflict with the type of program one would expect if the transfers were gained by recipients as a result of their political power. One possible difficulty with this inference is that producers of the goods made available to the poor also benefit; therefore, such programs may be the result of their political power. Both the first Food Stamp Plan, begun in the late thirties, and the one begun in 1964 attempt to augment total domestic food consumption by increasing the consumption of the poor. The purpose of the first of these programs, at least in part, was to raise the price of farm products. According to Samuel Herman, writing in 1940,

Since 1933, the United States Department of Agriculture has adopted as a major premise that for most foods the economic supply has exceeded the economic demand. The question on the threshold of administrative action has been: Do the farmers obtain "parity price" for their products? Farmers have not often obtained parity price since 1924. By concentric patterns of legislation, the New Deal has variously attempted to reduce the economic supply of food, and thus regressively to meet demand, or to raise the economic demand by progressively increasing consumer purchasing power, or both. The Food Stamp Plan was the first thoroughgoing attempt by the Department of Agriculture directly to increase effective economic demand for food among the underfed.[54]

The price-support objective was highlighted by the use of both orange and blue stamps. The required purchase of orange stamps, which could be exchanged for any type of food, was intended to equal the amount that persons receiving public assistance normally spent on food. The blue stamps, issued free and in a fixed proportion to orange stamps, were intended to stimulate additional consumption of certain food items that the Secretary of Agriculture found to be in "surplus." In a statement before the American Farm Federation Bureau in 1939, Milo Perkins, president of the Federal Surplus Commodities Corporation, noted:

> Nearly 20 million people are included in the total number of families which are now receiving some form of public aid. If the same percentage of persons took part in a national program as has been the case in experimental cities, the group of participating eligibles would include about 15 million individuals....On the basis of the foregoing assumptions, it is interesting to note that with current prices the Stamp Plan offers a potential annual market for about 294 million bushels of wheat in the form of flour, over 6 million bushels of corn in the form of corn meal, about 120 million pounds of rice, approximately 78 million pounds of prunes, 88 million pounds of raisins, and about 213 million pounds of dry beans."[55]

Thus, while the plan was viewed as aid to both underprivileged consumers and farmers, the benefit to the latter group seems to have been given predominant weight.

The second Food Stamp Plan, begun in 1964, also benefits farmers to the extent that food consumption is actually increased, but the absence of any attempt to stimulate consumption of "surplus" commodities suggests a shift in emphasis in the direction of placing more weight on benefits to recipients. Publicity about the extent of hunger and effects of malnutrition on children in the 1960's may well have aroused a latent utility interdependence. It is significant that the current Food Stamp Plan (along with the other nutrition programs and housing subsidies) makes low income the sole criterion for eligibility, possibly suggesting that when aid is given in a form taxpayers prefer their concern for the poor is less selective. Whether this inference is correct or not, strong evidence for the interdependence hypothesis is provided by the widespread support given to food stamps. In a Gallup Poll sampling opinion of a proposal by George McGovern to liberalize the current program,[56] the advocated change was supported by a two-to-one margin at all income levels.[57]

Evidence from Voting Behavior
and Opinion Polls

A second source of information useful in assessing how well the alternative models of redistribution explain existing welfare programs is the voting behavior of representatives and the expressed opinions of individuals provided by poll results. Since the welfare programs discussed above are not voted on in referenda, expression of preference is available only in opinion polls. However, local referenda have occurred on programs that provide disproportionate benefits to low-income persons, and voting results in such referenda provide useful information. Congressional voting on welfare programs is not considered here.[58]

The narrow self-interest model predicts that people will support programs that yield them direct net benefits (gross benefits less taxes) and oppose programs that do not. If direct net benefits can be calculated (and if people perceive the net benefits correctly), those supporting any program and those opposing it can be predicted. If information can then be gained about who actually supports the program and who opposes it, the narrow self-interest model can be tested. If no one supports a measure except those predicted to support it and if the opposition is composed of those predicted to oppose it, the theory is confirmed. If, on the other hand, the program gets substantial support from those who would be predicted to oppose it (in addition to those who the theory predicts will support it), the theory is called into question. In particular, if the support predicted for a proposal by the narrow self-interest model is not sufficient, given the voting rule for the proposal's adoption, the existence of the program cannot be explained exclusively in terms of that model (abstracting from log-rolling, which is not expected to be prevalent in referenda). This does not mean that the model is discredited; part of the support is surely explained in terms of it. What this does mean, however, is that for a more complete understanding of what has occurred additional considerations, such as those indicated in Models 2 or 3 above, must be a part of the explanation.

We begin by citing the evidence available from opinion polls. The widespread support given to food stamps has already been indicated. Other poll results indicate that popular criticism of existing welfare programs stems from the reports of fraud and laxity in applying eligibility criteria, rather than an opposition by the nonpoor to any program at all. This is suggested by a recent poll on attitudes toward welfare programs in which only 2 percent of the respondents rejected any form of welfare program, and only 4 percent mentioned the tax burden as an unfavorable aspect of welfare programs (although this was in response to an open-ended question).[59] In another poll the statement that "money spent on welfare programs is just wasted" was rejected by 65 percent and accepted by only 25 percent of the respondents.[60] And finally, in yet another poll, individuals were first asked whether they would favor a program that would guarantee enough work to families with employable wage earners so that a yearly income of $3,200 could be earned. For the nation, 79 percent favored this plan. By income class 80 percent of the respondents with incomes between $5,000 and $10,000 favor this; 76 was the percentage in favor for respondents with incomes exceeding $10,000. However, only 30 percent of the former group and 24 percent of the latter favored a minimum guaranteed annual income plan (negative income tax) that would assume an annual income of $3,200.[61] One surprising additional result is worth noting: Only 43 percent of those persons having an annual income of less than $3,000 favored the guaranteed income plan, as compared with 44 percent opposed to it. Apparently, even many persons who would be the potential recipients of the negative income tax have an aversion to transfers representing an outright gift.

In sum, expressions of preferences in opinion polls on welfare programs and proposals are not in complete accord with the narrow self-interest hypothesis. The number of supporters is too extensive, including many that would be predicted on self-interest grounds to oppose such redistribution. Also revealed are definite preferences about the nature of the welfare programs that is desired.

A second kind of evidence about preferences for vertical redistribution is provided by voting behavior in local referenda. When a referendum is held on a particular program, the self-interest hypothesis predicts that a person will vote for adoption if the monetary or service benefits perceived by the program exceed the costs he expects to bear.[62] Therefore, local programs that concentrate benefits on lower-income groups but either spread costs over all voters or focus them on middle- and upper-income groups would generate "yes" votes by the former individuals and "no" votes by the latter. If a different voting pattern emerges, say, with upper-income groups along with those with low incomes supporting the program, the narrow self-interest hypothesis is not confirmed. The "yes" vote by the upper-income group can be interpreted as an expression of preference for vertical redistribution as predicted by Model 3 or perhaps Model 2.

A study of voting behavior with the explicit purpose of testing the narrow self-interest model was undertaken by Wilson and Banfield. The results of this study indicate two criteria that are important in determining whether behavior will be consistent with the self-interest hypothesis. These are the income level of the voter and the ethnic group to which he belongs. With respect to income level, it was found that low-income groups almost invariably support all expenditure proposals:

> We have examined returns on thirty-five expenditure proposals passed upon in twenty separate elections in seven cities and have found no instance in which this group (the lowest income people) failed to give a majority in favor of a proposal. Frequently, the vote is 75-80 percent in favor; sometimes it is over 90 percent. The strength of voter support is about the same regardless of the character of the proposed expenditure."[63]

Most local public expenditures are financed by a property tax, and low-income groups own little or no property.[64] If we assume that these persons regard such expenditures as imposing no cost on themselves, the observed voting pattern of the low-income group confirms the self-interest hypothesis.[65]

Voting responses by homeowners and nonhomeowners yield further support of the hypothesis: The percentage "yes" votes in a suburb or ward were found to be inversely correlated with the percentage of voters who are homeowners. Furthermore, the percentage of middle- and low-income homeowners voting for a proposal was sensitive to the type of financing in the expected direction. The former group was more favorable if a state-wide sales tax was the financing method, as opposed to a property tax; for the latter group the opposite was true.[66]

In contrast to these results, which tend to confirm the income or wealth maximization hypothesis, are those found in comparing the behavior of high-income and middle-income homeowners. There tended to be positive correlation between median family income for a ward and the percentage of "yes" votes on various measures. Since (*a*) the taxes levied to pay for a proposed expenditure rise, theoretically at least, in proportion to the value of the property owned, (*b*) the value of property owned is positively correlated with income, and (*c*) the direct benefits for most of the expenditure proposals do not rise in proportion to income level,[67] the self-interest hypothesis would predict a result the reverse of that actually found.

The other variable having a significiant influence on voting behavior was ethnic groups. When other variables (median income, percentage of home ownership) were held constant, a negative relation was found between the percentage of voters who are of foreign stock (Polish, Irish, and Italian) and the percentage of "yes" votes. The Negro, Anglo-Saxon, and Jew, to put the result in another way, tended to be more favorable to expenditure proposals than the individual of foreign stock, with economic position held constant.

In attempting to explain the inconsistency of voting behavior with the self-interest hypothesis and the ethnic influences on the vote, Wilson and Banfield reject the notion that individual voters act irrationally by not calculating benefits and costs or make erroneous calculations and that irrationality is a function of ethnic status.[68] They argue rather that voters in certain income and ethnic groups are more concerned with the welfare of others and, in particular, community welfare, than are other groups. Furthermore, it is not income level *per se* that determines how "public-regarding" a voter is but rather the ethnic and cultural attitudes empirically associated with a given income level. But since ethnic groups and income groups overlap (for example, upper-income voters tend disproportionately to be Jews and Anglo-Saxons), the ethnic and income influences are hard to separate. An attempt was made to do this, however, and it was found that at low-income levels, ethnic influence mattered very little but it made a conspicuous difference at higher income levels.

III. CONCLUSION

In this paper three different models have been considered to account for income redistribution and it has been argued that the vertical and equalizing transfers carried out through public-welfare programs are not explained exclusively or even largely by the political demand of recipients. Such programs have characteristics that the nonpoor want them to have, and the nonpoor give verbal support to the programs. Evidence from voting behavior, although not entirely free from ambiguity, also reveals a redistributive preference. The precise nature of this preference, however, is too complex to be represented by simply putting the income levels of the poor (or their consumption levels of particular goods) in the utility functions of those who have larger incomes. Preferences toward redistribution appear to be heavily influenced by the Puritan ethic of individual responsibility and the moral virtues of work and industry. This heritage of ideas serves in part to explain the distinction between the "deserving" and "undeserving" poor and the stigma associated with welfare payments (as well as the lack of any stigma associated with redistribution achieved by special government favors to particular industries).

The relative importance of interdependence preferences and the insurance motive in explaining the preference of the nonpoor for welfare programs is uncertain. The existence of a welfare program does offer some degree of security against having one's income fall below a minimum amount, provided that other eligibility requirements are also met. Whether a given nonpoor person receives sufficient benefits from this reduction in risk to make it rational for him to support welfare programs on these grounds alone depends on his distaste for risk, the probability that he will ever be eligible for the program's benefits, and his estimate of his share of the tax cost of the program. This broader kind of self-interest may be sufficient to account for the programs that exist. Yet for many upper-income persons the insurance provided by current welfare programs is probably a bad bargain, and the support given must be the result of utility interdependence of some kind. This conclusion is reinforced by the fact that receiving welfare payments is not a right to which a person is legally entitled, as are social security benefits. The barriers erected to prevent the "undeserving" poor from getting welfare and to prevent cheating serve also to prevent the system from serving as a source of potential benefit to the currently nonpoor. Hence the insurance benefits of a welfare program may be negligible in reality or at least viewed as such by the nonpoor who would find it very distasteful to suffer the stigma of being "on welfare."

NOTES

[1]See Anthony Downs, *An Economic Theory of Democracy* (New York: Harper and Row, 1957).

[2]G. J. Stigler, "Director's Law of Public Income Redistribution," *Journal of Law and Economics* (April, 1970), pp. 1-11.

[3]W. Breit, "Income Redistribution and Efficiency Norms," Paper 1 in this book.

[4]J. R. Davis, "On the Incidence of Income Redistribution," *Public Choice* (Spring, 1971), pp. 63-74.

[5]G. Tullock, "The Charity of the Uncharitable," *Western Economic Journal* (December, 1971), pp. 379-92.

[6]These data are taken from *The President's Commission on Income Maintenance: Background Papers* (Washington, D.C., 1970), pp. 131-34.

[7]Downs, *An Economic Theory of Democracy*, pp. 200-1.

[8]These two variables are interdependent. Disincentive effects may work to reduce investment, not only causing everyone's income to grow at a slower rate than in the absence of such effects, but also changing the rate of growth in incomes of different groups.

[9]See Stigler, "Director's Law of Public Income Redistribution,"

[10]There are only three public assistance programs, making up together about one-fourth of federal expenditures for public assistance, that have need, i.e., low income, as the exclusive criterion for eligibility. These are food stamps, other nutrition pro-

grams, and housing subsidies. A fourth program of aid to needy students other than veterans also makes need the only basis for eligibility. All other income support programs either have other elibility requirements in addition to need (e.g., previous employment) or they base eligibility on other requirements exclusively (e.g., the farm program). See Charles L. Schultze et al., *Setting National Priorities: The 1973 Budget* (Washington, D.C.: Brookings Institution, 1972), pp. 176, 196.

[11]Gordon Tullock, "Problems of Majority Voting," *Journal of Political Economy* (December, 1959), pp. 571-79.

[12]J. M. Buchanan and G. Tullock, *The Calculus of Consent* (Ann Arbor: University of Michigan, 1962).

[13]Individual wealth is probably an important variable, since, as Downs has emphasized, wealth gives one a bargaining advantage.

[14]G. J. Stigler, "The Theory of Economic Regulation," *The Bell Journal of Economic and Management Science* (Spring, 1971), pp. 3-21.

[15]For the development of the theory of groups employed here, see Mancur Olson, *The Logic of Collective Action* (Cambridge: Harvard University Press, 1965), especially ch. 6.

[16]Stigler, "The Theory of Economic Regulation."

[17]*Statistical Abstract of the United States* (Washington, 1971), pp. 450, 452.

[18]See M. Friedman and L. J. Savage, "The Utility Analysis of Choices Involving Risk," *Journal of Political Economy* (August, 1948), pp. 279-304. See also I. Erlich and G. S. Becker, "Market Insurance, Self-insurance, and Self-protection," *Journal of Political Economy* (July-August, 1972), pp. 623-48.

[19]See "Risk Spreading and Distribution," by Richard Zeckhauser, Paper 8 in this book.

[20]K. J. Arrow, "Uncertainty and the Welfare Economics of Medical Care," *American Economic Review* (December, 1963), pp. 947-48.

[21]M. Pauly and T. D. Willett, "Two Concepts of Vertical Equity and Their Implications for Public Policy," *Social Science Quarterly* (June, 1972), p. 12.

[22]J. M. Buchanan and G. Tullock, *The Calculus of Consent* (Ann Arbor: sity of Michigan, 1962), p. 193.

[23]See also "Intertemporal Redistribution through the Tax Structure," by A. Mitchell Polinsky, Paper 9 in this book.

[24]See M. Pauly, "The Economics of Moral Hazard: Comment," *American Economic Review* (June, 1967), pp. 531-37.

[25]Arrow, "Uncertainty and the Welfare Economics of Medical Care."

[26]*Ibid.*

[27]For example, if the government sold fire insurance, it could refuse to pay benefits to homeowners who were found to have put pennies in fuse boxes. This restriction is also applicable to private insurance firms.

[28]See, for example, G. S. Becker, "A Theory of Social Interactions," mimeographed, September, 1969. Also H. M. Hochman and J. D. Rodgers, "Pareto Optimal Redistribution," *American Economic Review* (September, 1969), pp. 542-57; E. O. Olsen, "A Normative Theory of Transfers," *Public Choice* (Spring, 1969), pp. 39-58; and R. Zeckhauser, "Optimal Mechanisms for Income Transfers," *American Economic Review* (June, 1971), pp. 324-34.

[29]For a rigorous definition of marginal relevance and of other externality concepts, see J. M. Buchanan and W. C. Stubblebine, "Externality," *Economica* (November,

202 James D. Rodgers

1962), pp. 371-84. These external effects, which might appropriately be called "distributional externalities," include a much wider range of nonmarket interactions than altruistic feelings of the nonpoor for the poor. This point requires emphasis because Breit, the author of Paper 1 of this book, seems to equate interdependent preferences exclusively with benevolence, while talking about other types of nonmarket interactions (represented, for example, by the situation where a measure of distributional inequality enters preference functions) as being consistent with independent preferences, which it is not.

[30]A distinction between the total amount of his gifts and the number of gifts might also be made.

[31]If making voluntary transfers become more prevalent, the utility E derived from engaging in the activity himself may actually fall. Transfers may be subject to "snob" appeal. See H. Leibenstein, "Bandwagon, Snob, and Veblen Effects in the Theory of Consumers' Demand," *Quarterly Journal of Economics* (May, 1950), pp. 183-207.

[32]If a "snob effect" were present, givers might desire government intervention in the charity market to reduce the amount of contributions. Instead of special tax advantages for charity, there might be pressure for tax penalties.

[33]See H. M. Hochman and J. D. Rodgers, "Pareto Optimal Redistribution," *American Economic Review* (September, 1969), pp. 542-57.

[34]With no transactions costs this price would equal unity.

[35]A third proposition that holds under any assumption about income elasticities is that a change making the initial distribution more nearly equal, holding total income $(Y_a + Y_e)$ constant, decreases the size of E's desired transfer.

[36]Note that any position satisfying

$$\sum_{i=1}^{N} (\partial U_i / \partial U_a)/(\partial U_i / \partial Y_i) \leq 1$$

is a Pareto-optimal point. See J. D. Rodgers, "Distributional Externalities and the Optimal Form of Income Transfers," *Public Finance Quarterly* (July, 1973), pp. 266-99.

[37]Ignored here are other circumstances such as family size that E would probably also desire to have taken into account.

[38]G. M. Von Furstenberg and D. C. Mueller, "The Pareto Optimal Approach to Redistribution: A Fiscal Application," *American Economic Review* (September, 1971), pp. 628-37.

[39]J. M. Buchanan, "What kind of Redistribution Do We Want?" *Economica* (May, 1968), p. 189.

[40]See M. Pauly, "Efficiency in the Provision of Consumption Subsidies," *Kyklos* (March, 1970), pp. 33-57; J. D. Rodgers, "Distributional Externalities and the Optimal Form of Income Transfers," *Public Finance Quarterly* (July, 1973), pp. 266-99; and G. Daly and F. Giertz, "Welfare Economics and Welfare Reform," *American Economic Review* (March, 1972), pp. 131-138.

[41]G. Peterson, "Welfare, Workfare, and Pareto Optimality," *Public Finance Quarterly* (July, 1973), pp. 323-38; J. D. Rodgers, "Distributional Externalities and the Optimal Form of Income Transfers"; and R. Zeckhauser, "Optimal Mechanisms for Income Transfers," *American Economic Review* (June, 1971), pp. 324-34.

[42]Lyndon B. Johnson, "*Message on Poverty*," March 16, 1964, in R. E. Will and H. G. Vatter, eds., *Poverty in Affluence* (New York: Harcourt Brace, 1965).

[43]Treating various activities or goods as inputs rather than as ultimate outputs has been suggested in a somewhat different context by G. S. Becker, in "A Theory of the Allocation of Time," *Economic Journal* (September, 1965), pp. 493-517, and by K. Lancaster, in "A New Approach to Consumer Theory," *Journal of Political Economy* (April, 1966), pp. 132-57.

[44]Several studies bear out the relationship between poverty and crime, although it is unclear what type of causal relationships exists. The slum areas of large cities show disproportionate amounts of juvenile delinquency. Yet, if low-income people were scattered uniformly over space rather than being highly concentrated in a single area, the crime rate might fall by much more than it would if everyone in a slum area were made eligible for a generous welfare grant. The empirical evidence simply suggests that low-rent, low-income areas have more crime per capita than other areas. See C. R. Shaw and H. D. McKay, *Juvenile Delinquency and Urban Areas* (Chicago: University of Chicago Press), p. 57. See also *Report of the Atlanta Commission on Crime and Juvenile Delinquency* (Atlanta, 1966), p. 24.

[45]Earl Rolph has argued that since productivity is a function of current and past consumption, being low for the poor and high for the nonpoor, the state should "redistribute as long as the value productivity of some people can be increased without reducing the value productivity of others." (See E. Rolph, "Controversy Surrounding Negative Income Taxation," *Public Finance and Social Security,* Travaux de l'Institut International de Finances Publiques, Congres de Turin, XXIVe Session (September, 1968), pp. 252-261). This is similar to the possibility noted by Graaff (J. de V. Graaff, *Theoretical Welfare Economics* [New York: Cambridge University Press, 1957]) that the community's production possibility depends to some extent on the distribution of income: "If workers are underfed, a redistribution of wealth in their favor may so increase efficiency that everybody benefits." However, this would require that the increase in productivity be sufficiently large to allow output to rise by more than the amount of the transfer. The conditions under which this would be the case may be rare. Moreover, the benefits of the transfer might remain with the recipient if some explicit action were not taken to recoup the taxpayers' "investment." In the absence of such remuneration agreements (i.e., loans), the taxpayers would not support transfers justified on "productivity" grounds unless they were concerned with the recipient's welfare or with reducing externalities of poverty.

[46]H. Aaron and M. C. McGuire, "Public Goods and Income Distribution," *Econometrica* (November, 1970), p. 907.

[47]W. Irwin Gillespie, "Effect of Public Expenditures in the Distribution of Income," in R. A. Musgrave, ed., *Essays in Fiscal Federalism* (Washington, D.C.: Brookings Institution, 1965).

[48]The English Poor Law is discussed in Karl De Schweintz, *England's Road to Social Security* (New York: A. S. Barnes, 1943), chs. III and IV. The operation of the poor laws in America prior to 1870 is discussed in W. Friedlander, *Introduction to Social Welfare* (Englewood Cliffs, N.J.: Prentice-Hall, 1955).

[49]In some American communities during the nineteenth century the relief recipient was required to publicize his status by wearing a pauper's badge, a letter "P" on the right shoulder. See A. P. Miles, *An Introduction to Public Welfare* (Boston: Heath, 1949), ch. IV.

[50]Public Law 90-248, Section 402(a) (19) (F), January 2, 1968.

[51]As of 1968, the number of states having residency requirements for OAA, AB,

AFDC, and APTD is, respectively, 42, 38, 39, and 40. Relative support is required in 40 states. See *President's Commission on Income Maintenance: Background Papers* (Washington, 1970), p. 241.

[52]These poll results were reported in R. E. Will and H. G. Vatter, eds., *Poverty in Affluence* (New York: Harcourt Brace, 1965), pp. 69-70.

[53]In New York City, for example, it has been estimated that the ratio of actual recipients of public assistance (excluding OAA) to the number of eligibles seldom exceeds 60 percent. See D. M. Gordon, "Income and Welfare in New York City," *The Public Interest* (Summer, 1969), pp. 64-88.

[54]S. Herman, "The Food Stamp Plan: A Study in Law and Economics," *Journal of Business* (October, 1940), pp. 331-32.

[55]The statement by Milo Perkins was cited by S. Herman on pages 337-38 of his study (see footnote 54 above).

[56]McGovern's proposal was to provide free food stamps to families with incomes below $20 a week and at greatly reduced cost to families with incomes between $20 and $60 a week.

[57]*New York Times*, April 20, 1969, p. 20.

[58]See Otto A. Davis and John E. Jackson, "Representative Assemblies and Demands for Redistribution," Paper 10 of this book.

[59]These results were, reported in W. Bateman and J. Allen, "Income Maintenance: Who Gains and Who Pays," Sar A. Levitas, ed., *Blue-Collar Workers: A Symposium on Middle America* (New York: McGraw-Hill, 1971). They were taken from W. E. Bicker, *Public Attitudes and Opinions of the Current Welfare System and Major Components of the Proposed Family Assistance Plan*, unpublished findings of a study undertaken for the Department of Health, Education, and Welfare, University of California, Berkley, July, 1970.

[60]*The Philadelphia Inquirer*, January 27, 1969, pp. 1 and 3.

[61]*New York Times*, January 25, 1969, p. 47.

[62]W. B. Neenan, *Political Economy of Urban Areas* (Chicago: Markham, 1972). Neenan has correctly emphasized the point that *perceived*, not necessarily actual, costs and benefits control behavior. But strictly speaking, testing requires either that perceived values equal known actual values or that information is available on what people's perceptions are. Otherwise, refutation becomes impossible.

[63]See J. Q. Wilson and E. C. Banfield, "Public-Regardingness as a Value Premise in Voting Behavior," *American Political Science Review* (December, 1964), pp. 876-87. Quotation on p. 876.

[64]The authors (Wilson and Barfield), present no correlation measures of property ownership and income for the wards of cities analyzed, although they determine the percentage of voters owning homes.

[65]The poor are assumed to reason in a very simple-minded manner: "If I own no property, I pay no property tax." Wilson and Banfield present no evidence that the poor actually reason this way. If past experience has indicated that new expenditures financed by the property-tax rate increases usually result in a subsequent rise in rents, the poor are unlikely to view their tax cost as zero.

[66]Again it should be noted, however, that Wilson and Banfield present no verification of the tax incidence views being attributed to voters.

[67]The proposals voted upon included a zoo, a county hospital, a welfare levy, public parks, a veteran's bonus, sewers, a courthouse, and urban renewal bonds. Rather

than there being any reason to expect direct benefits from such programs to increase in proportion to income, one might well expect an incidence of benefits inversely related to income. A county hospital providing free medical service would be expected to have a regressive benefit pattern. Higher opportunity cost of time might also produce a regression benefit pattern for parks and zoos, since these forms of recreation are relatively time intensive.

[68]Wilson and Barnfield argue convincingly that this observed relation is not explained by a falling marginal utility of income that would tend to reduce the utility loss resulting from tax payments of high- relative to middle-income groups. Even if the marginal dollar is worth relatively less to the wealthy, support for expenditures providing trivial direct benefits is not explained. Furthermore, low marginal utility of income cannot explain different responses to different proposals. Moreover, the hypothesis itself may be disputed for the income range considered.

8

Risk Spreading and Distribution

————◆●◆————

RICHARD ZECKHAUSER

The plight of retarded children—twice stinted, first by nature's lottery and again by society's stinginess in providing them resources—well represents the unfortunate outcome that results when a risk cannot be adequately spread. The magnitude of this risk dwarfs those we economists traditionally consider; and our theoretical constructs, such as contingent claims markets, risky assets, and so on, hardly seem to capture the major elements of the situation. Why this example by way of introduction? First, it dramatizes the asymmetry in individuals' *ex post* positions in contexts where risks are spread minimally or not at all. And, second, it shows clearly the narrow bias of economists' traditional investigations into worlds of uncertainty.[1]

This analysis attempts to expand the scope of such investigations by looking at a more general theory of risk pooling, and by directing particular attention to the implications of that theory for the distribution of income. Despite the potential of risk spreading to (1) improve planning, (2) reduce the anxiety caused by persistent uncertainty, and (3) redistribute income in a more egalitarian way—three positive aspects discussed in the first half of this paper—markets to spread risks have had rather limited success. The reasons for their failure are the concern of the second half of the following discussion.

Richard Zeckhauser is Professor of Political Economy at the Kennedy School of Public Affairs, Harvard University. He is indebted to Carole Edelstein, George Peterson, Howard Raiffa, and Thomas Schelling for helpful comments.

I. THE MARKET EFFICIENT OUTCOME
IN AN UNCERTAIN WORLD

What could be achieved in an ideal world where appropriate markets could be established for the spreading of risk? Arrow and others have shown, assuming risk aversion on the part of all individuals, that "any optimal allocation of risk-bearing can be realized by a system of perfectly competitive markets in claims on commodities."[2] The required markets yield allocations of goods to individuals that are contingent upon the state of the world; hence their name, contingent claims markets.

The achievement of risk spreading markets is most easily seen in a one-good world. An individual will receive a random amount of manna, *m*. Say he will receive either 50 or 150 units, each with one half probability, and that his utility function is log(m). Then he would pay up to 13.4 units of manna to participate in an actuarially fair market for contingent claims: a for-sure consumption of 86.6 units of manna yields him the same expected utility as his present 100-unit-expectation lottery on manna.

II. THE TWINNING OF TIME AND UNCERTAINTY

Economists' uncertainty models, for the most part, deal with situations in which all lotteries are resolved immediately. In the real world, presently uncertain situations may not be decided for years. This elapsing of time until full resolution introduces a new richness into the analytic structure of risk-spreading situations. It allows consumption and saving to be planned and also affects the level of anxiety experienced during the wait for resolution. The concept of elapsing time has a substantial impact as well on the distributional accomplishments of markets that spread risks, as will be discussed later.

A. Risk Spreading To Improve Planning

Extend the earlier example to allow the individual two periods in which to comsume. His first period manna supply is known to be 100. For the second period he faces the lottery mentioned above. He wishes to decide how much to save to maximize the expected sum of his utilities over the two periods.[3] His problem is to find the

$$\underset{s}{\text{MAX}}[\log{(100 - s)} + .5 \log(50 + s) + .5 \log(150 + s)]$$

It is optimal for him to save 11.24. His expected utility is the same that he would receive if he had a certainty income of 93.92 in each period.

If the individual can learn how much manna he is going to receive in the second period, his situation improves. He would then save 25 if his received income were to be low and −25 if it were to be high. The expected utility he would then receive would be equivalent to what he would get with an income of 96.82 in each period. The gain results because he can make present allocations with certainty information about his future allocations. After the fact, his decisions will always turn out to have been ideal ones.[4]

In the best of all possible (actuarially fair) worlds, one which would enable the individual to trade on a contingent claims market, his expected utility rises to match an income of 100 in both periods. Here, it would be possible to trade away 50 should his second period income be high in return for 50 should it be low.[5] Thus, he need not know what his second period income will be, nor will he care.

B. Risk Spreading to Reduce Anxiety

The resolution of uncertainty may provide a reduction in anxiety, a type of gain that fits poorly in the economist's conventional expected utility framework that relies on immediate resolution of uncertainty. (Psychiatrists' models are well structured to deal with anxiety reduction. Naturally, they devote substantial efforts in this direction.) What is needed is an analytic framework that explicitly recognizes the timing and sequencing of decisions, that gives individuals time to be concerned about the nonresolution of future lotteries.

One solution would permit anxiety, *a*, to enter as a separate argument of the utility function. Assume that a lottery is to be resolved at the end of one period, with eventual payoffs x_1 and x_2. The individual's expected utility for the lottery is

$$p_1 U(a,x_1) + p_2 U(a,x_2)$$

where it is understood that a is a function of x_1, x_2, p_1, and p_2, and the time, t, until resolution of the lottery.

In general format,

$$a = f(X,P,t)$$

where $X = (x_1, x_2, \ldots, x_n)$ and $P = (p_1, p_2, \ldots, p_n)$. The case where anxiety does not exist is a special one where for all lotteries a receives some constant value.[6]

Some analysts claim rational individuals should not be concerned with anxiety.[7] A hypothetical medical example effectively rebuts this claim. An inoperable cyst has been diagnosed and the patient told that the probability is 0.98 that it is benign, in which case his life will proceed as normal. If it is malignant, he will die suddenly at the end of one year. For $500, he can commission a diagnostic test that will reveal the outcome of the lottery he faces. Should he buy it?[8]

If your answer for him is yes, you might consider a second question. How does willingness to pay for the diagnostic test vary with the probability of the malignant outcome? For many people, the relationship between the two is far from proportional. If the probability of malignancy was 0.98, isn't it possible that one would not only choose ignorance, but pay for that choice?

This series of observations provides some insights into some classical debates about decision theory. In particular, it calls into question the axiom that lotteries can be substituted for their equivalents in any compound lottery.[9] In traditional decision theory, you should be willing to spend no sum at all to remove the uncertainty of your medical condition, for the probability that you will pass the diagnostic test (98 percent) is just the same as the probability that the cyst is benign.

Our common-sense notion of anxiety deals with the fear that outcomes may be bad and the relief that ensues when we are assured they will not. There is no salient probability cutoff point, but it would seem for the most part that anxiety relates to situations where the probabilities of these unfortunate outcomes are low, say less that 0.25. Much of course will have to do with the familiarity of the bad outcome and to the individual's accustomed method of dealing with it. This will be reflected in the x's being multi-dimensional vectors, not merely single values.

If the probabilities of the bad outcomes were very large, our mind set would change. We would be rooting instead for the unlikely favorable outcomes. If people will pay some positive amount to eliminate their need to live some period without knowing whether some small probability bad outcome will occur, what will happen when the small probability event is favorable? It might very well turn out that individuals would pay not to have the outcome of the lottery known. They might like to be able to keep their hopes up during the intervening time period. We might refer to this positive pleasure as value in anticipation. Our previous formula for anxiety generalizes. The hypothesis just set forth is that nondetermination of the lottery outcome offers a positive contribution to utility when the low-probability event is a strongly positive outcome and a negative contribution when the low probability event is severely unfavorable.

The existence of positively valued anticipation would explain the existence of individuals who simultaneously insure themselves yet gamble.[10] It is possible to distinguish between this hypothesis and the traditional one of a two-humped utility curve. If individuals will take actuarially unfair gambles when the odds are long, but not when they are short, the anticipation hypothesis garners support.

I shall illustrate with just two examples. A lottery is identified by its subscript and its time argument. An individual's preference ordering $L_A(0) > L_B(0)$ states that he prefers lottery A to lottery B if the chosen lottery is to be resolved immediately. Yet this same individual might select $L_B(1)$ over $L_A(1)$. This could occur, for example, if L_A offered a small probability of a very bad outcome, a possible source of anxiety, and a factor that would reduce his utility during the period before the lottery was resolved.

Matters get more interesting when we consider substitution possibilities. The individual might find the compound lottery $L_C(1)$ which offers a 50-50 chance at $L_A(0)$ or $L_B(0)$ less attractive than $L_D(1)$ which offers a 50-50 chance at $L_B(0)$ or $L_B(0)$ (that is $L_B(0)$ for sure), this despite the fact that C has substituted the preferred $L_A(0)$ for an $L_B(0)$ in D. The reason is that $L_C(1)$ has lottery A as one of its components, and the possibiliby of the future bad outcome is a source of anxiety. (This reversal of preferences is more evident if another $L_A(0)$ is substituted for the final $L_B(0)$ in lottery C, for this new comparison is in effect between $L_A(1)$ and $L_B(1)$.) At first glance, this may appear to violate the substitutability axiom of rational choice, although it does not. That axiomatic system was developed for situations where lotteries receive immediate resolution, and "until resolution" feelings such as anxiety and anticipation play no role.

One significant aspect of the presence of anxiety is that it creates an area where risk spreading can play a useful yet inexpensive role. Through appropriate spreading of risk we can reduce or eliminate anxiety, and that may be a very useful thing to do.

C. Risk Spreading to Redistribute Postlottery Income

In addition to its achievements in improving planning and reducing anxiety, risk spreading has the potential to improve the postlottery income distribution. No exogenous social-welfare function need be invoked to make this judgment of improvement. It relies rather on a contractual notion, where each party to the risk-spreading pool is guided by his own expected welfare.

To take the most extreme case, consider a situation in which all risk spreading had been instituted at the first possible instant. It is profitable here to employ a construct developed by John Rawls, the notion of an original position.[11] It is understood as a purely hypothetical situation that is characterized to lead to a certain conception of justice. Among the essential features of this situation is that none of the contracting parties knows his place in society, his class position or social status, nor his fortune in the distribution of natural assets and abilities, his intelligence, strength, and the like. It even assumes that the parties do not know their conceptions of the good or their special psychological propensities. The principles of justice are chosen behind a "veil of ignorance." This ensures that no one is advantaged or disadvantaged in the choice of principles by the outcome of natural chance or the contingency of social circumstances. Since all are similarly situated and no one is able to design principles to favor his particular condition, the principles of justice are the result of a fair agreement or bargain.

In the original position individuals can get around to some real risk spreading. Since nothing has been determined in advance, strictly egalitarian, actuarially fair contracts will emerge.

III.   A MANNA MODEL

The simplest contractual uncertainty model offers each individual an uncertain endowment in the desired good, manna, m. Each individual is confronted by the same probability density function, $f(m)$. His concave utility function for m, $u(m)$, displays the traditional properties of risk aversion. The individuals have an incentive to establish a redistributional arrangement. Whatever endowment an individual has received, he will give or take from some central pool the difference between his endowment and the average endowment of all the individuals.[12] The desirability of this action is expressed by the inequality

$$\int_0^\infty u(m)f(m) \; dm < u(\bar{m})$$

On an *ex ante* basis everyone gains by agreeing to redistribute at some future time after the lottery has run. The outcome is completely egalitarian.[13]

IV.   THE FAILURE OF RISK SPREADING TO ACHIEVE AN EGALITARIAN OUTCOME

What is significant about this manna model is that it produces an extraordinary amount of redistribution, solely by working through trades on free markets. Why do we not observe this outcome in the real world? The remainder of this paper attempts to confront reality by answering this question. First we will explore the major difficulties encountered in the establishment of markets to spread risks. Then, we will consider the most attractive outcomes available in the second-best world where these difficulties pertain.

A. Why Markets That Spread Risks Completely Cannot Be Established

There is a variety of explanations for the rather limited success of markets to spread risks. (1) Certain goods such as intelligence and health are not redistributable. (2) Under the best of circumstances, contingent claims markets are difficult to establish and run. (3) Risk-spreading contracts are drawn up after some lotteries have been conducted. (4) It may be difficult or impossible to monitor the information required for the efficient functioning of a contingent claims market. Each of these factors alone would be sufficient to prevent the emergence of a completely egalitarian world. Together, they create a situation that is decidedly unequal.

1. Goods That Cannot Be Redistributed. The nonredistributable goods problem is the one confronted at the beginning of this paper. There is no way we can give retarded children, say, 30 extra IQ points in return for one from each of 30 average-IQ individuals. Given our inability to carry out this redistribution, it is natural to ask whether redistribution of some other good could be used to compensate. It may be that no amount of money and the goods and care it would purchase could bring a retarded individual to the average level of welfare in the society. Even if it could, there is the question whether skewing the money distribution in this way is what would be contractually agreed upon in, say, the original position.

This problem can be formalized a bit in terms of the contractual manna model. Extend the lottery to include the individual's health in addition to his manna receipts. Although only manna can be redistributed, the risk-spreading policy will also wish to observe health. The form of the market contract will be a transfer function $g(x_1, x_2)$, where x_1 is manna endowment, x_2 is health, and the amount of manna determined by the function is the transfer that an individual with a particular health and manna status receives. The constraint on manna transfers is that they sum to 0, that

$$\int_0^\infty \int_0^\infty g(x_1,x_2) f(x_1,x_2) \, dx_1 dx_2 = 0$$

The objective would be to find the $g(x_1,x_2)$ function meeting this constraint that maximizes the individual's expected utility.

$$\int_0^\infty \int_0^\infty u(x_1 + g(x_1,x_2); x_2) f(x_1,x_2) \, dx_1 dx_2$$

Although the manna payment depends upon health in this instance, the optimal $g(x_1,x_2)$ function will preserve a property of the outcomes achieved in a manna-only world. The marginal utility of manna will be the same in all ex post positons. However, it need not be the case that after the lotteries are run and the payoffs are made all individuals reach equally desirable outcomes.

In the special case where the utility function is separable in manna and health, the optimal function will lead individuals to have the same after-redistribution manna totals.[14] The result will be that people who are unfortunate enough to receive poor health in the lottery will end up with a total utility substantially below that of individuals who are blessed with health.

Depending on the signs and magnitudes of the various derivatives and cross derivatives, all outcomes are possible. Individuals who would have been worst off in the absence of a policy may come off best after redistribution. Alternatively, the policy could work to aggravate inequalities. To see this consider a situation in which only health is variable, $(f(x_1,x_2) = 0$ for $x_1 \neq C)$. It might turn out that individuals in better health have a higher utility for manna, that u_{12} is positive. Then the policy would be what Arrow has labeled output regressive.[15] The optimal policy is output regressive if and only if the following condition holds: when initially expenditures have been so adjusted to ability that all individuals have the same utility, then the cost of achieving a given increment of utility is less for individuals of higher ability. Risk spreading to maximize expected utility could produce a less equal distribution.

2. Why Contingent Claims Markets Are Difficult To Establish. Even for those goods that are redistributable, there will be great difficulty creating the contingent claims markets on which they can be traded. (*a*) The quantities of commodities that change hands depend on the uncertain state of the world that occurs at some future date. In essence, this adds a new attribute to the descriptions of goods being traded on the market. (*b*) Trades must be recorded in advance, to be consummated at some future date. (*c*) Traders' preferences must be defined in advance so that trades contingent on future outcomes can be arranged. (*d*) Preferences must be specified under a large range of circumstances, the vast majority of which will never occur. (*e*) Procedures must be developed so that individuals can specify relative intensities of preferences under different (perhaps mutually exclusive) circumstances. (*f*) Monitoring procedures must be developed that will allow the market mechanism to determine which outcomes occur, so that agreed-upon trades can be implemented.

This is just a suggestive half dozen. The major point is obvious: contingent claims markets are most difficult to establish, and when established work most imperfectly.

3. Risk-Spreading Contracts Are Drawn Up After Some Lotteries Are Run. If we recall that the original position comes well before birth, for a contractor knows neither his potential parents nor indeed his country of residence, it is clear that real world risk spreading starts well after individuals have departed from their positions of full equality. In essence, some lotteries have already been conducted. Neither is birth the appropriate starting point. In most societies individuals are not allowed to contract with one another until they reach some age of majority. By that time most of the most significant lotteries have already been resolved. In some instances, the total society will enforce a lottery, with parents contracting for their children. But even here, only a limited amount of equality can be achieved through any contractual system. In virtually every social system there is a high degree of correlation between the success of parents and that of their children. Parents cannot be counted upon to lay their children's welfares in the hands of some giant lottery. To sum up in simple terms, when we get to the contingent claims market, we find that individuals face very different lotteries. Those blessed in this regard, assuming that they are many, will have no incentive to contract with the cursed.

This relationship can be formalized just a bit. Start by considering cases where information monitoring is perfect on the outcomes of lotteries conducted to date. This eliminates the problems of adverse selection and adverse incentives we shall get to later, and allows for the possibility of actuarially fair markets. If individuals deal on these markets, then the sooner risks are spread, the greater will be the degree of equality in the postlottery, postmarket outcome. Once the time of contracting arrives, all participating individuals are guaranteed the mean of the lottery that they face at present. However, there is no way to recover the variability that has already crept in to be reflected by the disparity among individuals' present means.[16]

Consider, for example, what would happen if contingent claims markets were set up in the earned income field. Lawyers would contract with other lawyers, or perhaps with business executives. Day laborers would surely wish to join these groups, but they would not be welcomed. The difficulty is the one cited earlier. We are too far along in the process of resolving lotteries. We know too much about our position.

This even applies as far as making policy for children and future generations. For genetic and environmental reasons, the exact balance of the two being a matter of great current debate, there are substantial correlations between the incomes and earning abilities of successive members of the same family. The rich man knows his son is likely to be rich, and conversely for the man in poverty. The variance in outcomes is decreased through various risk-spreading policies, but the decrease is still insubstantial in relation to the "between class" variance. The rich man might prefer no contingent claims market at all to one that maximized expected utility for a randomly selected son.

One might wish to ask the question what would happen to the structure of our society if the between-generation correlation in earning ability were very low, if rich men did not know whether sons would be "more likely to succeed." There is at least strong *a priori* reason to believe that redistribution would increase substantially. It would increase even more if we could somehow make the rich man confront the lottery as well, say, for the second half of his life.

One can almost look at the resolution of uncertainty as a process of entropy. Over time things run down, in the sense that from indi-

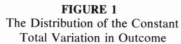

FIGURE 1
The Distribution of the Constant
Total Variation in Outcome

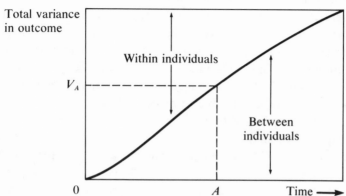

viduals' standpoints there is less future variability to be expected. If actuarially fair risk spreading is invoked at time A the terminal variance after lotteries are run and contracts satisfied will be V_A. Individuals' means, of course, are receiving ever-increasing dispersal. The graph makes this clear.

4. *Information Monitoring Difficulties and Imperfect Risk Spreading.* We have talked about the difficulties that arise because contracts cannot be drawn until a number of lotteries have been conducted and the results become known. A related set of problems arises because it is not always possible for the manager of the market to acquire all the information known to individuals at present. If we follow the contingent claims market terminology, the difficulty is that we cannot observe directly a full description of the state of the world. A number of nasty problems come to the fore. They can most easily be understood in the context of traditional insurance models, where they travel under the titles adverse selection and adverse incentives.

a. *Adverse Selection and Risk Spreading.* Adverse selection occurs because the insurance scheme may be unable to distinguish among different individuals who face different lotteries. Quite naturally, those who will benefit most significantly from any risk-spreading policy will become joiners. To put the difficulty in an analytic context, the lottery faced by an individual might be represented as $f(x,\gamma)$, where γ is a parameter known to the individual but not the insurance scheme.[17]

There are two ways to confront the problem of adverse selection. The first is to make participation in the policy mandatory. The second is to do a more effective job of screening, of gaining further information on γ. Then different policies can be offered to different classes of individuals, as identified by the values of their γ's.

Does the problem of adverse selection reduce or increase the amount of redistribution that is carried out? Unfortunately, there is no unambiguous answer. It is a problem of trade-offs. With adverse selection, there will be more equality among the people participating in the scheme. However, fewer people will participate in the scheme. The greater is the variance about each individual's mean, the less incentive there will be to drop out of the scheme. This would seem to suggest that inability to avoid the adverse selection problem may be favorable when individuals' variances are high, unfavorable when they are low. A graph provides an easy way to see these relationships. The graph is drawn for a particular common utility function $u(x)$, a present distribution of means $g(M)$, and a distribution about each mean $f(x,M)$.

Without the risk-spreading agreement, an individual with mean M will have expected utility

$$I(M) = \int_0^\infty u(x)f(x,M)\,dx$$

Let $\hat{M}$ be the average mean of all individuals with means up to M. Then if a risk-spreading agreement attracts everyone with mean up to M, a participating individual will receive an expected utility

$$R(M) = u(\hat{M})$$

If an individual will receive a higher utility from the pool than he will in isolation, he will join. (Unless the variance associated with high means is relatively high, all the joiners will be individuals up to a certain cutoff point.) In the graph all individuals with means up to M_0 will participate in the risk-spreading pool.

The situation that we have considered of no monitoring ability is an extreme version of a frequently occurring situation where moni-

FIGURE 2
Expected Utility if All Individuals Whose Means
Are Below You Join the Pool—
For a Particular Pair of $g(M)$, $f(x,M)$

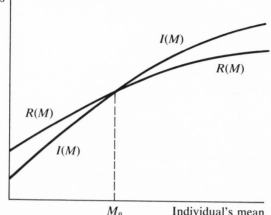

toring is limited. In general, in such situations people who yield the same signal participate in the same risk-sharing category.

There may be other ways to group individuals. If, as our model has assumed, terminal outcomes can be observed but not present means, we may wish to restrict participants to individuals whose outcomes fall within certain limits, or above specific cutoff points. To be passive about outlyers would not enable you to overcome the adverse selection problem completely. What might be worthwhile would be to penalize "underachievers." The scheme could be of this form: If you receive a prize less than z_1, you pay the pool a penalty of K. Individuals who receive above z_1 divide evenly the sum of their total received prizes plus the penalty payments from the unfortunates. Even if the penalty could not be worked out, or if it were ruled illegal, cutting off people who receive a prize below a certain limit can serve to allow substantial risk spreading among individuals whose present means are favorable but unobservable to others.

b. Adverse Incentives and Risk Spreading. The adverse incentives problem arises if the individual can take an action that influences the parameter that is observed by the risk-spreading agency.

With medical insurance, for example, policies traditionally have their payments depend on the level of the insured's medical expenditures. But this is a variable over which the individual has some control; it is not a random occurrence determined solely by chance. Thus the individual will have the opportunity to distort his expenditure to reap a larger payment from the insurance scheme. To eliminate this adverse incentive the payoff from the policy could depend solely upon the individual's medical condition. Unfortunately, this variable is difficult and expensive to monitor directly.[18]

B. Selecting Second-Best Outcomes

It is instructive to sequence the steps that will be taken by an identical group of citizens contracting to construct an optimal risk-spreading policy in a situation where the adverse incentives problem is inherent. First they must check for consistency, to see whether a considered policy can meet its requirements. With medical insurance, this might demand that the premiums cover the costs. With an optimal income tax, the requirement might be that the government manage to raise sufficient funds to meet its expenditures.

V.   A CONSISTENCY CHECK FOR A POLICY

1. Establish a policy, P.
2. Conduct the hypothetical lottery faced by each individual.
3. Allow each individual, in knowledge of the outcome of that lottery, to choose his maximizing action, z. This can be understood as $z = g(x,P)$.
4. Look at the outcome produced. The lottery outcome, choice pairs $x,g(x,P)$ will have the distribution $f(x)$. The constraint works on an expected value basis. If per capita estimation is what we are interested in, then if numbers are large this is a reasonable approximation. These pairs together with their distribution define an outcome, Y.
5. See whether Y is consistent with P. If it is, say that P belongs to P^*, the class of consistent policies.

The object is to select the one among the class of consistent policies that maximizes expected utility. This goal can be represented to find the

$$\underset{P \epsilon P^*}{\text{MAX}} \quad \int_0^\infty u(x,g(x,P),P)f(x) \; dx$$

where it is understood $z = g(x,P)$ is the maximizer of

$$u(x,z,P)$$

The problem comes in because we cannot specify in advance the action that an individual must take when a particular x occurs. If we could so specify, we could do better. The problem would become to find the

$$\underset{P \epsilon P^* \, , \; g(x,P)}{\text{MAX}} \quad \int_0^\infty u(x,g(x,P),P)f(x) \; dx$$

a formerly exogenous behavioral equation would become included in the maximization process. The way the gain is achieved is a bit deceptive. For any given policy and lottery outcome, not selecting $g(x,P)$ as the maximizer hurts utility. However, it offers an externality elsewhere; it substantially expands the range of acceptable policies.

The appendix examines the way this process of optimization over consistent policies would work in the context of a redistributive income tax. But that is primarily a mathematical and numerical effort. It is more appropriate to conclude the text on a philosophical note.

CONCLUSION—RISK-SPREADING POLICIES AND DISTRIBUTION

A major argument of this paper is that early and extensive risk spreading could bring about a more equal, contractually preferable income distribution. The factors that account for our present skewed distribution can be classed under three headings. (1) Structural elements in our society prevent disadvantaged groups from securing their equal opportunity market incomes. (2) The natural distribution of abilities in our society leads to dispersion in the income distribution. (3) Given an individual's abilities, education, etc., there is still a strong random element in the amount of income earned.

What sort of risk-spreading policies have we established to deal with these income randomizing factors? Some redistribution is carried out privately, but that hardly appears to be the paying off of an implicit or explicit *ex ante* contract. The government has a number of redistributional programs that have a risk-spreading aspect; these have more of a contractual element. Unemployment insurance clearly belongs in this category, as does compensation for natural disasters. Welfare is a less clear case. Finally, a number of government risk-spreading programs not primarily oriented toward redistribution achieve redistributional effects (not always progressive).[19] Still, the final income distribution is decidedly unequal. The market imperfections cited throughout this paper are together sufficient to prevent risk-spreading markets from accomplishing their redistributional tasks.

Despite the observation of the rather minimal performance of risk spreading in the income distribution area, the risk-spreading approach would seem to offer great promise. This promise is not as a redistributional tool, however, but rather as a guide to the types of outcomes we might like to see.

Looking backward we can surely speculate on the types of redistributional contracts we would have agreed upon had we less knowledge of our present positions. The further we could recess into ignorance, the more egalitarian would be the outcome of our voluntary contract. But this is a thought experiment, and we would hardly agree to such a contract now after so many lotteries have been run.

But perhaps this thought experiment could prove instructive for our ethical valuations of income distributions. If so, they could serve as our model in drawing up redistributional policies. To look for a contractual "would have been" may be more successful and more acceptable than to continue the search for the elusive social-welfare function. The welfare of retarded children, I would bet, would come out much improved.

APPENDIX
AN OPTIMAL INCOME TAX STARTING
IN THE ORIGINAL POSITION

In the original position, no individual knows his future earnings or earning capability. Each perceives on a subjective basis that he faces a common lottery on his ability to earn. The objective is to formulate an income-tax policy to maximize expected utility. The constraint is that the policy be consistent; in this case, just break even financially.

When dealing with income taxes, the payoff from the risk-spreading policy depends upon a variable over which the individual has some control, his income. He can choose how much to work. This introduces the presence of the problem of adverse incentives and insures that an inefficient outcome will result. To be efficient, the tax scheme would have to levy lump-sum amounts on different individuals, the size of the lumps to depend solely upon the random element, their ability to earn.

The objective, to use the terminology of human capital discussion, is to charge an individual a tax that depends only upon his exogenously given stock of capital. Noncontrollable changes in his capital stock, such as heart attacks, would also affect tax impositions. (If widgets decrease in price, a well-trained widget maker suffers a decrease in human capital.) What an individual does with his capital, or what he adds to it, could not affect his tax, lest this affect his income-earning or capital-accumulation decisions.

Why do we not employ a scheme of this sort? We cannot monitor exogenously given endowments and changes in capital supply sufficiently closely. Recognizing the fallibility of our monitoring powers, we might decide to make taxes depend upon individuals' incomes. Assume that each individual is free to earn as much or as little as he wants, in full knowledge of the amount he will be taxed on any particular amount of earnings. The good competing with income is leisure; there is no satiation with either good. For this discussion, taxes have only a redistributive purpose. The constraint on taxes then is that the total imposed on all individuals must be zero.

One possibility would be to adopt a completely leveling tax

scheme. Unfortunately, if the size of the community is large, so that each individual gets negligible benefits from his own tax contribution, it will reach a competitively lazy, no-work equilibrium. The difficulty, of course, is that the government in imposing its taxes is being too responsive to individuals' incomes, variables that are subject to their own control.

The other extreme would be to have no redistribution whatsoever. Each individual would keep all of his earnings. The objection to this scheme is that some people end up too poor because the government fails to assess taxes in response to individuals' incomes.

What is needed is something in between, a scheme in which taxes are somewhat responsive to income. The outcome of each possible scheme will be characterized by a utility value for each member of the community. If the individuals had identical utility functions and prospects, the problem of evaluating each outcome might be simplified. Assume, as with the manna model, that they contracted before any of them knew their earning capabilities. They might agree to select the scheme that maximizes expected utility. Let us see how such a scheme would work in a particular format.

Let w represent an individual's wages. The individuals have identical prospects before wages are determined. They all face the lottery on future wages given by the density function $f(w)$. If the government could base its taxes directly on wage rates, the sole variable that distinguishes individuals and one over which they have no control, an efficient outcome could be achieved. Unfortunately, the government in this example can base its taxes only on income y, and its tax scheme $T(y)$ must be the same for all individuals.

Each individual is told the wage he receives and the government's tax scheme before he selects the number of hours, h, he wishes to work in, let us say, a 100-hour period. This determines his pre-tax income, $y = wh$. The common individual utility function U has as arguments after-tax income $v = y - T(y)$, and leisure, $z = 100 - h$. An individual selects the number of hours he works to maximize this utility function given his particular wage rate and the government tax scheme. Denote this maximizing h as h^*. We have $h^* = g(w, T(y))$.

The constraint on the tax scheme (what is equivalent to the constraint above that $P \epsilon P^*$) is that total taxes equal 0. That constraint is

$$\int_0^\infty (w)T(wh^*)\, dw = 0$$

The tax scheme is selected to maximize expected utility, which is given

$$\int_0^\infty f(w)U(y - T(y),\ 100 - h^*)\, dw$$

subject to that constraint.

This is a complicated problem because the h^* for a particular w depends as well on the function $T(y)$. This makes the problem one stage more complex than traditional calculus of variations problems. Fortunately, computer approximations can yield nearly optimal results. Quadratic tax schemes are sufficiently diverse in shape to provide a close approximation to the optimal scheme of general form.

A Numerical Example[20]

Assume that the utility function is $U(v,z) = v^{1/2}z^{1/2}$. There are four possible wages: 1, 2, 3, or 4 dollars per hour. The probability an individual receives a particular wage is $\frac{1}{4}$ for each. The optimal quadratic tax scheme in this example is

$$T(y) = -\,0.0007y^2 + 0.372y - 30.125$$

The outcome under the scheme is given in the table.

TABLE 1

Values for the Optimal Scheme

Wage Rate	1	2	3	4
Leisure	72.178	58.500	63.316	50.347
Before-tax income	27.822	83.000	140.052	198.614
After-tax income	48.139	87.072	131.809	182.468
Average tax rate	−0.730	−0.049	0.059	0.081
Marginal tax rate	0.333	0.256	0.176	0.094

The marginal tax rate, which is an index of the responsiveness of the government's reaction function, at any particular point, falls continuously over the relevant range. The average tax rate rises throughout, which means that the tax scheme is progressive. This is what we would expect. The scheme is least responsive at the margin to those whose working decisions we want to influence the least, the high wage earners. To get the progressivity which is required because of the decreasing marginal utility of income, there is a large negative constant in the tax scheme; it represents a lump sum payment from the government to each individual.

This tax scheme produces results remarkably like those of the negative income tax at the bottom end of the income scale. Unfortunately, there is a strong work disincentive because of the high marginal tax rates imposed on low incomes. One solution suggested by our analysis would be to have more than one tax scheme, more than one reaction function for low-income individuals. Individuals with little or no earning potential would receive a lump-sum payment but would be taxed significantly at the margin. Individuals who could earn income might forfeit the lump sum but receive instead a wage supplement, what in effect would be a negative marginal tax rate on earnings. The choice of reaction function could be left to the low-income individuals. This would obviate the need to have the government discriminate on the basis of wage rate, a variable proscribed as an argument of the government's reaction function.

NOTES

[1]The distinction I draw between situations that are traditionally classified as those of risk and those of uncertainty is that it may be worthwhile to acquire information when there is uncertainty. Given this understanding, individuals should behave in the same manner when they confront a one-play lottery situation whether their probabilities are defined on a subjective or an objective basis. In betting situations rational individuals will wish to distinguish between objective and subjective probabilities. With the latter, other bettors may possess more information, and hence have an edge.

[2]Kenneth Arrow, *Essays in the Theory of Risk-Bearing* (Chicago: Markham, 1971), p. 123.

[3]A positive discount or interest rate would complicate the problem but not change its essential aspect.

[4]See M. Spence and R. Zeckhauser, "The Effect of the Timing of Consumption Decision and the Resolution of Lotteries on Income," *Econometrica* (1972), for an elaboration of this point.

[5]This is a "fair trade" if the individual's outcome in the second period is independent of the rest-of-the-world's outcome. If the reason this consumer has low second-period income is that the economy as a whole goes bad, the "fair price" for a contingency claim will involve the exchange of more-than-fifty units, if times are good; for less-than-fifty units, if times are bad.

[6]An alternative model that factors anxiety out of the analysis allows for its existence, but assumes that it is a linear function of P.

[7]Thomas Schelling, in commenting on this paper, provided a number of queries on this sentence. They reinforce the theme elucidated here, and to some degree answer themselves. "Do you mean that a 'rational' individual should not be subject to anxiety, or that he should ignore his own anxiety? If anxiety is uncomfortable or disabling as it usually is, then the rational person has to be concerned with it, just as he should be concerned with the pain and disablement of a broken bone. If you mean that a rational person should not be subject to anxiety, then we're back to the old question of where we draw the line between the 'rational individual' and the body he lives in. Am I a rational individual who resides in a nervous body, whose nervousness I cannot effectively control; or am I an irrational individual because the fear of death can keep me from sleeping, spoil my digestion, and make it hard for me to enjoy music?"

[8]There is a second, confounding factor that enters here. You might be able to change some decisions depending upon the information you receive. (This is a problem considered earlier.) To eliminate this factor, structure your thought problem to assume that you are bound to all decisions you would take if you did not know the lottery outcome.

[9]Without this axiom, for example, the troubling Allais Paradox is no longer either troubling or a paradox. In the real world, individuals confront decisions in sequences where elapsed time is significant. It may be that some "paradoxes" of decision theory arise because individuals train their thinking for dynamic cases and cannot easily convert their patterns of thought to the instanteous-resolution problem proposed by the experimenter.

[10]For a different explanation, see Friedman and Savage, "The Utility Analysis of Choices Involving Risk," *Journal of Political Economy*, vol. 56, (1948), pp. 279–304.

[11]Rawls's analysis rapidly diverges from the thoughts presented here. I am indebted to him for the loan of his framework.

[12]Numbers are assumed to be large enough that there need be no worry that the average for the group exceeds $\bar{m}$ by a significant amount.

[13]This risk-spreading system would be egalitarian, but would not always yield $\bar{m}$, if the risks that different individuals were exposed to were positively correlated. This would be the case, for example, with wars or large floods.

[14]The optimal plan redistributes x_1 so that its marginal utility is constant across situations. If fulfillment of this property leads to an equal x_1 endowment across all states of the world, that implies that the marginal utility of x_1 is solely a function of the level of x_1, that

$$u_1(x_1,x_2) = h(x_1)$$

Multiplying both sides of the equation by dx_1 and integrating, we get

$$\int_0^\infty \frac{d}{dx_1} u(x_1, x_2) \, dx_1 = \int_0^\infty h(x_1) \, dx_1$$

which shows that

$$u(x_1, x_2) = H(x_1) + I(x_2)$$

The second function is introduced because each value of x_2 may have a different constant of integration. Note the reciprocal nature of this relation. If health were redistributable but not manna, and individuals had this utility function, they would all receive equal *ex post* health.

[15]Arrow, "A Utilitarian Approach to the Concept of Equality in Public Expenditures," *Quarterly Journal of Economics* (August, 1971), pp. 409-15.

[16]See "Insurance, Information and Individual Action," for a more comprehensive treatment of the information monitoring problem as it relates to insurance-type problems. Spence and Zeckhauser, *American Economic Review* (May, 1971), pp. 380-87.

[17]There may be multiple equilibria; those that are stable will have the $I(M)$ curve cut the $R(M)$ curve from below. With multiple equilibria, all citizens will prefer that the rightmost equilibrium, call it M_r, be in effect. This can be achieved if the risk-spreading authority announces that it will pay each participant M_r.

[18]Even with direct monitoring of health condition, some might argue, the adverse incentives problem does not disappear. Individuals with health insurance might become less careful with their health.

[19]It is worthwhile to distinguish between programs that spread risks by compensating after a bad outcome has occurred, and those that spread risks by preventing bad outcomes. Dike building or pest control would fall in the latter category. The prevention programs hurt everyone's welfare just a bit (paying for the project) to prevent a few from being hurt severely.

[20]This example was used in a different context in "Uncertainty and the Need for Collective Action," in *The Analysis and Evaluation of Public Expenditure: The PPB System*, Joint Economic Committee, U.S. Congress, 1969.

9

Imperfect Capital Markets, Intertemporal Redistribution, and Progressive Taxation

————◆◆————

A. MITCHELL POLINSKY

Suppose we observe the government at a particular point in time redistributing income from rich persons to poor persons via the "tax structure" (generically used throughout this paper to refer to the tax, transfer, and expenditure sides of the public budget). What might we conclude about the effect of the tax structure on the income distribution? With respect to the distribution of current incomes, the unambiguous answer is that incomes are partially equalized. With respect to the distribution of lifetime incomes,[1] there is no unambiguous answer without further information. For example, consider a hypothetical economy in which all individuals live the same length of time (but are born at different times) and have the same income profile. For concreteness assume that each person's income grows continuously over his lifetime. Furthermore, assume that the net lifetime effect of the tax structure is neutral with respect to each individual, i.e., benefits (negative taxes) received when young are just canceled out by taxes paid when old (with appropriate adjustment for discounting). In this hypothetical economy the distribution of lifetime incomes is unaffected by the tax structure even though at every point in time we observe redistribution from the rich to the poor—

A. Mitchell Polinsky is an assistant professor, with a joint appointment in the Department of Economics and the Law School at Harvard University.
He wishes to thank James M. Buchanan, Peter A. Diamond, Roger H. Gordon, Robert E. Hall, David Harrison, Harold M. Hochman, Duncan MacRae, George E. Peterson, Jerome Rothenberg, Lester Thurow, and Burton Weisbrod for criticism and help.

due solely to the fact that individuals are born at different times. The essential point is that focusing on the current redistributional impact of the tax structure is incomplete and may be very misleading.

A given tax structure has three direct redistributional effects. It redistributes current incomes among different individuals, lifetime incomes among different individuals, and income between different periods of a given individual's life.[2] The first effect is the one conventionally treated. The second effect I have discussed elsewhere.[3] The focus of this paper will be on the third effect,[4] which will be referred to as intertemporal redistribution. With the exception of social security, intertemporal redistribution through the tax structure is probably unintended (a question I shall return to later) and is not generally recognized.[5] Unfortunately, its empirical magnitude is yet to be substantiated owing to the lack of direct information on before-tax and after-tax lifetime income profiles.[6] However, on indirect evidence, it is probable that this effect is empirically relevant.[7]

In Section I the intertemporal redistributive effect will be illustrated by means of some simple examples. Then, in Section II, the case for the importance of recognizing this effect, and the role of government in the light of it, will be stated. Its importance rests on the imperfection of capital markets in terms of the difficulty of borrowing against future income. Given such imperfections, a tax structure that merely redistributes income from later periods to earlier periods of an individual's life can increase his real lifetime income. A formal analysis of the implications of the role of government as intertemporal redistributor will be undertaken in Sections III and IV. It will be shown that, given reasonable assumptions about actual income and desired consumption profiles, optimal intertemporal redistribution implies a progressive tax structure. In Section V the question of whether or not this normative theory is also a valid positive theory will be treated. The conclusion is that the observed progressivity in the United States tax structure cannot be attributed to intertemporal redistribution goals. Some policy implications of the intertemporal redistributive role of the public sector will be examined in Section VI.

FIGURE 1
Hypothetical Pre-Tax and Post-Tax Income Profiles

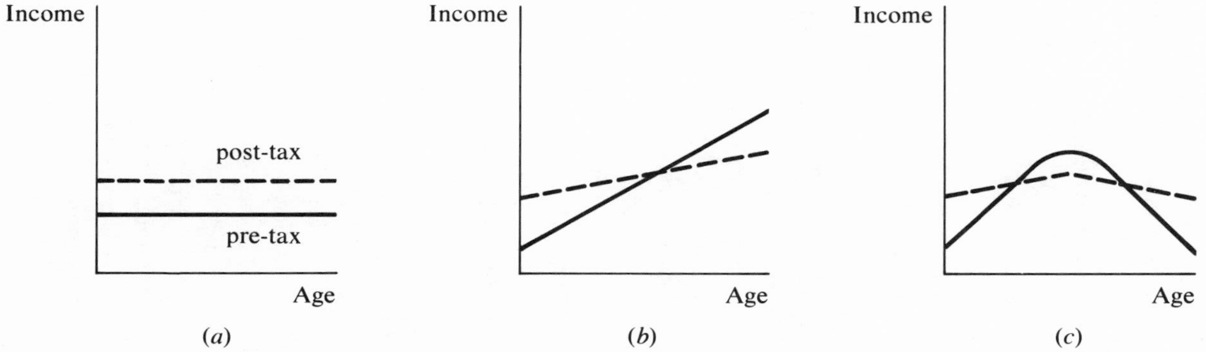

I. WHAT DOES A PROGRESSIVE TAX STRUCTURE
DO TO LIFETIME INCOME PROFILES?

The usual distributional question asked about the tax structure concerns its impact on the interpersonal distribution of incomes during some accounting period, usually taken to be a year (in practice) or the lifetime (in principle) of the taxable units (households, individuals, etc.). The question posed here, which is of a supplementary nature, concerns the impact of the tax structure on the shape of a given unit's income profile. (Why this is thought to be an interesting question will be discussed in the next section.)

The answer to this question depends both on the income profile and on the tax structure chosen. Because the tax structure in the United States is progressive,[8] a structure with this property will be used. In terms of a balanced-budget public sector this implies that there will be a net positive transfer to low-income households, that is, negative taxes. The choice of a representative income profile is much more difficult because profiles differ so much across individuals and are particularly sensitive to occupational choice. Three hypothetical profiles will be examined: a constant income profile, a growing income profile, and an inverted U-shaped profile. The examples are illustrated in Figure 1.

In the first case (Figure 1a) a relatively poor person's profile is presented. His before-tax income is constant over his lifetime, and his after-tax income is also constant. Aside from a vertical shift, there is no impact on the distribution of income over the individual's lifetime. In the second case (Figure 1b) the individual's income is growing, and the effect of a progressive tax structure is to flatten the profile. Income is transferred from later periods of his life to earlier periods. In the third case (Figure 1c) the individual's profile is again flattened, with the flattening occurring both on the growing and on the declining portions. Income is transferred from middle age to both earlier and later periods.

The general point to be made is that when there is any deviation from a constant income profile, a nonproportional (progressive or regressive) tax structure will affect the relative timing of income over an individual's lifetime. A progressive structure flattens the income profile, whereas a regressive structure accentuates the curvature of the profile. The intertemporal redistributive effect occurs simultaneously with both interpersonal redistributive effects. All three are associated with any particular progressive (or regressive) tax structure and may be confused if annual measures of tax incidence are used.[9]

II. CAPITAL MARKET IMPERFECTIONS,
LIFETIME ALLOCATION, AND THE ROLE
OF THE PUBLIC SECTOR

Why should we be concerned with the intertemporal redistributive effect of the public sector, in addition to its interpersonal redistributive effects? In principle, in an ideal intertemporal economy with perfect foresight, an individual would be indifferent among all income profiles that had the same value when discounted to the present at the market rate of interest. In such a setting only lifetime income (defined as the discounted income stream) matters. A tax structure that merely rearranged income over the individual's life but did not change his lifetime income would have no impact on his lifetime utility (to be defined more precisely in Section III). Given any income stream, an individual could transform that stream into his desired consumption profile by borrowing and lending in a perfectly operating capital market. Thus, in the ideal setting, intertemporal redistribution is of no substantive consequence.

This ideal is far from being realized in the world we live in. It is generally agreed that capital markets operate imperfectly and asymmetrically:

> Individuals can easily redistribute consumption into the future by saving, but they cannot easily borrow for present consumption. The high risks associated with expected earnings make borrowing difficult .... Consequently the current flow of income may dominate current consumption expenditures.[10]

If under perfectly operating capital markets many individuals borrow more than they currently do, there is likely to be a widespread

FIGURE 2

Average Money Income After Taxes and Expenditures
for Current Consumption

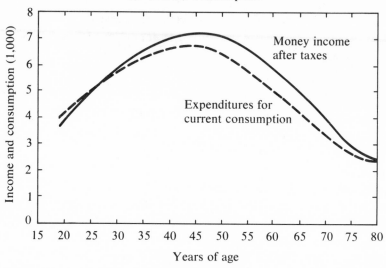

Source: Thurow (1969, Fig. 1, p. 325)

intertemporal (lifetime) misallocation of resources. Whether this potential misallocation exists depends on the relationship between the individual's actual income stream and desired consumption stream. If they coincide, there is obviously no problem. Moreover, if income exceeds desired consumption in the early part of an individual's life, there is still no problem since he could easily save current income for future consumption. There is a problem only when there is a desire to transfer future income to the present. However, it is usually assumed that this desire is widespread, as illustrated by the "textbook model" of the consumer's lifetime allocation process.

A "typical" consumer might dissave and go into debt during the early years of his earning life while he is earning a comparatively low income, buying a home, and raising a family; then save to retire his debts and establish a positive bond position during the remainder of his working life; and finally dissave and liquidate his bonds during retirement.[11]

Unfortunately, it is extremely difficult to test empirically the

FIGURE 3
Actual and Optimal Distributions of Income for Urban Families

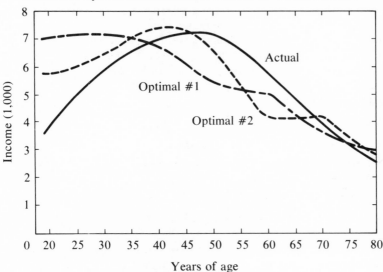

Source: Thurow (1969, Fig. 2, p. 328)

presumption that individuals would borrow substantially more if capital markets operated perfectly. Market data can give information only about actual levels of current income and consumption for a representative cross section of families in a given year.[12] Such information for 1960–1961 is illustrated in Figure 2, where it is seen that average income dominates average actual consumption. In order to demonstrate that more borrowing would have been undertaken than that observed under imperfect capital markets, information about intertemporal tastes is necessary. These, of course, are not observable data. However, it is possible to draw inferences about such tastes using market data if one is willing to make some rather strong assumptions. To my knowledge, the only attempt to pursue this line of development is a study by Lester Thurow.[13] In essence, he argued that the average desired consumption level at each age may be derived by finding that level of income in each age group at which there is zero saving.[14] The results of this study, using two different concepts of current consumption, are illustrated in Figure 3.

He concluded:

> Families desire a substantial amount of lifetime income redistribution over and above that done in 1960–61 and this redistribution is heavily weighted toward the younger years of a family's life. The actual lifetime pattern of income is a severe constraint on desired lifetime distribution of consumption expenditures. Based on the results of this analysis, lifetime welfare levels might be substantially increased if the constraints on lifetime income redistribution could be lifted.[15]

If we are willing to accept the results given above,[16] some important consequences may follow for designing a tax structure. As was seen in the previous section, a tax structure usually will affect the relative timing of income over an individual's life. In fact, the tax structure could be designed to have the effect of transferring income from the future to the present. For example, for a representative individual whose income grows to middle age and then declines (Figure 1c) this will be accomplished by a progressive tax structure. Thus, if capital markets are imperfect, the tax structure may be used to achieve intertemporal (lifetime allocation) efficiency.[17]

A single tax structure will be incapable in general of achieving multiple goals simultaneoulsy. Trade-offs would have to be made, or other instruments would have to be found. In order to highlight the public sector's role as intertemporal redistributor, conventional equity targets of the fiscal structure hereafter will be ignored. The last point deserves some elaboration to avoid confusion later. It will be assumed that equity goals are formulated in terms of lifetime incomes and that the initial distribution of lifetime incomes is optimal.[18] Consequently, in what follows, the government will undertake no interpersonal redistribution of lifetime incomes. However, since capital markets are imperfect, a given individual may not be able to achieve independently his optimal lifetime profile of consumption. The tax structure will be designed to transfer income from one period of his life to another period of his life. However, because different individuals will be at different stages in their life cycles at any given point in time, the government may still undertake redistribution of annual incomes between individuals. This will not be inconsistent with the assumption that the distribution of lifetime incomes is unmodified by government actions (as illustrated in the hypothetical example in the opening paragraphs of this paper.

Abstracting from the usual equity target of the tax structure, we shall assume that the only purpose of the public sector is to bring the consumer's income path into line with his optimal consumption path. The tax structure that achieves this goal will be called the "optimal tax structure." In the next two sections the characteristics of the optimal tax structure will be derived formally from a simple model of the consumer's lifetime allocation process. It will be shown that under plausible conditions the optimal tax structure will be progressive for the particular model employed. Two common notions of progressivity will be analyzed: in terms of the tax rate structure (Section III) and in terms of the impact on the income distribution (Section IV). The reader who is less inclined towards technical details may proceed directly to Section V with little loss of continuity.

III. THE OPTIMAL TAX STRUCTURE:
A ONE-CONSUMER ECONOMY

In this section a simple and well-known model of the consumer's lifetime allocation process will be presented. From this the optimal consumption stream can be derived and compared to an assumed income stream. Given these two streams, the tax structure that exactly transforms the latter into the former can be found. The one-consumer case is of little interest in itself, but it will be easier to start with it before treating the many-consumer case in the next section.

In spite of the simplicity of the textbook view of the typical consumer (as indicated in the quotation on page 234), it is still too complicated to be represented in simple analytical terms. Since our focus will not be on capturing reality as closely as possible, it will be useful to take a more simplified view of the lifetime allocation process. The most realistic characterization is that the consumer desires to transfer income from rich periods of his life to poor periods, both forward and backward in time (for example, as in Figure 1c). The formal model developed below will satisfy this condition only with respect to a desire for forward or backward shifting, but not both. It also differs from reality in that it does not include a retirement period and in that it assumes the individual's income grows or declines monotonically over his lifetime. The monotonicity assumption is for analytical convenience, and the omission of a retirement period is not serious for our purposes, since it will be assumed that an individual can easily save for retirement, thereby imposing no need for governmental interference to shift income forward. The conclusions of this paper will not be affected qualitatively by these simplifications.

We now proceed to the formal model, based in general on Yaari's exposition on the lifetime allocation process.[19] The reader should note that Yaari's model assumes perfectly operating capital markets. This will be modified below in a trivial way. The model may be developed most easily by explicitly setting forth its assumptions.[20]

Assumption 1: The capital market in our hypothetical country is perfect—it is possible to save and/or borrow at the "world" interest rate j (which is constant over time).

For reasons that will soon become apparent, the interest rate should be thought of as the "world" rate, that is, the rate set in a perfectly operating world capital market in which there is free trade in all factors and goods (at zero transport costs), and in which our hypothetical country is a relatively small member. This grossly unrealistic setting will greatly simplify the analysis in a way that is not detrimental to the issues of primary interest.

Assumption 2: The consumer's income grows (or declines) at the constant rate i starting from some initial level, m_0

(1) $$m(t) = m_0 e^{it}, \ 0 \le t \le T, \text{ and } i \gtrless 0$$

Given this assumption, the consumer's lifetime income, M, is defined as

(2) $$M = \int_0^T e^{-jt} m_0 e^{it} \ dt = m_0(i - j)^{-1} \left[e^{(i - j)T} - 1 \right]$$

Assumption 3: The consumer's preferences are representable by a utility function, denoted by V, of the form:

(3) $$V(c) = \int_0^T e^{-rt} \log c(t) \, dt$$

where the closed interval $[0,T]$ is the consumer's lifetime, r is his subjective rate of time preference (assumed to be constant over time), $c(t)$ is the rate of consumption at time t, and $\log c(t)$ is interpreted as the utility associated with the rate of consumption at every moment of time. Assumption 3 is implicit in much of the literature on the long-run consumption function, and often is used explicitly in the literature on optimal savings.[21]

If we assume that the consumer leaves no bequests at the end of his lifetime and that he starts with no assets, his lifetime allocation problem is to maximize (3) subject to non-negative consumption and a lifetime income constraint. Assuming that a solution to this problem exists and is unique, let $c^*(t)$ represent the optimal consumption plan. It is relatively straightforward to show that the solution to this problem has the following general form:

(4) $$c^*(t) = c_0 e^{(j-r)t}, \ 0 \le t \le T$$

where the constant c_0 is determined from the initial condition, $c^*(o)$. In other words, the consumer's optimal consumption stream grows (or declines) at the constant rate $(j - r)$ over time, starting from some initial level c_0.[22]

The optimal consumption stream (4) has been derived on the assumption that the individual can save and borrow at the interest rate j, and we would expect that the individual would thereby transform his income stream (1) into (4). The role of the public sector as intertemporal redistributor is interesting only when some constraint is imposed on saving or borrowing, and, as argued in Section II, the most realistic constraint is on the ability to borrow. For purely expositional reasons, the most extreme form of this constraint will be assumed. Replace Assumption 1 with

Assumption 1': The capital market in our hypothetical country is perfectly asymmetrical—it is possible to save current income at the "world" interest rate j, but impossible to borrow against future income.

It is not *a priori* certain that this additional constraint will be binding. It will depend on the relationship between the income and desired consumption streams. If the borrowing constraint is not binding, we are back to our original problem in which there is no role for the public sector. It will therefore be assumed that our representative consumer would desire to borrow if he could. As noted in Section II, this is the usual presumption and is consistent with Thurow's empirical evidence.[23] However, it rules out certain relationships between the income and desired consumption streams. Since the two streams will cross only once,[24] it rules out the possibility of income exceeding desired consumption before the crossover, and vice versa after the crossover. By considering each possible relationship between the two streams it will be seen that this leads to:[25]

> *Assumption 1''*: The borrowing constraint is binding, which implies that $(j - r) < i$, where $(j - r) \gtreqless 0$ and $i \gtreqless 0$.

Using the above model of the consumer's lifetime allocation process (Assumptions 1', 1'', 2, and 3), we may now derive the tax structure that transforms his actual income stream into his preferred consumption stream, thereby circumventing the difficulty (impossibility) of borrowing. In the present context the assumption that the interpersonal distribution of lifetime incomes is optimal (see Section II) may be reinterpreted to mean that the consumer's before-tax and after-tax lifetime incomes are the same. By construction, if the tax structure exactly transforms the consumer's actual income into his preferred consumption at every point in time, it will have a neutral lifetime incidence. (This follows since the budget constraint requires that the discounted value of consumption equals lifetime income.)

Letting $\Phi(m)$ be the average tax rate, we seek an explicit expression for $\Phi(m)$ such that at each point in time his income, minus his tax payments (which may be negative), equals his desired consumption, that is,

$$(7) \qquad m(t) - \Phi(m) \cdot m(t) = c^*(t)$$

where the tax rate function does not have age as an argument. This may be solved for $\Phi(m)$:

(8) $$\Phi(m) = 1 - \frac{c^*(t)}{m(t)}$$

The next step is to find an expression for c^* as a function of m, independent of age. Since $m(t)$ and $c^*(t)$ are uniquely determined for a given t, we may solve these expressions for t and then set them equal to each other. For (1) and (4) respectively, we have:[26]

(9) $$t = [1/i] \log [m/m_0]$$

(10) $$t = [1/(j - r)] \log [c^*/c_0]$$

Setting (9) equal to (10) and solving for c^*, we obtain

(11) $$c^* = c_0 \left[\frac{m}{m_0} \right]^{(j-r)/i}$$

And finally substituting (11) into (8) gives the desired result

(12) $$\Phi(m) = 1 - \left[\frac{c_0}{m} \right] \left[\frac{m}{m_0} \right]^{(j-r)/i}$$

We can first compute a measure of average rate progression[27] of the tax structure by differentiating (12) with respect to m:

(13) $$\frac{d\Phi(m)}{dm} = \left[\frac{c_0}{m^2} \right] \left[\frac{m}{m_0} \right]^{(j-r)/i}$$

$$- \left[\frac{1}{m_0} \right] \left[\frac{(j-r)}{i} \right] \left[\frac{c_0}{m} \right] \left[\frac{m}{m_0} \right]^{(j-r-i)/i}$$

The tax structure is said to be progressive in average rate terms when $d\Phi(m)/dm > 0$. It is easily shown that

(14) $$\frac{d\Phi(m)}{dm} > 0 \text{ if and only if } \frac{(j-r)}{i} < 1$$

By assuming that the borrowing constraint is binding in the context of the present model (Assumption 1''), and therefore that $(j - r) < i$, it follows that the tax structure will be progressive if the income and desired consumption streams are both growing, or the income stream is growing and the consumption stream is declining. If both streams are declining and the borrowing constraint is binding, the optimal tax structure will be regressive. In each of the three cases, the tax structure will transfer income from the future to the present. The most unlikely of the three cases is probably the one leading to a regressive tax structure. This requires that the desired consumption stream be steeper than the income stream, contrary to much empirical evidence on the long-run consumption function, which supports the conclusion that individuals desire to smooth consumption over time. I will therefore refer to the "usual" case as ruling out this possibility.

A secondary result is also of some interest. First differentiate (13) with respect to m:

$$(15) \quad \frac{d^2\Phi(m)}{dm^2} = - \left[\frac{2c_0}{m^3} \right] \left[\frac{m}{m_0} \right]^{(j-r)/i} + \left[\frac{2}{m_0} \right] \left[\frac{(j-r)}{i} \right] \left[\frac{c_0}{m^2} \right]$$

$$\left[\frac{m}{m_0} \right]^{(j-r-i)/i} - \left[\frac{1}{m_0{}^2} \right] \left[\frac{(j-r)}{i} \right] \left[\frac{c_0}{m} \right] \left[\frac{(j-r-i)}{i} \right] \left[\frac{m}{m_0} \right]^{(j-r-2i)/i}$$

It can be shown that

$$(16) \quad \frac{d^2\Phi(m)}{dm^2} < 0 \text{ if and only if } (j-r) < i \text{ or } (j-r) > 2i$$

Thus, given Assumption 1'', it follows that the degree of progressivity declines with income.

We may thus conclude that (for the particular model employed) if the inability to borrow is a binding constraint, the optimal tax structure is "usually" progressive, and the degree of progressivity declines with income.

IV. THE OPTIMAL TAX STRUCTURE: A MANY-CONSUMER ECONOMY

In this section the simple one-consumer model will be extended to a simple many-consumer economy. The first step will be to specify the characteristics of the population in order to derive a before-tax income distribution at some arbitrary point in time. Then the tax structure will be applied in order to derive the after-tax income distribution. The incidence of the tax structure will be defined in terms of the relative degree of inequality of these two distributions. Although the assumptions about the population and the economy are highly unrealistic, they are made in order to focus on the intertemporal redistributive effect of the tax structure and to simplify the analysis as much as possible. More realistic assumptions would probably not change the qualitative results.[28]

Before we set forth the formal model, a brief discussion of the second concept of incidence is in order. Rather than defining progressivity in terms of the rate structure (as in Section III), we now find it possible and appropriate to measure progressivity in terms of the relative degree of inequality of the before-tax and after-tax income distributions. A widely used measure of inequality is the Gini coefficient of concentration, based on the Lorenz curve.[29] A natural measure of progressivity (or regressivity), referred to as "effective incidence," is the ratio of the before-tax Gini coefficient to the after-tax Gini coefficient.[30] The tax structure will be defined to be progressive, proportional, or regressive as the ratio is greater than, equal to, or less than unity, respectively.

The many-consumer model to be studied is completely described by two additional assumptions:

> *Assumption 4*: All individuals are identical except for the
> date of their birth.

Starting with a world of equals will be helpful in sorting out the interpersonal from the intertemporal effects of the tax structure. By construction, there will still be no interpersonal redistribution of lifetime incomes. Furthermore, all interpersonal redistribution of current income will be explained by the fact that two individuals (with identical lifetime profiles) may be at different points in their life cycles at a given point in time.[31]

> *Assumption 5*: The population is constant over time.

Assuming that there were a nonzero population growth rate would not affect the qualitative results unless the growth rate were unreasonably large.[32]

It is now relatively easy to derive formally the income distribution from the model developed in the previous section. Let $y(p)$ be the current income (at the point in time at which the Lorenz curve is constructed) of individuals in the pth percentile of the population, ranked from lowest to highest. The subscripts "ex" and "cum" will denote before-tax and after-tax incomes. Given the present assumptions of a constant population and a world of equals, the cross-sectional income distributions at a given point in time will be identical to the individual lifetime profiles, with a simple change of variables. The crucial relationship is

$$(17) \qquad \frac{p}{100} = \frac{t}{T}$$

Solving for t and substituting into (1) and (4), respectively, gives the before-tax and after-tax income distributions:

$$(18) \qquad y_{\text{ex}}(p) = m_0 e^{ipT/100}$$

$$(19) \qquad y_{\text{cum}}(p) = c_0 e^{(j - r)pT/100}$$

For purposes of the Lorenz curve, the actual number of individuals in the economy is irrelevant. We might just as well assume that there are 100 individuals, one in each percentile. Let $\hat{Y}_{\text{ex}}$ denote aggregate income before the tax. Then

$$(20) \quad \hat{Y}_{\text{ex}} = \int_0^{100} y_{\text{ex}}(p)\, dp = \int_0^{100} m_0 e^{ipT/100}\, dp = 100 m_0 (iT)^{-1}(e^{iT} - 1)$$

Similarly, for aggregate income after the tax

$$(21) \qquad \hat{Y}_{\text{cum}} = 100 c_0 (j - r)^{-1} T^{-1} \left[e^{(j - r)T} - 1 \right]$$

Let the before-tax Lorenz curve relationship be denoted by $Y_{\text{ex}}(P)$, the cumulated income percentage as a function of the cumulated population percentage. Then

$$(22) \qquad Y_{\text{ex}}(P) = \left[100 \int_0^P y_{\text{ex}}(p)\, dp \right] / \hat{Y}_{\text{ex}}$$

Then substituting (18) and (20) into (22) and solving gives

$$(23) \qquad Y_{\text{ex}}(P) = 100 \left[e^{iTP/100} - 1 \right] \left[e^{iT} - 1 \right]^{-1}$$

Similarly, the after-tax Lorenz curve is

(24) $\quad Y_{\text{cum}}(P) = 100[e^{(j-r)TP/100} - 1] \, [e^{(j-r)T} - 1]^{-1}$

The next step is the derivation of an expression for the Gini coefficients of the before-tax and after-tax Lorenz curves. The area under the diagonal (Figure 4, p. 257) is equal to 5,000 (in percentile-squared units). The area under the before-tax Lorenz curve is

(25) $\quad \displaystyle\int_0^{100} Y_{\text{ex}}(P) \, dP = 100(e^{iT} - 1)^{-1} \int_0^{100} (e^{iTP/100} - 1) \, dP$

$$= 10,000(e^{iT} - iT - 1) \, [iT(e^{iT} - 1)]^{-1}$$

Letting G_{ex} denote the before-tax Gini coefficient, we have

(26) $\quad G_{\text{ex}} = 2(e^{iT} - iT - 1) \, [iT(e^{iT} - 1)]^{-1}$

Similarly, the after-tax Gini coefficient is

(27) $\quad G_{\text{eum}} = 2(e^{(j-r)T} - (j-r)(T-1)(j-r)^{-1}T^{-1} \, [e^{(j-r)T} - 1]^{-1}$

It should be noted that in general (26) and (27) are also functions of time. However, because of the nature of the steady state assumed, we have abstracted from this aspect. And finally, we may derive the incidence measure, denoted by N:

(28) $\quad N = \dfrac{G_{\text{cum}}}{G_{\text{ex}}} = \dfrac{[i]}{[(j-r)]} \ \dfrac{[e^{(j-r)T} - (j-r)T - 1]}{[e^{iT} - iT - 1]} \ \dfrac{[e^{iT} - 1]}{[e^{(j-r)T} - 1]}$

As in the analysis of the rate structure, the most interesting question concerns the conditions under which the tax structure is progressive. This now corresponds to the conditions under which $N > 1$. The derivation is not as straightforward as before, but after making some approximations it can be shown that:[33]

(29) $\quad\quad\quad N > 1$ if and only if $\left| \dfrac{i}{(j-r)} \right| > 1$

Except for one not very plausible exception that will be discussed, the conditions under which the effective incidence (N) of the tax structure is qualitatively the same as the rate structure incidence

$(d\Phi(m)/dm)$ are identical, provided the borrowing constraint is binding. The only exception can occur when the income stream is growing and the desired consumption stream is declining at a faster rate (that is, $|(j-r)| > i$, where $(j-r) < 0$ and $i > 0$). In this case the rate structure incidence is progressive, but the effective incidence is regressive. This will occur because there is so much redistribution from the rich to the poor that before-tax rich persons become after-tax poor persons and vice versa, and because the rate structure is so steep that the after-tax income distribution is more unequal than the before-tax distribution. This is certainly not an empirically plausible case, and I will rule it out in practice.[34] Again, we may thus conclude that (for the particular model employed) if the inability to borrow is a binding constraint, the optimal tax structure is "usually" progressive.

V. USEFULNESS AS A POSITIVE THEORY

Within the context of our hypothetical economy, it has been assumed that the government behaves in a particular way in response to capital market imperfections and the lifetime consumption preferences of the members of the society. The question naturally arises whether it is reasonable to impute a similar motive to the Congress of the United States. The explanation of progressive taxation in the United States is far more complex than the simple model developed above. It probably is best explained as a mixture of conflicting power relationships, altruistic preferences, and inertia.

Whether intended or not, there is still a substantial amount of intertemporal redistribution through the United States tax structure, particularly because of the inclusion of the incidence of expenditures at all levels of government. A significant portion of federal-state-local government expenditures goes directly or indirectly to programs benefiting young (and relatively poor) persons. Education is probably the best illustration of this: there currently exists free primary and secondary education, highly subsidized college education, and highly subsidized graduate training. Given the relationship between education and lifetime income prospects, persons who benefit from free or subsidized educational programs when they are young and have low incomes probably pay back a substantial portion because of their higher incomes later in their lives, which are subject to relatively high marginal tax rates. The relationship between subsidized educational consumption, lifetime incomes, and lifetime tax payments implicitly illustrates the progressive character of intertemporal redistribution.

Even though intertemporal redistribution may not be among the important positive explanations of progressive taxation, it may still be useful to see whether or not the normative theory developed here is even consistent with reality. Any positive theory of the public sector must be consistent with the following empirical observations about the degree of average rate progression and effective progression. Musgrave and Thin found that for the tax structure (now used in the narrower sense) in the United States the slope of the average rate curve was positive, and that it "declines more or less continuously ... when moving up the [income] scale."[35] For the one year in which they computed the effective progressivity of the United States income tax structure (in 1948), they found a coefficient of progression of 1.02. Although this may appear very low, they noted (p. 511 of their article) that the Gini coefficient is "rather insensitive to changes in distribution." In studying the incidence of the public sector Gillespie examined the expenditure side as well as the revenue side.[36] His results are more recent, and indicate a higher degree of effective progression, if both sides are included.[37] For the federal sector alone, the coefficient of progression is 1.07. If the state-local sector is also included, this coefficient rises to 1.11.

Any theory of the tax structure therefore should be at least consistent with the following facts: an average tax rate that rises with income at a decreasing rate, and an effective incidence greater than unity. If we collect the results derived in Sections III and IV it is evident that the present model "usually" meets all these requirements if the borrowing constraint is binding. However, to infer from this that the United States tax structure is progressive because of intertemporal redistributive goals would be fallacious. Without a direct test of the intertemporal redistribution model, nothing can be said about the usefulness of the model as a positive theory. The model still may be used to suggest policy prescriptions, provided the assumptions on which it is based are more or less accepted. Although many of these assumptions are unrealistic, I believe a more realistic model will give results of the kind derived here. I shall therefore proceed on this basis.

VI. POLICY IMPLICATIONS

In keeping with the emphasis on intertemporal efficiency the policy implications will focus on this consideration. In reality, there will of course be a mixture of interpersonal and intertemporal redistributive effects.

(1) One obvious implication of the preceding analysis is that the government should correct the imperfections in the capital market. With such corrections, the analysis and conclusions of this paper will no longer be relevant, but this should not obscure the fact that the first best solution is a world with perfectly operating capital markets. Although this is the preferred outcome, there are some second-best alternatives that have similar outcomes.

In practice it is impossible to design a tax structure that can achieve intertemporal efficiency for everyone when income and desired consumption paths differ. It is therefore necessary to consider alternatives that either permit each household itself to choose the desired timing of the tax structure's impact or allow a fixed tax structure to be accommodated to households in different circumstances with respect to age (analogously to "formula flexibility" in stabilization policy). Two alternatives of each type will be considered.

(2) The so-called Yale Plan to finance private higher education is a model of the kind of public program that would improve intertemporal efficiency by permitting each household (or individual) to borrow voluntarily against expected future income. For each $1,000 borrowed, a very small percentage of income is repaid each year during a long repayment period. Although the Yale Plan has interpersonal redistributive effects, since those who end up with below-average incomes are subsidized by those with above-average incomes, its primary intent is to promote intertemporal redistribution.

The public sector might promote programs of this type for education or any other socially beneficial good that individuals desire to consume while young but that requires large expenditures. Although this scheme will promote intertemporal efficiency it may be partly at the expense of labor market efficiency. As more and more activities are financed in this manner the percentage of future income that will have to be returned will have large substitution effects on labor supply. Because of the potentially offsetting income effect, it is impossible to predict *a priori* whether such a plan will affect labor supply seriously.

(3) A similar plan in which each household would choose individually the level at which it desires to use the option is a deferred tax payment provision. In general, such a provision would allow each household to postpone a certain fraction of its tax payments, under the condition that both the taxes postponed and compounded interest on them would be due when actually paid. (There could be numerous variations of this general scheme, but these will not be discussed.) A deferred tax payment provision would not affect the present value of tax burdens, but would permit each household to allocate its tax burden over time. Note also that there will not be a deadweight burden of the kind associated with the Yale-type plan, since the part of the tax liability at some future date due to previously postponed taxes is independent of current income at that date. (There will still be the usual potential deadweight burden associated with the part of the tax liability due to current income.) Some limitation on ability to postpone taxes must be imposed in order to prevent taxes from being continuously postponed until death and to prevent tax liabilities due to previously postponed taxes from greatly exceeding current income. In principle, the latter consideration is not necessary, although in practice, given the uncertainty of future income and of death, it would be desirable to prevent a household from being swamped by high tax liabilities when its income unexpectedly declines (permanently or perhaps even temporarily). One limitation of the tax deferment plan is that it is not capable of actually augmenting incomes, in contrast to the Yale-type plan. Consequently, it may be only a partial remedy for intertemporal inefficiencies.

There are two other alternatives that achieve similar objectives but are not tailored to voluntary household choices.

(4) An age-related annual income tax structure could be designed to take account of the assumed widespread desire to transfer income from middle age to earlier ages. In essence, there would be a separate tax schedule applicable for each age of the taxable unit. A detailed proposal for such a plan would have to consider (among other things) how to treat different taxable units (individuals, households, etc.), how to relate the tax schedules of different years for the same taxable unit, and how to treat persons whose tax unit status changes. It would be possible to have progressive marginal rates in each year's schedule, with lower average rates for earlier and later periods of the unit's lifetime. Alternatively, one might desire to use a proportional income tax for each age, with the rates varying by ages. This would decrease the possible deadweight burden due to high marginal rates, yet still permit tax burdens to be shifted over time by an appropriate choice of the rates as a function of age.[38] Whether the rate structure for any given age should be proportional or progressive will depend primarily on considerations other than intertemporal efficiency. One advantage of an age-specific income tax structure is that it imposes no additional deadweight burden, since an individual or household has no control over its age. Unlike the deferred tax payment plan, this alternative also could be used to increase income above its pre-tax level by employing negative average rates for some ages (presumably for young and old households). The primary disadvantage of the age-specific approach is that it cannot be tailored to the needs of individual households, as can alternatives (2) and (3). Also, it would entail greater administrative costs than the present tax structure, although such additional costs do not appear to be excessive.[39]

(5) The last alternative to be considered is some form of income averaging.[40] Income averaging is usually desired because it improves horizontal equity with respect to lifetime income. However, averaging also will have an effect on the profile of taxable income, and therefore on the pattern of tax payments over time. The precise impact will depend on the preaveraging income profile, the method of averaging, and the tax structure. For an inverted U-shaped in-

come profile, a moving average, and a progressive tax structure, the effect of averaging will be to shift the pre-tax income profile "to the right," and therefore to shift tax burdens to later periods in life. Given the ease of saving, this cannot decrease lifetime utility, and in general will improve it.[41] Like alternative (4), an averaging scheme cannot be tailored to the circumstances of individual households. Its additional administrative burden is small, particularly for cumulative lifetime averaging as opposed to moving averaging.[42]

The last implication to be discussed has to do not with alternative means of improving intertemporal efficiency, but with improving the awareness of the lifetime allocation effects of tax, transfer, and expenditure policies.

(6) Existing and proposed tax and expenditure programs should be described both in terms of their impact on current incomes and on lifetime income profiles. Although it is natural to illustrate these effects explicitly for such programs as social security,[43] where benefits and payments are related and occur in different periods of a given individual's life cycle, the same analysis should be undertaken for tax and expenditure programs generally. An individual as *homo economicus* behaves in such a way as to maximize his lifetime utility. His decision to save or borrow (to the extent he can) at any point in time is part of a lifetime consumption plan. Similarly, the tax and expenditure incidence of the public sector at any point in time should also be seen as part of a lifetime incidence plan.

VII. CONCLUDING REMARKS

Although there are many related matters that could be discussed in terms of the approach and implications of this paper, their theme would be the same. When the public sector is viewed in terms of its impact on lifetime income and consumption profiles, some new insights are gained. For example, even if the government, through the tax structure, does not change an individual's lifetime income, it can improve his lifetime utility by affecting the pattern by which he receives his income. Moreover, the progressivity of the public sector at any point in time may not be closely related to any notion of vertical equity, either in terms of annual incomes or lifetime incomes. To the extent that it reflects intertemporal redistribution, it might also be explained by such socio-economic factors as the rate of growth of individual incomes and the rate of time preference.

The fundamental basis for the results of this paper were the assumptions of the difficulty of borrowing, and of a rate of time preference high enough for our hypothetical consumer to desire to borrow (given his income stream). A similar model could be developed for other sets of assumptions, and the conclusion that a progressive fiscal structure is required for efficient intertemporal allocation might be tempered. Although the assumption that it is easy to save and difficult to borrow is probably acceptable to most,[44] the assumption about relatively high rates of time preference is much more questionable. Obviously, this assumption is not easily subject to empirical observation. However, it is possible to draw indirect inferences from observable phenomena, as Thurow has done.[45] To my knowledge, his study is the one that is empirically most relevant to this assumption, and fortunately supports it. However, it is too big a step to go from the conclusion that the hypothetical tax structure developed here is progressive because of intertemporal redistribution to the conclusion that United States tax structure is progressive for the same reasons. Unfortunately, the latter conclusion does not seem amenable to empirical testing. The purpose of this paper has not been to suggest a positive theory of progressive taxation, but to propose a different way of looking at the tax structure. It is a viewpoint that has not received very much attention but that may be very important.

APPENDIX A. SUMMARY OF NOTATION

t	time (or age)
$[0,T]$	lifetime of each individual
j	(constant) rate of interest
i	(constant) rate of growth of individual income
r	(constant) subjective rate of time preference
$m(t)$	income at time t
m_0	initial income of an individual

M	lifetime income
$c(t)$	consumption at time t
$c^*(t)$	optimal consumption
c_0	initial consumption
C	lifetime consumption
$V(c)$	utility function
$\Phi(m)$	average percentage income tax rate
$\hat{Y}_{ex}$	aggregate income for before-tax Lorenz curve
P	population percentile
$Y_{ex}(P)$	before-tax Lorenz curve (cumulated income percentile)
G_{ex}	before-tax Gini coefficient
N	measure of effective incidence

APPENDIX B. PROOF OF THE INCIDENCE
RESULT IN THE MANY-CONSUMER ECONOMY*

Equation (28) can be written in the form $N = f((j - r)T)/f(iT)$, where

$$f(x) = \frac{(e^x - x - 1)}{x(e^x - 1)} \tag{30}$$

We therefore need to know whether $f(x)$ is increasing or decreasing in x. First calculate

$$\frac{df(x)}{dx} = \frac{x(e^x - 1)^2 - (e^x - x - 1)(e^x - 1 + xe^x)}{x^2(e^x - 1)^2}. \tag{31}$$

Since the denominator of (31) is positive, the sign only depends on the numerator which, after some manipulation, is $\gtreqless 0$ as

$$x^2 e^x \gtreqless (e^x - 1)^2. \tag{32}$$

At $x = 0$, (32) holds with equality. Differentiate both sides of (32) with respect to x:

$$\frac{d}{dx} x^2 e^x = xe^x (2 + x), \tag{33}$$

---

*The first part of this proof was suggested by Robert M. Solow.

$$\frac{d}{dx}(e^x - 1)^2 = 2e^x(e^x - 1) \cdot \qquad (34)$$

It will now be shown that (33) is less than (34) for all $x > 0$. This will be true if

$$x(2 + x) = 2x + x^2 < 2(e^x - 1) = 2\left(x + \frac{x^2}{2!} + \frac{x^3}{3!} + \dots\right)$$

$$= 2x + x^2 + \left(\frac{x^3}{3!} + \dots\right), \quad (35)$$

which certainly is true for all $x > 0$. Thus, $f(x)$ is decreasing in x for all $x > 0$ and (29) follows without approximation for $i > 0$, $(j - r) > 0$.

Suppose, however, that $i < 0$ and/or $(j - r) < 0$. It is claimed that the problem in this case is approximately equivalent to the problem for $|i|$ and $|(j - r)|$, which satisfy the conditions required in the first part. This will be true if the Gini coefficients associated with i and $(j - r)$ are approximately equal to those associated with $|i|$ and $|(j - r)|$. This follows from (26) and the following result which can be proven to a third-order approximation:

$$\frac{e^x - x - 1}{x(e^x - 1)} \doteq \frac{e^{|x|} - |x| - 1}{|x|(e^{|x|} - 1)} \text{ for } x < 0 \cdot \qquad (36)$$

This establishes (29).

NOTES

[1]As used here, an individual's lifetime income refers to his discounted income stream.

[2]Of course, these are not independent effects. They are related through the lifetime income profiles of the individuals in the economy.

[3]A. Mitchell Polinsky, "A Note on the Measurement of Incidence," *Public Finance Quarterly*, (April, 1973), pp. 219-30.

[4]This issue was first explored by James Buchanan in an unpublished manuscript in 1964. A later version of this paper was published as Chapter 15 in his *Public Finance in Democratic Process* (Chapel Hill: University of North Carolina Press, 1967).

[5]For a discussion of the empirical significance of intertemporal redistribution through the social security system, see Elizabeth Deran, "Income Redistribution under the Social Security System," *National Tax Journal* (September, 1966), pp.

276–85, and Henry Aaron, "Benefits under the American Social Security System," in Otto Eckstein, ed., *Studies in the Economics of Income Maintenance* (Washington, D.C.: Brookings Institution, 1967), pp. 61–72. As the reader will see, the primary issue in this paper is quite different from the concerns underlying social security. I shall focus on the difficulty of transferring future income to the present, whereas the social security system transfers income in the opposite direction.

[6]For a review of the indirect evidence, see James Morgan, "The Anatomy of Income Distribution," *Review of Economics and Statistics* (August, 1962), pp. 270–83.

[7]For this argument and a review of more recent evidence, see Polinsky, "A Note on the Measurement of Incidence," *Public Finance Quarterly* (April, 1973), pp. 219-30.

[8]This conclusion is based on the empirical study by Gillespie. See W. Irwin Gillespie, "Effect of Public Expenditures on the Distribution of Income," in Richard A. Musgrave, ed., *Essays in Fiscal Federalism* (Washington, D.C.: The Brookings Institution, 1965), pp. 122–86. The study includes all three components of the public budget (taxes, transfers, and expenditures). We should note, however, that it is extremely sensitive to certain arbitrary assumptions. See Henry Aaron and Martin McGuire, "Public Goods and Income Distribution, *Econometrica* (November, 1970), pp. 907–20.

[9]Polinsky, "A Note on the Measurement of Incidence," *Public Finance Quarterly* (April, 1973), pp. 219-30.

[10]Quotation is from Lester C. Thurow, "The Optimum Lifetime Distribution of Consumption Expenditures," *American Economic Review* (June, 1969), p. 324. For an extensive documentation of the widespread belief that capital markets are imperfect, see George J. Stigler, "Imperfections in the Capital Market," *Journal of Political Economy* (June, 1967), pp. 287–92. It should be noted, however, that Stigler is skeptical of the conventional belief that capital markets operate imperfectly.

[11]The quotation is from James M. Henderson and Richard E. Quandt, *Microeconomic Theory*, 2d ed. (New York: McGraw-Hill, 1971), p. 299. It should be noted that this statement is somewhat misleading, since most families mortgage their homes, which is not the same thing as borrowing. It is relatively difficult to borrow against future income because we do not permit individuals to mortgage their human capital.

[12]Data of this kind do exist for longer periods, but not nearly so long as a lifetime and not for a representative sample. For a brief review of this evidence see James Morgan, "The Anatomy of Income Distribution," *Review of Economics and Statistics* (August, 1962), pp. 270–83.

[13]Lester C. Thurow, "The Optimum Lifetime Distribution of Consumption Expenditures," *American Economic Review* (June, 1969), pp. 324–30.

[14]*Ibid.*, p. 326.

[15]*Ibid.*, p. 329

[16]For a critical discussion and defense of Thurow's methodology and conclusions, see Kan Hua Young, "The Optimum Lifetime Distribution of Consumption Expenditures: Comment," *American Economic Review* (September, 1970), pp. 736–37; Brian Motley and Samuel A. Morley, "The Optimum Lifetime Distribution of Consumption Expenditures: Comment," *American Economic Review* (September, 1970), pp. 738–43; Thurow, "The Optimum Lifetime Distribution of Consumption Expenditures: Reply," *American Economic Review* (September, 1970); and "Errata," *American Economic Review* (March, 1971), pp. 248–49.

[17]Obviously if every individual's income profile is different, this cannot be achieved for everyone. In this case, to choose a second-best tax structure on intertemporal efficiency grounds one may have to consider interpersonal equity goals to decide who should bear the deadweight burden of lifetime allocation inefficiencies.

[18]The question of what discount rate to use in computing lifetime income is not obvious since capital markets are assumed to be imperfect. This issue will be considered below.

[19]Menaham E. Yaari, "On the Consumer's Lifetime Allocation Process," *International Economic Review* (September, 1964), pp. 304–17.

[20]Definitions of all variables are summarized in Appendix A of this paper.

[21]Earl A. Thompson, "Intertemporal Utility Functions and the Long-Run Consumption Function," *Econometrica* (April, 1967), pp. 356–61. Yaari, "On the Consumer's Lifetime Allocation Process," has demonstrated that if the elasticity of consumption at each instant with respect to lifetime income is unity (at all points in time), then only two functional forms (or some linear combination of them) are admissible as indicators of utility at each instant: the logarithm, as used in the present paper, or some power function. This result assumes that the optimal consumption stream is nonconstant.

[22]Given the assumption that the consumer spends his entire income, we can solve for c_0 in terms of the other variables. The present value of the consumer's lifetime consumption is

$$(5) \qquad C = \int_0^T e^{-jt} c^*(t) \, dt = \int_0^T e^{-jt} c_0 e^{(j-r)t} \, dt = c_0 r^{-1} (1 - e^{-rT})$$

Setting (5) equal to (2) and solving for c_0 gives

$$(6) \qquad c_0 = r m_0 (i - j)^{-1} (1 - e^{-rT})^{-1} \left[e^{(i-j)T} - 1 \right]$$

[23]Thurow, "The Optimum Lifetime Distribution of Consumption Expenditures," *American Economic Review* (June, 1969), pp. 324–30.

[24]Although this could be proved rigorously, the intuitive argument is straightforward. Ignoring discounting, we know that the areas under the income and desired consumption profiles must be the same, and we have assumed that both streams are exponential functions. First, it should be intuitively obvious that they must cross at least once; otherwise, the areas under the curves could not possibly be the same if they are both monotonic. But can they cross just twice (or any finite number of times)? This is ruled out by the assumption that each function is exponential. However, they may "cross" an infinite number of times if they just happen to coincide.

[25]The equality of $(j - r)$ and i is also permitted, but this is not an interesting case since it leads to zero tax rates everywhere.

[26]For convenience, the argument "t" will not be written out for $m(t)$ and $c^*(t)$.

[27]Average rate progression is defined as the slope of the average rate tax structure. See Richard A. Musgrave and Tun Thin, "Income Tax Progression, 1929–1948," *Journal of Political Economy* (December, 1948), pp. 498–514.

[28]In an earlier version of this paper a more complicated model of a many-consumer economy was developed. However, it quickly became analytically unmanageable and had to be solved by computer for particular values of the parameters. Since those results were qualitatively no different from the ones derived in the simpler version, I have opted for simplicity and an analytical solution.

[29]"A Lorenz curve is a plotting of the cumulative proportion of units arrayed in order from the smallest incomes to the largest against the cumulative share of the aggregate income accounted for by these units" (Morgan, "The Anatomy of Income Distribution," p. 281). Two different Lorenz curves are illustrated in Figure 4, where P is the cumulated population percentage and Y is the cumulated aggregate income

FIGURE 4
Hypothetical Lorenz Curves

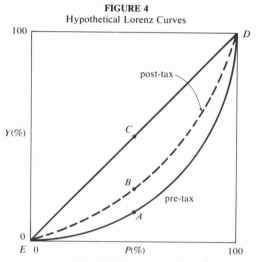

percentage. If there were complete equality, the distribution would be represented by the diagonal ECD. The curve EBD indicates some inequality, and the curve EAD shows even more. The Gini coefficient is defined as the ratio of the area below the Lorenz curve to the area below the diagonal. A coefficient equal to unity indicates perfect equality. (Some authors define the Gini coefficient as the ratio between the Lorenz curve and the diagonal to the area below the diagonal.)

[30]See Musgrave and Thin, "Income Tax Progression, 1929–1948," *Journal of Political Economy* (December, 1948); also Musgrave, *The Theory of Public Finance* (New York: McGraw-Hill, 1959), p. 224.

[31]It should be noted that the model does not constrain the budget to be balanced at every point in time. The government may have a surplus of deficit due solely to its role as intertemporal redistributor. Because this issue is not of central importance to our investigation, it will be assumed that a surplus at any point in time is redistributed in proportion to the distribution of income at that time, so that it leaves the size distribution unchanged. A similar assumption applies for the use of tax increases to finance any deficit. Alternatively, deficits or surpluses may be eradicated by government lending or borrowing in the "world" capital market.

[32]In the earlier more complicated version of the model the population grew at a constant rate. This had no effect on the qualitative results except in some pathological cases (such as rates over 50 percent a year).

[33]A proof of (29) to a third-order approximation is provided in Appendix B.

[34]That such a large redistribution from the rich to the poor might show up as regressive is a strong conceptual indictment of cross-sectional measures of incidence in general, and the Gini coefficient measure in particular.

[35]Musgrave and Thin, "Income Tax Progression, 1929–1948," p. 500.

[36]Gillespie, "Effect of Public Expenditures on the Distribution of Income," in Musgrave, ed., *Essays in Fiscal Federalism* (1965).

[37]Since Gillespie did not present his results in terms of Gini coefficients, these were computed by the author from his data. The raw data used were contained in: Table 11—line 1; Table 13—line 13; Table 14—lines 6, 14; Table 15—line 17; and Table 16—line 17. The Lorenz curve was approximated by linear interpolation between the seven points determined by the data.

[38]These points were suggested to me by James Buchanan and Burton Weisbrod.

[39]The additional administrative requirements of an age-specific plan are quite similar to cumulative income averaging (to be considered below). William Vickrey has argued in some detail that the administrative burdens from cumulative averaging would be surprisingly small. See Vickrey, "Averaging of Income for Income-Tax Purposes," *Journal of Political Economy* (June, 1939), pp. 379–97. Also Vickrey, *Agenda for Progressive Taxation* (New York: Ronald Press, 1947).

[40]For a discussion of various forms of income averaging, see Vickrey, *Agenda for Progressive Taxation*, pp. 169–74.

[41]I am abstracting from the problem of the uncertainty of death and the technical details of how to average at the beginning of the accounting period.

[42]See Vickrey, "Averaging of Income for Income-Tax Purposes." Also Vickrey, *Agenda for Progressive Taxation.*

[43]See Elizabeth Deran, "Income Redistribution under the Social Security System," *National Tax Journal* (September, 1966), pp. 276–85. See also Henry Aaron, "Benefits under the American Social Security System," in Otto Eckstein, ed., *Studies in the Economics of Income Maintenance* (Washington, D.C.: Brookings Institution, 1967), pp. 49–72.

[44]For numerous citations reflecting this viewpoint in the economics literature, see George J. Stigler, "Imperfections in the Capital Market," *Journal of Political Economy* (June, 1967), pp. 287–92.

[45]Thurow, "The Optimum Lifetime Distribution of Consumption Expenditures," *American Economic Review* (June, 1969).

IV

Redistribution and the Public Choice Process

10

Representative Assemblies and Demands for Redistribution: The Case of Senate Voting on the Family Assistance Plan

OTTO A. DAVIS AND JOHN E. JACKSON

Whether representatives vote in accordance with the desires or preferences (somehow defined) of their constituencies is probably the oldest and most central issue in the study of democracy. Certainly, all the rational models of politics assume that representatives do somehow represent the interests of their voters. When this assumption is joined with the commonplace observation that a narrow definition of self-interest should indicate that a majority of almost any constituency might benefit from redistribution, one has what appears to be an obvious paradox. Voters should demand redistribution. Democratic institutions should produce a response to these demands. Yet very little explicit redistribution seems to occur in those countries governed by representative assemblies.

What is the explanation of this apparent paradox? Do representatives somehow refrain from responding to the desires of their con-

Otto A. Davis is Professor of Political Economy and Associate Dean of the School of Urban and Public Affairs at Carnegie-Mellon University. John E. Jackson is Associate Professor of Government at Harvard University. Professor Davis is indebted for support to the National Science Foundation for a grant to Carnegie-Mellon. Professor Jackson is indebted for support to Resources for the Future for a grant to Harvard University. For helpful comments thanks are due Professor James S. Coleman, University of Chicago; J. Patrick Moynihan, Harvard University, and at present Ambassador to India; A. Myrick Freemann, III, Bowdoin College; and George E. Peterson, The Urban Institute.

stituents on this issue? Are voters motivated by something other than a narrow view of their own self-interest? This paper attempts to cast some light upon such questions by an examination of a particular case where specific legislation with redistributive intent was considered by the Senate of the United States.

The particular case to be studied here is the voting in the Senate that is associated with the proposal to establish the Family Assistance Plan (often referred to as FAP). The effort to enact FAP terminated, at least temporarily, on December 28, 1970, when the Senate voted 49 to 21 to kill the part of HR 17550 dealing with the proposal of President Nixon as it was amended by Senator Ribicoff and other Senate liberals.

Equal proportions of the Senate Republicans and non-Southern Democrats voted against killing the plan whereas all the Southern Democrats voting favored its demise. Does this represent the work of one or two powerful Southern committee chairmen, the opposition of Southern Democrats to a plan proposed by a Republican president, or the strong opposition of constituents in the Southern states to a guaranteed income plan? The truth or falsity of these various explanations is important in designing strategies to pass or defeat a version of FAP in the future. They also have implications for the efficacy of the legislative process as it operates in the United States.

In this paper we argue that the evidence suggests that the influence of the constituency is probably the appropriate explanation. Later in the paper attention is given to an explanation of some of the factors contributing to people's support or opposition to the Family Assistance Plan. This later part of the paper is admittedly speculative. However, it may be of general interest since it raises some questions about the meaning that can be attached to self-interest as this concept is used to explain the attitudes of voters. In terms of our organization of the paper, it is necessary to give a very brief outline of the proposed Family Assistance Plan and a summary of its intended benefits. After this, responses to a survey that asked people whether they favored or opposed substituting a minimum family income plan for the current welfare system are analyzed to determine which factors are associated with opposition to or support for the plan. This analysis is used to construct a variable assessing the support within each state for FAP. This variable is an important part of the basis for our explanation of senators' voting on the parts of the HR 17550 relating to FAP. Our speculative concluding argument and some additional data suggest that the most evident opposition to the plan, as observed in the explanations of Senate voting, may be based on a misunderstanding of, or lack of information about, the intent and likely impact of the plan.

THE FAMILY ASSISTANCE PLAN

The essential ingredient of the Family Assistance Plan was a guarantee by the Federal Government that families who qualified would have a specified minimal income. Under the Nixon plan a family of four with no income would have received a payment of approximately $1,600. Families with some earnings, the working poor, were to be eligible on a decreasing scale until their annual incomes reached $3,920.

Insofar as incomes in the South are relatively lower than in the rest of the country, it appears that the South would have been the major beneficiary. According to one estimate, roughly half the families affected would have been in the South.[1] In addition, a high proportion of these families would be black. The direct benefits to the Northern states were estimated to be considerably less. In fact, some Northern states already provide more in benefits under existing AFDC programs than those proposed in the FAP legislation. The Federal Government would have picked up 10 percent of the costs of existing programs in these Northern states.

DATA AND ANALYSIS OF SUPPORT
FOR FAMILY ASSISTANCE

This very limited discussion of the proposed Family Assistance Plan suggests patterns of support for the program. Support should be related to a person's income, race, possibly region of residence, and

TABLE 1
Proportion Favoring Family Assistance Plan
Income in Thousands of Dollars

Whites

	Urban Sample/Income Class						Rural Sample/Income Class					
	<3	3-5	5-7.5	7.5-15	15-25	>25	<3	3-5	5-7.5	7.5-15	15-25	>25
West												
Favorable %	0.90	0.57	0.64	0.43	0.67	0.00	0.72	0.56	0.42	0.39	0.50	0.00
Cell size	10	7	11	30	3	1	18	16	31	67	18	3
North Central												
Favorable %	1.00	0.60	0.25	0.53	0.82	0.40	0.69	0.55	0.50	0.40	0.43	0.10
Cell size	3	5	8	45	11	5	42	31	38	103	28	10
Northeast												
Favorable %	0.83	0.63	0.47	0.62	0.50	0.62	0.64	0.58	0.52	0.45	0.50	0.67
Cell size	12	8	19	60	16	13	11	12	23	74	8	3
South												
Favorable %	0.40	0.83	0.36	0.36	0.50	0.29	0.58	0.50	0.59	0.39	0.39	0.14
Cell size	5	6	11	28	12	7	43	38	66	94	23	7

Blacks

	West		North Central		Northeast		South	
	Urban	Rural	Urban	Rural	Urban	Rural	Urban	Rural
Favorable %	0.69	0.67	0.90	0.68	0.90	1.00	0.85	0.59
Cell size	16	3	10	25	19	2	13	41

location of his residence in a metropolitan or a rural area. These elementary propositions can be tested with data from an economic survey taken by the Survey Research Center of the University of Michigan in the fourth quarter of 1969. One of the questions in this survey was: "Some say that welfare should be replaced by a system in which the government raises the income of the poor so that every family in the country would have an income at least equal to some minimum poverty standard. What do you think of this proposal?"

Responses were coded in the following fashion:

1. Good idea.
2. Good idea, with qualifications (if they make it fair; if they make a person work, etc.).
3. Both pro and con.
4. Bad idea (other reason, or no answer why).
   Bad because:
5. Too expensive a plan.
6. Impossible to do; can't fairly decide who needs it, and some people would take advantage of it.
7. DK: undecided.
8. NA.

These responses were recoded into the trichotomous responses of Favorable (items 1, 2), Unfavorable (items 4, 5, 6), and No Opinion (items 3, 7, 8). Of the total sample, 46 percent favored the plan, 13 percent had no expressed opinion, and 41 percent opposed it. Thus a very high proportion of the respondents expressed an opinion on the basic idea underlying FAP. The remainder of this analysis will concentrate solely on those individuals who expressed an opinion. From other data in the survey the proportion favoring the plan could be analyzed by the respondent's race, region, and metropolitan or rural residence, and income for whites only. The black sample was not large enough to make a comparison by income. Table 1 shows the cross-tabulation of percentage favoring FAP by race, region, urban or rural residence, and income, along with the number of people in each cell. Unfortunately, in a sample size of only 1469, many of the cells have small frequencies. However, even allowing for this difficulty, there are indications that the probability of favoring the

Family Assistance Plan does vary systematically with our explanatory variables. The most obvious difference is between blacks and nonblacks. The proportion of blacks favoring the plan varied from 59 percent among rural Southerners to over 90 percent among urban North Central and Northeastern blacks, and 72 percent of all blacks having an opinion favored the plan, compared to 50 percent of all whites. There are also detectable income and urban-rural differences, with support decreasing as incomes rise and among rural residents. There does not appear to be any easily detectable regional variation.

These casual observations can be examined systematically, using the logit analysis described by Theil.[2] The application of this technique means essentially that the proportions shown in Table 1 are used as estimates of the probability (P) that a person with a given set of characteristics will favor FAP. With this technique, which converts these estimated probabilities to the log of the odds [the log of $P/(1 - P)$], the effect of each of the classifications shown in Table 1 upon this logit value can be estimated and systematically related to the odds of favoring FAP. Ideally, one would like substantially larger cell sizes. However, the procedure has the advantage of giving considerably less weight to cells with small frequencies, so that it also takes these small cell sizes into account when estimating the variance of the coefficients. Those coefficients that relate to cells of sizes consistently small enough will have relatively larger estimated variances. As a matter of fact, this effect applies additionally in an absolute way so that all our estimated coefficients will have large variances due to our unfortunately small cell sizes.

Table 2 gives the estimated coefficients for this logit model and their estimated variances. These coefficients estimate the change in the logit value, the log of the odds of favoring FAP, associated with each of the different classifications constructed in Table 1. For example, a white who earns less than $3,000 and lives in the rural West has an estimated logit value of 0.62; this estimate corresponds to a probability of 0.71 that he favors adoption of FAP. Other coefficients indicate that residence in an urban as opposed to a rural area increases the value of the logit by 0.30 for whites and 1.11 for nonwhites.

Also note that these estimates indicate that the probability of

TABLE 2

Estimated Coefficients for the Logit Model

Region

	Const.	*North Central*	*Northeast*	*South*	*Urban*
Whites Favor	0.62	0.04	0.26	−0.10	0.30
Standard Error	0.23	0.18	0.19	0.18	0.14
Blacks Favor	−0.14	0.94	1.27	0.54	1.11
Standard Error	0.71	0.76	0.91	0.71	0.60

Income (thousands of dollars)

	3-5	*5-7.5*	*7.5-15*	*15-25*	*>25*
Whites	−0.47	−0.68	−1.01	− 0.81	−1.36
Standard Error	0.26	0.23	0.21	0.27	0.40

favoring the Family Assistance Plan decreases markedly with increasing income. With the exception of the 15,000 to 25,000 dollar range, where there was an absolute decrease in the (negative) value of the logit coefficient, the absolute magnitude of these negative coefficients increased with each income range. This pattern indicates that the income class that gave most support to the proposal was the group with an income less than $3,000. Since those with low incomes are more likely to benefit and those with higher incomes are more likely to bear the cost burden of the plan, the general pattern or direction of these results is consistent with the notion that a narrowly conceived view of one's self-interest is a major determinant of individual attitudes, although the negative sign of the coefficients on the lower income groups is not obviously derivable from this notion.

Blacks were also more likely to support the plan than whites. Although the data on incomes are not sufficiently detailed to allow a full analysis of the nonwhite parts of the sample, the probability of a black of any income (except in the rural West) favoring FAP is higher than the probability of whites in the under 5,000 dollar category, and in two of the classifications this probability is higher than that for whites in the very lowest income class, under $3,000. Since the median income for both rural and urban blacks is 5,000 dollars or slightly higher, this would suggest that, with only minor exceptions, blacks have a higher propensity to favor the plan than whites in the same region.

All three of these results are consistent with the notions of self-interest discussed above and implicit in the variable classifications in Tables 1 and 2. These notions are not meant to be complete explanations of individuals' attitudes. Thus one might draw upon certain sociological and *ad hoc* arguments to indicate that blacks and urban dwellers (in addition to the poor) are the most likely supporters of FAP. It is important to note, however, that these explanations are complementary to, and certainly do not contradict, the idea that narrow self-interest is an important determinant of attitudes.

The results for regional effects are a striking contrast to the picture above. Since the idea of FAP clearly aims at the redistribution of income, and since there are obvious regional income differences within the United States, the aggregate redistributional consequences of the plan are clear. One might think *a priori* that these consequences would be reflected in the estimated coefficients. The major recipient of the transfer would be the South, and the largest donor would be the Northeast. True a very large proportion of the Southern families receiving aid from FAP would be black, but a most elementary knowledge of spending habits and multiplier theories leads to the conclusion that Southern white families too would obtain a large benefit through indirectly increased incomes. More will be said about this later. For the moment it is sufficient to note that a narrow view of self-interest as a major determinant of attitudes should imply that both white and black Southerners should lend relatively the largest support to the plan, whereas whites in the Northeast should be the least favorable. In fact, or at least according to these estimates, whites in the South were less likely to support the FAP than were whites from any other region. At the same time, whites from the Northeast were more likely to favor the plan than the argument above would indicate. Note that the logit for a white Northeasterner is 0.26, which is the largest of the regional logits. In addition, there appears to be little difference between whites with the same income level from the West and North Central regions. Thus not only are the differences in regional coefficients not as statistically significant as might be expected on *a priori* grounds, but such differences as there are tend to be in the opposite direction from what is implied by a narrow view of self-interest. White persons in the South appear to be more opposed to the program and those in the Northeast appear to me more likely to favor FAP than is consistent with the self-interest hypothesis.

Although the black and white patterns of support for FAP are not identical, the black pattern too appears somewhat paradoxical. Western blacks are least likely to favor the program, followed by those in the South, the North Central, and then the Northeast regions. Thus Southern residents are again less likely to favor the program than Northerners. It is also interesting to note from Table 1 that the group of blacks least likely to favor FAP are those living in the rural South. Although we are not controlling for income here, it is clear that black rural Southerners are the group likely to benefit most from the program. The two groups most strongly in favor of the plan were the urban blacks in the Northeast and North Central areas. Thus the results for blacks are relatively similar to the results for whites on a regional basis. Certainly, these are not the results that one would predict if one believed that narrow self-interest is the only determinant of basic attitudes and opinions. Although not wishing to overdo the point, we devote the latter part of this paper to a more systematic examination of at least one part of this seeming contradiction between self-interest and attitudes.

DATA AND MODELS CONCERNING
SENATE VOTING ON FAP

The next question is whether these systematic differences in support for FAP among different income groups, places of residence, races, and regions can be used to explain the observed differences in Senate voting. At least at a conceptual level it is easy to incorporate this information to estimate a constituency variable by using the results from the previous analysis. If data on the income distribution within each state by race and urban-rural areas were available, it would be a straightforward task to use our estimates of the probability of support within each income and urban-rural classification to estimate support for FAP among each state's electorate. These data are usually prepared by the Census Bureau as part of the decennial census. Unfortunately, the Census Bureau is falling badly behind its projected dates for making the data available.

The only state data available at this time concern the family income distribution for whites and nonwhites and for metropolitan and nonmetropolitan residents. These data do not give the white income distribution separately for metropolitan and nonmetropolitan areas. In order to get around this deficiency, white income distributions for metropolitan and nonmetropolitan areas were estimated from the available data. Within each income category, the distribution of whites between metropolitan and nonmetropolitan areas was assumed to be the same as that for all the people in that income category. For example, if there were N white families in an income category, and if 60 percent of all the state's families in this income category lived in metropolitan areas, it was assumed that $0.6N$ white families lived in metropolitan areas. This same calculation was continued over all the income categories shown in Table 1. From these calculations, the percentage distribution of whites by income class in both the metropolitan and nonmetropolitan areas of each state was estimated.[3]

The approximations above make possible the construction of a constituency variable for each senator — the proportion of the people in each state expected to favor the Family Assistance Plan. Consider the following definitions:

$F^w_{i,j,k}$ = proportion of metropolitan ($i = 1$) or rural ($i = 2$) whites in income class j and region k who favor FAP.

$Y^w_{i,j,m}$ = proportion of metropolitan or nonmetropolitan whites in income class j in state m (which is in region k).

$N^w_{i,m}$ = number of whites in state m who live in metropolitan or nonmetropolitan areas.

$F^B_{i,k}$ = proportion of metropolitan or nonmetropolitan nonwhites in region k who favor FAP.

$N_{i,m}^B$ = number of nonwhites in area i and state m (in region k).

N_m = total population in state $m = N_{1,m}^w + N_{2,m}^w + N_{1,m}^B + N_{2,m}^B$.

By using these definitions, the income distribution data estimated by the method outlined above, the number of whites and nonwhites in metropolitan and nonmetropolitan areas in each state, and the proportion of each group expected to favor a Family Assistance Plan derived from Table 2, one can estimate the constituency variable (denoted C_m) for each two senators (one estimate for each state) by the following formulation:

$$(1) \quad C_m = \left(\sum_{j=1}^{6} F_{1jk}^w * Y_{1jm}^w * N_{1,m}^w + \sum_{j=1}^{6} F_{2,j,k}^w * Y_{2,j,m}^w * N_{2,m}^w \right. $$
$$\left. + F_{1,k}^B * N_{1,m}^B + F_{2,k}^B * N_{2,m}^B \right) \Big/ (N_m)$$

Although there are problems inherent in the formula above, the estimates it gives appear to be the best that can be obtained from available data, and these will be used in the analysis that follows.

The support that senators gave to the proposed assistance plan will be measured by their votes on three different roll calls taken at the end of December relating to the welfare parts of HR 17550 rather than the single vote on the motion to kill the part of the bill containing FAP. The first of these votes was taken on Long's (Democrat, La.) motion to table Ribicoff's (Democrat, Conn.) amendment to HR 17550 establishing the Family Assistance Plan. Long is Chairman of the Senate Finance Committee that had voted earlier to keep FAP out of the legislation. Ribicoff is also a member of the Finance Committee and had been the leader of a group of liberals trying to gain consideration for FAP. The second vote was taken on a proposal by Harris (Democrat, Okla.) to delete from consideration several proposals added by the Finance Committee that strengthened eligibility rules for the current welfare plan. For example, the Committee proposals would have re-established a one-year residency requirement and the "man-in-the-house" rule, both of which had been struck down by the Supreme Court. The third vote was the one discussed previously that in effect killed the FAP proposal.

These three votes were used to construct a Guttman scale measuring senators' support for FAP, which included the Harris amendment attempting to kill certain restrictive eligibility proposals. The scale might be viewed more as a welfare-reform scale than a simple FAP scale. However, since the enactment of FAP certainly would have effectively lightened eligibility requirements and prevented the residency and man-in-the-house criteria, one can argue that the votes above can be used to constitute a scale that does effectively represent the degree of support for Family Assistance. There were 83 senators who cast a sufficient number of votes to be scalable. Table 3 shows the distribution of senators by scale score, where zero constitutes the least support for FAP and represents those senators who voted to kill Ribicoff's amendment. This would have had the effect of preventing the Senate from considering FAP. Thus zero represents those who are totally opposed to even considering the proposal.

There were 6 nonscale votes cast out of a total of 247. This total includes pairs and announced votes. The coefficient of reproducibility is 0.976, and the minimal marginal reproducibility is 0.729. These are two figures often used to assess the content of Guttman scales. The first is simply the percentage of the votes that fit the scale pattern, and the second is the proportion of votes that would have been predicted correctly just on the basis of every vote's being cast with the majority. By conventional standards this must be considered a good scale. This variable constitutes our measure of a senator's support for FAP and is the behavior to be explained with our constituency variable.

The equation that will be used to relate estimated constituency preferences to senators' voting is very simple and straightforward. In an article trying to assess the systematic influence of constituency and leadership on senatorial voting, Jackson showed that there were in fact clear differences in the effects of the formal and informal leaders upon the members of various regional groupings of the senators

TABLE 3

Distribution of Scale Scores on the FAP Guttman Scale

Score	0	1	2	3
Number of Senators	13	39	14	17

from each party.[4] In these results non-Southern Democrates were more likely to give weight to the various internal or leadership variables, whereas Republicans and Southern Democrats generally were more constituency oriented, with the Southerners being more so than the Republicans. Unfortunately, these results were based on a sample of bills from 1961 and 1962. At that time the Democrats had control of the White House for the first time in eight years. Thus one might reasonably expect greater responsiveness among non-Southern Democrats to the leadership variables, and less among Republicans. In 1970, when the FAP was being considered, there was a Republican in the White House although the Democrats still controlled the Senate. In addition, many of the senatorial leaders and the individual senators themseleves had changed. Consequently, Jackson's detailed results may not be an exact representation of the influence patterns operating in 1970. However, the general pattern of relative leadership and constituency effects represented in his results, if not their exact magnitudes, should be an integral part of the behavior of senators during all recent periods of time.

The implication of Jackson's study for our model of FAP voting is that each of the three groups of senators (Southern and non-Southern Democrats and Republicans) may have systematically different constituency and leadership coefficients. Ideally, we should like to allow for the (possibly) different behavior by permitting different intercept and constituency coefficients to be estimated for each of the three groups. This objective could be accomplished by the provision of a complete set of intercept and slope dummy variables. Unfortunately, our early attempts to estimate such a model provided evidence that the complete set of variables could not be included in our equation because of extreme multicollinearity. The simple correlations between the intercept and slope dummies for both the Republicans and Southern Democrats exceeded 0.99. Consequently, the model was re-estimated in an acceptable and interesting but less than perfectly ideal form.

The re-estimated model is given below as equation 2. In this equation, V represents the support a senator gave to the FAP proposal, R is a dummy that is one for all Republicans and zero otherwise, S is a dummy variable that is one for all Southern Democrats and zero otherwise, and C is the constituency variable that is our estimate of the proportion of each state's population favoring the substitution of FAP for the current welfare plan.

$$(2) \qquad V = a_1 + a_2 R + a_3 S + a_4 C$$

In this regression-type model with dummy variables the constant term a_1 is associated with the group for whom there is no dummy, the Northern Democrats. The coefficients a_2 and a_3 for the respective R and S variables measure the effect of merely being a Republican or a Southern Democrat upon the votes of FAP. Thus, given the same constituency support, these coefficients measure the systematic differences in the behavior of the three groups of senators arising from ideologies, different leadership effects, and other causes. Obviously, the coefficient a_4 measures how a senator's support of FAP changes as his constituents' preferences change.

ESTIMATION AND INTERPRETATION OF
THE SENATE VOTING MODEL

It is not appropriate to use a standard ordinary least squares regression to estimate the Senate voting equation above because of the presence of the Guttman scale scores as the dependent variable. These Guttman scale scores are merely ordinal measurements of the senators' positions on FAP so that is is not proper to interpret them as interval measures. In addition these scale scores contain some measurement error because they group together senators whose positions are different but fall between the same two amendments. This difficulty is illustrated in Figure 1, where V is the possible positions on FAP and X is the constituency position on the bill. The line

FIGURE 1
Senator's Votes and Constituency Interests

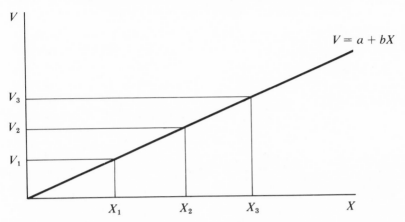

$V = a + bX$ represents the true relationship between a senator's position on FAP and his constituency's preference, assuming that V could be measured precisely and that the senator could be induced to reveal his actual position. Unfortunately, neither of these is possible.

A workable alternative is to use Guttman scales to provide an approximation to the various senators' positions as they are revealed by the pattern of their yes and no votes on different roll calls. Again with reference to Figure 1, the lines marked V_1, V_2, and V_3 represent the three amendments. Any senator whose preference falls below V_1 will vote no on all votes and will be scored a zero. Any senator with preferences falling between V_1 and V_2 will be scored a one, etc. In fact, senators' preferences will be scattered above and below the line $a + bX$ so that some senators will have the "wrong" score. An immediate objective is to use the Guttman scores and estimates of the constituents' sentiments about FAP to estimate the coefficients a and b in Figure 1. The particular procedure utilized for this task, which was designed for Guttman scales of this type, estimates the values for the coefficients a and b and the locations of the votes making up the scale V_1, V_2, and V_3 that make the actual observed scale scores most likely, assuming the senator's actual preferences are distributed normally about the line $V = a + bX$. This procedure, developed by Zavoina and McKelvey,[5] provides estimates for these five values as well as estimates of the variances. Their program was used to provide the estimates reported below.

The results are shown in equation 3. The negative intercept term indicates that if nobody in a state favors FAP (for example, $C = 0.0$), there is very little likelihood that a senator from that state will vote for the plan. Furthermore, the negative coefficients for the R and S variables indicate that even with equivalent constituency attitudes, Republicans and Southern Democrats exhibited less support for FAP than Northern Democrats. This was particularly true for Southern Democrats. These coefficients are statistically significant by most standard tests. The large and highly significant constituency coefficient indicates that

(3)
$$V = -6.62 - 0.96R - 2.86S + 17.07C$$
$$(1.89) \quad (0.30) \quad (0.47) \quad (3.69)$$
$$V_1 = 0.00 \quad V_2 = 2.11 \quad V_3 = 2.92$$

a senator's votes were quite sensitive to his constituency's opinion on the bill. This estimate indicates that for each additional 10 percent of the people who favor FAP, a senator's position on the bill increases by 1.71 points. To establish a benchmark, note that this increase can be compared to the difference of 2.11 between the first two amendments and 0.81 between the last two. These differences mean that it would take a change of 17 percent in the proportion of the constituency that favors the plan to get a senator voting against considering the plan to support it. The results obviously imply that consituencies did exert an important influence over how senators were voting on the Family Assistance Plan.

In order both to further the richness and to reduce the difficulties of interpretation implicit in these results, consider the case of the Southern Democrats. Note that there is substantial initial opposition indicated by the negative coefficient. This opposition may either be the result of the influence of Senator Long, who strongly opposed the plan and is the chairman of the Senate Finance Committee, or reflect a set of personal preferences of the Southern senators against the Family Assistance Plan. This evidence does not allow one to distinguish between these two different (and not necessarily mutually exclusive) explanations.

Since models never fit perfectly, one obvious strategy to determine the reasonableness of the results is to examine deviations from the prediction of the model. There were thirty-four senators who had votes that were not predicted correctly. These senators can be grouped into four categories. The first is the group of future (for 1970) Democratic presidential contenders. There were seven of these men in the Senate and voting on these bills.[6] All these senators come from states whose constituencies were basically opposed to the plan, and all but McCarthy were underestimated by at least one vote. Undoubtedly these men were responding to the wishes of the constituency needed to win the Democratic nomination rather than their home state constituency.

A second group of deviants were five Southern Democrats, —Senators Fulbright and McClellan of Arkansas, Spong and Byrd of Virginia, and Talmadge of Georgia. These were also underestimated by one vote. One might argue that Arkansas and Virginia are not in the core South and, with the exception of Florida, have a lower percentage of blacks in their population than other Southern states. This observation suggests that Southern senators' opposition to the plan may be directly related to the size of the black population, which is likely to be the main beneficiary.

The last systematic group of senators whose votes deviated from the model's predictions were a set of liberal, industrial-state Republicans, whose actual votes were more "pro-FAP" than predicted. They were Case (New Jersey), Scott and Schweiker (Pa.), Brooke (Mass.), Griffin (Mich.), and Hatfield (Ore.), although the last named is obviously from a Western state. There are two possible explanations for these errors. One is that since Scott and Griffin are the Republican leaders in the Senate and FAP was originally a Nixon proposal, these senators are simply supporting their president. An alternative explanation is that each of these Eastern senators was responding to the interests of a particular group in his constituency. Recall from Tables 1 and 2 that urban blacks in the Northeast and North Central regions gave FAP considerably greater support than did any other group. Most of these senators have a sizable urban black population in their constituencies. Thus they might be trying to obtain the support of their black constituency by voting for the Family Assistance Plan. Obviously, these two explanations may be complementary. These senators would find it very easy to support the president if they suspected that an important part of their constituency also liked the proposed legislation. One might note, however, that most of these senators voted against the president on such issues as Supreme Court nominations, which the president pushed much harder than he pushed FAP. Indeed, popular accounts explained their votes against the Administration nominees on the grounds that blacks and liberals in their constituencies were strongly opposed to those nominees. One can argue that these residuals lend further support to the contention that the Senate votes on FAP were strongly tied to constituency opinions.

The remaining fourteen senators whose votes were not predicted correctly did not fit into any noticeable pattern. They consisted of both Republicans and Democrats from all regions but the South. There did not appear to be any systematic explanation for these errors in prediction, and they may be the result of statistically random effects such as logrolling with other legislation and personal opposition to the plan.

Given the explanation above, it appeared appropriate to respecify the equation in an effort to incorporate at least some of the effects indicated in these explanations of predictive error. One obvious way to do this is to take into account the fact that seven senators were presidential aspirants and may have behaved in a manner that differentiated them from their colleagues. Hence, let P represent a dummy variable that takes on the value of one when the senator in question is a presidential aspirant and zero otherwise. Clearly, this variable should have a positive coefficient associated with it. The other way, which appears to be related to both Republican and Southern Democratic predictive errors, is that a black (or nonwhite) constituency may have an influence that is not at all identical with the influence of a white constituency. Let N represent the proportion of a state's nonwhite population that is predicted to favor FAP from Table 2 times the proportion of the state's population that is nonwhite. This variable incorporates both the support for FAP among nonwhites and their potential political strength. Since the different groupings of senators might be expected to behave differently with respect to their nonwhite constituency, the equation should allow for such a differential effect. Consider the following specification:

(4) $\quad V = a_1 + a_2R + a_3S + a_4C + a_5P + a_6N + a_7NS + a_8NR$

where V, R, S, and C are the variables used previously, P is the presidential aspirant dummy, and N is the nonwhite variable defined above. The NS and NR variables are the values of N when it is multiplied by the dummy variables for Southern Democrats and Northern Republicans. The five Southern and Border State Republicans are excluded from this last variable so that NR represents only the nonwhite effects for Republicans outside the Southern and Border States.[7]

The interpretation of these coefficients is similar to that given for the earlier specification (equation 2). Accordingly, although a full discussion is not warranted here, it may be desirable to discuss the newly introduced variables. The interpretation of the coefficient for presidential aspirants is straightforward and simply measures the special support that those senators gave to FAP beyond what would otherwise have been predicted for them. The nonwhite support variables measure the difference in the weight accorded nonwhites' preferences by our three groups of senators — Southern Democrats, Northern Republicans, and all others (predominately Northern Democrats). For example, a_6 measures the difference between the weights given to whites and nonwhites by Northern Democrats and Border and Southern Republicans and a_7 and a_8 estimate how this difference changes if one considers Southern Democrats or Northern Republicans respectively. To illustrate, a_4 is the weight each senator gives his white constituents, $a_4 + a_6$ is the weight a Northern Democrat gives his nonwhite constituents, and $a_3 + a_6 + a_7$ is the weight a Southern Democrat gives the nonwhites in his state. The equation is specified this way because we are primarily interested in a_7 and a_8, the coefficients on the NS and NR variables, because our hypothesis is that Northern Republicans and Southern Democrats behave differently from other senators with respect to their nonwhite constituents.

The estimated coefficients for this specification of the model are given in Table 4. The Southern Democrats' dummy variable, S, was deleted because it was no longer important or statistically significant. The standard error of the coefficient on this variable was considerably larger than the coefficient itself in the re-estimated model. The results are good and in general agreement with those of the earlier specification. The sign of the coefficient for the presidential aspirant variable is positive, as was expected. The estimated coefficient on the preferences of the nonwhite population for Northern Democrats is rather surprising. The coefficient suggests that as the proportion of the state's population which is nonwhite increases. the weight given the constituency decreases! Thus the effect on a Northern Democrat's vote if an additional 10 percent of the population favors FAP is 2.39 if the attitude change is among whites and 1.39 if the change is among the black populace.

The Southern Democratic coefficient indicates that this group of senators gives even less weight to nonwhites than do their Northern colleagues. The Republicans outside the South and Border States, on the other hand, have a positive coefficient and appear to give more weight to nonwhites than either of the other groups. In fact, these coefficients imply that on this bill Republicans gave slightly more weight to nonwhites in their constituency than to whites. The implicit coefficient on nonwhite preferences was 24.31. This fact does not mean, of course, that Republicans in general were more likely to support the proposal than Democrats. It only makes sense to compare the expected support of a Republican and a Northern Democrat by assuming that both came from the same state. In this case, if 75 percent of the nonwhites support the plan, the state's minority population must exceed 15 percent before the Republican senator is more likely than the Northern Democrat to support the plan. Alaska and Maryland are the only non-Southern states whose proportion of nonwhites exceeds this number. In states with less than one percent nonwhite, a state with a Republican senator must have an additional 5 percent of the people in favor of FAP

TABLE 4

Coefficients in the Respecified Senate Voting Equation

Variable	Coefficient	Standard Error
Constant	− 9.68	2.57
Republican	− 1.15	0.42
Presidential candidate	1.56	0.53
Constituency	23.91	5.19
Nonwhite preference	−10.09	4.39
Southern democrat nonwhite preference	−11.11	4.10
Republican nonwhite preference	10.49	5.38
$V_1 = 0.00$	$V_2 = 2.49$	$V_3 = 3.50$

to get its senator to exhibit the same support of the plan as a Democrat.

Before one definitely concludes that Northern Democrats give less weight to blacks than to whites, an alternative explanation for the negative coefficient on the nonwhite preference variable for these senators should be examined. Pat Moynihan, when showed an early draft of this paper, commented that he thought the data in Table 1 overestimated black support for the proposed Family Assistance Plan. He added that we should "be sure to point out that the members of the black caucus in the House voted against the plan when it came up again" as partial evidence that black support was not as strong as the survey makes it appear to be. Blacks' support of the plan may have declined substantially between 1969 and 1970 because of the increased emphasis on the workfare aspects of the bill. In this case the constituency variables would overestimate a senator's constituency support for FAP by an amount directly proportional to the black percent of the state's population and the estimated black support for the bill. A variable measuring these proportions would then adjust for this systematic bias in the constituency variable by having a negative coefficient. In this case, unless one has an estimate for the magnitude of the change in black attitudes, there is no way to estimate and remove any bias from the coefficient on the nonwhite preference variable. The relative differences in the coefficients for the three groups of senators should still stand, however, unless there happened to be a systematic pattern to the change in black attitudes that is correlated with the senators' parties. Except for Southerners, this is unlikely since many non-Southern states had both a Republican and a Democratic senator: for example, Massachusetts, New Jersey, Michigan, Iowa, and Idaho. Consequently, it seems reasonable to conclude that Republicans outside the Southern and Border states were most sensitive to nonwhite preferences on this issue whereas Southern Democrats were least sensitive, with non-Southern Democrats between the two groups.[8]

Aside from the negative coefficients for the nonwhite population's preferences, for the Southern and non-Southern Democrats, the major result to be noted in Table 4 is that the constituency coefficient remains positive, large, and significant. Thus, aside from the Democratic anomaly, the evidence associated with these votes on the Family Assistance Plan indicates that the preferences of the constituency do count and, indeed, are more influential than any other variable examined here in affecting the behavior of senators in their consideration of this redistributive measure. In this sense the paradox that was posed earlier is partly resolved. The preferences of the population are important in determining policy for the redistribution of income.

SELF-INTEREST AND THE PARADOX
OF SOUTHERN PREFERENCES

It is obvious, of course, that the positive conclusions, (1) that constituency preferences are taken into account and (2) that voting behavior can be explained by the variables discussed above, do not constitute a resolution of the paradox. The question of constituency attitudes remains. Why do the regional differences discussed earlier appear to be inconsistent with what might be expected from the narrow self-interest point of view? Why do Southerners appear to be more opposed to Family Assistance than persons residing in other parts of the nation? This section is devoted to an examination of these and related questions. In order to make the discussion meaningful, it is necessary to consider briefly some of the consequences of FAP.

Clearly, one of the prime objectives of Family Assistance is to transfer income from those who have some to those who do not. Since there are substantial regional differences in income distributions, especially at the lower end of the scale, it makes some sense to think about the regional consequences of FAP. According to a report compiled by the Bureau of the Census (1970), the Southern States have by far the largest concentrations of families whose incomes fall below the poverty line. This statement obtains no matter whether one thinks in terms of absolute numbers or percentages. Hence there can be no doubt that the regional essence of FAP is the transfer of income from the rest of the Nation to persons who reside in the South. Kain and Schafer estimate that the aggregate incomes of low-income Southern households would have increased by just over 1.5 billion dollars if FAP had been enacted.[9] Approximately 0.5 billion of this increase would have come from southern taxpayers, leaving approximately one billion dollars as a regional transfer.

There is nothing complicated about the direct benefits of this regional transfer. Low-income families, including a large part of the greater than 35 percent of the black Southern population that is below the poverty line, receive direct subsidies. We do not have to be very sophisticated, however, to realize that the story does not end with direct benefits. Poor people tend to spend their money. Hence a net transfer to the South implies that Southern retailers, wholesalers, and manufacturers will have increased revenues. As adjustments in the economy occur, the net transfer would act as a stimulant to Southern economic development. Kain and Shafer argue that a multiplier of 2.5 is reasonable, so the one billion transfer implies that Southern incomes would be raised by approximately 2.5 billion dollars by the enactment of FAP.

The fact that the direct and indirect effects of Family Assistance would be to raise average incomes in the South, with the negative net transfer to the other regions having the opposite implications for them, raises questions about the predictive power of the narrow version of the self-interest hypothesis. After all, and especially if other considerations were held roughly equal, this view of self-interest would seem to imply that one should find a greater degree of support for Family Assistance in the South than, say, the Northeast. On balance, the latter are net givers and the former the net receivers. In fact, the actual pattern of regional support is almost the opposite of that predicted by self-interest. Are there explanations for this seeming contradiction?

The non-Southern part of this contradiction does not appear to be nearly so interesting as the Southern part. After all, charity is relatively common and is seldom explained by narrow views of self-interest. Economists often argue that such behavior is consistent with a broad view of self-interest when the well-being of third parties is an argument of individual utility functions. Here, however, those who stand to benefit most, both black and white, tend to be more negative than those who are bearing the burden.

There are many myths about the attitudes of Southerners, and especially white Southerners, that might be presented as explanations of this paradox of preferences. First, there is the issue of prejudice. At the most elementary level, some might argue that Southern whites simply do not want poor Blacks to receive assistance. Although this argument clearly has little explanatory power for the pattern of Black preferences, it overlooks the fact that in absolute terms a larger number of white families might benefit. Hence, if the argument is true, it must be augmented with a willingness to sacrifice the benefits to fellow whites.

At a more sophisticated level, some might argue that Southern white opposition to Family Assistance is based upon migration patterns. Of course it is no secret that the last decades have witnessed a massive migration of blacks from the rural South to urban areas, particularly those in the North. As the mechanization of agriculture took place, black families looked for their best opportunities and found them in the urban North and West. Thus the sophisticated version of this argument might have it that prejudiced Southern whites favor this migration and are opposed to anything that might alter it. They see their area of the Nation getting rid of its major social problem. Let the disparity between the Northern and Southern welfare programs continue. Let the South, at least outside the major metropolitan areas, become white. Don't take a chance on disrupting the migration by adopting a Family Assistance Plan.

The fault with the above argument is that it does not appear to be based upon a full understanding of the facts. It does appear to be true, of course, that the adoption of FAP would tend to slow the rate of black migration. Kain and Schafer estimate that the Plan would decrease black out-migration from the South by 2.2 percent.[10] However, black migration is only part of the story. Since the early 1960's there has been a substantial white migration into the South as the area has become increasingly industrialized. Since the net regional transfer would help to speed up the process of industrialization, it probably would also increase white migration into the South. Kain and Schafer estimate that white in-migration would increase by 3.5 percent. Since this latter figure is applied to a larger base, the adoption of the Family Assistance Plan would mean that the Southern region would on net become more white than it would otherwise be. It would be curious, indeed, for a prejudiced Southern white to reject an opportunity to make the region more white.

Another version of this argument is associated with the work ethic. Some persons may simply feel that it is wrong to perpetuate or increase welfare programs and that it is even more wrong to provide the level of benefits associated with FAP to people who might choose not to work. Why people of such persuasion might be concentrated in the South is not entirely clear, but in any event the beliefs do not appear to be fully in accordance with what seem to be the facts. The tentative evidence from the Negative Income Tax Experiment indicates that insofar as such a program has a net effect on incentives for work they are positive.[11] The popular versions of the results associated with this experiment, reported in such periodicals as *Business Week,* suggested that people get hooked on money and desire more, even to the extent of being willing to work for it. In any event, there were substantial workfare provisions in the bill.

We could go further and concoct additional theories to explain the attitudes of our citizens of the South, but it is probably more appropriate to admit that, with one possible exception, they would be largely concoctions and might not merit our attention. The exception concerns information. Suppose the citizens of the South do not know that the adoption of FAP implies an increase in their average incomes. Suppose that they do not understand that Family Assistance means that their region will become more white. Suppose that they are not aware of the tentative evidence and conclusions from the negative income-tax experiments. Then the situation becomes somewhat less of a paradox. Somehow it seems more rational to be opposed to something if one is not aware that it will result in personal benefits.

If the guess above is correct, it has strong implications for the future of some version of a Family Assistance Plan. We might predict that over time some learning may take place and the regional consequences of Family Assistance may become better known. A knowledge of the benefits for the South may then lead to changes in attitudes. In fact, as this discussion has indicated, the country is offering the South a substantial monetary incentive to alter these attitudes. Obviously, one of the strategies available to those who favor Family Assistance is to attempt to inform people of the consequences of the plan. Our Senate voting model implies that the more people in the South become convinced that Family Assistance is in their interest, the more likely their senators are to vote for the plan.

CONCLUDING REMARKS

This case study does shed some light upon the questions that were raised in the introduction. The constituency variable proved extremely important in explaining Senate votes, although it was by no means the only significant variable. On the issue of representation, however, it appears to be fair to conclude that Senate voting behavior on redistributive measures is basically similar to Senate behavior on other issues. The explanation of constituency attitudes, on the other hand, is much more puzzling. Although we might not expect a narrow view of self-interest to be the sole determinant of individual attitudes, we can argue that attitudes should not be expected to come directly into conflict with self-interest. On a regional basis, however, such a conflict does appear to be documented by the data in this instance.

NOTES

[1]Congressional Quarterly Inc., *Congressional Quarterly Almanac*, Vol. XXVI (1970), Washington, D.C.: Congressional Quarterly, Inc., 1971), pp. 1030-41.

[2]Theil seems to have been inspired to develop this technique by some sociological examples cited and analyzed in James S. Coleman's *Introduction to Mathematical Sociology* (New York: Free Press, 1964). See H. Theil, "On the Estimation of Relationships Involving Quantitative Variables," *The American Journal of Sociology* (July, 1970).

[3]Income data were not available for four states — California, Colorado, North Carolina, and Pennsylvania. In these cases the white income distributions were assumed to equal the white distributions for the region in which the state was located. These were obtained from the U.S. Department of Commerce, Bureau of the Census, *Consumer Income*, Current Population Reports, No. 80 (Oct. 4, 1971), p. 60.

[4]John E. Jackson, "Statistical Models of Senate Roll Call Voting," *The American Political Science Review* (June, 1971).

[5]William Zavoina and Richard McKelvey, "A Statistical Model for the Analysis of Legislative Voting Behavior," Paper delivered to the Annual Meeting of the American Political Science Association, September 1-6, 1969, New York, N.Y.

[6]Senators McGovern, Jackson, Harris, Bayh, Hartke, Hughes, McCarthy. Muskie was absent for two of the votes, and Humphrey had not yet taken McCarthy's place.

[7]The excluded senators were Guerney (Fla.), Baker (Tenn.), Thurmond (S.C.), Tower (Texas), and Bellmon (Okla.).

[8]How does this picture change when the Southern and Border Republicans are treated differently? Intuitively, one might think that since there are only five such senators, the results must be robust on this dimension. The facts appear to confirm one's intuition although there are some changes. If one argues that the Southern and Border Republicans should be placed with the Southern Democrats (instead of being lumped with the Northern Democrats, which is where they are in the results reported above) so that the relevant variable changes its interpretation to be simply Southern without a party label, then the results are almost identical to those reported in Table 4 except that the Southern coefficient is less negative. Similarly, if one argues that the Southern and Border Republicans should be lumped with the Republicans, then the results are very similar to those reported in Table 4 except that the Republican coefficient is less positive. In summary, one might conclude that the behavior of the

Southern and Border Republicans in regard to the Family Assistance Plan more closely corresponds to that of the Northern Democrats than any other group.

[9]John F. Kain and Robert Schafer. "Income Maintenance, Migration and Growth," *Public Policy* (Spring, 1972).

[10]*Ibid.*

[11]For a tentative report, see Harold W. Watts, "The Graduated Work Incentive Experiments: Current Progress," *The American Economic Review* (May, 1971).

11

Public Policies for Private Profits: Urban Government

JULIUS MARGOLIS

Economic analysis of the economy has proved to be powerful, with its assumption of a simple, strong motivation to man (rational egotism) and a simple institutional structure in which men interact (impersonal exchanges in markets). But as we extend the analysis to nonmarket behavior, to urban government in particular, it is probable that the models will have to be transformed. Nonmarket institutions are different; behavior patterns should reflect this difference.

The major shortcoming of the economic models of urban government is their excessive attention to voting behavior. Voting is surely important, but it is only a small part of government. The relationship between the election of officials and the behavior of the bureaucracy is barely discussed. (Unfortunately, in this paper, I too err and have little to say about the bureaucracy.) Voting occurs every two or four years, incumbents are generally returned to office, and only a minority of the electorate vote. Voting is a weak institution on which to hang a model of government.

Associated with voting is the assumption that the objective of the candidate is solely to get elected. Since the pay of these officials is deplorably low, this would seem to be a strange objective indeed. I would hazard a guess that if the incomes of legislators were restricted to their salaries, very few would stand for office in the next election. Certainly, there are payoffs other than the vote that motivate their behavior.

Julius Margolis is Director of the Fels Center of Government and Professor of Economics at the University of Pennsylvania.

The urban political economic model, like that of the national economy, should start with the individuals of the society: households and firms. Their political actions are costs they incur to procure services or favors from the government. They can choose among a variety of political acts, or they can choose to eschew political acts and respond to government via economic and social behavior. Whichever decision they take will be based upon the familiar utility-maximizing model of the household or on the profit-maximizing model of the firm.

Prices in the political domain are taxes and extra payments of time or money to alter the behavior of officials. Not everyone pays these prices, but if he does not, then he does something that alters the price others pay. In any case, political costs are incurred, and these are transformed into gains and costs for public officials. The officials, like all unincorporated businessmen, do a poor job in separating their business and personal accounts, but they are keen on profit maximizing, which they do.

These are the elements of the appropriate model. Unfortunately, what follows is not the full-blown model. It is a more discursive treatment of the elements of the model, especially of the characteristics of the political profit-maximizer.

The first Section of the paper is a digression (before I have even begun). It deals with the neglected role of government and political officials in the classic models of economic theory. The next two sections (II and III) discuss the role of government and of the political official and some of his characteristics. Section IV presents a sketch of the model that should be developed to help explain metropolitan governance, and a few impressionistic hypotheses are offered.

I. ECONOMISTS' UTOPIA
AND GOVERNMENT

Generally, the government enters into the economists' model as a purely exogenous factor. A typical solution for a problem would be for the government to assess a price against the polluter, or for a government to issue orders to restrain a monopolist. The feasibility conditions for the government to act are not explored. This becomes especially distressing when we deal with public goods supplied by the national or local governments. It is difficult to be indifferent to the behavioral conditions of the supplying agency. In this section we shall briefly characterize two of the approaches of economists to government that are found in their normative writings dealing with the optimality conditions of the economy.

In the pure form of the Economists' Utopia there is no mention of the government. The government is ignored because there is a precise matching between property rights, incentives, beneficiaries, and information, and therefore voluntary exchanges in markets are sufficient to reach Utopia. But even in this ideal world, where private and social gains are coterminous, it is implicitly assumed that there would be a role for government. Since the existence of the conditions of perfect competition does not rule out the private advantage of such socially disruptive behavior as violent crime, fraud, or contract violations, a law-and-order government is necessary. Therefore, even in the perfectly competitive Utopia there has to be an agency that would prevent some types of exchanges, especially coercive ones. Utopia has rules, and a government is needed to enforce the rules.

It has always been recognized that Utopia would have rules, that is, there would be a Constitution. It has been argued that unanimous consent would be forthcoming to adopt these rules. (Let us ignore how we are to get consent about the distribution of property.) What has been completely neglected is the nature of the Enforcer of the constitutional rules.

If the Enforcer is to be part of the Utopia, we have to ask what are his property rights and his incentives. It would be difficult to design a pricing system for the public good he provides, and it is equally difficult to design a mechanism to restrain him from enforcing the rule to his private advantage. However, we can guess at his property rights and how he would exercise them. Since the economic units of a world of perfectly competitive producers and consumers are without any power at all and only the Enforcer could enforce contracts or prevent unconstitutional exchanges, the Enforcer would have a monopoly of power; he would be a dictator. As the dictator he would control the distribution of property and, if he is an egoist like all other actors in the economy, we can assume that the economy will function for his benefit. The perfectly competitive Utopia plus an Enforcer does not look very attractive; the Enforcer would extract all surpluses in the society. The perfectly competitive economy might be Pareto efficient, but it would be an abomination.

Can we rescue Utopia through the device, familiar to economists, that it is incumbent upon our colleagues the political scientists to design the Enforcer role? If so, we then ignore him. Unfortunately the logic of Utopia severely constrains the definition of the Enforcer, and we have given the political scientist an impossible task. If the perfectly competitive economy is to be truly Utopian, the Enforcer must be a Saint who is devoted to the enforcement of the constitutional rules. Since he would require no incentive, other than the knowledge of a job well done, and since he would neither consume nor accumulate worldly goods, he would not have any property. The Saint could be the Enforcer for Utopia.

Would it be possible to make the Saint endogenous by having him elected? No, the stability of the Utopia would be in doubt if the Enforcer had to be elected, since the number of Saint Pretenders far exceeds the the number with grace, and the egotistical economic actors might elect a False Saint. No, it would be necessary to make the Saint completely exogenous, eschew democratic participation by economic men, and allow him to be chosen by God.

The Saintly Utopia fails once we introduce the conventional market failures: externalities, public goods, squabbles about distribution, and so on. The government would be no longer solely a rule enforcer, but it would become a resource allocator, an income distributor, and so on. The ruler would have to be more than a judge; he would have to be endowed with the qualities of knowledge and insight that go beyond any sainted earthling. He must be God.

Without God the Computer, the government could not gather all of the relevant information on production and preference functions.

Without God the Psychoanalyst, we could not assign "true preferences" to individuals since there is no behavioral mechanism to get individuals to reveal their evaluations.

Without God the Strategic Analyst, we would not know when in-dividuals are bluffing.

God the Governor is necessary to achieve optimality in the imper-fect world, but what if God is not part of the feasible set? What if He refuses to submit and administer our unanimously adopted rules? We would be pressed to a second-best solution for a government, and for the economy that is to be directed by the government. A Saint might be less intractable than God, but Saintliness would be insufficient. Even in the static world, the informational requirements and distributional judgments would be beyond his capacity. If we considered the dynamic world where preferences and production functions are continually changing it would be clear that only the omniscience of God would do.

But let us stop speculating about the special characteristics of the exogenous government man. It would be more fruitful to assume that the political leaders, be they enforcers or allocators, should be as egotistical and corruptible as their siblings who are entrepreneurs, managers, workers and consumers. We know that those who reach the top in the government pyramid are as industrious, tough, and ruthless as their peers in the private sector. Survival and success will be as demanding of strong egos in either case. A self-abnegating deference to the utilities of others is unlikely to be rewarded by a series of elections to higher posts. In other words, it would be rea-sonable to assume the obvious: government leaders have objective functions not very unlike the rest of us. It is likely that there are dif-ferences between the utility functions of public and private leaders, but these differences probably are small relative to the similarities.

All economic models, especially normative ones, are heavily dependent upon implicit theorizing about government. The assump-tions about government have been inconsistent with the assump-tions about the economic actors, and therefore we have an attractive set of normative and positive models of the economy, which are po-litically unfeasible. Fortunately, the tools of economic analysis are still useful and can be very helpful in understanding a model of gov-ernment and how to relate it to the economy.

A second approach to normative theorizing about the dilemmas of public goods has dealt with the creation of tribal settlements, by letting men vote with their feet. If the philistines of San Francisco harass the flower children of Haight-Ashbury, the children can pack up and cross the bridge to find a more hospitable ruler. If the Mother wants a sidewalk where her children can tricycle with safety, she will find a satisfactory suburb. It would seem that we would no longer require Saints to head governments, but a fixed distribution of leaders with known tastes, and then the space occupiers could reshuffle themselves until they settled down with their ideal government.

This is a mechanism extremely suggestive of solution for the problem of public goods production, but it does not eliminate the necessity of developing a theory of the political process. Without a model of the political process, there is no reason to assume that the set of governments will produce an optimal set of public goods.

Citizen mobility sets economic constraints on the behavior of officials, but it does not transform the political process to a market process. Even if we ignore the political process, mobility would be insufficient since there is a hierarchy of governments within a nation, and therefore all cities will share some similarities. In fact, the central governments are becoming more powerful, and therefore an escape to a city that is individually optimal is becoming rarer.

Given the set of cities there will remain a need to understand the political system that will have established the packages of municipal services among which the citizens can choose. Furthermore, the political process within each of the cities may be such that none can supply a package optimal to any set of residents who have reasonable differences.

Citizen spatial mobility is an insufficient but a necessary part of any model of a political system. Government is organized territorially. Representation, the distribution of power, and the payoffs have spatial dimensions. The movement of resources, citizens, and capital affects spatial payoffs and, thereby, the behavior of political leaders and the government. In a tight dictatorship, mobility, to be influential, may have to take the extreme form of fleeing across borders, but in the pluralist democracies rather small moves have political consequences.

Mobility is an economic act. The political counterpart of mobility — voting — has been stressed in the economic literature. In practice, however, there is a very wide spectrum of political acts, other than voting, that are influential on public decisions, and movement is only one of these acts. The citizen may relocate his residence, but he may work, shop, recreate in his former city, or choose a third city. What is absent in economic analysis, with the exception of Albert Hirschman's excellent book, *Exit, Voice and Loyalty*,[1] is a joint consideration of the full range of citizens' behavior plus the mechanism by which these acts have political consequences. The citizen, even the non-voting recluse, chooses among a range of political acts. These choices affect the behavior of political leaders. However, not all acts have equal import for the political leader, nor are all individuals equally effective in making their preferences felt. There remains facing citizens the central question of alternatives, political and economic. There remains also the questions of how these are transformed to gains and costs to public leaders; and how public and private outputs are thereby affected.

II. THE PECULIAR INSTITUTION
OF GOVERNMENT

The behavioral characteristics of government, as we know it, give rise to an excess demand by individuals for public services and, thereby, to a revenue flow to political leaders. Although political leaders are paid salaries from taxes imposed on individuals, the more significant revenues they receive come from "voluntary" contributions. The relevant government characteristics are: (1) its monopoly position in regard to many services; (2) its refusal to use a pricing mechanism; (3) its philosophy of reasonably uniform treatment of citizens; and (4) its very limited range of alternative products. In essence, the government is an unsatisfactory institution, where there are always possibilities of improvement to all parties via a "political" act. The political acts from which contributions are made may take the form of a general rule or of a specific favor.

The monopoly power of government is far greater than any of our traditional private monpolies. The monopolistic government, when it aggressively defends this privilege, imposes severe sanctions on its competitors. For example, jail sentences are meted out to counterfeiters and fines to those who compete with the post office in delivering messages. If a group of firms should try to regulate themselves without the sanction of a regulatory agency, they would be subjected to fines and imprisonment. Only the government can kill with impunity. For some government services the individual does have private alternatives that make the government somewhat like a private monopolist, but the alternatives are usually severely regulated by the government. Unlike the alternatives to private monopoly, the consumer must still pay to support the government products although he chooses the private alternatives—for example, private schools and security guards. He must pay because the public service is financed through taxes rather than through voluntary pricing.

The high cost to individuals of using alternatives to government products gives ample incentives to pressure the government to amend the public services. For example, to most of us, migration because of objections to specific public services is too costly a private alternative to be chosen. The excess demand for some change in public services will be great.

Although government is usually a monopolist, there often are alternatives that affect government behavior. There are many private adaptations that are not very conscious or costly, like shifting purchases among commodities in response to taxes, or shifting residences in response to service differentials. These indirect responses are of political consequence since they affect the distribution of gains and costs within the community. Therefore, even when individuals make private adaptations to government, there will be others in the community who will try to influence government because of the consequences of these private adaptations. For instance, storekeepers may appeal to officials for a zoning policy change to increase density and thereby to increase sales.

Although many persons may respond to government as though its actions were exogenous and make individual adaptations, there will be others who will try to change government policy or programs.

Both types of responses may provide revenues to the officials. The political costs that citizens will incur will be a function of what they consider to be the net gains of changes in the behavior of government. A similar calculation will be the basis of their choice of private adaptation or a political act. Whether the individual acts privately or publicly there are costs, and as a consequence there will be a flow of revenues to the monopolist.

Uniformity in distribution of the government's product, which itself has a limited range of variation in quality of output, creates further excess demands on government and thereby a role for political leadership. If the government differentiated its product in response to the consumer and assessed taxes so as not to disturb marginal conditions in distribution, its monopoly powers would be so mitigated that the individual gains associated in changing the government's actions would be small. Revenues of political leaders would be low. Fortunately for the political leaders, the government rarely uses prices; instead, it has a variety of rationing devices, with a spirit of uniform and equitable treatment dominating. Since individual preferences vary greatly, there are strong incentives for individuals to seek a change in the patterns of government allocations.

The modern bureaucratic government has a dominating philosophy of equality and uniformity in the distribution of services. Of course we are all aware of "glaring inequalities" between public services for the poor and the rich or the black and the white, but these differences are trivial to the differences that prevail in the private sector. Certainly the Park Avenues are cleaned up better than the Bowerys, and the judge listens more carefully to the rich than the poor. But consider the differences between the furnishings of the Park Avenue apartment as against the Bowery flat or the quality of the legal services to the rich as against the quality of those to the poor. The City Planning Commission may not listen closely to the gripe of the poor tenant, and the doors of the best restaurants are closed to him.

The philosophy of equity and uniformity of treatment by the government is buttressed by the many well-known virtues and vices of bureaucracy. The even-handed professional bureaucrat can be viewed as an unresponsive, sluggish follower of rules rather than a provider of services. The bureaucracy's preference for simple rules for distribution is matched by their preference for a very limited range of quality variation in the product. Uniformity over persons and over products is the least bothersome solution.

To illustrate the above, consider the rules established to license a business, provide a school, establish a traffic light, petition for a variance, obtain a building permit, or repair a street. The inefficiency of the rules may be patent, but they will survive. Changes occur, but they are costly. It is more efficient to seek the individualized treatment afforded by a political intervener. The American legislator has been called an ombudsman. The term may be apt, but in the American scene it is associated with corruption—the bending of procedures in exchange for favors to constituents and revenues to officials. The political leader becomes the channel for favors requested and bestowed to alter the public services to fit individual preferences without the laborious work of new legislation or new operating rules.

Government rigidity gives rise to many private exchange operations where the directly involved parties can be made better off. The same process can also lead to a situation where the political leader can prey on the citizenry. The gatekeeper for favors may not be easily deposed. What might be viewed as benign corruption to generate flexibility can grow into a feudal tyranny where the official can exact prices for all the privileges he bestows. There is a delicate balance between the rule of law with inefficient but evenhanded outcomes and a rule of men with greater efficiency but subject to private exploitations. A symbiotic relationship exists between the political leader and his community, and it is not always clear who is the parasite and who is the host.

III. THE UTILITY-MAXIMIZING
ELECTED OFFICIAL

The political decision maker maximizes utility. He may get satisfaction from his work, like many of us. He values income and the private goods it purchases, and the leisure with which to enjoy the goods. And like all men who seek gains, he must incur costs. The costs as well as the gains take peculiar forms.

A useful way to view the elected official is to think of him as a small-scale unincorporated businessman. Like other small businessmen his economic life is perilous; bankruptcies are most common in the early years; he finds it difficult to separate his business and private accounts. It is useful to distinguish between two sets of small businessmen: the independent and the franchised dealer. In another society with stronger party control we could think of chain stores and even monopolies, but the independent and franchised dealer is more appropriate to our political system.

Although I cast the image of the politician in a business mold this is not to deny the presence of noncommercial motives. A tavern keeper may consider the friendship of his regulars as important for their conversation as for his sales. The cabinet maker may enjoy the compliment for his work as much as the price he charges. However, these nonpecuniary gains to small business, private or public, do not destroy the value of the model.

The financial structure of the elected official has peculiar short-run and secular cycles. His short-run cycle is set by the term of office; the secular trend is a function of his development of a personally committed electorate base. Loyalty of followers, developed over time, completely changes his possibilities for profit.

In the short, electoral cycle he has investment and operating costs. He invests at election time, and he incurs operating costs between elections. His equity investment is usually small, with the bulk of his funds coming in the form of contributions. Since his investors have made gifts rather than loans, he has no legal obligation to repay, but if he does not repay he will not have gifts in a future period. Therefore, he must repay with an appropriate set of favors.

The magnitude of investment funds he requires and the rate of return he must pay on the gifts are an inverse function of the citizens' support that he receives because of his anticipated performance. The greater the support he has from the voting public, the smaller the amount of gifts he must raise and the lower the rate of return to his financiers. Normally, an elected official must devote his early years in office to the payment of his debts, and his later years are the ones in which he can exercise greater discretion and reap gains for himself. Often this becomes difficult if his candidacy is part of a machine. Under those circumstances, the political boss becomes the financial intermediary. The official does not negotiate the bargains, and he may never be able to free himself from the obligations to the donors.

The payoffs to the political officials come after elections. He has many favors to dole out. Some of the "favors" are repayments of obligations incurred because of prior gifts, and others can create profits for him. The strategy of the maximizing official is to be free of obligations to financiers and other supporters and thereby be able to bring in profits. He has a period between elections to create a support base to make him independent. During this period he can dole out favors so that recipients become indebted to him and also to complete transactions that are profitable to his private account. Like the typical entrepreneur, he is paying debts, earning profits and investing for the future.

More common than the profit-maximizing independent politician is the "satisficing" franchised dealer — the political hack. He receives a "normal" salary via the allocations of the party. Franchiseships exist because of imperfections in the capital market, the difficulties of coalition formation, and scale economies in the electoral process.

A political party managed by career professionals can provide more certainty of a return to contributors. Even if a candidate loses, a party has some winners and therefore some capacity to supply favors. Although the gift to a party still does not carry any legal obligation, the party is a more secure agent if it has a stable of candidates. The party does reduce the market imperfection.

The credibility of the party is heightened by the number of its adherents. The friendship of one legislator in a body of many legislators does not ensure that legislative influence can be exerted. The probability of success is dependent upon the legislator's position in the set of coalitions that operate the legislature. The party leadership is specialized in these functions, and their goodwill may be more effective than contributions to a single legislator.

Specialization in coalition formation and uncertainty reduction are a few examples of scale economies. Further examples would be the reduction in marketing costs, since one meeting or mailing can easily deal with several candidates; or the reduction in recruitment and training costs because of the variety of jobs that a party has available to it.

Although it is clear that the party plays a major role in the political process, I shall concentrate in this paper on the independent politician. This may be less of an error for local government where nonpartisan elections are fairly widespread. Of course nonpartisanship is oftentimes more symbolic than real.

The preceding remarks may be considered a vulgar caricature of the elected official. After all the country has had centuries of political reform to weed out the venal, and of political education to elevate the moral level of political life. It is true that political reforms associated with good government complicate his life, since his freedom to maneuver is reduced. It makes him more dependent upon his initial backers to the point where he may never get out of political debt. He operates in a highly constrained environment where almost everything he does is considered unethical by many and often illegal (to say nothing of being fattening). There are high payoffs to the elected official, but first he must surrender his compunctions. Fortunately for his self-respect, the American credo contains many maxims extolling the pragmatic and in praise of compromise to get things done. He can, therefore, find some solace despite his violations of his oath of office.

What are his revenue sources? He has six principal sources of revenue: cash contributions to his electoral fund, cash contributions to his private account, contributions of time, indirect contributions via patronage of a business he controls, organizational support, and public esteem. (We will ignore his private satisfactions in getting a "good job done" or molding the government to conform to his values. There are few craftsmen who work solely for the joys of their products.)

For each of these revenue streams, he must incur costs. What are the relationships between the flow of revenues and costs and the behavior of the government and its officials? What are the relationships between the behavior and the structure of government? What are the relationships between the structure and the behavior and the value of public output? Obviously, these questions go beyond this paper, but let us sketch out some of the elements.

The Revenues of the Political Entrepreneur

The revenues of the political entrepreneur are financial, contributions of time, psychic returns, and organizational support. The nonaccountability of any of these flows make it difficult to distinguish between contributions to support his election and those that enter into his personal account. In principle there are reasonably clear differences; in practice there may be little difference. The dollars earned by an unincorporated businessman are used to cover costs, and if they are greater than costs, they become profits; but every dollar of sales is from a customer who is satisfied. The official is as grateful to the contributor to his campaign fund as he is to the donor of a new personal car (assuming that they are of equal value). Both provide necessary resources. The blurring of the distinction between personal and official revenues is probably overstated, but it is more important to stress their similarities than to explore their differences.

Previously I listed six types of revenues: cash contributions to election funds, psychic income, contributions of time, cash contributions to personal account, indirect payments via private business, organizational support. These are useful categories, although in practice they will often appear as a package—for example, an organization may contribute time, money, and business to an official's private firm.

The major inflows have been studied by political scientists: the costs of elections and the psychic motivations of officials. Neither of these has been related to the behavior of political leaders, except in most general terms. The costs of elections have been deplored as wasteful since they raise the price of entry to political office. The high campaign costs are recognized as a "corrupting influence," and, although there are many anecdotal reports, systematic analysis is absent. There is even less known about the role of psychic motivations.

James Payne identifies six different incentives for political participation: status, adulation, program, mission, obligation, and game.[2] Other political scientists have constructed similar classifications for psychological payoffs for political leaders. They are undoubtedly useful in explaining the styles of different leaders, and it is possible that motivations for governors will be different from those for legislators, and those for councilmen will differ from those for mayors. However, it is unlikely that these payoffs will prove very helpful in explaining public outputs.

The absence of studies of the payoffs to political leaders is very strange. There is a huge literature on politics and political behavior but hardly any studies on the behavioral determinants of the elected officials who are the central figures in the drama. The formal studies of the electoral process simply assume a single goal — to be elected — but no motivation and, therefore, no analysis of the gains and costs of being elected. Certainly, officials respond to incentives other than voters' support. In the formal model of voting the only differences the candidates show are their perceptions of what the majority of voters want.

Obviously, the ability to be elected is important to a political leader, but there are many men who run with little hope of election. Furthermore, almost every elected official will take actions that are disapproved of by the majority of his electorate. Payoffs, rather than being elected, are important, and they are often of sufficient importance for a man to risk defeat.

Candidates receive revenues in anticipation of election. These are the investments of supporters who believe that thereby they bind the candidate. Three types of investment are most important: cash contributions to the campaign fund, voluntary contributions of free time, and organizational support. Since each of the investors anticipates a return if the candidate is elected, the successful candidate, once in office, will incur costs to produce a product for his investors. Which groups in the community will make which type of investment and what rates of return can be expected for each type of investment are major empirical questions. I will suggest some hypotheses in a later section after we discuss the costs to the public officials.

During his period of office the official is besieged with pleas for favored treatment, and his revenue prospects are good. If he is a governor, he can make a life or death decision by commuting a sentence, but even a less visible county commissioner when he wields the power to locate a dam or a highway is perceived by many of the affected public to be deciding their fate. A favorable response could lead to a grateful vote, to investment in his future campaign, to trading a favor, or to a payment to the private account of the official.

Private payments to officials can take many forms, and since much of it is illegal, there are few systematic studies of its magnitude or effects. Newspapers and grand juries tell us repeatedly about cash payments. We hear less frequently about how the private business associations of an official benefit from the patronage of grateful recipients of public grants. It is only fitting that the contractor with the successful bid in a government project should buy his insurance from the councilman who votes favorably for the project. What better way to get a zoning variance than to employ the law firm of a local councillor to represent you?

Organizational support is less reliable than cash, but it may be very important. Since an organization such as a union or church group cannot be fully controlled, its resources may not be used most effectively, but they prove to be invaluable at points where it is necessary to influence specific persons. An organization becomes an efficient way to extend access to a great many persons.

The contribution of time is one of the most valuable of all favors. When we discuss costs, we shall see that time is a most precious commodity. The elected official does not have a large personal organization. His personal staff grows at election time and evaporates during the working years. During both periods he is harassed and he cannot administer a major staff. Voluntary labor that relieves him of his many burdens is a blessing. Lobbyists and government agencies are more than eager to help him, and he must rely on these potentially embarrassing donors if he cannot amass his own aides.

Most of his revenues cover his costs of campaigning and serving his constituency, and flow through him as an intermediary to arrange favors for others. Some will accrue to his personal account. Although it would be instructive to try to estimate the private rate of return, it is sufficient for our purposes to describe the gross flows. They influence the behavior of the public official. A net rate of return is necessary to explain career choice.

There is one major constraint on his revenue that is especially important in modern governments. The elected official sits on the top of a bureaucracy, and it is their cooperation that is necessary. In fact, the bureaucracy can prove to be a very effective competitor to the official on the sale of favors. An individual may often find that a favor by a bureaucrat may be far less costly than the passage of legislation, or intervention by the legislator. It is far easier to bribe the arresting officer than to change the definition of a crime. Therefore, the legislator must take steps to suppress the competition of bureaucrats.

However, the creation of a professionalized, noncorruptible civil service reduces the flexibility of the elected official to use the bureaucracy. This is a dilemma. Professionalism reduces the competition of the bureaucrat for the official, but it makes the bureaucrat a less willing tool of the elected leader.

The elected leader has a variety of ways to influence the bureaucrat. Even though the official has the opportunity to harass the bureaucrat through budgetary hearings, personal actions, and so forth, the profitable opportunities for the elected official are still limited.

The elected executive is the key figure in bending the bureaucracy, but even he is a weak ruler over the bureaucracy. The favored domain of the legislature is in the seemingly innocuous special terms of legislation that have differential effects upon the constituency. The complex tax code, the impossible building codes, the multicolored zoning maps all create situations where the legislator may intervene to serve individual clients.

The history of government reform has been one of insulating the bureaucracy from the intervention of elected offcials. At the same time, the demands upon the government have grown greatly. If reforms in the form of professionalization are successful, the excess demand for individual treatment will grow in accord. Are movements such as community control and suburbanization partially a response to a frustrated demand for individualization? Has excess demand for political favors been stifled, with a resultant reduction in profits to political leadership and thereby a decline in its quality? Has there been a reduction in the amount of custom-made solutions for individuals with the result that there has been a greater concern for the quality of government and a general improvement — despite the loss of revenues to political leaders? Or have more subtle channels for revenue been opened up so that the rate of return is still constant? The survivability of the military-industrial complex and pork-barrel legislation imply that the last hypothesis warrants further examination.

Political Costs

I shall not elaborate on political costs. There are the obvious resource costs of running an election campaign and of maintaining a staff to establish contact with the constituency. The more interesting costs are those associated with his limited time and with the product of the legislator — favors to parts of his constituency while he maintains a coalition of a majority. It is well known that a favor creates more enemies than friends. The typical decision benefits only a few, and therefore it has the potential of irritating the many who are not recipients. I shall discuss first the question of time, and then the costs of dispensing favors.

The public official, if he is ambitious, is one of the most hardworking of our politicians. He must be elected, and the more people he speaks to and can respond to, the more likely will his election be. Wherever a group gathers in his territory, he must be part of it. It is inefficient to meet persons individually, and therefore he seeks out events; and once there, he must meet as many people as possible.

His work consists of negotiations — bargaining and persuading. Few things are more time consuming than bargaining. Among elected officials, only the chief executive offical has a line of authority. Therefore every time a legislator must perform a favor, he must spend heavily of his time, which could be spent being friendly to possible supporters.

His time is a precious, limited resource. Unfortunately, he has little time left to inform himself adequately about the legislation he must vote on, or the bureaucracy he must supervise. His hours can be squandered by an action that disturbs his constituency. He cannot be aloof from his critical voters. Not only does he hate to lose a vote, but he does not know how extensive the damage of the critic might be. He cannot easily delegate responsibility since his assistants are anonymous and carry little credibility. He must be accessible to petitioners, but, at the same time, he must study the issues in an unhurried way.

I have stressed the time costs of the political leader because the resource costs are reasonably well known, and we know very little about time costs. We observe that the political leaders respond on the basis of what would seem to be minimal information. Everyone respects the adage that the squeaking wheel gets the oil. The squeaking may be sufficient to alert the official to the existence of a problem; and even if he knew that the solution lay elsewhere, he would seek to appease the squeakers, both to make them happy and to get them out of his office. The squeaks take time. Hours spent on complaints are hours lost from time he might have spent on speaking to donors or on searching for ways to generate new revenues.

The marginal productivity of the time of elected officials (of top bureaucrats as well) is extremely high, far higher than the salaries they are paid. It is not surprising that an informal market develops for their time. The formal centralization of the public sector means that top decisions have extensive consequences for a large part of government activity. The delegation of authority is severely constrained by the courts so that the top decision makers find it difficult to get relief. Of course, in pratice, they are forced to exercise their authority in a perfunctory fashion; they become captives to their advisers, public and private Although their decisions are of great importance, their time is limited. The public official's "friends" pay well to have access to him, and his "enemies" know how to impose on his time to influence his decisions.

Minorities with perceived injuries have power beyond their votes. Their disruptive powers can consume most of the time of officials. The need to reduce their demands on the time of the officials may get extensive concessions for them.

There are no studies on the allocation of officials' time, but the importance of access is revealed in many anecdotes. Many businesses contribute heavily to campaign funds so that an official will listen to an appeal when they try to get the bureaucracy to act. Irate citizenry who besiege the official with their complaints prevent him from carrying on the lucrative missions of dispensing favors to his supporters.

The second major cost (second to time) is the invidious nature of a favor. A contributor to a political official considers himself to be in a "most-favored person" position; favors done unto others should be done unto him. But, of course, in some cases, a favor to more than one donor may be infeasible because they are mutually exclusive, for example, the granting of a franchise to more than one firm in a circumscribed area.

Avoiding the envy and the wrath of donors is made more difficult because favors are dispensed over time, and a favor granted two years ago may not reduce envy engendered by favors done for others since then. A politician knows too well that his constituents have short memories. They want to know what has been done for them lately.

The political leader is beset with the problem of having to do less than the best for each of his constituents, and, at the same time, make credible the argument that if anyone of them joins another coalition, the defecting individual will do even worse. This is no mean task, which is made increasingly difficult as the leader doles out favors to a few. Political capital deteriorates rapidly.

IV. THE SKETCH OF A METROPOLITAN POLITICAL-ECONOMIC MODEL

The governance of the metropolitan area is illuminated by viewing the incentive structure of public officials. At the federal level issues often seem to transcend the restricted domain of favors, and payoffs and an economic model may seem to be crude. At the local level the direct benefits and costs to constituents are clear; unfortunately the data on payoffs to officials are anecdotal. Fortunately, the set of cities contained in a metropolitan area provides an appropriate world to test out hypotheses about political behavior. There are tens of thousands of cities in the United States, most of them located in interdependent metropolitan areas. These are excellent circumstances that give rise to interesting hypotheses and data to verify them. It is not strange that the study of urban politics and urban public finance, which were the dullest specialties in their disciplines, have begun to attract students of the disciplines.

Before I discuss the political leaders I shall sketch some behavioral characteristics of the households and firms of the city. After all it is their behavior that creates the revenues and costs for the officialdom. An individual in choosing a residential site or a firm in choosing a plant site makes a complicated calculation of the various benefits and costs to them. The house searcher usually accepts as given most important elements such as distance to jobs, social-economic characteristics of neighbors, land uses, recreational facilities, tax rates, and public services. The firm gives great weight to the same "facts," but it often considers as well the business climate — the willingness of public officials to accommodate to his special needs. These differences are reflected in the fact that the city's sales pitch to potential residents is left in the hands of private realtors whereas promotion for firms will be put in the hands of a public agency or a publicly supported chamber of commerce. The differences are also symptomatic of the differences in political activity of the two groups.

A land occupier in a city will be affected by any change in public programs. There will be a change in taxes and in benefits. The benefits may take several forms. A resident's private costs may be reduced, for example, if more police protection eliminates his need for a watch dog. His satisfactions may be increased, for example, if cleaned streets make walking more pleasant (if he is a walker). A third, ambiguous, benefit may be in the change in the value of his property. Let us explain this last benefit. If the benefits above exceed costs to nonresidents as well as residents, there will be an increase in demand for space in his city. The public program may lead to an increase in land values, which are good; but higher values also mean a higher opportunity cost for occupying that site, which is bad. We can imagine many cases of differential private evaluations of benefits and costs of a public program, but the only point I want to make is that the demand and supply for sites will be affected, and thereby land values.

The Household

Let us assume that the benefits and costs to an individual were positive. A park was built near his residence, he welcomed it, and the increment in taxes was less than his benefits. If other residents and nonresidents shared his views there would be an increase in demand for sites near the park and an increase in land values. This would force our sample individual to recalculate. Since his home has increased in value, he has received a windfall gain; but if he does not sell his property, he will be paying a higher opportunity cost to remain there — the foregone interest cost on his equity will have increased. Will he remain at the site? His decision will be based partly upon the value he placed upon the park as against the values the others in the market placed upon the park, as well as the other advantages of remaining in the neighborhood. He may be in the paradoxical position of voting for the park but then, discovering that he cannot afford it, of having to move to a more distant point.

If the gains of the park were slight to him relative to the gains to others, he would be tempted to sell because he would not find it worthwhile to spend so much for the benefits of the park. However, he might not sell if he has other attachments to the site that more than offset his loss — for example, friendly neighbors, a car pool, knowledge about tradesmen. If he is locked into the site because of heavy personal investment in the neighborhood, he will not leave but will suffer the losses due to the park. If the benefits of the use of the park did not exceed his tax costs, he would be doubly embittered since his private and public costs would have risen with no offsetting gains at all.

There are many combinations of gainers and losers in this simple illustration, but I shall not consider them because all I need for this sketch is the motivation for the structure of a model. There are individuals who will be differentially affected by the government.

The arguments in the utility function of the resident should contain the usual elements of private and public goods, and also other commodities such as the accessibility to jobs, shopping, and recreation, usefulness of physical facilities, compatibility of neighbors, proximity of friends, and knowledge of how to use the services of the community. These may appear to be strange commodities, but they are procurable by "prices," they are important in locational decisions, and they affect political behavior.

The budget constraint on individual behavior should contain time as well as income or wage rates. Some of the commodities above, like friendship, are bought by the expenditure of time rather than money.

The characteristics of the individual that we need to capture are those that lead him to feel pressed to behave politically rather than economically in response to the actions of the political leadership that governs him. The more perfect the substitutibility of other cities, the less will be his willingness to spend money or time in influencing public outcomes. Other variables will also affect his decision. Size of electorate should affect his feeling of effectiveness, for example, but this is only a sketch.[3]

The formal conditions for the maximization of utility for the resident are the traditional ones: the marginal rates of substitution for any two goods should be equal to the ratio of prices for these two goods. The problem we face in constructing a satisfactory theory is the specification of the dimensions of "prices" for all the goods desired by the residents and of the best way for the individual to procure those goods.

For instance, friendship is a highly valued commodity, but what is the price and what are the many ways to get friends? A minimal way to describe the price would be the time that an individual must give to nurture a friendship. He must have a search process to discover a candidate; he must invest time to nurture the friendship; he must continue the flow of time to keep it alive. The opportunity costs of time would be only a minimal estimate of costs. Certainly an individual will incur great psychic costs if he is to spend of himself sufficiently to warrant others to reciprocate. Enough on friendship. All I want to establish is that there is a set of prices, although we may have to strain our ingenuity to discover them.

The longer an individual remains in a community the greater will be his investment in nonmarketable assets versus marketable assets, and therefore the less substitutible will be other cities. House improvements are marketable, but he cannot market the invest- ments in friendships or his accumulated information about the com- munity. Longevity will be one of the factors that account for a willingness to participate politically rather than to seek an economic solution to public services by moving.

Longevity is of special importance in the world of a set of cities, since the growth of the metropolitan area gives rise to fairly rapid changes in the distribution of population and industry. Densities will change, and public services will change in accord. Many studies have pointed out the existence of an "old guard" of residents who are politically active in their resistance to growth. This is to be ex- pected since old residents have fewer good substitutes, and, therefore, political activity becomes more desirable relative to movement.

The Businessman

The differences among households in their proclivity to political activity are small relative to the differences between households and businesses. Although businesses in general have a much greater fixed investment in a city, not all of them are politically active. Some businesses produce for a national market and employ workers throughout the metropolitan area. They have little attachment to their community although they may be very concerned about such specific services as sewage and street capacity. Other businesses in- vest very heavily in the community — for example, merchants who know the shopping habits of the residents; realtors who are depen- dent upon local suppliers and subcontractors; bankers who hold local mortgages and know the business clientele; land owners who have been accumulating parcels of land and plans for its develop- ment; lawyers and insurance brokers who serve the local business community.

Unlike the national firms, the local businessman is an active parti- cipant in the local political scene. The home office of a national firm may make a contribution to the campaign of the congressman, sena- tor, or president, but the local businessman will be active in the city. A variance in zoning, or a realignment of a street, or the location of a

park, or the redistribution of fire engines is very quickly transforma-
ble into sales, commissions, or capital gains. Property taxes are a
burden to them, but they recognize the benefits of services.

The local businessman is an extreme form of the man for whom
other cities provide imperfect substitutes. Often he has more of a
stake in the city than do its top bureaucrats. The city planners or city
manager or police chief or city engineer all have career lines that dictate movement to larger cities if they are to advance in their profession. The fate of the local businessman lies in the growth of economic
activity in the territory of his city. He is grandly indifferent to the welfare of the metropolitan area. The wealth of the metropolitan area is
great enough from his perspective. The problem he faces is to get his
share relative to the share of other cities within the metropolitan area.

The land of the cities is occupied by men with varying stakes in
their specific cities. The greater the difference among cities for an
occupier, the more likely will he be to participate in the political life.
Given similar incentives for political action, the business leaders are
more likely to be active than the householder.

Political action is a public good. One man's contribution has little
effect unless it is matched with enough others to make a difference.
Although businessmen are few in number compared to the general
electorate, they have a community through their associations that
enables them to meet and to create the credibility that contributions
will be matched by others.

Now let us link this brief discussion of political participation to our
previous discussion of political leaders.

Households and Firms as Political Demanders

Each of the parties in a city will choose his own pattern of political
contributions. The businessmen can and do make cash contributions, and, equally important, they can direct private business to the
official's firm. This capacity of the businessmen not only gives them
an advantage in the amount of resources that they can direct to political use but it also has a serious effect on the supply of public officials. A surgeon can barely benefit from the munificence of a local
banker, but an insurance agent can prosper. A contractor on a public
project knows where to buy his insurance, and a banker can guide

borrowers to reliable insurance agents. The broker is far more likely to invest his time and financial resources in a political career than a surgeon is. The result will be an over-representation of those who can be influenced by local business and, because of their own occupations, would share the goals and assumptions of local business.

Households also contribute: the higher-income ones with money, and the lower-income ones with work time. Since noncash contributors make up the majority of the electorate, the official must satisfy their preferences also, but his fungible profits lie with business and those with upper incomes who can invest in him or who can pay for favors.

Fortunately for the local official, the electorate is generally apathetic about local elections. Approximately 30 percent vote in local elections. Therefore, if he can gain support of the right 20 percent, he can satisfy the electoral requirement. This is not to say that the silent 70 percent is not represented. Far from it — they are a potentially aroused voting body, and the local merchants and realtors who speak to the council are concerned about the silent voters who are their shoppers. However, their interests are filtered through profit calculations of the local businessmen, and therefore they will not be well represented. For instance, the transformation of the old downtown city corporation yard into a park might be welcomed by the apathetic residents, and lead to an increase in adjoining property values, but the business interests may be opposed because they object to the loss of developmental opportunities on the lot as well as the loss in taxable real property under frustrated private development. These losses, they may fear, will be greater than the gains in the value of land adjoining the park development. Thus business will not necessarily prove to be an effective transmission belt for residents who act only economically.

The citizenry can operate directly on the public official by voting, by attending council meetings and neighborhood meetings, by disruptive political actions, and, of course, by contributing time to his opponent. Since the wage rates of lower-income persons, housewives, and retired people are low, they are more likely to devote time rather than money to politics. However, if they are aroused to oppose the government, the value of the sum of their time could outweigh the cash contributions received by the official — for example, the huge amount of time spent in the anti-busing program. Fortunately for the profit-max-imizing political official, it is far more difficult to organize the lower-income groups for political action than it is the businessman.[4] The possibility of effectiveness of a single worker is low, and therefore the likelihood of participation is slight.

Anyone who observes local government in action cannot help but be impressed with the effectiveness of a small group of irate citizens who are willing to contribute time to represent themselves. The City Council will many times defer to their wishes in order to get on with their business. The time spent in political action by a lower-income opposition group can impose heavy costs on public officials whose profits lie elsewhere.

In the central cities, where there is a large repository of unem-ployed, the political effects of a low-income population are different. Again, it has proved difficult to organize a sustained political in-volvement. Sporadic outbursts in the form of demonstrations and riots have wrenched some concessions, but as weeds grow over burnt-out buildings, so can officials ignore the complaints as time passes.

The deprived of the central cities have other channels of protest and use of their time than political behavior. Delinquency, crime, disorders are their protests that prove immediately effective. Their incomes are increased, and they are not dependent upon the cohesiveness of a group or promises from a distant public official. Possibly it is far fetched to view deviant behavior as political, but formally one could view deviance as migration-in-place. The dis-sident chooses an economic alternative — migration — and the deviant chooses a social alternative — crime. The deviant's behav-ior is economically far more costly to the city than the migrant's. Both acts have economic and political consequences. A public of-ficial who allows either to grow imperils his job.

Efficiency, Equity, and Metropolitan Governance

Given the structure of government, the behavior of households and firms, incentives to political leaders, and the fractionation of the territory into many governments, what can we anticipate about met-ropolitan governance? First, it is clear that the division of the territo-

ry into municipalities with independent electoral districts would dis-
courage the elected officials from being concerned about the status
of the whole and thereby there would be nonoptimal policies. As we
mentioned earlier, there is enough wealth in the metropolitan area
for any city to gain considerably by having a larger share, and
therefore it need not be moved to worry about the welfare of the
total area. However, a city's preoccupation with its own welfare
need not mean that the total welfare is thereby reduced. The
hypothesis that competition among the municipalities would lead to
gains for the entire area must be disproved. Surprisingly, the
hypothesis has not been disproved, but the arguments disparaging
the competitive solution are strong enough to make it reasonable to
assume that the weight of proof should rest with those who praise
the competitive solution. Technological externalities, such as pollution and accessibility, dominate the metropolitan area. Competition
is a poor mechanism with which to solve these problems. Furthermore, population mobility is a necessary condition for a competitive
solution to be desirable, but many constraints are put on the mobility
of the poor, the fertile and unpleasant industry. The need for governance of the metropolitan area, although there is no government,
seems to be a reasonable statement. In fact, we shall find that the absence of metropolitan government has given rise to very imperfect
solutions to public problems within the metropolitan area.

Suburbanization, as a historical trend of the horizontal spread of
the urban area, can be explained by economic forces. Suburbanization, as sorting out of socio-economic groups and land users into
separate governments, is political economy.

The growth of suburbs that have very different characteristics and
internally are relatively homogenous is explainable by the typical
urban phenomena of social segregation and the formation of governments to protect these areas. The socially segregated neighborhoods
of the central cities have been traditional, but they have not been
able to survive the onslaughts of the immigration to the urban areas
and consequent shift of populations. The poor with their willingness
to accept much greater density have been able to outbid the well-to-
do for their neighborhoods. In general, the municipal governments
favored the "better" neighborhoods. The higher-valued properties

had lower assessment ratios and they had better public services. This discrimination arose from the greater political contribution of the well-to-do and their greater mobility. However, the inability of the municipal government to protect the "better" neighborhood drove the residents outside the city limits, where they could establish their own protection societies in the form of suburban governments. The movement of population had a cumulative effect. The tax base was spread over fewer high-income residents, who had to pay a still higher rate for services that were increasingly directed towards lower-income populations, and therefore there was a strong fiscal incentive to accelerate a flow of the higher-income population to the suburbs. The central city retained the bulk of the valuable business property and the residences of the poor. Revenues to the political leadership came from the absentee business owners, but the accumulation of an imbalance of voting strength in the hands of the poor meant an inability of the local political leader to deliver on promises.

In the suburbs land-use controls became a mechanism through which to filter those who wished to vacate the central city. Growth became the dominant theme of the suburb. It was growth that provided the gains in land values around which local decisions gravitated. Speculative gains were widespread but not universal. Most of the residents sought the suburbs for their residential virtues (attractive landscaping, better public services), and although they were not entrepreneur minded they were very concerned with the value of their major asset, their house. The marriage between the protective preferences of households and the speculative goals of the developers has been effected via the planning instrument called the cost-revenue study. This analysis consisted of a demonstration of the public costs that would arise because of land use and the tax revenue it would generate. If the land use was to be fiscally profitable all landowners would achieve a fiscal dividend. Of course the suburbs rigidly adhered to their line of approving only fiscally profitable activities, but despite the consultants' fees paid to planners, local taxes rose. Although the fiscal goals were not realized, the goal established a consensus that permitted the land developers to use the government for private gains.

The capture of local suburban governments was insufficient to achieve the full land speculative gains; intervention at a higher level was necessary. There were heavy public investment costs for the opening of new areas. The suburbs were too small to achieve scale economies in services like water supply and sewage treatment. They were too limited to be able to manage the vital function of accessibility. A metropolitan government could have managed these, but a metropolitan government with this range of power would have resulted in a sharing of power with those who had been deemed fiscally unprofitable — the central-city residual population: the poor, the fertile, the socially inferior. The solution took two forms: subsidies by federal and state governments for new public investment, primarily in the suburbs, and the formation of "businesslike" special districts to provide services without concern for the broader range of public policies. These solutions have had two harmful effects: the subsidy of suburbs had changed relative prices of location in favor of suburbs, and this was intensified by concentration of problem populations and businesses in the central city.

The structure of payoffs and therefore of political revenues and costs in the central cities and suburbs are different. In the suburbs the developmental gains generate political revenues; in the central cities a smaller volume of revenues is offset by the political costs of the lower-income groups seeking greater access to public services. The two different patterns of revenues and costs are analogous to the classical conflicts between efficiency and equity. In the metropolitan case the problem has been intensified by the policy of subsidizing the suburbs and thereby biasing efficient "solutions" in their direction. In the classic political situation the gains of efficiency create revenues sufficient to compensate the losers of the changes. However, this exchange has to be managed through a political forum where the losers can impose disruption costs on the gainers. The territorial separation of losers and gainers has led to a transfer of the market place of political exchanges to the federal and state levels and the judiciary.

The intervention of the higher-level governments has reduced pressures to create local political institutions to manage policies. The conflicts over transportation and environmental deterioration are resolved by federal subsidy. The politically unbearable burdens of the low-income population will be resolved by federal subsidy. The incentive structure in the metropolitan area encourages each of the localities to seek their own payoffs, with the federal treasury providing the funds to reduce the political costs that would have created political instability.

The incentives for the institutionalization of metropolitan governance via a formal metropolitan government are slight so long as the federal government absorbs the costs to avoid political instability. If revenue sharing were adopted in an extreme form, the situation would change drastically. Then the federal government would not be arranging bargains, and the advantages of cooperation would provide payoffs to institution building.

NOTES

[1] Albert Hirschman, *Exit, Voice and Loyalty* (Cambridge, Harvard University Press, 1971).

[2] James Payne and Oliver Woyshinsky, "Political Incentives," April, 1970, mimeographed study.

[3] For an interesting report of results of a houshold survey see John M. Orbell and Toru Uno, "A Theory of Neighborhood Problem-Solving: Political Action vs. Residential Mobility," *American Political Science Review* (June, 1972).

[4] But widespread patronage in working class wards of big cities has been the backbone of political machines. In this case, the contributed time to political clubs is rewarded with a job.

12

Rule Change and Transitional Equity

—•—

HAROLD M. HOCHMAN

Too often the professional analyst, in seeking a remedy for inefficiency or injustice, rests public policy discussion on simplified comparisons of the actual and the ideal. The costs of transition from the actual state to the ideal are de-emphasized. Still, the normative significance of these transitional costs which arise because pre-existing rules and institutions have legitimized claims and expectations is clear, and even a casual analysis of the legislative process verifies their importance in determining the terms on which governments enact change.

Such transitional effects raise the question of when it is appropriate to compensate those who suffer losses as a consequence of change in public policy, and on what terms. Where compensation is not desirable or feasible, transitional considerations illuminate the difficulties of obtaining an ethical consensus. In specific cases, they place constraints on the manner in which the inequities which are implicit in existing rules and institutions can be corrected.

The description and discussion of such issues of transitional equity form the objective of this paper. Because of transitional costs, we may have no unambiguous way to resolve inconsistencies between demands for rule changes which foster social justice or economic efficiency and the consensus which the Pareto criterion requires. The customary, but facile, way around this is to appeal to a social welfare function that assigns weights or social values to individual utili-

Harold M. Hochman is Senior Research Associate, The Urban Institute, and Visiting Member of the Faculty, Graduate School of Public Policy, University of California at Berkeley. He is indebted to the National Science Foundation for a supporting grant to The Urban Institute. For comments on earlier drafts, he wishes to thank Richard Bird, Martin Bronfenbrenner, Peter Brown, Cathy Gilson, George Peterson, A. Mitchell Polinsky, Edward Rastatter, Claudia Scott, and Walter Williams.

ty or wealth levels. But, given the difficulties of ascertaining a consistent social decision function of this kind, this merely begs the question.

Fortunately, to identify transitional equity issues and formulate distinctions that clarify them, so well-defined a criterion as a social welfare function is not needed. This paper addresses itself to such questions. Its focus is on the problems inherent in deciding when compensation of those who suffer interim losses can be foregone because a higher-level constitutional rule guarantees Pareto optimality in terms of a broader frame of reference. It tries to ascertain when it is legitimate in this broader sense to violate the Pareto criterion, defined in issue-by-issue terms. And it gropes toward an answer to how this might be done at least cost.

The discussion begins by inquiring into the notions of fairness and opportunity, interpreted in terms of a social contract that a community of self-governing individuals would find acceptable. The second section, focusing on a number of specific policy issues, places in context the normative problems of transition and highlights the potential for conflict between equity in the interim and the ultimate efficiency and equity objectives of social policy. The paper then turns to real-world political and economic mechanisms that mitigate the negative side effects of change and reduce transitional deviations from the Pareto criterion. The final section shows how transitional equity issues, which serve to confound public choice, have arisen in certain public education decisions of the federal judiciary.

I. SOCIAL JUSTICE AND LEGAL TRANSITION

Equity is a matter of well-being, which depends on the interpersonal distribution of entitlements to the returns from property and human capital. Usually communities hold some differences in well-being to be legitimate, while denying the fairness of others. The criteria used in evaluating legitimacy or fairness are a matter of social choice. Even so, whether equity is defined in terms of current or permanent income or some such broader but vaguer concept as opportunity (which permits stochastic variation in the relationships among prospects and outcomes) is a matter of values and intuitions. And, even if a proper measure of well-being could be agreed upon, it is essentially impossible to define a uniquely Pareto-optimal distribution when individuals have the prior benefit of endowments, whether these take the form of wealth, position, or some other measure of status.[1]

Transitional equity is a more limited concept. Its concern is with entitlements to certainty that pre-existing rights and endowments sanctioned by a social contract will continue undiminished. The basic issue is the fairness of windfall declines in the absolute wealth of some individuals that occur when the community-at-large, in its quest for a preferable long-run allocative or distributional income, alters its rules and institutions.

To gain perspective on transitional equity as a problem, one must consider the process of "constitutional choice" (that is, the process through which the high-level or general rules that govern conduct in a community are chosen) and relate it (as modern, but not elitist, theories of political economy do) to "social justice." One interpretation of this relationship, attributable to the political philosopher John Rawls, is that a "fair" (a just or equitable) distribution is one to which individuals, choosing freely, would agree in the "state of nature," in which neither rules nor endowments pre-exist. Acting behind this "veil of ignorance," no individual can identify his own distributional income, even in the probabilistic sense.[2] The social contract individuals agree upon in such ignorance of personal prospects sets up rules and institutions that govern claims to personal property and human capital and that determine, aside from random variation, the distribution of income. This distribution, moreover, carries the sanction of consensus, and being uniquely optimal (in the circumstances defined) it is socially just. Thus grounded, social justice, "indeed ethics itself is part of the general theory of rational choice."[3] There is no conflict between equity, which implies consent, and allocative efficiency. With distribution undetermined, all men prefer more wealth to less.

Under a "just" social contract, each individual, in Rawls' view, has "an equal right to the most extensive liberty compatible with like liberty for all." Included in this right, presumably, is the freedom to achieve a given standard of living: ". . . inequities[4] as defined by the institutional structure or fostered by it are arbitrary unless it is reasonable to expect they will work out to everyone's advantage and provided that the positions and offices to which they attach or from which they may be granted are open to all."[5] This right does not require that distribution be equal. But to be consistent with it, distributional inequalities must be justifiable in advance, as leaving the least-advantaged individual in the community at least as well off as he would be under strict equality. Since in a Pareto-efficient system, *ceteris paribus*, more output is available to be distributed than in an inefficient system, efficiency fosters justice and is desirable on its own merit. The thrust of this paradigm, given its probabilistic focus, is that distributional opportunities, not actual results, are what fairness is ultimately about. Clearly, many real-world practices that are consistent with democratic political constitutions fail this test.

Although social justice, thus conceived, may be the proper end of public policy, real-world decision making does not share its philosophic luxury. Once a "social contract" exists, as codified in rules and institutions, reality violates the assumption of probabilistic agnosticism, an assumption that is critical to the "fair game" interpretation of the choice of social rules contained in the Rawls paradigm. Most often, individual behavior presumes the permanence of pre-existing rules. Indeed, if law and the concept of rules are to be credible,[6] individuals must hold this presumption with a high degree of confidence. Not just existing rules of conduct, but changes in these rules, must be justifiable, and the process through which change is effected must itself be fair. Failing direct or indirect compensation, the fairness of a rule change is unambiguous only if the pre-existing rule was clearly inconsistent with the social contract or "constitution" that underlay it and if those whom the change has harmed have had an opportunity to anticipate and adjust to it. Public policy, in its overall concern with equity, must consider not only the beneficent effects of rule changes on individuals whom existing rules have disadvantaged but the fact that the process of change, if considered arbitrary, can itself make individuals feel it is irrational to accept the limits on behavior that rules imply.

Although Rawls provides us a backdrop against which to judge whether rules, *de novo*, are fair, he neither resolves nor claims to resolve this conflict. Rules, even if unfair or inefficient, may as custom underlie reasonable expectations. Rule changes that disappoint such expectations may themselves be considered unjust because they violate the equi-probability assumption implicit in the definition of a just practice. The problem of transitional equity is, therefore, all pervasive. Only if the present beneficiaries of an unjust practice have attained their positions through illegitimate means is the case clear-cut. Once a social system is in motion, there is no simple logical device through which the ideal can be defined or, even if it could be defined, through which the actual can be equated with it.[7]

To illustrate the pervasiveness of transitional equity problems, consider slavery, a practice that is clearly inconsistent with fairness. Even here, where the argument is one-sided, transitional considerations, although hardly compelling, are relevant, and the factors involved are much the same as those with which policymakers must deal in considering far less dramatic rule changes than the abolition of slavery.

Consider, for example, the preferences and choices of a benevolent man, living in a regime that permits slavery, who observes a slave being beaten by his master. His preference, abstracting from benevolence, is to purchase a Rolls Royce that he himself would drive. Given his benevolent concern for the slave, however, he purchases a less expensive automobile, buys rights to the slave from his sadistic master, and installs him (still a slave) as chauffeur. In doing this, he expects that the practice of slavery, which the political constitution sanctions, is permanent and that the slave, under the old master, would have continued to suffer regular beatings. The following day, the community abolishes slavery with no compensation to slaveowners, thus subjecting this man, who had entered the practice of slavery out of benevolence alone, to a windfall loss.[8]

The point, farfetched though the example may be, is clear. Even in a less fantastic setting the same issues remain. Because of these issues proposals to change existing rules are unlikely to be acceptable, much less fair, if public policy ignores their transitional implications. Situations in which ends fully justify any and all costs of transition, however great, are uncommon. From both the practical and normative perspectives the fairness of rules for changing rules is crucial.

II. FAIRNESS AND EFFICIENCY:
CONCEPTS, CASES, AND AMBIGUITIES

With few exceptions, changes in established rules and practices create transitional equity problems. Only rarely is change Pareto-efficient in the simple sense.[9] Even if all men might prefer the long-term outcome under altered rules, some will fear decreases in wealth and the foreclosure of options in the short run and, for this reason, oppose change. Interim effects may dominate, making the present value of a change negative not just because time preference is positive but also because a man's life span is finite and intergeneration utility interdependencies are imperfect. In these cases compensation must be paid if the Pareto criterion is to be satisfied, regardless of the fact that without it the new equilibrium could leave all parties better off than they would otherwise be.

It is useful, for heuristic purposes, to distinguish (even if imperfectly) between changes in the "effective" constitution, correcting its aberrations or inconsistences, and the more restrictive modifications of rules and practices with which most public policy deals. Issues of human rights, where moral overtones predominate, are in the first category. Although such practices as slavery and *de jure* segregation, practices that use unacceptable criteria to discriminate among individuals, may emerge and endure in a world in which power is correlated with endowments, there is a strong presumption that they would not have been chosen in a world of equals. Whether there is an orderly and accepted procedure for introducing and enacting change and whether those who might be harmed have long been on notice may determine whether compensation is necessary. In the second category the focus is on current outcomes of market and political processes rather than on fundamental human rights, and the issues are more routine. Not elemental freedoms but the terms on which transactions are conducted are at issue. Distributional considerations, although important, do not dominate from the start. It is in this paper more useful to focus on this second class of issues, for here men are more likely to agree that transitional cost considerations must temper positive action. Advocates of reform may be more willing to honor the Pareto criterion and accept a requirement that losers be compensated.

In determining whether compensation must be considered an ethical requirement, the ability of individuals to anticipate change and adjust their behavior to curtail potential losses is crucial. Consider the distinctions encountered in sorting out the negative effects of a rule change on private wealth. One distinction is between effects on existing wealth (the expected returns of those already engaged in the practice) and the potential losses (in an opportunity cost sense) implicit in denying privileges to new investors. A second distinction is between eliminating gains from continuing a practice (which is, say, monopolistic or discriminatory) and, by imposing change retroactively, redeeming the prior effects of this practice. Thus suburban residents, evincing concern with the quality of local schools, may well oppose interjurisdictional busing if they believe it will leave their children worse off. At the same time they may well hold that disparities between central city and suburban schools, both in finance and in facilities, derive from rules and practices that are unfair. The first distinction differentiates between the attitudes of current and potential residents of the suburbs toward busing. The second differentiates between the revealed and the abstract preferences of current suburbanites. It suggests that such individuals are quite rational in opposing policies that they may consider to be fair in principle because they do not wish to bear (or inflict on their children) concentrated transitional costs.

In practice whether compensation (for past or for future losses) is appropriate, is a far more subtle issue. Although the Pareto criterion strictly interpreted requires compensation, it seems absurd to argue that individuals unjustly deprived of rights under an existing rule should compensate its beneficiaries if the rule is changed.[10] Several countervailing considerations (some already mentioned) may be relevant. One is whether individuals harmed by an unfair practice participated in the "consent" process that established it. If not, the argument for compensation is less convincing. A second is whether the beneficiaries of the practice can reasonably be expected to have anticipated the change. Finally, the appropriateness of compensation may depend on whether the practice concerned involves the constitutional rights of identifiable persons or attributes of transactions that are logically distinct from the individuals who engage in them.[11]

With a rule change that is efficient in the sense that it is expected to produce net benefits it seems appropriate, even aside from ethical considerations, to compensate those who are harmed. There is little argument about compensating owners for private property "taken" through condemnation in the highway construction and urban renewal cases. But it is often unclear whether these are the only rights infringed. Destruction of familiar neighborhoods is itself costly, and many of the social difficulties of such programs derive from their effects on the intangible human capital of residents who are not property owners.[12] The ethnic or racial characteristics of these residents may, moreover, be well-defined. Can it then be said that they are not identifiable and that the rule change, in the first instance, affects the terms of transactions rather than the rights of specific individuals?

In general, the requirement that compensation be paid to neutralize distributional effects (because failure to compensate inflicts "demoralization costs") must be tempered by the proviso that the costs of violating the Pareto criterion exceed the costs of its assessment and implementation.[13] This utilitarian issue is, however, quite different from the ethical one. If public policy is concerned with compensation because interpersonal utility comparisons are impossible, the fact that transactions costs may render compensation uneconomic has no bearing on the ethical issue at stake.

Turning, for illustration, from general considerations to specific examples, consider the effort to control pollution, which deals with rights to a "common property resource." Although the objectives of such control in the long term are efficiency and equity, some individuals are sure to suffer short-run distributional harms as a consequence. Can it be argued, in this respect, that past pollution is one issue (whether retroactive compensation is appropriate) and potential pollution another? Need potential polluters be compensated for the expected effects of controls on their wealth? Might not fairness require that polluters and the community-at-large share the costs of clarifying rights to common property resources during a transition period? Can the law differentiate in logic between owners of existing firms that have capitalized known opportunities, and new or potential firms that have not? This seems at first blush a sensible course, but because it would not only spare existing firms from capital losses but provide them with a newly created source of economic rent it does not hold up.

Other rule changes, much the same in their appeal to the economist, have similar transitional equity implications. One such proposal, the elimination of quantitative restrictions on the number of taxicab franchises or "medallions" that cities authorize, is classic in its apparent simplicity. Under restricted supply the medallions sell for a high price and taxicab fares are higher than under free entry. Rationalization to the contrary, simple price theory suggests that standards of service suffer. Nonetheless, the recommendation that a community rid itself of this restrictive practice invariably raises significant political objections. These objections are justifiable because deregulation, without compensation, would inflict severe transitional losses on those who own franchises. These potential inequities would disappear, however, if the current cohort of franchise owners had instigated the medallion restrictions.[14] (Similarly, if participants in an illegal activity suffer losses when it is legalized, as private bookmakers do when public gambling ventures are created, such effects can be dismissed as fair outcomes of risky ventures.) By and large, however, current taxicab operators invested in existing franchises at the market price and did so with reason to believe that the licensing rules under which these franchises had been capitalized were both permanent and legitimate.[15] Indeed, there seems no reason (assuming that contrary legislation had not been pending and under active discussion) why they should not have considered such rules in this light, despite the fact of their inefficiency. Nor does it make any difference, in opportunity cost terms, whether the franchises have just been purchased and are yet to produce returns or whether they have already returned profits sufficient to justify the original outlay. Analytically, investment must be viewed as a continuous process and the investment decision as a choice just made.[16]

The transitional equity issue is no less important in explaining the reluctance of Congress to act on tax reform. It can be argued that many provisions catering to special interests (like percentage depletion) or to a wide class of taxpayers (like the preferential treatment of capital gains) are a travesty of distributive justice. But no tax change, however desirable it may appear in the abstract, is free of transitional effects on asset values. The fact that the community has adjusted to the established tax code is, in itself, sufficient to explain the tendency of its apparent aberrations to persist. Had active discussion of depletion reform not given wealth owners ample reason to anticipate it, it would be difficult to argue that present holders of mineral shares can justly be penalized (by failing to compensate them for the transitional effects of reform) for benefits that percentage depletion awarded to original investors in mineral properties. Nor, lacking a more definitive basis for interpreting voter preferences, have we any proof (despite ample presumption) that the political community actually prefers "statutory" to "effective" tax rates (or something in between) and that the disturbing compromises that seem endemic to the tax legislative process are unjustifiable.

It is, therefore, amply clear that the deliberation of reform proposals in isolation, without due regard for preconditions and due attention to the decision-making process from which existing institutions have emerged, risks substantial normative danger. To undo inequities without causing harm is no simple matter. Nor is it always self-evident whether the harm of transition is more or less severe than the harm of the *status quo*. For this reason, advocates of institutional change must, perforce, grant prominence on the agenda of reform to the rules that govern change. That inequity may be clothed in the garb of "justice" is small consolation.

III. PUBLIC CHOICE AND THE
PROBLEM OF TRANSITIONAL LOSS

It is neither accidental nor inappropriate that prospects of transitional loss are taken into account in the political arena. Legislators can be counted on to temper the pleas of reform-minded liberals. This is not because the *status quo* is desirable and Pareto nonoptimal change is to be avoided at all cost. It is, rather, because the prospect of transitional inequities implies that a more airtight case is required to justify rule changes than to rationalize existing rules and practices.

A variety of mechanisms, contained in the political process itself, can or do operate to reduce transitional inequities. These political mechanisms are, in a sense, imperfect substitutes for compensation and, when it is not feasible, perform a part of its function. Their effect is to make change less likely to "effectively" bankrupt specific individuals—a consequence that is irretrievable—and to reduce the concentration of transitional losses among subgroups of the population. These mechanisms, however, are not costless, for they also create political opportunities for influence and power that are more available to the strong than to the weak. Thus, whereas they help to alleviate the ethical compensation problem, they by no means eliminate it, and, depending on one's values and preferences, their overall effect may be to increase dissatisfaction with the general distributive milieu.

To focus this discussion, it is useful to refer to a simple model, constructed by Professor Buchanan, to rule out the transitional equity problem.[17] In this model the current generation defers the implementation of the rule changes it enacts until a full generation (or, to be less extreme, a decade or two) has elapsed. In consequence, individuals acting on rule changes can abstract from effects on their own status. This narrows the conflict among the alternative patterns of rights and opportunities that satisfy the Pareto criterion and brings the process of reform into closer conformity with the Rawls paradigm. Forward projection, by formalizing expectations, enables individuals to adjust to enacted change, thus softening its unintended distributional effects; and intergeneration utility interdependencies assure that time preference, through discounting, does not leave individuals indifferent to the distant future.[18]

Though a useful heuristic device, this "simple delay" model is clearly inadequate as a guide to practice. First, when the resolution of social problems is deferred, dissent is unsatisfied. The risks to a tranquil and free society that delay entails cannot help but affect the ultimate outcome. Second, for future generations, the deferral (even constitutional) of reform not only violates consent,[19] but also precludes them from changing the institutions under which they live. Third, if the effects of change can make everyone better off over time, postdating, which reduces the present value of such benefits, is inefficient—unless transitional costs alter the balance. These criticisms notwithstanding, partial delay does have its place in the real world, as in the "grandfather clause" (which permits the original rule to continue to govern on-going activities) and in explicit procedures for the gradual phase-in of rule changes.[20]

Within the more general frame of political reference, logrolling (the grouping of issues in public choice) is the primary mechanism through which the legislative process softens and mitigates transitional effects.[21] For logrolling to operate, individuals must differ in the importance they attach to issues, so that the outcome in multi-issue decisions can differ from the single-issue outcome. Although the single-issue decisions might offend some constituents, their net effect may be acceptable to all or nearly all,[22] in much the same way as the discounted effects over time of a single-issue decision may prove positive even though its short-run effects do not.[23]

The deficiencies of logrolling suggest, in themselves, certain criteria that are appropriate in weighing the likely benefits of change against its transitional costs. Rule changes with concentrated negative effects should, if possible, be avoided. If the effect on a given individual is so negative that it "bankrupts" him, issue-grouping is useless in countering transitional inequities. Consider, for argument's sake, a rule change that denies, for but a limited time, the consumption that sustenance requires. There is no way in which an individual thus affected can be compensated through issue-grouping or intertemporal logrolling and end up a net gainer. Similarly, logrolling neutralizes transitional inequities more effectively if the policies chosen have diffused rather than concentrated negative effects. Political reality, however, is quite the opposite. Despite aberrations, strength resides in numbers in a one-man—one-vote system. Legislators are more responsive to large numbers of constituents (even if these are a minority in the wider sense) who suffer well-diffused losses than to isolated individuals or local minorities. Within these groups, wealth itself is the best assurance of protection. Individuals with little capital are subject to transitional inequities as well as distributive injustice.

To carry the argument a step further, majority rule, applied in a succession of issues, is itself a means through which transitional inequities are reduced. Issues decided under this collective choice rule can, if unrelated, be considered episodes in a "convergence process," itself displaying the effective properties of logrolling.[24] Individuals, in evaluating political alternatives, trade off dissatisfaction with one rule or rule change for satisfaction with another, knowing that in some cases they will be in the majority and in some they will not. More restrictive decision rules than simple majority, such as a two-thirds rule or Wicksellian "relative unanimity," leave it less likely that a particular individual will always find himself in the minority and more likely that transitional effects, summed over issues, will be non-negative. They do this, however, at the cost of making change even more difficult to enact.[25]

Interjurisdictional mobility, within metropolitan areas (as the Tiebout model suggests) and among national communities, can also help to reconcile dissatisfaction with rules and rule changes. Individuals, over the long run, respond to (and help to bring about) majority-sanctioned changes by opting in or out of particular political communities. But in neither financial nor psychological terms are such moves costless. Moreover, their patterns are significantly affected by individual wealth. Thus, even in the potential sense, mobility is at most a partial offset to transitional costs.

Such defenses against transitional inequity, all of which hinge on the ability to delay the effects of change and to group issues, inhere in individual and legislative action, but not in judicial action. Judicial intervention, which by its nature applies on an issue-by-issue basis, thus precluding issue-grouping, is appropriate in constitutional discussions, where high-level rules for making rules are defined, and in cases where the risk is high that the pursuit of one objective will unduly compromise others. It is in these cases that the system of public choice is weakest. If negative effects are concentrated, legislative inaction (as with segregation in public education) or legislative action (legalizing the death penalty for certain convicted offenders) may "bankrupt" specific individuals or groups. Concern for their welfare may justify the dangers (in terms of side effects) inherent in the case-by-case and issue-by-issue interpretations that characterize judicial decision making.

IV. PUBLIC EDUCATION AND THE LAW:
A TRANSITIONAL DILEMMA

Perhaps the most far reaching of the transitional dilemmas in current public policy is the public education issue, and, in particular, the controversies surrounding educational finance and busing. To foster equal opportunity, both in market and in political transactions, and thereby to satisfy the Rawlsian preconditions of fairness, the courts have rendered a number of landmark decisions in the education area[26] (although as of this writing some of these are subject to reversal by the Supreme Court). A side effect of these decisions, taken to redress long-standing grievances, has been the attenuation of property rights. These have left legitimate expectations disappointed and closed or restricted channels of opportunity open to some members of the community.[27]

Consider, first, the *Hobson v. Hansen* and *Serrano v. Priest* decisions, which deal with whether differences in per pupil expenditures are consistent with equal opportunity. The *Hobson* decision, which concerns school finance within a single jurisdiction, requires the approximate equalization of per pupil spending among schools.

Intrajurisdictional differences in income and wealth are not considered a justification of expenditure differences, as they would be if taxation were benefit based and the output of the educational process were partially a private good.[28] The *Serrano* decision extends this logic to the state as a multijurisdictional region. It links opportunity with education and argues that interjurisdictional differences in burdens of the local property tax are not consistent with equal opportunity. Education, *Serrano* claims, is different from other public activities, being more like voting rights, a constitutional prerogative, than such conventional services as fire protection and trash collection. Local differences in public education spending are, then, justifiable only if the wealth basis of educational finance has first been normalized.

Turn now to the transitional equity issues implicit in these decisions. *Serrano* to the contrary, it is clear that public education is resource-using, unlike voting rights and like fire protection, and that it must be financed, in real terms, through means that attenuate private property. To substantiate the argument that education is different from other resource-using and tax-funded public activities, the educational finance issue must be raised to the constitutional level. Otherwise, if its "public-good" dimension is externality based, as the definition of a public good implies, it seems inconsistent to single education out for special treatment, enjoining equal services and rejecting wealth as the basis of its finance while permitting differential expenditures and the wealth-related financing of other public services that share its externality characteristics. Moreover, to the extent that public action is (and is supposed to be) a reflection of individual preferences, the case for consistent evaluation of resource-using activities carries over to private goods. If equal opportunity is a sufficient basis for questioning the appropriateness of the distribution of wealth as a basis of educational finance, it leaves us uneasy about permitting private resource allocation to be governed by endowment-related preferences.

This clearly leaves us in an uncomfortable quandary. Benefit distributions of municipal services like trash collection and the maintenance of municipal yacht harbors (much less the benefits of private goods) surely differ, both directly and in the externalities they produce. Moreover, there are difficulties in distinguishing equal opportunity arguments for equal provision from arguments that are little more than a particular minority's desire to extract more income redistribution than the community, acting through its political process, is willing to provide. An avid egalitarian might argue that advantages attributable to initial position have no redeeming social value, but so outright a rejection of property rights that are sanctioned in the prevailing constitution is hardly constructive. It seems more reasonable to seek a middle ground, to treat education as a public trust, managed by the community-at-large for the benefit of generations yet unfranchised and, in particular, for minors whose interests cannot adequately be represented by their parents. On this interpretation, there is, so far as the trade-off between transitional equity and social justice is concerned, substantial common ground between the public education decisions discussed and the abolition of slave holding.

If the constitutional case for equal educational opportunity (and, to the extent it is valid, other public services) could be satisfied through guarantees of minimum levels of provision, the transitional side effects of the Hobson and Serrano decisions (and others like them) would be far less significant. Augmentation of these minimum levels through endowment-related purchases of private or public education by resident taxpayers would restore the parity between private and public choice.[29] Still, such a scheme, while assuring opportunity, would not equalize it. In a free society in which rights to private property pre-exist—indeed, in any society that does not separate children from parents at birth—no way exists to reconcile fully all the dimensions of equity.

Provided the discussion is restricted to the equal opportunity criterion on which the *Hobson* and *Serrano* decisions focus, neither neighborhood schools nor "community control," nor public subsidies to private schools, are in themselves inconsistent with fairness. To object to these delivery systems on equity grounds, an additional consideration, "equal access" to public facilities, must be introduced. This leads to an inquiry as to whether truly equal opportunity requires not only fiscal equalization but also a heterogeneity in classroom composition that implies, ironically, homogeneity of such units of production. It is with this issue of equal access that the debate over the fairness of busing within and among jurisdictions concerns itself.

Swann v. Charlotte-Mecklenburg Board of Education, written by Chief Justice Burger, deals with intrajurisdictional busing. The thrust of this decision is that equal access to physical facilities in which human capital can be formed is essential to equal opportunity and that equal expenditure is insufficient to remedy past injustices. *Swann* holds, moreover, that transitional inequity problems, so far as the matter at hand is concerned, are subordinate to the ultimate objective, the dismantling of a dual school system that is segregated by race. It concludes, more generally, although implicitly, that efforts to correct past injustice cannot accept current differences in status as a base point. Its argument is pragmatic. There is no implication that property or initial endowments are in themselves illegitimate. It simply avers that injustice cannot be corrected without infringing on endowments.

Absent a constitutional violation there would be no basis for judicially ordering assignment of students on a racial basis. All things being equal, with no history of discrimination, it might well be desirable to assign pupils to schools nearest their homes. *But all things are not equal in a system that has been deliberately constructed and maintained to enforce racial segregation. The remedy for such segregation may be administratively awkward, inconvenient and even bizarre in some situations and may impose burdens on some; but all awkwardness and inconvenience cannot be avoided in the interim period when remedial adjustments are being made to eliminate the dual school system.*[30] (emphasis mine)

In homing in on the equal access objective, Swann links the present defects of the system of public education to prior decisions on school location and construction. Its argument, however, need not be confined to such narrow terms of reference, limited to the public education case. Residential location is itself inextricably intertwined with school construction and classroom composition and has itself been shaped by exclusionary practices, including restrictive covenants, zoning and jurisdictional boundary decisions. Whatever their intent, the total effect of these practices, given the neighborhood school concept, has proved closer to *de facto* segregation than to equal opportunity in many cases.

Clearly, the total integration of educational finance and educational production, as Swann directs, would substantially attenuate the rights of self-contained communities (which could thereby be self-contained no longer) to establish and control their own school systems and finance them through wealth-related taxes. Residential sites in areas hitherto sheltered from the disadvantaged would suffer in value. Since most owners of such homesites, like the taxicab operators of our ealier example, purchased their properties with good reason to expect rules to be firm, such losses are fair reason for concern with transitional equity.[31] Moreover, the effect of busing from suburban communities to the inner city may, for many children, reduce educational opportunity, without assuring improved service to the disadvantaged, at least in terms of their preferences.

Since *Swann, Carolyn Bradley v. The Richmond School Board*, its reversal, and presidential initiatives calling for a busing moratorium have kept the busing issue in the public limelight. The *Bradley* decision ruled that satisfactory integration requires busing on a metropolitan-wide basis and ordered consolidation of the public-school systems of Richmond, Virginia, and its contiguous suburban counties. The court argued that busing cannot achieve equal access and its overriding objective of dismantling the dual school system if it continues to be constrained by jurisdictional boundaries.

Transitional equity considerations suggest, other factors aside, that the *Bradley* decision (notwithstanding its reversal) is appropriate. Areawide busing would assure that transitional effects of both property values and the quality of public education are well diffused. Since the entire metropolitan community is responsible for the *de facto* segregation implied by jurisdictional boundaries,[32] it may be appropriate for the whole metropolitan area to share in the transitional losses incurred in satisfying the constitutional guarantees of equal protection and equal access. Other than the historical accident of existing boundaries, there seems no basis in logic for requiring high-wealth residents of central cities, the political communities in which the disadvantaged are concentrated, to bear such costs, as the

Hobson decision implies. To the contrary, if "equal access" is truly a condition of justice, the unquestioning acceptance of existing local boundaries is itself arbitrary.

V. CONCLUSION

The transitional issues that the public school decisions raise are conceptually much the same as the transitional implications of other changes in social rules, institutions, and practices.[33] The illustrations of Section IV make clear the fact that on-going societies cannot often correct unfair outcomes without creating collateral harms. Indeed, one can go farther and argue that the interim effects of well-intentioned change are important not only because transitional fairness is a matter of serious normative concern but also because they may substantially alter the final outcome of the change. Concern for social justice can hardly be expected to endure unless nonmalevolent individuals believe it to be in their interest to accept legal strictures. Thus, for reason of pragmatism as well as principle the undoing of past harms must do more than shift the onus of inequity.

I hope that my inquiries, admittedly Talmudic, have surfaced a much-neglected facet of public policy. The transitional equity implications of rule changes surely deserve more scholarly attention than they have hitherto been given. For narrowly defined policy problems, at least, the clarification of transitional implications, to make clear such trade-offs, may lie within the purview of economic analysis.

NOTES

[1]See discussion of this point in Harold M. Hochman, "Individual Preferences and Distributional Adjustments," *American Economic Review* (May, 1972), pp. 353-60

[2]See John Rawls, "Justice as Fairness" in *Philosophical Review,* 1958, reprinted in Laslett and Runciman, *Philosophy, Politics and Society,* Series 2, (Oxford: Basil Blackwell, 1959), 132–57, and *A Theory of Social Justice* (Cambridge: Harvard University Press, 1971). The same construction has been developed by

John Harsanyi in "Cardinal Utility in Welfare Economics and the Theory of Risk Taking," *Journal of Political Economy* (October, 1953), pp. 434-35.

³John Rawls, "Distributive Justice," in Laslett and Runciman, *Philosophy, Politics and Society*, Series 3, (Oxford: Basil Blackwell, 1969).

⁴I interpret the word "inequities," as used here, to mean "inequalities."

⁵Rawls, "Distributive Justice."

⁶This dilemma in the theory of public policy is also discussed in Worth Bateman and Harold Hochman, "Social Problems and the Urban Crisis: Can Public Policy Make a Difference?" *American Economic Review* (May, 1971), pp. 346–53.

⁷The argument, as stated, reflects my methodological "public choice" preference for relating social practices to individual preferences. One might, in judging such practices, appeal to more "basic," nonutilitarian criteria, but these, it seems to me, are difficult to rationalize as anything more than one man's (or men's) preferences regarding the rules that govern their relationships with others. I think it preferable to remain within the social contract frame of reference as long as one can—confronting such pitfalls as the transitional equity problem as they arise rather than papering them over at the outset with strong value judgments.

⁸Another uncomfortable question—again a matter of transitional equity—arises here. When rights are established that had previously been unfairly denied to an individual or group, can this individual or group justifiably direct reprisal, retribution, and demands for reparations at individuals who might have benefited, but had not designed, the unfair practices under which the rights had been denied?

⁹Basic traffic regulations, which curtail certain rights (like driving at unlimited speeds) in exchange for the physical protection the law can provide, are such an exception.

¹⁰This is not to say that the disadvantaged, given the wherewithal, would not offer such compensation if it were essential to bring about such change. And, although it is worth little from a normative perspective, it is worth noting that such a division of the gains from the removal of injustice would be Pareto optimal.

¹¹This distinction implies, for example, that housing covenants, which exclude financially capable individuals from participating in a market, are somehow different from ghetto retail prices that exceed the community average because sellers can separate low-income from high-income markets or because costs are higher in the low-income market.

¹²Thus, in addition to compensating residents, one recent suggestion is that public-housing authorities construct new housing before razing old structures, permitting residents to respond voluntarily to new housing opportunities as they are created.

¹³This point is made clearly in Frank Michelman's justly classic paper "Property, Utility, and Fairness: Comments on the Ethical Foundations of 'Just Compensation,'" *Harvard Law Review* (April, 1971), pp. 1165-1258. But although Michelman's discussion of the ethical aspects of the compensation problem is first-rate, it leaves open the even less tractable problem of implementation. Too often, the cost of compensating is prohibitive. It is difficult to identify those to whom benefits and costs of rule changes accrue, and valuation is bound to be substantially affected by the identities of the individuals (the political entities) charged with measuring the gains and losses.

¹⁴But would the appropriate conclusion be different if the restrictions had derived

from a distributional compromise giving nonfranchise owners other privileges in return? This way out of the maze, however, is more apparent than real. Whatever the terms of such a distributional compromise, the "inefficiency" of its effect suggests that the logrolling coalition has left some parties worse off.

[15]To charge investors with responsibility for full discounting of the risk of changes in "inefficient" rules is, for my taste, too facile. It turns public confidence in property rights into a gamble, thus making mockery of the rule of law. It also implies that public choice models are tautological. There is no way around the fact that it is more difficult for communities to extricate themselves from error than to commit it.

[16]Similar arguments apply, in a more topical context, to the licensing of Cable Television franchises. Regulatory authorities cannot ignore the effects of new franchises on current licensees. (The earlier invasion of the radio market by television can be viewed in the same light.)

[17]James M. Buchanan, *Public Finance in Democratic Process* (Chapel Hill: University of North Carolina Press, 1967), ch. 4.

[18]Without such interdependence, it is difficult to reconcile simple discounting with a concern for the distant future. Even moderate interest rates would render outcomes as few as twenty years away insignificant. But this does not square with individual behavior (in investing, for example, to reforest timbered areas). See Harold M. Hochman, "Individual Preferences and Distributional Adjustments," *American Economic Review* (May, 1972).

[19]This objection, however, may be less forceful than it appears. If intergeneration utility interdependencies are sufficient, the constitutional preferences of a given social or demographic cohort may be an appropriate surrogate for the preferences of its children. See Bateman and Hochman, "Social Problems and the Urban Crisis."

[20]A variation of this, which focuses on the difficulty of assuring "reasonable expectations" when rules are subject to change, is to predetermine time limits at which all rules must be reconsidered. Thus, since individuals are on notice that changes might occur, they can discount the implied risk.

[21]The essence of logrolling is compromise based on mutual self-interest. Two individuals, with opposing preferences, each strongly in favor of one rule change and mildly opposed to another, are likely to prefer enactment of both to enactment of neither. See James M. Buchanan and Gordon Tullock, *The Calculus of Consent* (Ann Arbor: University of Michigan Press, 1962) and Roland McKean, "Public Spending and the Unseen Hand in Government," *Public Spending* (New York: McGraw-Hill, 1968), ch. 2, pp. 10–30. If queried, many social scientists, ironically, fail to see the virtue in logrolling.

[22]"Omnibus" tax legislation is a case in point. Taken singly, some provisions of such legislation seem inappropriate. Together, however, the implicit compromise that underlies them is apparent. Unfortunately, this is also true of its costs.

[23]See A. Mitchell Polinsky, "Probabilistic Compensation Criteria," *Quarterly Journal of Economics* (August, 1972), pp. 407–25.

[24]This argument is weakened if the positions that given individuals take in a series of issues are correlated. See John Jackson, "Politics and the Budgetary Process," *Social Science Research* (April, 1972), pp. 35-60.

[25]Such safeguards as the requirement that three-quarters of all state legislatures approve constitutional amendments provide little protection in more routine legisla-

tive matters. Nor do they help groups that are invariably minorities, for example, American Indians or, in the internment of World War II, the Nisei.

[26]Julius W. Hobson, individually and on behalf of Jean Marie Hobson and Julius W. Hobson, Jr., et al., v. Carl F. Hansen, Superintendent of Schools of the District of Columbia, the Board of Education of the District of Columbia et al., in the U.S. District Court for the District of Columbia, Civil Action 82-66, May 19, 1970.

John Serrano, Jr., et al., v. Ivy Baker Priest, as Treasurer of the State of California, L. A. 29820, Superior Court No. 938254, filed August 30, 1971.

Swann et al. v. Charlotte-Mecklenburg Board of Education et al., Supreme Court 402 U.S. 1.

Carolyn Bradley et al., v. The School Board of the City of Richmond, Virginia et al. In the U.S. District Court for the Eastern District of Virginia, Richmond division, filed January 5, 1972 Civil Action 3353.

[27]The transitional equity problems that these decisions imply are more acute because the rule changes they require do not operate through market transactions, permitting a smooth transition, but through discrete administrative actions.

[28]To restrict this discussion to the transitional equity implications of the education decisions, I assume that equal expenditure implies equal opportunity and ignore the question of whether equal input implies equal output in terms of educational attainment.

[29]Even if transitional equity is ignored, equal service cannot eliminate the effects of endowments as long as private education is a viable alternative. Some individuals, turning to private suppliers, will simply "waste" their tax contributions, or relocate elsewhere. Since such individuals are likely to be net contributors to the fiscal system, this behavior will exacerbate the educational finance problem.

[30]Swann et al. v. Charlotte-Mecklenburg Board of Education, pp. 23-24.

[31]There seems, after all, no reason to presume that suburban residential location is based entirely on simple prejudice, rather than a justifiable desire for access to better public services, especially education.

[32]In no way does this blame suburban residents for acting in self-interest. If the existing system of property rights is considered legitimate, the formation of communities with a preferred environment, including a fiscal base adequate to finance desired levels of public services without a great deal of intrajurisdictional redistribution, cannot be considered objectionable in its own right. However, to the extent that the formation of suburban communities masks a desire to give legal sanction to prejudice, the broader issue of whether the prevailing system of property rights is consistent with fairness is raised.

[33]The same transitional issues as the public education decisions pose arise, for example, in the preferential employment of disadvantaged minorities. In this connection, the New York *Times*, June 30, 1972, reported that Benjamin Epstein, the National Director of the Anti-Defamation League of B'nai B'rith, and Ms. Naomi Levine, acting Executive Director of the American Jewish Congress, condemned the use of the preferential quotas to equalize employment and educational opportunities for racial and ethnic minorities, calling them a distortion of antidiscrimination policies. "The fundamental wrong in preferential treatment," said Mr. Epstein, "is that individuals who have no responsibility for past discrimination are made to sacrifice their opportunities for self-fulfillment to pay the debt that society owes."